Miletos, the Ornament of Ionia

Miletos, the Ornament of Ionia

A History of the City to 400 B.C.E.

Vanessa B. Gorman

Ann Arbor

THE UNIVERSITY OF MICHIGAN PRESS

Copyright © by the University of Michigan 2001
All rights reserved
Published in the United States of America by
The University of Michigan Press
Manufactured in the United States of America
⊗ Printed on acid-free paper

2004   2003   2002   2001   4   3   2   1

A CIP catalog record for this book is available from the British Library.

Library of Congress Cataloging-in-Publication Data

Gorman, Vanessa B. 1963–
    Miletos, the ornament of Ionia : a history of the city to
400 B.C.E. / Vanessa B. Gorman.
        p.   cm.
    Includes bibliographical references (p.   ) and index.
    ISBN 0-472-11199-X (cloth: alk. paper)
    1. Balat (Ayd,i çli, Turkey)—History.   2. Balat (Ayd,i çli,
Turkey)—Antiquities.   I. Title.
DF261.M5 .G67 2001
939'.11—dc21   2001041479

1007083565

To Robert Joseph Gorman,
sine quo non

Preface

This history of Miletos has been a long time in the making. It began in 1988, when I started work on my doctoral dissertation about fifth-century Miletos. In the years since then, many people have helped me in composing and assembling this book. A. John Graham served as mentor and dissertation advisor, and he has continued to read and criticize various chapters as I have progressed toward completion of this manuscript. I also wish to thank Martin Ostwald and Keith DeVries for the suggestions they made in the course of reading my dissertation and to note that this whole project arose as a result of a seminar paper I wrote for Martin Ostwald about the Athenian Regulations for Miletos. In the later stages, Kurt Raaflaub and Madeleine Henry were extremely helpful in reading a draft of the whole book as it neared publication and for recommending its publication to the press, while Ellen Bauerle was instrumental in getting it accepted.

The logistics behind producing such a book are monstrous. Accordingly, I wish to offer my gratitude to many people who made matters easier. I thank Paul Dangel and Sonja Rossum for producing maps for this volume. Audiences at the Association of Ancient Historians, the American Philological Association, the University of Wisconsin-Madison, and elsewhere have heard and commented on talks derived from this work. The archaeologists working on Miletos graciously entertained my husband and myself for two weeks during the summer of 1995; I wish to thank particularly Volkmar von Graeve, Berthold Weber, Hans Lohmann, Carsten Schneider, and the other inhabitants of Alman Kulasi for their assistance and hospitality. In addition, I have been financially sustained throughout this endeavor by the Department of Classical Studies at the University of Pennsylvania, which supported my graduate education generously with fellowships and assistantships, and the Department of History at the University of Nebraska-Lincoln, which has provided miscellaneous research funds. The Mellon Foundation gave me a graduate fellowship, while the

Nebraska Research Council awarded me a substantial grant to visit Germany and Turkey in 1995. My colleagues have been supportive and helpful as I labored away, and the following people have been especially generous with their advice and friendship: Elizabeth Beckwith, Joseph Farrell, James O'Donnell, and Ralph Rosen. Finally, Bob Gorman has labored long and diligently as chief editor and sounding board. I fear he now knows much more about Miletos than he may ever have wished.

Contents

Introduction

Miletos is located in southwestern Turkey, a few miles from the Aegean coast and slightly to the south of the island of Samos. The city marked the southern limit of the region in Anatolia that stretched north to Phokaia, an area the Greeks called Ionia. For several centuries, Ionia was the chief arena of Greek cultural development, and Miletos was its first city and leading light. During the Archaic period—roughly 750 to 490 B.C.E.—it easily surpassed Athens and Sparta in power and prosperity. Most especially, Miletos could boast of the remarkable number and vitality of its colonies. It was the most prolific mother city in Greek history, sending out at least forty-five known primary and secondary settlements into the Sea of Marmara (Propontis) and the Black Sea (Pontos), some of which have lasted into the modern era: Varna in Bulgaria; Bursa, Samsun, Sinop, and Trabzon in Turkey; Kerch and Feodosiya in Ukraine. Its success abroad was matched by extraordinary achievements at home: Miletos has been recognized as the birthplace of Western science and philosophy. Thus, it is without exaggeration that the first historian, Herodotos, could describe the city as τῆς Ἰωνίης πρόσχημα [the ornament of Ionia] (5.28).

If Miletos is most widely known for its achievements in the Archaic era, its importance was certainly not limited to that period, since for more than a thousand years it was a paramount center of Aegean culture in Asia Minor. As early as ca. 1700 B.C.E., it received its first significant settlement as an outpost of the flourishing Minoan civilization. Although Minoan cultural influence spread widely through the eastern Mediterranean, actual Cretan foundations are rare outside the home island. Therefore, Miletos is of special interest since it was the site of the only certain Minoan colony in southwest Anatolia to date. Later, the Mycenaeans, too, recognized the advantages the site offered to those who controlled it: the city became a foothold for the Bronze Age Greeks on the east coast of the Aegean. From this base, the Mycenaeans exerted their influence further toward the interior, so that Miletos became the focal point of the relationship between the Greeks and the powerful Anatolian empire of the Hittites.

This position at the juncture of two worlds—at the meeting place between Greece and the Near East—presented the Milesians with dangers as well as opportunities. After four centuries of independence, Miletos fell into the hands of Eastern powers: it was first conquered in the sixth century B.C.E. by the Lydians under Kroisos; shortly thereafter it joined the Persian Empire under Cyrus the Great. While a subject of the Persians, the city continued to exercise inordinate influence on the course of Greek history, instigating and leading Ionia in a bloody revolt against the Persian king. This uprising was of momentous importance, for the Greeks themselves saw it as the provocation for the Persian invasions of the Greek homeland, one of the defining moments of the Classical age. Not even the destruction of Miletos in 494 B.C.E. by the vengeful Persians completely ended this influence. The city was soon revived and rebuilt, providing the Greeks with the most noteworthy model of a completely planned city. While Miletos never again regained the prominence it had enjoyed in the Bronze Age and Archaic period, memory preserved its great glory in a popular saying among later Greeks: πάλαι ποτ᾽ ἦσαν ἄλκιμοι Μιλήσιοι [Once, long ago, the Milesians were mighty men] (Ar. *Plut.* 1002; Ath. 12.523e–f).

Today the site of Miletos is obscured under centuries of mud and debris. For many years it was occupied by the small Turkish village Balat, whose name derived from the Byzantine word *palation,* or "fortress," after a fortification built into the third tier of seats in the Milesian theater. Because of the importance of the ancient city, this site was a prime object of interest for the nascent discipline of archaeology, and the Berlin Museum initiated excavations at Balat at the end of the nineteenth century, funding the dig from 1899 to 1914. After various interruptions, the Deutsche Forschungsgemeinschaft provided the backing in 1955 so that the dig continues to the present day.[1]

The archaeologists have encountered tremendous difficulties: the first director of the site, Theodor Wiegand, was faced with excavating a marsh. He had to construct a system of ditches into the Maiandros River to remove much of the excess water for part of the year, enabling his team to initiate the ongoing multivolume work *Milet: Ergebnisse der Ausgra-*

---

1. Kleiner 1966, 5–11.

bungen und Untersuchungen seit dem Jahre 1899. When Carl Weickert succeeded Wiegand as director of the Miletos site in 1938, his task was greatly facilitated by two events. Shortly after World War II, the plain near Balat was planted with cotton, and Weickert used pumps to irrigate the fields while, happily, draining the city site, if only for a portion of the year. Then, in 1955, an earthquake destroyed the village of Balat. The inhabitants built a new home, called Yeni Balat (New Balat), a kilometer to the south on the road to Akköy and Didyma, abandoning Eski Balat (Old Balat) to the farmers and archaeologists.[2] Work continues today under the direction of Volkmar von Graeve, and although the problem with the groundwater is still considerable, valuable new information continues to be discovered year by year.

Difficult as it may be, the efforts of the archaeologists have brought to light the situation of the ancient city. Originally a series of small islands, by the time of its earliest habitation, Miletos was situated on the coast of the mainland. Over the centuries since then, it has been transformed into an inland marsh by silting of the wandering Maiandros River, a development already noted in antiquity by the geographer Strabo (12.8.17), writing in the first century B.C.E.[3] Slow deposits between ca. 3875 and 450 B.C.E. gave way to a more rapid progradation in the Hellenistic and Roman periods, so that the city was located in a swamp by the Early Byzantine era. Today the Maiandros deposits enough silt to advance the coastline by some twenty feet per year. Due to this factor, combined with a general rise in the groundwater level, Miletos is now nine kilometers distant from the sea, and the ancient Gulf of Latmos has become a freshwater lake called Bafa.[4]

The ancient city was located on a peninsula 1 km. wide that extended 1.8 km. north-northeast into the Gulf of Latmos.[5] Three smaller fingers of land jutted north out of the main peninsula; these spits shaped three of the four natural harbors of Miletos (Ephor. *FGH* 70 F 127 = Str. 14.1.6). The westernmost of the three extensions is fairly flat, but toward the interior it contains a slight elevation that scholars call the Stadium Hill, after the chief

2. Kleiner 1966, 8–9; Bean 1966, 219.

3. Cf. Str. 12.8.19, where he discusses lawsuits brought against the god of the river for altering the borders of the countries on his banks by sweeping away projections of land.

4. Brückner 1998, 251–53; Bean 1966, 219; Kleiner 1966, 10; Müller-Wiener quoted in Mitchell 1984/85, 86.

5. See the maps at the end of this volume. Voigtländer (1985) offers a reconstructed model of the city, which can be seen on display at the Pergamum Museum in Berlin. Cf. Voigtländer 1986a, 30–36.

architectural feature of that neighborhood. The middle spit of land is quite steep and is usually called the Theater Hill, or Kaletepe. Finally, the easternmost finger, also fairly steep, is called the North Hill, or Humeitepe. Miletos also had four harbors; only two were of much importance. The eastern harbor, which is unnamed, and the harbor on the far southwest, called the Athena Harbor after the nearby temple of the goddess, were used very little. The remaining two, the Theater Harbor and the northern Lion Harbor, were the commercial centers of the city. The Lion Harbor was named for the two Hellenistic stone lions installed on either side of its narrow mouth: a chain could be drawn up between them, effectively closing the harbor to intruders. Locations on the peninsula are usually described in relation to these harbors and hills, as well as a number of later structures that serve today as landmarks, especially the North Market, the Bouleuterion (Council House), the Baths of Faustina, and the southern cross wall. Beyond the city proper, to the southwest, rise four hills named, from west to east, Zeytintepe, Degirmentepe, Kalabaktepe, and Kazartepe. To the east of these hills lay the course of the Sacred Way, which ran from the sanctuary of Apollo Delphinios at the base of the Lion Harbor in Miletos, over the large mountain plateau known as Stephania, ending at the Oracle of Apollo at Didyma, fourteen kilometers to the south.[6] In the distance to the west rises what was once the island of Lade, now a part of the Turkish mainland.

A history of Miletos is overdue: despite the significance of this city in antiquity and the important results of the ongoing excavations, the modern reader in search of a detailed treatment cannot fail to be disappointed by the scholarly offerings up until now. The last full-scale discussion of the city was written by Dunham in 1915 and was not widely published. Meanwhile, more than eight decades of scholarly research, innovation, and archaeology have rendered her book largely obsolete. In that interval, other scholars have produced specialized works about Milesian trade (Röhlig 1933), colonization (Ehrhardt 1983), and archaeology (Kleiner 1966, 1968). However, the tight focus of these works prevents them from offering an integrated view of Milesian history, and they are particularly difficult for the general reader, since their argumentation is often esoteric and they are available in only a few libraries. Equally, Miletos is always treated in more general books, such as works about Ionia (Cook 1962;

---

6. Schneider 1987; Brückner 1998, 251 (eastern harbor).

Huxley 1966) and Greek trade and colonization (Boardman 1980), but there exists no modern, comprehensive history of Miletos itself.

The reasons for this gap are several, but they all relate to the fact that Miletos's rise to distinction and fall back into obscurity took place before the dawn of the Classical age, before alphabetic writing was widely adopted by the Greeks, and certainly before it was used to write history as we know it. As a result, pertinent literary and inscriptional evidence is relatively scarce, and as historians not surprisingly tend to concentrate their efforts on topics with an abundance of information, Miletos has drawn much less attention than, for example, Athens of the fifth century. Because of the paucity of documentary evidence, archaeological data takes on an even greater significance for historians of Miletos. Excavation at the site has been proceeding for one hundred years and is still ongoing. Each season yields new and exciting finds that not only must be integrated into the larger picture but also tempt the historian to wait just a little longer for fear of missing out on something of crucial importance. However, in addition to these problems, the principal reason why a history of Miletos has not been written is the difficulty inherent in the source material available for the study of the Hellenic world before the Classical era.

The ancient Greek mind divided the past into two periods: the heroic past and the era that encompasses the present day, also sometimes distinguished as the Age of Gods and the Age of Men.[7] The one contained the ageless, universal truths of poetry, while the other consisted of specific human events in a clear context. It was generally accepted that both were grounded in fact: even the distrustful Thucydides believes unquestioningly in King Minos and the Trojan War (1.4, 8–9). However, the ancients did not have a clear dividing line between myth or legend, on the one hand, and history, on the other. The advent of alphabetic writing, ca. 750, could have provided a boundary between the two, since before that time everything was clearly transmitted through oral tradition. However, the alphabet was not immediately used to record events and chronologies systematically, so the next few centuries continued to be shrouded from view, their histories subject to the vagaries of oral transmission. Only with the invention of history as a genre in the fifth century did authors start to record events of their own day more accurately. Before that,

---

7. The discussion that follows is heavily indebted to Finley 1975, 24, and Graf 1993, 131–36. Cf. Hesiod's Five Ages of Men (*Op.* 105–202).

everything was in confusion. As Moses Finley says,[8] "The plain fact is that the classical Greeks knew little about their history before 650 B.C. (or even 550 B.C.), and that what they thought they knew was a jumble of fact and fiction, some miscellaneous facts and much fiction about the essentials and about most of the details." Accuracy about earlier events was of far less importance to a story than was its ability to explain and justify present circumstances, whether political, religious, ethnic, or otherwise, so the transmission was marked by not only mutation but even outright creation. Literature—which before 550 B.C.E. generally means epic or lyric poetry—strove to make the past intelligible by making its truths permanent and universal.

All this changed radically with the fifth-century writings of Herodotos (ca. 480–ca. 420), often called the Father of History. Of course, Herodotos does not invent history ex nihilo. He is influenced in part by the genre usually called logography, early Ionian prose writing in two basic categories: individual city chronicles and mythology.[9] These works are not critical, scientifically conceived compositions but merely stories—poetry without meter, to paraphrase Dionysios of Halikarnassos—either literary adaptations of city records or mythological material from the period of the *Homerika*. However, Herodotos's other important influence came from the Ionian philosophical writers of the sixth century, many of them from Miletos itself. These men introduced both a skepticism about mythological explanations and a rational method of investigation to an examination of the physical world around them. Herodotos takes their methodology and applies it to the human past, producing what he calls ἱστορίη, "investigation." He writes on a typically mythological topic, the cause of a great war, but he uses skepticism about myth and a systematic method of inquiry that features human (not divine) matters and focuses on secular and political causes. He begins in the mythological past, but he also recognizes the limitations of such a beginning, as evidenced by his hesitation to assign precise dates to the events of the distant past: he thinks, for example, that Homer lived about 400 years before his own time (2.53.4). He is content to record the events from ca. 700 to ca. 550 B.C.E. in a very rough sequence.[10]

One characteristic of Herodotos's remarkable break with past practice is his insistence on using evidence in the form of eyewitness accounts.

---

8. Finley 1975, 18.
9. Pearson 1939; Fornara 1983a, 1–46.
10. Finley 1975, 17–18.

Although he nowhere specifically defines his methodology, he frequently refers to informants—named or, more often, unnamed—to establish the validity of his claims.[11] This is not to say that he believes everything he is told. He often reports varying accounts of the same event, sometimes expressing a preference and sometimes leaving the judgment up to the reader. The natural result of such a method of investigation is that Herodotos's historical perspective was strictly limited to the length of the living memory. He could only write with any kind of certainty about the events that happened in the lifetime of the people with whom he came into personal contact, usually thought to encompass about three generations or about a century (back to ca. 550). More distant events become increasingly more and more fantastic with the recession of time. As one scholar puts it, the subject chooses the historian and not vice versa; a particular history could not be rewritten once the people with direct access to the memory of that generation had died, because the evidence for that period died with them.[12]

While Herodotos concentrates on human—even political—events investigated through eyewitness accounts, in one very prominent way his work still resembles the poetic genres that came before him: he indicates in his proem that he is less interested in creating an annual digest than in presenting a didactic lesson for all time (ὡς μήτε τὰ γενόμενα ἐξ ἀνθρώπων τῷ χρόνῳ ἐξίτηλα γένηται [so that the deeds done by men should not be forgotten in time]). That principle, for Herodotos, is usually tied up in the Greek notion of the cycling nature of events, the rise and fall of fortune (1.5.3–4). Herodotos accomplishes this moral agenda primarily through the invention of speeches that act to guide the reader to the moral point that he is trying to make, as well as through the selection of events he will relate.

Whereas Herodotos allows morally instructive tales to color his narrative, his successor Thucydides encloses his account in a strict chronological frame, marked off annually into summers and winters, and analyzes events rigorously, emphasizing that which was secular and political rather than mythological. Like Herodotos, he uses eyewitness accounts (1.21–22) and writes about his own times. Also like Herodotos, he begins in the mythological past, but that treatment, abbreviated (1.2–19) and cautious, offers not so much a history as what Finley calls a "general

11. Lateiner 1989, esp. chaps. 1–4.
12. Collingwood 1956, 25–28.

sociological theory" about power and progress.[13] Thucydides scorns
people who believe the first account that they hear and make incorrect
assumptions about the distant past (1.20–21), and he praises his own
account of past events over that of other writers, the poets and logographers, who he says prefer to offer an entertaining story rather than the
truth (1.21.1). His own aim is to present a κτῆμά τε ἐς αἰεί [possession
for all time] (1.22.4).

Thus Herodotos and Thucydides establish history as a genre that es-
chews myth and divine matters, concentrates on human affairs, and em-
ploys a critical investigative method to arrive at the facts of a given incident. Though a far cry from the history practiced in the modern world,
certainly the seed has been planted. Aristotle first defines the technical
meaning of history by contrasting it with poetry (*Poet.* 9.1451a36–b11),
and his definition is still acceptable to the modern mind: while poetry gives
general truths, history offers particular facts (καθ' ἔκαστον λέγει).

With the advent of the Hellenistic Age, the nature of history changes,
as the distinction between Greek and barbarian fades and the world as
they knew it is brought—at least briefly—into a single political unit. The
idea of a universal, shared history developed among the writers of that
era, but it was only accomplished by redefining the historical method.
Historians no longer interviewed their own witnesses or recorded the
accomplishments of the present. Now they drew on the authorities of
ages past—such as Herodotos and Thucydides—extracting selected passages from those earlier authors to compile a patchwork history that
extended beyond the living memory into the far distant past.[14] As a
consequence, their work is only as trustworthy as the least accurate of
their sources, who are often used without attribution. With the passing of
time and a repetition of this process over and over again, the original
authority not only loses credit for his work but may easily become four or
five times removed from the scholar who is excerpting it. With both
context and attribution lost, the late scholars cannot intelligently judge
between reliable and unreliable information other than by estimating
plausibility based on their own experience. Myth and history blur together once more.[15]

---

13. Finley 1975, 18–19.
14. Collingwood 1956, 31–33.
15. An example of a serious misunderstanding that arose in the process of excerption is
the incorrect modern attribution of the invention of city planning to the Milesian architect
Hippodamos. See chap. 4 and Gorman 1995.

The purpose of this very brief outline of ancient historiography is to establish the challenges inherent in the primary sources, particularly those containing information that dates before ca. 550 B.C.E. How are we, as modern historians, to judge the accuracy of the ancient sources? We must not accept each account unquestioningly, without evaluating the author's own sources, his aims, and his general reliability. We must ask, especially: Is he writing a history based on eyewitness accounts of events from his own age? Is he compiling a universal history from scraps of other peoples' work? Is he reporting events from the Classical era and later, or has he crossed over into the shadowy region of pre-500 B.C.E.? The historian must account for all of these factors and maintain a skeptical outlook.

The problems are only exacerbated when dealing with incidents that are clearly mythological. It would be naive to include such accounts in toto: clearly the ancients were not expecting historical accuracy with these stories, and neither should we. However, there are so many instances in which myths have been shown to contain some kernel of historical truth that we can scarcely discard them unmentioned. Often certain broad features ultimately prove to be remarkably accurate, but those features cannot be identified prima facie. Instead, we must use other evidence to point to the element of truth contained in what is otherwise fantastic. It is incumbent on the historian of early Miletos to employ, in addition to literary sources, inscriptional evidence, building remains and artifacts, and comparative evidence, especially from elsewhere in Ionia and from the Milesian colonies, to draw the most accurate picture of events in the city.

The myth of the Dorian Invasion may serve as an example of this cautious use of what is clearly a mythological account of history.[16] To give a simplified version of the myth, the sons of Herakles were exiled from the Peloponnesos and took refuge in Doris, in northwest Greece. After three generations, three Heraklid brothers returned with a Dorian army, conquered the Peloponnesos, and divided it among themselves. The Argolid and Messenia were allotted to two of them, while Sparta was shared by the two sons of the third brother, who had been killed. When this account is compared with other evidence, we see that it contains a surprising amount of truth. According to the generally accepted theory

16. D.S. 4.57–58; Apollod. 2.167–80. Cf. Thuc. 1.12. Graf (1993, 131–36) and Malkin (1994, 33–45) explicate this myth more fully.

today, the border people of northwest Greece migrated slowly into the Peloponnesos early in the Dark Ages, filling the power vacuum left after the collapse of the Mycenaeans in the eleventh century B.C.E. Thus, the main outline of the Dorain Invasion myth is probably correct: the pottery styles and the dominance of the Doric dialect in the later Peloponnesos ensure this fact. But other elements of the story are surely later embellishments, for example, the idea of conquest rather than gradual infiltration, the mythical link to the hero Herakles, and the etiological explanation of the dual kingship at Sparta.

The lessons of the myth of the Dorian Invasion must be applied rigorously to the source material about Miletos, especially when it refers to the world of the heroic past. Elements that evoke folktale motifs or are obviously etiological are probably invented, whereas the broad pattern may be trustworthy, and material that is unexpected and inexplicable may well be true. Reliable components can only be determined by outside confirmation: arguments cannot be allowed to rest on the foundation of myth alone. Miletos was a remarkably important city in antiquity, and it is both necessary and possible to piece together its history. However, the results, to paraphrase Aristotle, can only be pressed to the level of detail that the material will allow, and from time to time we must step back and admit that Miletos will hide some secrets forever.

Miletos, the Ornament of Ionia is designed to provide a Milesian history that takes into account the most recent scholarship and that is therefore suitable to the specialized needs of the ancient historian and classicist. In this work, I have collected and scrutinized the sources about Miletos and their interpretation for the years from its first signs of habitation until 400 B.C.E. While I rely heavily on the important research of earlier scholars, I have found many of their results weakened by their failure to take into account the wider ramifications that their particular theories have within the broader outlines of Milesian history. I have tried always to keep my eye on the Big Picture as well as the details, and the expert reader will find much that is new. At the same time, I hope that this book will be within the grasp of the educated nonspecialist who is patient and persistent amid the sometimes difficult argumentation of ancient history.

Several conventions assumed in this work must be mentioned at the start. First, I have tried to minimize the number of names of modern scholars that appear in the text, especially when I disagree with them. I have taken their arguments nonetheless into account, and the proper references will always be found in the footnotes. In addition, while re-searching the history of Miletos, I have discovered a distressing number of instances in which a cautious conjecture or even an offhand remark made by a prominent scholar has in subsequent years come to be accepted by others as a matter of fact. Typically, such an interpretation quickly attracts a large supporting apparatus, and later, when contrary evidence comes to light, what started out as speculation or hypothesis is often doggedly maintained, even at the cost of grossly complicating the resulting histori-cal conclusions. I have tried wherever possible to follow important inter-pretations back to their inception, to present the evidence fairly, and to let the arguments speak for themselves. As a result, I have offered many significant revisions to the chronology and interpretation of events in Milesian history, with the hope that the reader will find them plausible on their own merits.

Second, any work dealing with the prehistory of the Aegean becomes entangled in the problem of assigning absolute dates to the different eras in the Bronze Age. Various systems are available, and none has won anything like universal acceptance in the academic community. In the text, I offer the relative dates (e.g., EM II, LH III A1), usually coupled with approximate absolute dates based on the high chronology of Man-ning (1995). I do this not to disparage the rival, low chronology of Warren and Hankey (1989) but simply to be consistent with the excava-tion reports published by the Niemeiers, who are the most recent excava-tors of the Bronze Age city.

Finally, I employ the standardized abbreviations for ancient authors and works (except that the spelling is Hellenized) and for modern refer-ence works as given in *L'Année Philologique;* the *Greek-English Lexicon* of Liddell, Scott, and Jones; and the *Oxford Latin Dictionary.* Proper names are transliterated with a Hellenic spelling (e.g., *Kroisos* instead of *Croesus*) except where they are already firmly established in the English-speaking world under their Latinate spelling (e.g., *Cyrus* instead of *Kouros*). All translations are my own unless noted otherwise.

1

Foundations

Μιλήσιοι δ' ἕως μὲν οὐκ ἐτρύφων, ἐνίκων Σκύθας, ὥς φησιν
Ἔφορος, καὶ τάς τε ἐφ' Ἑλλησπόντῳ πόλεις ἔκτισαν καὶ τὸν
Εὔξεινον Πόντον κατῴκισαν πόλεσι λαμπραῖς, καὶ πάντες ὑπὸ
τὴν Μίλητον ἔθεον. ὡς δὲ ὑπήχθησαν ἡδονῇ καὶ τρυφῇ,
κατερρύη τὸ τῆς πόλεως ἀνδρεῖον, φησὶν ὁ Ἀριστοτέλης, καὶ
παροιμία τις ἐγεννήθη ἐπ' αὐτῶν, πάλαι ποτ' ἦσαν ἄλκιμοι
Μιλήσιοι.

[As long as the Milesians did not live luxuriously, they conquered
the Skythians, as Ephoros says [FGH 70 F 183], and colonized the
cities on the Hellespont and settled the Black Sea with shining
cities, and everyone prospered under Milesian protection. But
when they were enslaved by pleasure and luxury, the manly
strength of the city collapsed, as Aristotle says [fr. 557 Rose], and
a certain proverb arose about them: "Once, long ago, the
Milesians were mighty men."] (Ath. 12.523e–f)

For the ancients, the history of Miletos presented a paradigm of a people
who achieved great wealth through their virtue but then, succumbing to
the allures of prosperity, fell into ruin. A good deal of historical truth lies
behind the proverb. We know that, from the Bronze Age onward, Miletos
was an important part of civilization in the Aegean. Particularly after the
upheavals of the early Iron Age, it emerged to become one of the richest
of all Greek cities, serving as the most important metropolis in the Hellenic world in the seventh and sixth centuries B.C.E. Then, after its long
acme, the power of Miletos collapsed, so that by the days of Ephoros and
Aristotle, the city that Herodotos had called the "ornament of Ionia"
(5.28) was noteworthy only for what it had been.

Though later Greeks attributed the rise and fall of Milesian prosperity
to the moral qualities of its people, historians find that the geographical
advantages were more important. With its peninsular site offering relative security and excellent harbors, the location of Miletos was very

13

desirable throughout antiquity, and the site was nearly continuously occupied from at least 1700 B.C.E. More important for its history than these strictly local features, Miletos was situated on the cusp between the emerging Aegean civilizations and the established states of Asia Minor. Thus, from the Bronze Age, Milesians were deeply involved in the nexus of international trade that would take Miletos to its place in the front ranks of Greek cities. However, Miletos's role as a link between West and East was also perilous. Repeatedly throughout its history, the rulers of Anatolia sought to exert control over this city, and it was in resisting one such inland force—not from moral degeneracy—that the power of Miletos was irrevocably broken.

This chapter examines the evidence pertaining to the foundations of Miletos. The plural is used advisedly, since circumstances did not allow the city to develop without interruption from its beginning. Instead, in the changing currents of Aegean history, Miletos was resettled several times. Evidence for these foundations varies. Some are remembered in the myths told by later Greeks, some are reflected in the physical remains at the site, and some are witnessed by both literature and archaeology. By sorting through diverse and sometimes contradictory evidence about the city, we are able to reconstruct a picture of its first millennium of existence, from ca. 1700 to ca. 700 B.C.E.

Indigenous People and the Bronze Age City

According to a Milesian tradition, the earliest inhabitants of the region were ruled by an autochthonous king, Anax, and his son, Asterios, a story that is preserved in the writings of Pausanias (7.2.5), a second-century C.E. traveler from the city of Magnesia on the Hermos.

Μιλήσιοι δὲ αὐτοὶ τοιάδε τὰ ἀρχαιότατά σφισιν εἶναι λέγου-
σιν· ἐπὶ γενεὰς μὲν δύο Ἀνακτορίαν καλεῖσθαι τὴν γῆν Ἄνακτός
τε αὐτόχθονος καὶ Ἀστερίου βασιλεύοντος τοῦ Ἄνακτος, Μιλήτου δὲ κατάραντος στόλῳ κρητῶν ἥ τε γῆ τὸ ὄνομα μετέβαλεν
ἀπὸ τοῦ Μιλήτου καὶ ἡ πόλις. ἀφίκετο δὲ ἐκ Κρήτης ὁ Μίλητος
καὶ ὁ σὺν αὐτῷ στρατὸς Μίνω τὸν Εὐρώπης φεύγοντες, οἱ δὲ
Κᾶρες οἱ πρότερον νεμόμενοι τὴν χώραν σύνοικοι τοῖς Κρησὶν
ἐγένοντο·

[The Milesians themselves describe the earliest events of their history as follows. For two generations the land was called Anaktoria, since Anax, a native man, and Asterios, his son, ruled it. But then Miletos landed with a fleet of Cretans, and the land and city changed its name to Miletos. Miletos and his army came from Crete, fleeing from Minos, the son of Europa. The Carians, who had previously occupied the territory, joined with the Cretans in their settlement.]

Pausanias offers a great deal of interesting information; unfortunately, most of it is not very useful. Details in legends concerning the distant past are a priori suspect, and in this case particularly, the names *Anax* and *Asterios* are clearly later inventions: *Anax* was certainly created as a personification of the Greek title *wanax,* meaning "master" or "lord," while *Asterios* means "starry." In addition, both men provide aetiologies for local place-names. *Anaktoria* is a name attested—albeit rarely—for Miletos,[1] and in another passage (1.35.6), Pausanias tells us that Asterios was buried near Lade on a small island that took his name. In addition, the mention of the Carians is also problematic, since the point of the πρότερον, "before," is ambiguous: it may refer to a time either before the rule of Anax and his son or before the arrival of the Cretans. Pausanias leaves unclear whether the Carians made up the people of Anax and Asterios or whether, displaced briefly by a discrete people called the Anaktorians, they returned with the help of the Cretans.

Whichever is the correct interpretation, it probably represents a projection into the past of contemporary circumstances, for the Carians were in fact the native people living in the environs of Miletos in historical times: as early as the works of Homer in the eighth century B.C.E., the Carians are listed as the inhabitants of Miletos and allies of Troy (*Il.* 2.867–75). Today some scholars arguing for the historicity of the Trojan War would draw far-reaching conclusions from the comments in the *Iliad.* However, Homer's memory of a non-Greek Asia Minor should be seen more as a reflection of the general ignorance of the later Greeks about their Mycenaean ancestors than as historical evidence about the Bronze Age.[2] By the time the historians begin writing, in the fifth century and afterward, the

---

1. Only here and in Steph. Byz. s.v. At Paus. 1.35.6, Anax is the son of the gods Ouranos and Ge, and the name is often given to underworld powers: see Dunham 1915, 35.
2. For a general discussion, see Starke 1997; Raaflaub 1998a, 1998b.

Carians are a pastoral people often occupying hilltop villages that were centered around religious sanctuaries. They settled in the mountainous interior of southwestern Anatolia, from Miletos on the north, southward to Kaunos, and inland up the Maiandros River valley and its tributaries as far east as Aphrodisias.

It is likely that the story reported by Pausanias was influenced by the later situation and that the idea that the Carians were the oldest inhabitants of the area is anachronistic. Herodotos (1.171.5) offers two versions about their origins, saying that the Carians moved from the islands to the mainland, according to the Cretan account, but that the Carians themselves claim to be indigenous. Neither of these origins fits well with the extant evidence. If the Carians were indigenous, they should have been in residence continuously from the Stone Age; however, the Stone Age settlements near Miletos have little in common with the later Carian settlements, and they ceased to exist around 2300 B.C.E. at the very latest.[3] In addition, early finds in the interior of Caria are very few. Thus, the archaeological evidence weighs in favor of the Carians being immigrants to the area. Those who favor an indigenous origin must argue that we simply do not have comprehensive enough data to give an accurate picture of Anatolian prehistory. However, the few Stone Age remains found at Miletos do demonstrate an affinity to finds in the Dodecanese. This connection indicates that contact was made between Miletos and the islands in the Chalcolithic period and would seem in harmony with an insular origin for the Carians. Yet it is impossible to say whether the influence went from the islands to the mainland or the reverse, and cultural affinity need not indicate population movements. Thus, the physical evidence is inconclusive: "the origin of the Carians is archaeologically inscrutable."[4]

Linguistic considerations may help decide the issue, though in favor of neither traditional view. It has recently been established that the Carian language is Indo-European, a member of the Anatolian language group that also includes Luwian and Hittite. This discovery weighs heavily in favor of an arrival date early in the Bronze Age, from the east and north. Thus, the Carians were neither aboriginal nor from the islands. One could contend that the indigenous Carians borrowed their language from other,

---

3. At least two prehistoric sites have been found in and near Miletos (see discussion following). Voigtländer (1982, 41) would like these settlers to be ancestors of the Carians, but Parzinger (1989, 424) disagrees.

4. Cook 1975, 794–95. Cf. Melas 1988, esp. 109: "The two areas [Caria and the Dodecanese] appear to have shared a more or less common culture in prehistory."

later Indo-European immigrants, but such an argument is both unnecessarily complex and unprovable. In sum, the evidence strongly favors the view that the Carians were a nonindigenous, Indo-European people, although the current state of the evidence does not permit certainty.[5]

Besides the Carians, the Leleges are the native people mentioned most often in connection with Miletos: Μίλητος πόλις Ἰώνων ἐπιφανής. Ἐκλήθη δέ ποτε καὶ Λελεγὶς διὰ ἐποίκους Λέλεγας [Miletos is a famous city of Ionia. It was once called Lelegis as well when it was occupied by the Leleges].[6] Greek authors often speak of the Leleges, but they know strangely little about them. For example, the geographer Strabo (12.8.5) attempts to clarify their role in Milesian prehistory as well as their relationship with the Carians.

καὶ οἱ Κᾶρες δὲ νησιῶται πρότερον ὄντες καὶ Λέλεγες, ὥς φασιν, ἠπειρῶται γεγόνασι, προσλαβόντων Κρητῶν, οἳ καὶ τὴν Μίλητον ἔκτισαν, ἐκ τῆς Κρητικῆς Μιλήτου Σαρπηδόνα λαβόντες κτίστην·

[Also, the Carians, who were formerly islanders, and the Leleges, as they say, became mainlanders with the help of the Cretans, who also founded Miletos, having taken as their founder Sarpedon from Cretan Miletos.]

Strabo also reports (7.7.2 = Pherek. *FGH* 3 F 155) that some equate the two people while others distinguish them, particularly by their geographic distribution: the Carians held the land from Miletos to Ephesos, while the Leleges occupied the coastal lands near Phokaia, Chios, and Samos.[7] Despite these attempts at precision, it seems that the Greeks used the name *Leleges* very much as they used the name *Pelasgians,* as a general term to designate the pre-Greek inhabitants of Hellas, Asia Minor, and the islands. Perhaps the Leleges were a genuine prehistoric people, but the evidence for them is entirely mythological and so unreliable.[8]

---

5. Mellink 1991b, 662–65 (later Carians); Hajnal 1995 (Indo-European).

6. The geographer Eustathius quoting from Steph. Byz. (*GGM* 2.361–62, para. 823, lines 13–14); cf. Str. 14.1.6.

7. Cf. Hdt. 1.171.2, which says that the Carians who were obedient to Minos were called Leleges.

8. Geyer 1924 (in general); Parthen. 14 (at Miletos), discussed later in this chapter. Dunham (1915, 37–38) suggests that the Leleges may have been the pre-Carian, autochthonous people, while the Carians were post-Mycenaean immigrants into the islands from the Asian mainland.

Archaeology has not yet been able to yield much data on this question. Stone Age remains—stone axes, obsidian, and obsidian flakes—have been found in four different areas of the Milesian city peninsula. Isolated discoveries on the southern plain and east of the Temple of Athena have been augmented by numerous finds indicating at least two settlements. One included the block just west of the later Bouleuterion and extended over to an area under the Roman Heroon near the Baths of Faustina; the other is located on the hill now called Killiktepe, 1.5 km. south of Kalabaktepe on a southwestern ridge of Stephania, where the discovery of tools is supplemented by the remains of Neolithic walls and some graves.[9] The pottery sherds from these different areas are most typically red monochrome ware with silver and gold glimmering particles embedded in the clay *(micacaeous)*. The ceramic was not made on a potter's wheel, although much of it was fired to be moderately hard. Stylistically, these finds can be compared to those discovered on the islands of the Dodecanese, at Chios, and in the Troad, causing archaeologists to conclude that the settlements at Miletos date to the Late Chalcolithic 2–3 period (ending ca. 3200) and extend down into the Bronze Age to Early Helladic II periods (ca. 2750/2300) at the very latest.[10] Thus, the Milesian peninsula was sparsely inhabited during the Stone Age until about 2300 B.C.E., but the evidence is insufficient to determine who those natives may have been.

The peninsula then stood empty for six hundred years before the attractive location lured settlers from Crete. From at least the time of Homer onward, the legendary doings of the Cretans played a large role in the Greek picture of their own prehistory in the Heroic Age. These early Cretans were thought to have dominated the Aegean through the power of their navy and to have led out numerous colonies, including one to Miletos.[11] Among the very oldest Milesian traditions (τὰ ἀρχαιότατα, Paus. 7.2.5) is the story of an eponymous founder from Crete; in one

---

According to Aelian (*VH* 8.5), the Mydonians were another native people near Miletos, but they never appear again in the extant tradition unless they are the same Mydonians who pay part of the Carian tribute to Athens from 453/2 to 438/7 (*IG* 1³ 259.6, 261.5, etc.). Ruge (1933) thinks that it is unlikely that they are the same, and the editors of the *ATL* do not even mention the possibility. Instead, they equate the Mydonians with the Amyzoneis of Hellenistic and Roman times. See *ATL* 1.170, 344–45, 521.

9. Wiegand 1911, 4–5; Weickert et al. 1957, 117–18; Schiering 1959/60, 16ff.; Kleiner 1966, 11ff.; Kleiner 1969/70, 113–14; Voigtländer 1982, 30–41; Voigtländer 1983; Parzinger 1989.

10. Mellaart 1966; Dickinson 1994, 9–22; Melas 1988 (Dodecanese).

11. Huxley 1968, esp. 10 (early myths of the Minoan Empire).

variation of this story, a son of Apollo named Miletos fled the envy of
King Minos and eventually settled in Caria, where he founded a city
named after himself.[12] Another account (Apollod. 3.1.2.1) recombines
three elements that we have already seen in different contexts: the name
Asterios, previously seen as the name of the son of Anax; the Cretan link
to Sarpedon and Minos; and the eponymous founder. According to this
story, Asterios was a Cretan nobleman married to Europa, who had
already borne to Zeus three sons: Minos, Sarpedon, and Rhadymanthos.
The sons quarreled over the love of a boy named Miletos, with the result
that Sarpedon and Miletos fled to Caria and there built a city. Yet another
version of the story connects the name of the city in Asia Minor to that of
the like-named city on Crete: according to Ephoros, the Homeric hero
Sarpedon led colonists from Miletos (or Milatos) on Crete to Miletos in
Asia Minor.[13] The details of these myths must be dismissed as folktale
elements, and one may be skeptical in accepting even the general thrust—
the idea of Cretan colonization—as historical fact.

Modern scholars call the early Cretans "Minoans," after their famous
king Minos, who was renowned in myth for his labyrinth and minotaur.
They were a non-Greek, non-Indo-European people who occupied Crete
from earliest known times until the fifteenth century B.C.E., when, according to the prevailing theory, they were overrun by the mainland Greeks,
called Mycenaeans. When the Minoans were in their prime (MM I B–LM
I B, ca. 1900–1490/70), their prosperity and cultural influence was undoubtedly very great. However, their thalassocracy, as it is often called,
probably owed less to a powerful navy and political domination than to
their far-flung commercial enterprises and their clear cultural superiority
throughout the Aegean. Of special significance here is the fact that, while
Minoan economic influence throughout the eastern Mediterranean has
been extremely well documented by archaeological excavations, there is
little credible indication that they settled the region extensively or controlled it militarily.[14]

At first glance, then, it might seem best to interpret these myths of the
Milesian foundation as later inventions, probably based on the similarity

12. Aristokritos of Miletos *FGH* 493 F 3 = Herodoros of Heraklea *FGH* 31 F 45 = Sch.
Ap. Rhod. 1.185.
13. *FGH* 70 F 127 = Str. 14.1.6; cf. Str. 12.8.5. Herodotos (1.173) says that the Lykians
were originally from Crete and came to Asia led by Sarpedon.
14. Some basic works include Desborough 1964; Stubbings 1975; Hägg and Marinatos
1984; Bryce 1989; Dickinson 1994.

of place-names, *Milatos* in Crete and *Miletos* in Asia Minor. Since these are the only two historical occurrences of this place-name in the Greek world (Eust. *GGM* 2.361–62, para. 823), the implication is unambiguous: because the names are the same, the one city must be founded by the other. The Greeks had further reason to connect Miletos to Crete: Apollo Delphinios, the patron god of Miletos, also played an important role in various Cretan state cults (see chap. 5). Thus, one is tempted to discard the entire tradition of a Cretan foundation as a later, false explanation for the similarity in names and patron cult.

However, an unequivocal reason to believe that Minoans settled the site can be found in the archaeological digs from the Stadium Hill and the region near the Temple of Athena. From 1938 to 1973, under the leadership first of Carl Weickert and then of Gerhard Kleiner, Minoan material was brought to light, especially in the latter area. Finds included Minoan ceramics covering a wide chronological range, from one handle possibly from MM II (ca. 1900/1875–1750/20) to a number of pieces from LM I A and I B (ca. 1675/50–1490/70). For some, this Minoan pottery seemed to be conclusive evidence for a Cretan settlement at Miletos, and this view has commonly been reflected in modern scholarship on the Minoans. Others, however, remained skeptical: since what is apparently Anatolian pottery has been uncovered in the same context as the Minoan finds, some scholars have interpreted the data as indicating a colony of Minoan traders in the midst of a native Carian community, others as pointing to Minoan cultural influence in a primarily Carian population.[15] In view of the incomplete publication of the excavations of Weickert and Kleiner, each of the preceding interpretations remained plausible.

In order to try to answer the questions about Minoan settlement that the earlier excavations left open, Barbara and Wolf-Dietrich Niemeier began new excavations into the Bronze Age layers in 1994 and 1995 under the overall supervision of site director Volkmar von Graeve.[16] They undertook to identify the character of Minoan influence at Miletos and, in particular, to determine whether or not one could legitimately speak of a "Minoan settlement" at Miletos and, if so, what kind of settlement.

15. E.g., Furumark 1950, 201–2 (Minoan cultural influence); Yaker 1976, 123 (trading colony); Taylour 1983, 132, 148 (colony); Melas 1988, 114, 118 (Minoan cultural influence). The Minoan evidence found at Miletos before 1984 is summarized in Schiering 1984. See Niemeier and Niemeier 1997, 193, for a discussion of differing views.

16. All of the discussion of Bronze Age archaeology that follows is based closely on Niemeier and Niemeier 1997 and Niemeier 1998.

They began by comparing their evidence to a set of strict criteria developed by Peter Warren to define a Minoan settlement outside of Crete. These criteria include a coastal location on a small and easy promontory; an irregular street plan; Minoan architectural features; Minoan tomb types; local pottery in Minoan shapes, especially conical cups; Linear A writing; and evidence of Minoan religious ritual.[17] According to Warren, the existence of a majority of these characteristics stands as definitive proof of a Mycenaean settlement.

The Niemeiers' excavation on the Stadium Hill and at the Temple of Athena was remarkably successful: in the First Building Phase of the Bronze Age city, roughly equivalent to LM I A–LM I B (ca. 1675/50–1490/70), they found the unmistakable features of a Minoan settlement at Miletos.[18] Architecturally, it includes a building whose walls were constructed using the standard Minoan technique of smoothing only the visible parts of the stone. There were signs of Minoan cult practice, including two imported Minoan vessels—an alabaster goblet and a serpentine stone vessel—both with ritual functions.[19] Fragments of several frescoes remain, including part of a griffin and part of a white lily on a red background. Such artwork is often considered an integral part of Minoan cult life and so offers further indication that Minoan ritual was being employed at Miletos. Moreover, the very presence of a fresco indicates that this was an important building: in other Minoan cities, frescoes only occur in palaces or villas of wealthy and prominent people.

Much of the modern disagreement over the presence of Minoans at Miletos in the First Building Phase has arisen because of the incomplete publication of the ceramic evidence. The excavations of 1994 and 1995 have, to a great degree, filled this gap. The site had produced a large number of Minoan-style ceramics, both imported and locally made. Noteworthy is the so-called Standard-Tradition ware (sub LM I), which, according to the excavators, is rarely found outside of Crete except in true Minoan colonies. Most significant of all is the discovery of a large

17. Niemeier and Niemeier 1997, 194; Warren 1975, 101.

18. The three building phases were established by Weickert and followed by others, including Schiering (1959/60) and Parzinger (1989), but are significantly modified by the Niemeiers. On the dating, see Manning 1995, 217–29. For the First Building Phase, in addition to Niemeier and Niemeier 1997, see Hanfmann 1953, 3–4 and n. 11; Weickert et al. 1957; Weickert 1959; Weickert 1959/60a; Desborough 1964, 162; Kleiner 1968, 24; Schiering 1986; Niemeier 1998.

19. Warren 1969, 166–67: "Many of the stone vases were clearly made for ritual use only."

amount of everyday Minoan household ware, including several hundred locally made conical cups that are recognized as absolutely indicative of Minoan presence, as well as tripod cooking pots, fire stands, scuttles, and disc-shaped loom weights.[20] All in all, the Niemeiers are able to estimate that 98 percent of pottery found in the First Building Phase is of Minoan character, whether imported or locally made, and they compare this percentage favorably to Trianda on Rhodes and Kastri on Kythera, also thought to be Minoan colonies. In contrast, the Minoan pottery at Akrotiri on Thera, Phylakopi on Melos, and Agia Irini on Keos is in a minority and reflects trade and cultural influence rather than a Minoan presence.[21] In addition, a number of kilns have been found that are unquestionably Minoan: the only other place where kilns of this style have been discovered is on Crete.

Finally, three pieces of a locally made clay pot were fit together to reveal an example of Linear A (MIL Zb1), the undeciphered script of the Minoan civilization. This find represents the earliest known writing sample from all of western Asia Minor. Of the three symbols recorded— AB56, AB41, and AB47—the last is very rare: there are only eight other extant instances of it, and all of those come from Crete itself. The presence of this sign at Miletos is taken to mean that Linear A and the Cretan language were very familiar to the earliest Milesians.

While it is nearly impossible to prove to everyone's satisfaction that Miletos was a Cretan site, the force of this newest evidence is difficult to resist: the Niemeiers' work has revealed five of Warren's seven criteria, lacking only the irregular street plan, which does in fact seem to be emerging,[22] and the Minoan tombs, which have not been found. Miletos was probably what some scholars classify as a *settlement colony,* a true Minoan city built on previously unoccupied land.[23] The architectural

---

20. Niemeier 1998, 27; Wiener 1984 (conical cups). Concluding his list of criteria for determining Minoan presence outside of Crete, Warren (1975, 101) says, "The presence of all or a majority of these features [the criteria already listed], especially the quantities of cheap but uniquely Minoan conical cups, should indicate a Minoan settlement."

21. Niemeier and Niemeier 1997, 238; Branigan 1981 (other Minoan colonies).

22. Niemeier 1998, 29 fig. 7.

23. Branigan (1981) defines three options: a *governed colony,* where a settlement of largely indigenous people are governed by a foreign power; a *community colony,* where the foreign settlers make up a significant element of the society but it is ruled by the indigenous people; and a *settlement colony,* founded by immigrants and ruled either by them or by their home power. According to his definitions, Akrotiri, Phylakopi, and Ayia Irini on Keos were all Minoan community colonies, while Kastri on Kythera was a settlement colony. Cf. the discussion in Schofield 1984.

style, the household pottery, the kilns, the religious objects, the implied wealth and prominence of the building that housed frescoes, and especially the Linear A symbols etched onto local pottery indicate that we must speak not of a Minoan influence on the native Milesian culture but of a dominating Minoan presence.

We cannot say with certainty when the Cretans arrived. The earliest remains include a fragment of a handle possibly from MM II and increasing numbers of imported ceramic beginning from MM III B, indicating a Minoan presence by ca. 1700 and influence as much as two centuries earlier.[24] However, the First Building Phase rests on a layer of rubble 1–1.5 m. thick that contains a jumble of earlier layers that have become unstratified, so it is impossible to determine when the Minoans first settled Miletos. The small Stone Age community that preceded them seems to have been long gone, and although it is possible that a small native population still occupied the site, their physical remains have been completely lost in the rubble. Thus, the Minoans either settled on an abandoned site or they expelled or absorbed a small, preexisting native community.

Around 1470/50 B.C.E., Minoan civilization suffered a disastrous decline throughout the Aegean. In Crete itself, the palaces were destroyed and the Greek-speaking Mycenaeans from the mainland took control of Knossos and many other sites. The cultural center of Aegean civilization shifted from Crete to the Mycenaean cities of Hellas, where it would remain until the end of the Bronze Age, ca. 1150 B.C.E.

The legends have nothing whatsoever to say about the end of the Minoan settlement at Miletos, but the archaeological record demonstrates that events at Miletos conform to the pattern observed at other sites.[25] Recent excavations have confirmed earlier reports that the First Building Phase ended in a destruction layer (LM I B, ca. 1490/70), while the pottery found in the two later Bronze Age levels—the Second Building Phase (LH III A1–2, ca. 1435/05–1330/25) and the Third Building Phase (LH III B–C, ca. 1320/1300–1050/30)—is predominantly Mycenaean in character. At the same time, it is thought that Miletos offers an excellent opportunity to study the transition from Minoan to Mycenaean settlements, since finds in the Second Building Phase point to continuing traces of Minoan influence. Certainly the plan of the settlement changed,

---

24. Schiering 1959/60, 16.
25. Kilian 1990 (Mycenaean colonization).

as the house walls of the Second Building Phase were not aligned along the ruins of the First Building Phase. However, a slight intermingling of Minoan pottery among the predominantly Mycenaean fragments indicates that the Minoan presence was not altogether obliterated. Furthermore, this continuity of cultural influence is supported by the discovery in each of the other two Bronze Age building phases of two kilns of a type that is only otherwise found on Crete.[26]

Investigation of the area of the Stadium Hill has yielded little clear architectural evidence for the Second Building Phase. The area is very poorly preserved, and while the unstratified remains indicate that the Stadium Hill was definitely occupied in the Bronze Age, so much damage has been done in later construction (this was the site of the old village of Balat until 1955) that it is nearly impossible to clarify the picture.

Although it has been hampered by a terrible groundwater problem, the excavation of the Second Building Phase near the Temple of Athena has been significantly more productive, yielding much Mycenaean-style pottery and uniquely Mycenaean-style kilns. A terracotta female figurine of the *phi* type indicates the probability of Mycenaean cult practices. Excavators have also found a building complex that existed in the Second Building Phase and was reused, at least in part, during the Third Building Phase, and the earlier part of this structure has been identified as *Oikos*-Type 2, a style of building that has parallels in Mycenae and Tiryns and in the Anatolian tradition.[27] In the later part of the fourteenth century, Miletos was destroyed by a conflagration: excavators have found a fire destruction layer 30 cm. thick both on the Stadium Hill and near the Temple of Athena. Of the unpainted and the painted pottery sherds found in the burn layer, which belongs to the transition between LH III A2 and LH III B (ca. 1330–1320), almost all are Mycenaean. In sum, the Niemeiers estimate that the ceramic finds of the Second Building Phase are 95 percent Mycenaean.[28]

The Third Building Phase is difficult to reconstruct because it was badly damaged by later construction: at times, the Geometric house foundations rest immediately on top of the burn layer from the Second Build-

---

26. Niemeier and Niemeier 1997, 194, 222–23, 228, 244; Niemeier 1998, 31–32.
27. Niemeier 1998, 30–31; Hiesel 1990, 59–67.
28. Second Building Phase: Schiering 1959/60, 10–11; Hommell 1959/60, 34–36; Niemeier and Niemeier 1997, 219–29; French 1971, 116–23 (*phi* figurines in general). Destruction: Schiering 1959/60, 5, 8ff.; Schiering 1979, 85–87; Mee 1978, 135; Niemeier and Niemeier 1997, esp. 196, 219.

ing Phase, and while there are a great deal of individual ceramic finds from the Third Building Phase, they are not preserved in a recognizable layer of their own. Some significant evidence, however, has been unearthed. From this period dates a fortification wall 4.4 m. thick, which would have enclosed approximately 50,000 sq. m. Other architectural remains include a so-called corridor house, a style that appears in large numbers in the Mycenaean world in the thirteenth century, and among the artifacts was found a Mycenaean *psi* type religious figurine and three animals of the Linear 1 variety.[29] In addition, possible Linear B symbols have been found on fragments of locally made *pithoi*, which were incised before they were fired. These symbols are problematic, and their identification as Linear B has not been universally accepted.[30]

One of the most surprising results of the Niemeiers' excavations in the Third Building Phase is negative in its implications. Earlier digs on the Stadium Hill uncovered what was said to be a Mycenaean *megaron*, with associated living quarters and courtyard. It has been suggested that this complex may be the Mycenaean palace, which, if correct, would have important implications for the interpretation of Mycenaean political organization. Unfortunately, the excavation of 1994 quickly revealed that the identification was mistaken. The walls of the so-called *megaron* belong instead to two separate phases of construction, and, furthermore, neither of them is Bronze Age. Distinctly Archaic sherds under the walls indicate that it was probably built after the destruction by the Persians in 494.[31]

In contrast to the disappointed hopes for a palace complex, a remarkable feature of this Mycenaean settlement is its extent, since the remains from the Third Building Phase are not confined to the small area dug around the Temple of Athena and the Stadium Hill. Instead, in another dig from the 1970s in the plain midway between the Theater Harbor and Kalabaktepe (between the later Round Church and the Hellenistic cross

---

29. Third Building Phase: *Milet* 1.8.73–77, 2.3.119; Weickert 1940, 328; Weickert 1959/60b (fortification wall); Weickert et al. 1957, 106–25; Hommell 1959/60, 31–38; Mallwitz 1959/60b (fortification wall); Mallwitz 1968; Kleiner 1966, 11–14; Kleiner 1968, 9, 38, 122–23; Kleiner 1969/70, 114–18; Müller-Wiener 1986a, 100; Mee 1978, 133–55 (135–36, area within the wall); Mellink 1983; Furumark 1950, 201–2; Desborough 1964, 161–63; Voigtländer 1975 (fortification wall); Mitchell and McNicoll 1978/79, 63; Stubbings 1975, 184; Niemeier and Niemeier 1997, 196–98 (corridor house), 219; French 1971, 126–42 (*psi* figurines in general), 157–64 (animal figurines).

30. Schiering 1979, 102–3; esp. Niemeier 1998, 37. One of the symbols especially may be an arrow-like sign found elsewhere on Hittite vessels.

31. Schiering 1975; Schiering 1979, 77–78 *(megaron)*; Mellink 1972, 175 *(megaron)*; Hommel 1975 (palace); Niemeier and Niemeier 1997, 195, 207–9 (Classical).

wall), at a location 500 m. south of the Mycenaean harbor wall, archaeologists have found numerous Late Mycenaean sherds, one large Mycenaean kiln and part of another, flues, and partition walls made of clay bricks.[32] This evidence is obviously limited, but so is the scope of excavation there, whereas the damage done by later levels is extensive. Certainly there is enough to indicate a Mycenaean presence, but there is not enough to tell us whether this settlement was discrete from the one by the harbor or whether the two represent parts of one very large settlement. This puzzle will only be solved when and if the archaeologists expand their Bronze Age explorations into the intervening areas. Meanwhile, the possibility of a large Mycenaean settlement is tantalizing.

Furthermore, a Mycenaean necropolis has been found on Degirmentepe, 1.5 km. to the south. It contains eleven Mycenaean-style chamber tombs, one of the determining criteria for a settlement colony. The contents of those tombs have never been properly published, and most were lost in Berlin during World War II. However, some items have recently been rediscovered in storage and may be published in the future. Meanwhile, the Niemeiers discuss (and offer photographs of) the more interesting finds, which include earthenware vessels, bronze weapons, horse bridles, plumb bobs, drilled boars' tusks, and jewelry.[33]

The evidence discovered to date, limited though it may be, supports the conclusion that Mycenaean settlers occupied Miletos from LH III A1 (beginning ca. 1435/05) to LH III C (ending ca. 1100/1090). The evidence of Mycenaean cult, the Mycenaean-style corridor house, and the masses of Mycenaean pottery, taken together with the chamber tombs on Degirmentepe, imply a significant Mycenaean colony. The character of the colony cannot be determined definitively, given the limited state of the evidence; however, two features in particular argue for a settlement colony.[34] The architectural and ceramic break that divides the Second Build-

---

32. Graeve 1973/74, 68–69; Kleine 1979, 111–15, 135–36.

33. *Milet* 1.8.12; Furumark 1950, 201–2; Kleiner 1966, 11; Kleiner 1968, 124–25; Bittel 1975 (bridles); Müller-Wiener 1986a, 104; Niemeier and Niemeier 1997, esp. 190–91, 244; Niemeier 1998, 36.

34. According to Bryce (1989), we must think of Mycenaean involvement in Anatolia in terms less of a colonizing movement and more of a quest for the resources that area had to offer, such as metals, livestock, and slaves: the population of the city may have been predominantly native, with a generous intermingling of Mycenaean adventurers and traders. Compare Stubbings (1975, 184), who thinks that under the Mycenaeans much of the population of Miletos was made up of native Carians. However, in recent years the Niemeiers' work has shown the opposite to be true: the Mycenaeans made up the majority of the settlement, probably even after the Hittites took control of the government.

ing Phase from the First Building Phase suggests that the people occupying the site were nearly completely replaced at the end of the Minoan era: greater continuity would be expected if the Mycenaeans had come as rulers over a population that was largely native or survivors of the Minoan era. Second, the predominance of Mycenaean pottery—95 percent in the Second Building Phase—signifies that the new population represented not a small enclave but the majority of what may prove to be a very large settlement. Although no pre-Geometric remnants have been found in other parts of the peninsula, indicating that the Bronze Age city probably did not extend over to the Lion Bay and the area immediately south of it, the finds near the Theater Harbor and on the southern plain, as well as the necropolis 1.5 km. from the harbor, lead to the conclusion that the Mycenaeans had developed Miletos as one of their most important and extensive colonies, one that proved to be an irresistible target for the other major power of the day.

During the time that Miletos belonged to Greeks from the mainland, most of Asia Minor fell under the sway of the Hittites. From his capital at Hattusa, near the river Halys, the Hittite king ruled an empire that stretched from northern Syria to western Anatolia. Miletos, linked to the interior by the valley of the Maiandros, could not fail to feel the influence of the great kingdom to its east. A witness to the relationship between the city and the Hittite Empire has been found in the evidence from the royal archives of the Hittites, thousands of clay tablets covered with cuneiform, which have been unearthed at the site of Hattusa (modern Bogazköy). These documents seem to indicate that in the fourteenth and thirteenth centuries, Miletos passed back and forth between Mycenaean and Hittite control.[35]

Among the Hittite documents are numerous references to the land and king of the Ahhiyawa. Already in the early days after the decipherment of Hittite in 1915, the suggestion was made that the word *Ahhiyawa* was the Hittite representation of the Greek word *Achaioi,* the term Homer uses to designate the Greek forces at the siege of Troy—in other words, the Mycenaeans.[36] Furthermore (and of special interest to this study), in several texts, the king of the Ahhiyawa is associated with the city and the land of Millawanda (or Milawata). Several scholars have advanced Miletos as the best choice among the possible locations of Millawanda, and if this

---

35. Bryce (1998, passim) discusses the entire matter in the context of his history of the Hittites.
36. Forrer 1924a, 1924b.

identification is correct, the Hittite archives constitute a resource of unparalleled importance for the investigation of Bronze Age Miletos.

It must, however, be admitted at the outset that the equations of Ahhiyawa with Achaioi and Millawanda with Miletos are by no means securely established.[37] There is no conclusive evidence either for or against these equivalences, but the arguments in favor seem convincing. In particular, supporters of the Ahhiyawa/Achaioi hypothesis point out that the denial of this connection would mean the absence of the Mycenaeans from all extant Hittite texts. This startling result is unacceptable in light of the increasingly substantial archaeological evidence for Mycenaean activity in western Anatolia. Furthermore, it is pointed out that if the equivalence is rejected, we must wonder who these Ahhiyawa could be.[38] This kingdom is so important that its king is listed as equal in rank to the kings of the Hittites, Egyptians, Babylonians, and Assyrians, yet we can come up with no candidates for this role in all that we have learned from the combined literature of all peoples.

The earliest document with implications for the relationship between Miletos and the Hittite kingdom is called the Madduwatta text (*KUB* 14.1), written by an unnamed Hittite king who has been identified as Arnuwandas I (ca. 1450–1430).[39] The text states that a certain Madduwatta had been driven from his home by "Attarissiyas, the man of Ahhiya" (*Ahhiya* is an early form of *Ahhiyawa*). Madduwatta took refuge with Tudhaliyas, the father of the current Hittite king, who protected Madduwatta and made him a vassal. Later, the Ahhiyawan Attarissiyas once again came against Madduwatta with one hundred chariots, a considerable force that would require a strong home base. Certain places mentioned in the text (e.g., Arzawa, Talawas) have been located in southwestern Anatolia, suggesting that Attarissiyas—and thus the Ahhiyawa—was active in that region as early as the second half of the fifteenth century.

---

37. For a list of those who support and deny the equation, see Bryce 1989, 3 nn. 12–14; Niemeier 1998, 17–25. Among those accepting it, in addition to Bryce and Niemeier, are Güterbock (1983, 1984, 1986) and Mellink (1983).

38. One cannot argue that the name *Achaioi* was an invention by Homer or later Greeks, because the name *Achaiwia* occurs on a Linear B tablet from Knossos (C 914): see Bryce 1989; Güterbock 1983. Niemeier (1998, 40) offers as evidence two other tablets that mention a woman from Miletos (*mi-ra-ti-ja*, from Pylos) and a man from Miletos (*mi-ra-ti-jo*, from Thebes). The tablet from Pylos denotes this woman in the context of a list of probable slaves from sites on the Asiatic coast and offshore islands, indicating that at least the Milesian woman came from Ionian Miletos, not Milatos on Crete.

39. Bryce 1985.

Another pertinent piece of information comes from the *Comprehensive Annals* of the Hittite King Mursili II (*CTH* 61, late fourteenth century B.C.E.). The passage in question relates the events of the third year of Mursili's reign. The text is badly damaged, but it is clear in the first line that Uhhaziti, the ruler of Arzawa, is sometime enemy and sometime vassal of the Hittites. The following line mentions both the land of Millawanda and the king of the Ahhiyawa. Next, Mursili reports that he sent two of his generals, who attacked and captured Millawanda. The accepted interpretation of this lacunose text is that Millawanda, a Hittite vassal, was enticed by Uhhaziti of Arzawa to shift allegiance to the king of Ahhiyawa. Mursili dealt with the rebellion harshly, by sacking Millawanda, then conquering Arzawa and ending its separate existence.[40]

By the time of the Tawagalawa letter (*CTH* 181), ca. 1265–1240, however, Millawanda had come under Ahhiyawan control. One scholar argues that the transfer took place sometime before 1275, for when Mursili's successor, Muwatalli (ca. 1296–1272), drew up a list of potential troublemakers as he prepared for the confrontation with the Egyptians at Kadesh (*CTH* 76), neither Millawanda nor Ahhiyawa was on that list. The suggestion is that the Hittites had peacefully ceded Millawanda to the Ahhiyawa as a diplomatic move intended to satisfy the king of Ahhiyawa and ensure against future aggression in Anatolia.[41] If this interpretation is correct, Muwatalli's efforts were unsuccessful, as the Ahhiyawa encouraged raids into Hittite territory. In the Tawagalawa letter—written by a Hittite king, probably Hattusili III (ca. 1265–1240), to the Ahhiyawan king—a Hittite renegade named Piyamaradu has taken refuge in Millawanda after carrying out raids on Hittite territory. The Hittite king sent a messenger to the king of the Ahhiyawa—whose sovereignty over Millawanda he clearly recognizes—to ask for the surrender of Piyamaradu. A king of the Ahhiyawa instructed Apta, his vassal in charge of Millawanda, to comply, and the Hittite king went to Millawanda to receive the renegade. However, Piyamaradu had escaped by ship to the king of the Ahhiyawa, perhaps with the connivance of Apta, who was the son-in-law of the fugitive. Thus, the Tawagalawa letter provides evidence that Miletos served as a base of operations for incursions against Hittite power. The actions of Piyamaradu were perceived as a serious enough threat against Hittite interests to warrant a journey to Miletos by the king

40. Singer 1983, 206 with n. 7.
41. Bryce 1989, 8–9.

himself. Elsewhere in the letter, we read that the brother of the Ahhiyawan king, the Tawagalawa who gave his name to the letter, was himself present in Millawanda and from there engaged in activities in the Lukka lands (possibly Lykia).

Two more letters seem to substantiate the raiding of Piyamaradu. These letters (*CTH* 191 and *KUB* 23.13) are written by the Hittite vassal ruler of the Seha River Land, which is probably an area on the Maiandros River. The vassal complains that with the help of the Ahhiyawa, Piyamaradu has put Apta over him; thus the letters imply that the Ahhiyawan vassal rulers are making indirect inroads into the territory of Hittite vassal rulers. The interpretation of a third missive, called the Milawata letter (*CTH* 182) and thought to be written by Hattusili III's successor, Tadhaliya IV (second half of the thirteenth century), is difficult, but it may indicate that Milawata had fallen into the hands of the Hittites.[42]

Bronze Age archaeological evidence is consistent with the identification of Millawanda and Miletos. The destruction layer that marked the end of the Second Building Phase may reflect the sack of Millawanda by Mursili in the third year of his reign, ca. 1318–1314; recently discovered information on the dating of the transition from LH III A2 to LH III B, marked by a thick ash layer, makes a date of 1318–1314 quite possible.[43] After the sack, Miletos fell into the hands of the Hittites and then passed back and forth between Hittite and Mycenaean control.

Certain finds from the Third Building Phase show an interesting convergence between the Hittite and the Mycenaean. The dominant architectural feature of that building phase is the thick fortification wall, which was constructed in the thirteenth century. It is controversial because it embodies characteristics of both Hittite and Mycenaean building design.[44] Other pertinent finds include horse bridles that could be Hittite and bronze swords that definitely are, all found in the context of the Mycenaean-style chamber tombs in the necropolis. Finally, one of the most interesting examples of the intersection of the two cultures can be seen in the fragment of a locally made krater from LH III B2–III C that was glazed

---

42. Singer (1983, 215) disagrees, claiming instead, "as far as we can tell from the Hittite texts, Milawata was never ruled by the Hittites."

43. Mellink 1983; Niemeier and Niemeier 1997, 200–205, esp. 246–48 (redating); Niemeier 1998.

44. Mallwitz (1959/60b) thinks it is Hittite, but Kleiner (1969/70, 114) denies this, calling it Mycenaean. Naumann (1971, esp. Appendix 1) may be closer to the truth when he calls it a compromise style. See discussion at Niemeier and Niemeier 1997, 196, 203.

according to a Mycenaean technique but features a picture of a Hittite horned crown, such as was worn only by gods and the Great King.[45] Thus the material evidence from Miletos supports the equation of that city with Millawanda. At the same time, the continuity of ceramic and architectural remains, both between the Second and Third Building Phases and within the Third Building Phase, suggests that the population of the city remained Mycenaean even during the periods when it may have fallen under Hittite control: the rulers may have changed, but the makeup of the community remained substantially the same.

The Ionian Foundation

Around 1200 B.C.E., disasters began to strike the Hittites, leading to the collapse of their civilization. However, the Mycenaeans were in no position to take advantage of the Hittite misfortune, because they too were faced with calamity: many settlements in the Peloponnesos, the heart of the Mycenaean world, were destroyed and abandoned. For some time, Miletos and the Aegean islands escaped the spreading catastrophe and remained fairly prosperous. Then, in the middle or near the end of the LH III C period (ca. 1130–1070 or ca. 1070/50–1030), the Bronze Age in Miletos came to an end, as it too was destroyed. There is no literary account of the downfall of the Mycenaean settlements, at Miletos or elsewhere (the Greeks seemed oblivious to the fact of their collapse). However, legend identified this period as the time when the people redistributed themselves into the patterns recognized by the later Greeks.

Miletos is given a leading role in the stories of the great population movements of this period, for it was the first Anatolian foundation established in the wave of resettlement known as the Ionian Migration. The Ionians are said to have originally inhabited the area in the northern Peloponnesos that was later known as Achaia. The tribe of Dorians, led by the descendants of Herakles, are supposed to have descended out of the north into the Peloponnesos, where they overran Lakedaimonia, Argos, and Pylos. When the Dorians entered the regions of Argos and Lakedaimonia, they set in motion a chain of events that led to the expulsion of the

45. Niemeier and Niemeier 1997, 203–5. The krater fragment is first published in Weickert 1959/60b, 65.

Ionians from their homeland, and these refugees fled to Attica (Paus. 7.1.1–9). Once there, legend joins the fate of the Ionians to that of the family of a certain Melanthos, a prince from Pylos in Messenia, the region in the extreme southwest corner of the Peloponnesos. The story is elaborated by Hellanikos of Lesbos, a logographer from the fifth century B.C.E. (*FGH* 4 F 125 = Sch. Pl. *Symp.* 208d). According to him, Melanthos migrated from Messenia to Athens and, through a feat of bravery, became king. His son, Kodros, and then his grandson Medon followed him on the throne. Meanwhile Medon's younger brother, Neleus, seeing no future for himself in Attika, led out a migration to Ionia and founded a league of cities there. Thus, in this tradition, Neleus, the leader of the Ionian Migration, is a member of the Pylian—and Athenian—royal house.

Several other historians confirm the basic story. Herodotos (5.65.3) confirms that Kodros, Melanthos, and Neleus were of Pylian ancestry: he probably got his information from a history of the Neleids and the colonization of Ionia written in six thousand verses by Panyassis of Halikarnassos, Herodotos's own uncle or cousin (Douris *FGH* 76 F 64). According to another version told by Pausanias (7.2.1–6; cf. Ael. *VH* 8.5), Medon and Neleus quarreled over the throne. When the Oracle settled in favor of Medon, Neleus and the remaining sons of Kodros left Attika, ἀγαγόντες μὲν καὶ αὐτῶν Ἀθηναίων τὸν βουλόμενον, τὸ δὲ πλεῖστόν σφισιν ἦσαν τοῦ στρατεύματος οἱ Ἴωνες [leading out with them any Athenian who wished to go, but the majority of the expedition was composed of Ionians] (Paus. 7.2.1). They founded the various cities of Ionia, and Neleus himself founded Miletos; either he killed the males of the old Milesians there (τῶν ἀρχαίων Μιλησίων, 7.2.5) and married the women or he expelled all the Milesians.

The myths also make it clear that the Attic-Ionians were not the exclusive settlers of Ionia. Rather, they provided the leaders and a significant enough proportion of the people in the migration to establish an ethnic cohesiveness, while many of the settlers came from elsewhere in Hellas. Herodotos describes one segment of the original group of settlers as οἱ δὲ αὐτῶν ἀπὸ τοῦ πρυτανηίου τοῦ Ἀθηναίων ὁρμηθέντες καὶ νομίζοντες γενναιότατοι εἶναι Ἰώνων [the ones who set out from the Prytaneion in Athens and believed themselves to be of the purest Ionian blood] (1.146.2). He continues, εἰσὶ δὲ πάντες Ἴωνες, ὅσοι ἀπ' Ἀθηνέων γεγόνασι καὶ Ἀπατούρια ἄγουσι ὁρτήν [They are all Ionians, whoever had come from Athens and celebrates the festival of the Apatouria]

(1.147.2).[46] However, he is also quick to point out the mixture of peoples involved in the expedition (1.146.1), listing the Abantes from Euboia; Minyans from Orchomenos; Kadmeians, Dryopians, and Phokians from Phokis; Molossians; Arkadian Pelasgians; Dorians from Epidauros; and other non-Ionic Greeks. Pausanias (7.2.1–4) agrees that the venture was primarily Ionian but that the sons of Kodros took with them any Athenians who wished to go along, as well as Thebans, Minyans from Orchomenos, all of the Phokians except the Delphians, and the Abantes from Euboia.

The essential features of the myths are recapitulated as follows: The Ionians left the Peloponnesos after the arrival there of the Dorians. They took refuge in Attica. Within a few generations, Neleus, son of the Athenian king and born of Pylian ancestry, led them across the Aegean to found the Ionian duodecapolis. Admittedly, refugees from much of Greece joined them in this endeavor, but the Ionians formed the core of the expedition and provided the basic organizational structure of the cities they founded.[47]

In evaluating these myths of the Ionian Migration, we can say little about the idea of a central group of refugees from the Peloponnesos. It is not implausible on the face of it, since the Peloponnesos was the population center of the Mycenaean civilization. Nor is it unlikely that the colonization effort was joined by settlers from throughout Greece, but without further evidence, we can make no firmer judgment.

Our position is more secure with regard to the Pylian origin of Neleus. Although modern archaeology has proven the importance of Pylos in the Bronze Age, the Messenian connection to Miletos is probably a fabrication based on a similarity of names. It is the nearly unanimous tradition in later Greece that Neleus led the Greeks to Ionia. Remembering that the only other prominent Neleus in Greek tradition was the father of Nestor, the king of Pylos who was immortalized in the epics of Homer, the ancient Greek would necessarily associate the two and feel obliged to connect them, concluding that Neleus, the founder of Ionia, must have had roots at Pylos in Messenia. Stories then were created to fit this

---

46. Connor (1993, 197–98) denies the connection, noting the absence of a month in Attica named after this festival and postulating from that that Athens was not part of the Ionian kinship group but only adopted the festival at a late date.

47. Cook 1975, 783–84. For other possible non-Attic Greek elements in Miletos in particular, see Sakellariou 1958, 39–76, 254–68, 367–79.

connection within the dominant tradition that Athens was the launching place of the Ionian Migration.[48] Until other evidence can be found to corroborate the Messenian connection, it should be discounted as an artificial construction.

However, the principal feature of the myths, the leading role given to Athens—one of the few cities not destroyed and abandoned in the upheavals of the early Dark Ages—is almost certainly historical. It is evidenced not only by traditional accounts but also by dialect, social institutions, and ceramic finds. To begin with tradition, the idea that Athens was the point of origin for the Ionian Migration is clearly quite old. It is first attested in the work of the Athenian leader Solon (Arist. *Ath. Pol.* 5 = fr. 4 Diehl), who portrays Athens as the ancestral home of Ionians (πρεσβυτάτην γαῖαν Ἰαονίης [oldest land of Ionia]). The existence ca. 600 B.C.E. of this belief in the Athenian ancestry of Ionia means that the idea was not an invention to serve Athenian imperial purposes during the zenith of that city's power in the fifth century.

The next appearance of the tradition in the historical record indicates the importance of the idea in the second half of the fifth century. In the Herodotean account, the belief in the Athenian mother city formed an integral part of the argument of Aristagoras of Miletos when he approached the Athenians to ask for help in the Ionian Revolt of 499. Herodotos relates how Aristagoras went first to Lakedaimonia, where his mission failed. He then proceeded to Athens, where, as at Sparta, his plea was based on a twofold appeal: to self-interest and to right.

ἐπελθὼν δὲ ἐπὶ τὸν δῆμον ὁ Ἀρισταγόρης ταὐτὰ ἔλεγε τὰ καὶ ἐν τῇ Σπάρτῃ περὶ τῶν ἀγαθῶν τῶν ἐν τῇ Ἀσίῃ καὶ τοῦ πολέμου τοῦ Περσικοῦ, ὡς οὔτε ἀσπίδα οὔτε δόρυ νομίζουσι εὐπετέες τε χειρωθῆναι εἴησαν. (2) ταῦτά τε δὴ ἔλεγε καὶ πρὸς τοῖσι τάδε, ὡς οἱ Μιλήσιοι τῶν Ἀθηναίων εἰσὶ ἄποικοι, καὶ οἰκός σφεας εἴη ῥύεσθαι δυναμένους μέγα. καὶ οὐδὲν ὅ τι οὐκ ὑπίσχετο οἷα κάρτα δεόμενος, ἐς ὃ ἀνέπεισέ σφεας.

[Coming before the assembly, Aristagoras said the things he had said at Sparta about the good things in Asia and about Persian

---

48. Str. 14.1.6 = Ephor. *FGH* 70 F 127; Ael. *VH* 8.5; Marm. Par. *FGH* 239 F 27; Polyb. 16.12.1–2; Polyain. 8.35; Kallim. *Art.* 225. Mimnermos (fr. 12 Diehl) says that the Ionian city Kolophon was founded by Pylos.

warfare, how they did not use shields or spears and were easy to conquer. In addition to these arguments, he said that the Milesians were colonists of the Athenians, and so it was fitting for them to come to help, since they were so mighty. And there was nothing that he did not promise that they might want until he persuaded them.] (Hdt. 5.97.1–2)[49]

Aristagoras could only appeal to the Spartans as fellow Greeks (ἄνδρας ὁμαίμονας [men of the same blood] Hdt. 5.49.3),[50] but at Athens he could invoke the ties of close kinship, saying that the Milesians were colonists (ἄποικοι) of the Athenians, and here he was successful. Aristagoras's tactic in this argument points to a widespread familiarity among the Athenian demos with the idea that Athens played a major role in the Ionian Migration.

It might be objected that Herodotos casts doubt on the veracity of the tradition that Aristagoras invokes, when, commenting on the Athenian decision to help the Ionians, the historian remarks, πολλοὺς γὰρ οἶκε εἶναι εὐπετέστερον διαβάλλειν ἢ ἕνα [for it seems to be easier to deceive many than one] (5.97.2). Clearly Herodotos thinks that Aristagoras is being dishonest in his argument. But it is equally clear that the deceitful element is not in the claim that the Milesians were colonists of the Athenians. Rather, since Aristagoras tried to trick both the Lakedaimonians and the Athenians, the dishonesty must lie in that part of the argument common to both speeches: the promise that the unwarlike Persians could be easily defeated and the riches of Asia readily attained. This conclusion is confirmed by Herodotos's words at 5.50. Here Aristagoras, who up to that point was successfully deceiving (διαβάλλων) the Spartan king Kleomenes about the situation in Asia, foolishly let slip the fact that the Persian seat of government was three months' journey from the Ionian coast. Kleomenes now realized the true difficulty of the undertaking Aristagoras was promoting; he saw through the Milesian effort at deceit. Thus, it is apparent that Herodotos's criticism of the gullibility of the Athenian demos implies skepticism not about the close affinity of Athens and Miletos but about the ease of the task Aristagoras proposed.

The strength of this tradition at Athens is confirmed by Herodotos's

49. Diogenes Laertes (1.44) records a purported letter of Thales to Solon in which Thales calls Miletos an Athenian colony.
50. Cf. Hdt. 8.144.2: τὸ Ἑλληνικόν, ἐὸν ὅμαιμον τε καὶ ὁμόγλωσσον [the Greek nation, being of the same blood and speaking the same language].

account of the fall of Miletos in 494 B.C.E. The Athenian reaction to the news amply illustrates the special relationship between the two cities; of all the Greek world, the Athenians were particularly moved and demonstrated publicly their intense emotion.

Ἀθηναῖοι μὲν γὰρ δῆλον ἐποίησαν ὑπεραχθεσθέντες τῇ Μιλήτου ἁλώσι τῇ τε ἄλλῃ πολλαχῇ καὶ δὴ καὶ ποιήσαντι Φρυνίχῳ δρᾶμα Μιλήτου ἅλωσιν καὶ διδάξαντι ἐς δάκρυά τε ἔπεσε τὸ θέητρον καὶ ἐζημίωσάν μιν ὡς ἀναμνήσαντα οἰκήια κακὰ χιλίῃσι δραχμῇσι, καὶ ἐπέταξαν μηκέτι μηδένα χρᾶσθαι τούτῳ τῷ δράματι.

[For the Athenians made it clear that they were extremely grieved at the capture of Miletos, in many other ways, and especially when Phrynichos made and produced a play, *The Capture of Miletos,* and the audience fell into tears and they [the Athenians] fined him a thousand drachmas for reminding them of their own personal disaster, and they decreed that no one was to stage that play ever again.] (Hdt. 6.21.2; cf. Str. 14.1.7)

The grief of the Athenians must be understood in the context of the indifference of the Sybarites, which Herodotos counterposes to the Athenian reaction (6.21.1–2).

παθοῦσι δὲ ταῦτα Μιλησίοισι πρὸς Περσέων οὐκ ἀπέδοσαν τὴν ὁμοίην Συβαρῖται, οἳ Λαόν τε καὶ Σκίδρον οἴκεον τῆς πόλιος ἀπεστερημένοι. Συβάριος γὰρ ἁλούσης ὑπὸ Κροτωνιητέων Μιλήσιοι πάντες ἡβηδὸν ἀπεκείραντο τὰς κεφαλὰς καὶ πένθος μέγα προσεθήκαντο· πόλιες γὰρ αὗται μάλιστα δὴ τῶν ἡμεῖς ἴδμεν ἀλλήλῃσι ἐξεινώθησαν. οὐδὲν ὁμοίως καὶ Ἀθηναῖοι·

[The Sybarites, who had lost their city and were living at Laos and Skidros, did not return a similar sympathy to the Milesians, who were suffering these things at the hands of the Persians. For when Sybaris was destroyed by the people of Kroton [ca. 510], all of the Milesian adults shaved their heads and assumed a posture of extreme grief. For these two cities especially, of all the cities I know, were bound to each other in friendship. But the Athenians did not act likewise.]

At this point, Herodotos relates the Athenian reaction, as just quoted. By the selection of these two cities out of all of the Greek world, Herodotos is pressing the particular point that they had the closest ties to Miletos. Of all the Greeks, the Sybarites are the nearest *xenoi* (ἐξεινώθησαν)—those bound by ties of friendship but not blood. The Athenians, however, consider the calamitous events at Miletos to be their own personal disaster [οἰκήια κακὰ].[51] Therefore, the contrast Herodotos establishes between Sybaris and Athens points to a particularly close blood relationship between Miletos and Athens.

Of course, the evidence of the literary tradition only establishes that the belief in the Athenian origin of the Ionian Migration was current at Athens from at least 600 B.C.E. It does not prove the substance of that tradition. However, other kinds of evidence support this view. Linguistically, the dialects of Attic and Ionic are certainly very closely related, so much so that they are usually treated under the same name, Attic-Ionic (Doric, Aiolic, and Arcado-Cyprian are the other three major language families). This affinity implies a common ancestry in the East Greek dialect that was already distinguished from West Greek dialect in the Mycenaean Linear B records from about 1400 B.C.E. Chadwick postulates that some of the differences between Attic and Ionic are West Greek elements resulting from "the mixture of populations common in colonial enterprises."[52]

The evidence from the calendar points in the same direction. Clearly the Ionian calendar and the Attic calendar share a common ancestry, probably of quite early date since the Greek calendar is a construct of the greatest stability and continuity, undergoing only occasional additions and even more infrequent alterations. While every Greek city-state had its own calendar and the basic structure was everywhere the same— twelve lunar months, alternating between twenty-nine and thirty days, leaving an annual deficit of eleven and one-quarter days[53]—the details of the different calendars can be useful in establishing affinities between cities. It is therefore significant that, outside of Ionia, the Milesian

---

51. According to an alternate interpretation (Roisman 1988), these evils are personal to the Athenians not because of the reference to Miletos as kin but because the play reminded the audience of Athenian problems having to do with the Persian threat in the first invasion. For yet another view, see Rosenbloom 1993.

52. Chadwick 1975, 811–12. For the origins and characteristics of Attic and Ionic, see also Buck 1955. For Milesian inscriptions in particular, see Scherer 1934.

53. Samuel 1972.

calendar most closely resembles that of Athens: six of the twelve months have very similar names, and in both cities they follow the same order. Because of the scanty Archaic remains from Miletos, its calendar must be deduced from the evidence of the colonies, and a remarkable confirmation of both the order and the names has been discovered only at Olbia, where a graffito lists the months written in a spiral on the inside of a fifth-century dish.[54] From this evidence, we conclude that the months at Miletos were, in order, Taureon, T(h)argelion, Kalamaion, Panemos, Metageitnion, Boedromion, Kyanepsion, Apatoureon (or Apaturion), Posideon, Lenaion, Anthesterion, and Artemision.[55] The year probably began in the spring, with the first visibility of the crescent moon after the equinox. The first month was Taureon, which opened with the main festival of Apollo Delphinios.[56]

In addition to the calendar, social divisions are also useful for identifying affinities between various Greek peoples, since the citizens of Greek poleis were commonly divided into several tribes, probably established at the time of the development of the polis throughout Greece and so not antedating the ninth or eighth century B.C.E. In the Archaic era, Miletos, as well as Ephesos, Samos, Teos, and probably much of Ionia, had six tribes, or *phylai* (φυλαί): Geleontes, Hopletes, Aigicoreis, Argadeis, Boreis, and Oinipes.[57] Because there is no inscriptional testimony for the existence of the six tribes in Miletos before the destruction of the city in 494, we must necessarily rely on indirect evidence: they are so thoroughly attested in so many of the Milesian colonies as to leave little doubt that

---

54. Rusjaeva 1979, 15–16; Ehrhardt 1983, 118 n. 247. A photograph of the bowl is available in Vinogradov and Kryzickij 1995, ill. 106–1. For copious colonial evidence for the month names, see Ehrhardt 1983, passim.

55. Samuel 1972, 114–18. For the month Kyanopsion, one also finds the names *Kyanopsion, Pyanepsion,* or *Pyanopsion.* Compare the Athenian months: Munychion, Thargelion, Skirophorion, Hekatombaion, Metageitnion, Boedromion, Pyanepsion, Maimakterion, Posideon, Gamelion, Anthesterion, and Elaphebolion. See Bilabel 1920, 70; Ehrhardt 1983, 114 n. 154.

56. The beginning of the year is a disputed topic. Rehm (*Milet* 1.3.230–34), followed by Samuel (1972, 114–15), thinks that the Archaic and Classical calendar began in the autumn in the month Boedromion, while the Hellenistic calendar began with the spring equinox, in the spring month of Taureon. Bilabel (1920, 67–80) disagrees and, on the basis of a comparison with Kyzikos, argues that Taureon was always the beginning of the year. Cf. Ehrhardt 1983, 113–26. That the Molpoi Decree establishes that Taureon contained the festival in which the eponymous officials change for the year (see chap. 5) is convincing evidence that the year began then.

57. Sakellariou 1958, 47–76, 254–58; Roebuck 1961; Harris 1971, 48–54; Roussel 1976, passim; Jones 1987, 320–27 and passim; Ehrhardt 1983, 98–103.

they were derived from the mother city (even though they probably do not date back to the time of the migration itself). The *terminus ante quem* for the presence of all six tribes at Miletos is the founding of Kyzikos in 679 B.C.E., because that colony possesses the same tribes: an inscription there dating to Roman times preserves the names of four tribes: Argadeis, Geleontes, Boreis, and Aigicoreis (*CIG* 3664.29, 61). A second inscription lists five of the tribes—Argadeis, Geleontes, Aigicoreis, Hopletes, and Oinipes—but omits Boreis (*CIG* 3665.13, 26, 32, 47).[58]

Only four of the tribes are directly attested in Classical Miletos. Three—Hopletes, Oinipes, and Boreis—come from the Molpoi inscription of the fifth century (*Milet* 1.3 #133.1–5), while a fourth, the Argadeis, is recorded in a Classical inscription from the theater (Wiegand 1904, 85 = Mil. Inv. 451). The remaining two tribes remain unattested in the few extant inscriptions from Classical Miletos, and because the government and tribal organization of Miletos were changed in the middle of the fifth century B.C.E., there is no possibility of later corroboration of them. The confirmation of four out of six of the Archaic tribes is sufficient evidence to postulate the existence of the remaining two tribes as well in Classical Miletos.[59]

These six tribes endured at Miletos into the Classical era, until the

---

58. Ehrhardt (1983, 100 n. 24, 102 nn. 45–53) lists copious other similar attestations at Kyzikos and at other Milesian colonies: inscriptions from Istros (founded 657) list Argadeis, Aigicoreis, Boreis, and probably also Geleontes, while Tomis (founded ca. 500) has attestations of all six.

59. The internal organization of the tribes is not well known, since there is no Archaic or Classical testimony at Miletos for the usual subdivisions fround in Greek cities: *phratrai, patriai,* or *demoi.* There is some indication that some sort of tribal subdivision did exist. Two inscriptions combine tribal names with ordinal numbers. The first, a fifth-century inscription on the back of a sixth-century statue of two seated women, reads Ὁπλήθων δεοτέρης [the second of Hoplethes] (Dunst 1961, 272 = Mil. Inv. 1623). Dunst dates the letter forms to ca. 400 B.C.E., but this is probably too late according to Piérart (1983, 4–5). The second inscription, on a stone from the area of the theater, reads Ἀργαδέων πρώτη [the first of Argadeis] (Wiegand 1904, 85). In addition, in the Molpoi Decree, two *prosetairoi* are said to come from each of the tribes Hopletes and Boreis (*Milet* 1.3 #133.2–3), which implies that they may represent subdivisions within each tribe. However, these subdivisions are not named, either by political unit or by proper name, nor do we know whether such subdivisions were original to the tribal division or enacted later.

The *demoi* existed in Hellenistic Miletos but were very different from their counterparts at Athens. In both states they were geographical units, but in Miletos they were dependent entirely on a citizen's current place of residence and changed when that citizen moved outside of that residence. They were probably not created at Miletos until the fourth or third century B.C.E., so they are outside the scope of this study. For a comprehensive discussion of the issue, see Piérart 1979, 1983, and 1985.

Athenian reorganization of the city in the middle of the fifth century. Because four tribes (Geleontes, Hopletes, Aigicoreis, Argadeis) correspond to the four pre-Kleisthenic tribes in Attica, they confirm the very ancient ties between Athens and Miletos. The other two tribes have no apparent connection with Athens: they may have been of Asian origin, although equally their names may well trace back to Boros and Oinopion, the legendary heroes who were remembered in Thessaly, Boiotia, and Crete.[60] Perhaps they represent the non-Attic elements of the population.

The evidence of social institutions is consistent with the tradition that Athens was the mother city of Miletos. However, this interpretation is not universally accepted. Some scholars oppose the prevailing view of kinship and colonization and maintain instead that this idea is a construct based on excessive admiration of Ionia in the Archaic period.[61] In short, they argue, it is impossible to determine from the evidence available either the timing or the direction of the influence between Ionia and Athens. According to this conjecture, the legends all assume an Athenian foundation for Ionia, but actually the idea of an Ionian identity developed gradually in Asia Minor and then spread back over to Athens, where it was at first embraced (before ca. 600) and then repudiated (particularly by the fifth century). This theory is certainly provocative, serving as a reminder that little can be said with much certainty about the early Dark Ages. However, strong considerations weigh against it. The archaeological record has indisputably established that in the Submycenaean period, Miletos was inhabited by a new people who were not closely related to the previous Mycenaean inhabitants who had to come from somewhere Greek. To maintain that Athens was not involved in this settlement, one must plausibly explain by other means the undoubtedly close relationship between Athens and Miletos reflected in our earliest post-Mycenaean evidence. It is best to argue that, as the legends say, Miletos was founded from Athens, a city famous for the continuity of its settlement throughout the Bronze Age and the Dark Ages. This closeness was preserved through-

---

60. Sakellariou 1958, 256–58; Roebuck 1961, 499–500.

61. Cassola 1957, 246–56; Sakellariou 1958; Connor 1993. Cassola believes that the transfer of tribal names worked from Ionia to Attica. This theory does not explain why the last two tribal names were left behind (perhaps they were late additions?); besides, there is no other concrete evidence of any such institutional transfer from east to west. Sakellariou (1958, 47, 255; refuted by Roebuck 1961, 498) minimizes the Athenian element by arguing that the four tribes were common to Greece in Mycenaean times, but the names have in fact only survived in Attica, the primary towns of Ionia, and Delos.

out the Dark Ages: since it is quite unlikely that tribal and calendar names, for example, were already in place in the Submycenaean period of the migration, they must have arisen as common customs of cities that reflected their close kinship by developing those institutions shared so prominently in the historical era.

Furthermore, the strongest support for the Athenian origin of Miletos lies in the ceramic remains of the period of the migration itself. Considering the earliest pottery found on top of the destruction in LH III C (ca. 1065)—pottery that is for the most part made of native clay—one scholar notes:

> One thing at least is clear, the very close similarity to the shapes and decorative motives that one finds in Athens—skyphoi with concentric circles, and an occasional central rectilinear panel, kraters with rectilinear panels, lekythoi with semicircles (one with hour glass filling), and vertical wiggly lines—some of the sherds could come from trefoil-lipped oinochoai—and amphora sherds with languettes and vertical lines on the shoulder. . . . [There are local peculiarities, but] on the whole, however, the parallels with Athens seem remarkable.[62]

Moreover, these affinities with Attic pottery are found in material that precedes the development at Athens of the widely influential Protogeometric ware. In all probability, the similarity is best explained by settlers moving from Athens to Miletos.

This same connection between Milesian and Athenian ceramic gives us the information necessary to assign an approximate date to the Ionian settlement of Miletos. Excavators have identified the earliest post–Bronze Age pottery as Submycenaean and early Protogeometric. The former, especially, points to a very early date for the Ionian Migration to Miletos, "by, or even before, the rise of Attic Protogeometric in c. 1050."[63] It seems, therefore, that the site of Miletos did not remain unoccupied for any length of time and that the tradition that Miletos was the first Ionian foundation (Ael. *VH* 8.5) may in fact be accurate.

According to the myths that we have already examined, when the Ionians arrived at Miletos, they found the Carians in possession of the

---

62. Desborough 1972, 179. Emlyn-Jones (1980, 13) describes a "very close dependence stylistically of the sub-Mycenaean and Proto-geometric pottery of Ionia on Athens."

63. Snodgrass 1971, 127.

site and either killed or expelled them. The tradition of colonization by force is known as early as Herodotos, who, to explain why Milesian women ate apart from their men, relates that Miletos was founded by Ionian settlers who married native Carian brides after killing their husbands (Hdt. 1.146.2; cf. Paus. 7.2.6). However, we must be very cautious when evaluating the veracity of an aetiological story such as this: it is told to explain the unusual customs of Milesian women. It cannot be taken to establish specific facts, like the marriage of the Milesian founders to Carian brides, especially since Herodotos is writing some five hundred years after the putative events. Instead, it only provides evidence for a general practice, the custom of the women eating separately.[64]

Since an indigenous population is thoroughly attested in the literature, the assumption has been widely made that the native peoples played a distinguished role in the life of Miletos, but there is no physical corroboration for it. The theory was advanced that the Carians inhabited certain oval buildings, dating back to the eighth century, that were found near the southern cross wall and that these people were then responsible for making the bronze artifacts with relief decorations and the local plain ware found in those places. However, the connection to the Carians has been thoroughly discounted for several reasons: curved houses were the norm in the Greek Dark Ages; plain ware was widespread and could have been made by any inhabitants; and further discoveries in Caria have lent little support to the idea of the early Carians possessing a flourishing art of their own.[65] The further suggestion that the Carians were responsible for the destruction that ended Mycenaean Miletos[66] requires some kind of corroboration that is currently lacking.

Therefore, because the Carians have left so few traces in Miletos, it is dangerous to assume that their presence was very large. We may consider the possibility of a small Carian population, either intermarried with the Greeks or living as noncitizens in the new urban center to take advantage of the economic opportunities the city offered them, just as the metics did at Athens. Perhaps a comparison can be made with the later Dorian colonists in Sicily, who violently destroyed native Sicel settlements and replaced them with Greek cities, leaving purely Greek remains and no signs of coexistence. The Sicels who remained "evidently lived as serfs

64. Graham 1980/81, 294–95.
65. Pro-Carian: Kleiner 1968, 10, 24; cf. Cook and Blackman 1970/71, 45. Anti-Carian: Cook 1967.
66. Hanfmann 1953, 5–8; Kleiner 1969/70, 115.

and lost their own cultural traditions."[67] In any case, the Carian presence at Miletos was not substantial enough to leave unequivocal indication of their influence on society there: no definitive Carian nomenclature or architecture has been unearthed.[68]

Little can be said about the physical arrangement of the city of Miletos from its resettlement until the end of the Geometric period. However, some evidence that has come to light bears on the question of the extent of the city at that time, mainly in the form of pottery sherds found in the debris layers under later strata and also remains of house walls. Submycenaean sherds were followed immediately by Protogeometric painted pottery of a type found in bulk here and at Smyrna and in lesser amounts at Phokaia, Klazomenai, and minor spots along the coast. Such sherds, ranging from Submycenaean to Late Geometric, have been found in abundance in the area around the Temple of Athena, west of the later Bouleuterion, on the southern plain near the Round Church, and even further to the south on Kalabaktepe,[69] while the same areas have also revealed house walls beginning in the eighth century. By the seventh century, the buildings are widespread, characterized by individual houses rather than the complexes of the Bronze Age. The unbroken pottery record reflects the short duration of the abandonment of Miletos after the fall of the Mycenaeans—if, indeed, it was abandoned and not sacked and immediately reoccupied—while the extent of the finds, both ceramic and architectural, suggests that by the end of the Geometric period, Miletos was a very large city (see chap. 5).

The Milesian Territory

The Milesian territory, or *chore,* consisted of a peninsula extending south to the coast past Didyma, abut 30 km. in all, and inland about 18 km. to Mt. Grion. It was bordered on the north by the Gulf of Latmos, along the west by the Aegean Sea, and on the south by the Gulf of Iasos, including the smaller inlet now called Akbük Bay. The peninsula was connected to the mainland proper by an isthmus that narrowed to about 8 km. Past the isthmus, to the east, began the mountains of the interior that set the

67. Schofield 1984, 46.
68. In contrast, at the neighboring Dorian city Halikarnassos in the fifth century, "Carian names were as common as Greek" (Cook 1975, 793).
69. Isolated pieces of ceramic have also come to light on the Theater Hill.

eastern limit to the *chore*. No exact boundary markers have been left for us, but we can decide the approximate extent of the territory by establishing the nearest neighboring cities.

Miletos was the furthest south of the Ionian duodecapoleis. Nearest to it, both in proximity and kinship, was Myous, located across the Gulf of Latmos on the north shore, ca. 16 km. directly to the northeast (more than 45 km. by land travel). Several myths report that Myous was founded from Miletos (Polyain. 8.35; Str. 14.1.3; Paus. 7.2.11). Myous remained an independent state until the third century. Then, because of a shrinking population base at Myous, it joined in an interdependency with Miletos that, in the second century, became a formal *sympoliteia,* and the territory of Myous was incorporated into that of Miletos (Str. 14.1.10).[70] In addition, Miletos may have briefly held the city of Magnesia (located on the far side of Myous, about 40 km. to the north-northeast of Miletos) when it was ruined by the invading Kimmerians in the seventh century (Str. 14.1.40), but no sources other than Strabo attest this account, and it may be false.

To the south, Miletos was bordered by non-Ionian Greek cities. Approximately 37 km. to the southeast of Miletos lies the city of Iasos. According to tradition, it was not Ionian but Argive in origin (Polyb. 16.12). The excavations there indicate that, before the Argives got there, it was originally occupied by Carians from the time of the Early Bronze Age and probably Cretans in the Middle Bronze Age.[71] Further to the south, about 35 km. in a direct line from Miletos, lay the Dorian city Halikarnassos, on the south side of the Gulf of Iasos.

Within Milesian territory, we know the names of a few towns or smaller settlements that formed part of the Milesian polity, but we have very little archaeological data confirming them. The only reasonably secure physical evidence for pre-Classical villages in Milesian territory is found at three sites: Didyma, Zeytintepe, and Mengerevtepe/Assessos. Didyma, a shrine and Oracle sacred to Apollo, was located toward the southern end of the larger Milesian peninsula. The first Greek pottery appears there as early as the eighth century B.C.E.[72] On the summit of

---

70. Demand 1990, esp. 141–42, 171–72; Ehrhardt 1983, 23 n. 114; Herrmann 1965, 91; Bilabel 1920, 55–56.

71. *PECS* 401–2; Ehrhardt 1983, 21–22, 26; Bilabel 1920, 99–100, 120, 128. Bean and Cook (1957, 100–106) describe this site in detail. Polyainos (16.12.1–2) records that, as they had done Magnesia, the Milesians helped refound Iasos after it was depopulated during Archaic wars with the Carians, but there is no corroboration for this story.

72. Parke 1985b, 24; Fontenrose 1988, 5–9. For legends of a pre-Ionian Didyma, see Paus. 7.2.6, 5.13.11; Parthen. 1; D.L. 8.5; *Orph. Arg.* 152–53; Quint. Smyrn. 1.283; Stat.

Zeytintepe, west of Miletos and 1 km. northwest of Kalabaktepe, archaeologists have recently found a sanctuary of Aphrodite that dates back to
the early seventh century.[73] However, the oldest Greek finds outside of
the city of Miletos proper are from Mengerevtepe, 5 km. southeast of
Miletos and almost certainly the site of ancient Assessos. It is identified
by its Temple of Athena, which contains Greek sculptural remains from
the Protogeometric through the Archaic periods.[74] In the literary sources,
Assessos is mentioned in the story about rival Neleid claimants to the
Milesian throne: Nicolaus of Damascus (*FGH* 90 F 52: see chap. 3) says
that the rulers of Assessos had been set in place by Leodamas, the king of
Miletos, and that when that king was murdered, his sons fled for refuge
to Assessos. With the aid of some Phrygians, they were able to use that
site as a base for successful operations against the usurper, Phitres. Later
still, Assessos is mentioned by Herodotos (1.19–22) in the context of
Lydian attacks on Milesian territory in the last decades of the seventh
century: when Alyattes fell ill after accidentally burning down the Temple
of Athena at Assessos, he had to make peace with the Milesians in order
to rebuild not one but two new temples at Assessos. Thus, the town must
have belonged to Miletos.

Carian villages have been discovered in the mountains near the
Milesian *chore* as well. The most famous of these is Pidasa. According to
Herodotos, after the Persians sacked Miletos in 494, they gave the highlands previously controlled by the Milesians to the Carians from Pedasa
(τὰ δὲ ὑπεράκρια ἔδοσαν Καρσὶ Πηδασεῦσι ἐκτῆσθαι, Hdt. 6.20). Two
Carian towns with similar names—Pedasa and Pidasa—stand in the vicinity of Miletos. The first, Pidasa (spelled in Greek with a iota), lies on the
east side of Mt. Grion, north of Iasos. It had close ties to Miletos in the
Hellenistic period, entering a *sympoliteia* with the city in 175 (*Milet* 1.3
#149). The other city, Pedasa (spelled in Greek with an eta), was located
in the hills above Halikarnassos. It was much more important at an earlier
date: Herodotos tells us, for example, that the Pedasians resisted the

Theb. 3.478–79, 8.198–200; Lykoph. 1378–81; Tzetz. *Chil.* 13.110–16. Parke (1985b, 2)
trusts the testimony of the ancient literature and believes that the sanctuary at Didyma
predated the Ionian Migration. Fontenrose thinks this unlikely, based on the archaeological
evidence. The earliest written evidence for Didyma dates to the sixth century, while the first
stone structures there were built in the late seventh century. They were probably proceeded
by wooden buildings, but there is no evidence that their existence predated the early eighth
century. See chap. 5.
    73. Gans 1991; Senff et al. 1992; Heinz and Senff 1995; Senff 1997a. See chap. 5.
    74. Senff 1995b; Weber 1995; Lohmann 1995. See chap. 5.

Persian general Harpagos in the 540s (1.175) and that in 499 the Carians ambushed a Persian army near Pedasa (5.121).[75] It is impossible to be certain which town Herodotos was denoting, but proximity favors the northernmost: Pedasa is too distant—on the far side of Iasos even—to have the allocation of Milesian land to them make much sense.

The remaining evidence for Milesian expansion on the mainland dates to the fifth century or later, although the process probably occurred earlier. Teichioussa, a town across what is now called Akbük Bay from Didyma, on the northern tip of Kazikli Bay, came into Milesian hands by at least the mid–fifth century, when the "Milesians from Teichioussa" are listed on the Athenian tribute lists.[76] Also, the Milesians extended their territory to the north, obtaining a small section of land across the Bay of Latmos to the west of Priene, including the town of Thebes, which Theopompos says (*FGH* 115 F 23) Miletos received in barter from Samos. While Thebes certainly existed in Archaic times, it is not known whether it was then a Milesian or Samian dependency or neither. By the fourth century, Thebes was definitely Milesian, and at yet a later date, it was again Samian.[77]

Thus, throughout the Archaic period, the mainland territory of Miletos was limited to the arable land on the large peninsula that extended west from Mt. Grion. It bordered on Myous and the other Ionian settlements to the northeast and on the Dorian settlement at Iasos to the southeast. Carian villages were scattered throughout the eastern mountains. Situated at this juncture of three distinct groups, Miletos was poised to step into a leading role in the growing Hellenic world.

---

75. Cook (1961, 90–96, esp. 91 n. 7). Radt (1973/74) looks at the northern site in more detail, concluding that there is no evidence of an Archaic settlement and that the Carians occupied the city from the fifth century until the beginning of the second. He, along with Ehrhardt (1983, 21 n. 100), opt for the southern town.

76. Ehrhardt 1983, 20–21, following Bean and Cook 1957, 106–16. Bean and Cook locate this city for the first time at Doganbelini. Voigtländer and Wiegand have consistently thought it was elsewhere. See the discussion at Lohmann 1995, 321 n. 246.

77. *IvPriene* #37.56–57, #361–63; Haussoullier 1902; Manganaro 1963/64; Cook 1975; Ehrhardt 1983, 24; Roebuck 1959, 13. The town has Milesian coins in the ruins, and a cult decree includes the Milesian *stephanephoros* of 189/88 (the date is slightly problematic, because the letterforms do not fit this time well). For all the evidence and argumentation, see Ehrhardt 1983, 14–15. Ehrhardt (1983, 21–22) thinks that Miletos also might have controlled the territory of Ioniapolis, situated on the south coast of the Latmian Gulf between Miletos and Herakleia, before the latter city was built in the Hellenistic era. For the location, see Cook 1961.

2

Trade and Colonization

In the tenth through eighth centuries, when the basis of the Ionian economy was still agricultural, the extent of good cropland at the disposal of the Milesians remained severely limited: they simply did not have the space necessary for cultivation on a level comparable to such cities as Ephesos and Kolophon.[1] As long as Miletos remained confined to the resources of its *chore*, its prosperity was tightly circumscribed. Therefore, near the end of the Dark Ages, Miletos turned the focus of its attention away from the hinterland, toward trade and overseas expansion.

Trade

The potential for Milesian trade was substantial. On the one hand, like most of Ionia, Miletos lacked papyrus, linen, hemp, a good source of slaves, various luxury items, and any sizable deposits of gold, silver, electrum, iron, copper, and tin. In addition, some scholars think that the region had inadequate grain to feed its growing population: the balance between food and population may have been reached in Miletos ca. 700 B.C.E.[2] On the other hand, Ionia was self-sufficient in clay for pottery, pitch, stone, less important metals (zinc and antimony), and colored earth for pigments. The region also had fresh seafood: bass, red mullet, and especially mussels, whose shells have been found littering the city. Miletos became particularly famous for exporting textiles, especially those colored with a purple dye derived from shells. It also produced furniture, olive oil, and probably wine: we know that the city had the usual olive industry, because it is remembered in a story passed down about how the

1. Roebuck 1959, 13.
2. Roebuck 1959, 19–20.

philosopher, Thales, cornered the market in olive presses to prove that he could be a successful businessman.[3]

The land route up the Maiandros River valley into the Anatolian interior—among the Carians and the Lydians—was probably little used until the time of the Persians in the sixth century. Instead, the chief markets of Asia Minor were at Sardis and in the Hermos River valley. Even under the Roman Empire, bulk goods were not much moved by the Maiandros route or by land at all except for military purposes. Any trade before the mid–sixth century between Miletos and the interior was on a very small scale and probably only dealt in small luxury items that could be carried easily, especially metal goods and ingots.[4] Intercourse with Lydia must have served as a major stimulus for the government of Archaic Miletos to begin minting its own coinage, since our initial numismatic evidence for the region appears in the second half of the seventh century in the area of contact. This find agrees with the literary accounts that attribute the invention of coinage to Lydia (Hdt. 1.94.1; Xenoph. in Poll. 9.83), although modern opinion is undecided about its exact origin. A common weight standard was shared between Lydia and Miletos, and electrum coinage was issued from Miletos as early as the beginning of the sixth century, most commonly featuring lions: the standard type by the Hellenistic era was marked by a standing or recumbent lion whose head is turned backward, with the lion gazing on a star.[5]

Since trade to the east was constrained by the difficulty of inland transportation, Miletos turned to the west and seaborne commerce. One of the first steps in this process was the acquisition of some of the nearby Sporades Islands immediately off the Carian coast. These islands—Lade, Tragia, and Pharmakoussa are closest to Miletos, while a second line

3. Fish: Ar. *Eq.* 361; Ath. 7.311a, 320a. Sheep and wool: *Carm. Pop.* 35; Ath. 12.519b, 12.540d; Ar. *Ra.* 543. Furniture: Ath. 1.28, 11.486e; Krit. 1.5–6; *IG* 1³ 421.202, 206; *IG* 1³ 422.295. Dye: Arist. *Hist. An.* 5.15.3 = 5.347a4–6; Herrmann 1965. Röhlig 1933, 12, 21–22; Noonan 1973; Roebuck 1959, 20–21. Thales: Arist. *Pol.* 1.1259a9–18.

Roebuck's otherwise excellent discussion is marred by one assumption: he believes that Ionia was probably self-sufficient in timber for shipbuilding because Chios and Miletos exported furniture. This is a troublesome hypothesis, because wood that is used for the manufacture of furniture is not necessarily appropriate for shipbuilding.

4. Roebuck 1959, 13–18; Dunham 1915, 11–15, 50. A sixth-century Lydian inscription found on Kalabaktepe may be a reflection of trade between the two peoples: see Adiego 1997.

5. Early coinage in general: Kraay and Hirmer 1966, 353; Wallace 1987. Archaic Milesian coins: Brett 1955, #1882–83; Kraay and Hirmer 1966, #588, #589(?), #591; Kraay 1976, #588, #589, #591.

consists of Ikaros, Korsiai, Patmos, Lepsia, Leros, and Kalymnos—contain a minimal amount of arable land: in general they are small, rocky, and undesirable except so far as they facilitated maritime trade. We would expect Miletos to establish an early domination over some of them for the land they offered and especially as first steps in establishing what would become an extensive network of trade. Unfortunately, the evidence for their settlement is for the most part lacking.

Leros is the best known of these islands and can stand as a model for Milesian relations with them, but even the history of Leros before the fifth century is virtually unattested.[6] Strabo (14.1.6) uses Anaximenes of Lampsakos (*FGH* 72 F 26), a fourth-century B.C.E. historian and rhetorician, as the authority for the Milesian colonization of Ikaros and Leros. Since this discussion is located in Strabo's section on Milesian colonies in the Troad and Propontis, it might seem reasonable to make a temporal connection as well and place the acquisition of the islands in the eighth or seventh century. Indeed, the earliest pottery—several Fikellura sherds and another piece that resembles Chian ware—dates to ca. 700,[7] giving us a rough *terminus ante quem*. We know that in the fifth century, Leros was already closely tied to Miletos, because Herodotos (5.125) recounts that when Aristagoras was suffering from declining popularity at Miletos during the Ionian Revolt, Hekataios advised him to flee to Leros, build a fort there, and use it as a base of operations. Certainly by the mid–fifth century, when Leros appears on the first Athenian tribute list, the Milesians were firmly in possession.[8]

The evidence for Milesian control over the other islands is much more tenuous. Besides Leros, the only two that are firmly linked to Miletos even as late as the Hellenistic era are Lepsia and Patmos. Judging from the pottery, Lepsia may have been Milesian as soon as the early Archaic period, but the evidence is not conclusive. Of the remaining islands,

---

6. Benson 1963, esp. 45–51. Bean and Cook (1957, 134–35) note the continuous occupation of Leros from the seventh century B.C.E. to Byzantine times. They also comment, "The absence of fortifications would correspond to the status of ancient Leros, which was not an independent city but a dependent colony of the Milesians" (135). They do not date this colonization.

7. The oldest inscription, however, is an honorary decree from the fourth century B.C.E.: L. Ross in *Inscriptiones Graecae Ineditae* 2.68ff., reproduced at Benson 1963, 31–32. Cf. Haussoulier 1902, 127–28.

8. *ATL* 2.81. A native historian of the island, Pherekydes, lived in the Classical or Hellenistic era (*FGH* 3 T 3). Dionysios of Halikarnassos (*Din.* 11.661) also mentions a certain Deinarchos, who may have written a history of Leros. For a discussion, see Benson 1963, 47 n. 13.

Ikaros was certainly Greek since at least the seventh century, but Strabo is the only direct evidence linking it to Miletos at any time: it may have been a Milesian settlement, or it may have been Samian. Kalymnos has Mycenaean and Archaic sherds but nothing to indicate the origin of the inhabitants. Korsiai was probably Samian, and we know nothing about the early history of Lade, Tragia, and Pharmakoussa.[9]

Most scholars presume that the Milesian influence on the islands— at least on Leros, Lepsia, and Patmos, and probably on Ikaros as well— must have begun in the late seventh century.[10] The argument is indirect: we know that the Milesians were founding colonies in the Propontis and Pontos before then, and it is not credible that they could have bypassed such important naval bases close to home. Again, Leros serves as an example. Not only are its harbors superb and thus difficult to overlook, but during the Peloponnesian War, it was used as a point of reconnaissance by both the Spartan and the Athenian fleets (Thuc. 8.26). In addition, anyone who controlled one or more of the nearest islands could use them as bases from which to threaten the city of Miletos (cf. Hdt. 5.125), so it was too dangerous to allow the islands to fall to others. This line of argumentation is persuasive, but its full implications are often overlooked in that it clearly points to an earlier date for the acquisition of the islands than is usually assumed: since the earliest known Milesian colonies date to the third quarter of the seventh century at the very latest—and may go back well into the eighth—it is better to date the Milesian occupation of at least some of these islands to the early seventh or eighth century.

Whatever role the Sporades may have played in Milesian economic growth, Miletos must have developed an extensive fleet, at least of merchant ships. According to Herodotos (1.17) and Diodoros Sikilos (fr. 7.11), Miletos had a thalassocracy—command of the sea—at the end of the seventh century. We cannot argue from this literary evidence that Miletos controlled and policed the Aegean Sea in the way Athens did in the fifth century, but we can deduce that Greeks had the memory of a strong Milesian navy, probably related to the extensive overseas trade

9. In general: Ehrhardt 1983, 15–20; Bean and Cook 1957, 116–38 (location, remains, and resources of the various islands). Lepsia: Ehrhardt 1983, 16–17; Bean and Cook 1957, 135–38. Ikaros: Roebuck 1959, 18; Bilabel 1920, 54–55. Kalymnos: Bean and Cook 1957, 127–33. Haussoullier (1902) lumps Korsiai in with other Milesian possessions.

10. Benson 1963, 49; Roebuck 1959, 18, 67–70; Ehrhardt 1983, 15–20; Haussoullier 1902; Manganaro 1963/64.

and colonization.[11] As Milesian interests abroad increased, the importance of communicating with them and carrying goods abroad would have grown apace, while increased maritime activity would have correspondingly opened new opportunities for trade. Because of this link, evidence of Milesian military activity overseas may point to some of these trade interests.

Miletos's earliest reliably recorded military venture abroad is its participation in the Lelantine War (ca. 710–650 B.C.E.),[12] which was, according to Thucydides (1.15.3), the largest land engagement of Greeks in the era between the Trojan War and the Persian invasions of the fifth century. The war was fought in Euboia over the Lelantine Plain, situated between the cities of Chalkis and Eretria, and Thucydides reports, μάλιστα δὲ ἐς τὸν πάλαι ποτὲ γενόμενον πόλεμον Χαλκιδέων καὶ Ἐρετριῶν καὶ τὸ ἄλλο Ἑλληνικὸν ἐς ξυμμαχίαν ἑκατέρων διέστη [Especially in the war that was once fought between the Chalkidians and the Eretrians, the rest of the Greek world sided with one party or the other].[13] Our sources tell us only that the war aligned Eretria and Miletos against Chalkis, Samos, Thessaly, and the Chalkidian colonies in Thrace.[14] Some scholars have followed the tone of Thucydides' comments and speculated that the war either was from its beginning or else gradually became a large conflict involving numerous Greece cities that chose sides according to certain trade relationships.[15] Since Samos and Miletos are natural adversaries because they are located so close to each other (cf. Hdt. 3.39.4), it is difficult to explain their participation in a conflict so far from home if it was not connected in some way to their trading interests abroad. However, it is also possible that the war preceded the formation of real trade alliances and was instead a simple border dispute between Chalkidians and Eretrians, aided by only a small number of Samian and Milesian

---

11. Wallinga (1993, 78) discounts the idea of a Milesian thalassocracy.

12. Parker 1997, 59–83. According to Konon (*FGH* 26 F 44.1–2), the Neleids were involved in raids against the island of Melos and Karystos on Euboia.

13. The most recent and comprehensive work on this topic is Parker 1997. See also Boardman 1957, 27–29; Bradeen 1947; Burn 1929.

14. Str. 10.1.11–12; Hdt. 5.99.1; Plut. *Mor.* 760e–761b = Arist. fr. 98 Rose.

15. Burn (1929) argues for the involvement of three trade leagues, while Bradeen (1947, 239–40) says, "The war became a series of more or less local struggles." Bradeen thinks that Eretria aligned with Miletos, Chios, Megara, Argos, and Aigina against Chalkis with Samos, Corinth, Sparta, Erythrai, Paros, Andros, and Athens. Burn has an even more extensive listing. Parker (1997, 119–52) is characteristically conservative, completely rejecting the idea of trade leagues.

noblemen who were induced to join in support of their guest-friends on Euboia.[16]

Apart from the Lelantine War, the evidence for a few early allies of Miletos indicates the unsteady and shifting nature of agreements between states or between powerful families within those states. In particular, Paros and Erythrai were allied with Miletos at different times. The city of Parion is reported to have been founded on the southern shore of the Propontis in 709 by Miletos, Paros, and Erythrai together, although Miletos may have played a lesser role: Paros named it, but Erythrai is usually remembered as the mother city (Str. 13.1.14; Paus. 9.27.1).[17] Moreover, the special relationship between Miletos and Paros is emphasized by the fact that the Milesians called in the Parians to arbitrate an extensive civil stasis, probably in this same period of the late eighth or early seventh century (Hdt. 4.28). Thus, as early as ca. 700, the Milesians were allied with Paros, itself one of the most prosperous cities of the day.[18]

Miletos also had a celebrated association with the city of Sybaris in Magna Graecia (southern Italy). Sybaris was jointly founded ca. 720 by Achaia and Troizen and enjoyed such prosperity resulting from trade

---

16. Tausend 1987; 1992, 137–45. Tausend attributes Thucydides' comments to an erroneous conflation of a series of local conflicts (especially between Samos and Miletos, Corinth and Megara, and Chios and Erythrai) into one larger war.

17. Parthenios (*Narr. Am.* 9) also remembers a story in which Miletos and Erythrai are allied against Naxos. In contrast, Plutarch (*Mor.* 244e–245a) recalls a war in which Miletos helps Chios against Erythrai, perhaps the same help that Herodotos refers to at 1.18.3. See Tausend 1992, 78–85.

18. Many scholars disagree with the Parian alliance, based on two arguments. One concerns the dating of the Parian arbitration at Miletos, which I have significantly revised (see chap. 3). The other concerns the fact that the Parians participated with Samos and Erythrai in ca. 650 in an arbitration between Chalkis and Andros over the colony of Akanthos/Sane (Plut. *QG* 30), leading some to assume that Paros must have been a Chalkidian ally in the Lelantine War and throughout the Archaic period. This conclusion forces those who adopt it to write off the evidence of the Milesian participation in the colonization of Parion. For example, Burn (1929, 17 n. 46) says, "The Milesian element at Parium, mentioned by Strabo [13.1.14], may be presumed (without further evidence, however) to be the result of Milesian seizure of an unfriendly port on the way to her Pontic possessions" (followed by Bradeen 1947, 231). The Parian participation in the arbitration over Akanthos may mean that Paros was one of the interested parties whose acquiescence was necessary for the stability of a peaceful process of colonization in the north Aegean: at about the same time as the Akanthian arbitration, Paros seized the very desirable north Aegean island of Thasos, after a fierce struggle with the Thracians who had inhabited it (Graham 1978). Paros was at its height in ca. 650, and its presence in Thrace could not be ignored.

with the Etruscans that, like Miletos, the very name *Sybarite* became a synonym for luxury (Timai. *FGH 566* F 50). The Milesian connection with Sybaris must have been commercial and probably dated back considerably, even to the end of the seventh century:[19] indeed, one of the marks of Sybarite luxury was the Milesian clothing that they wore (Ath. 12.519b). The relationship was very close by the end of the Archaic period: in a passage already quoted in chapter 1 (Hdt. 6.21.1), the Sybarites, who are called the particular friends of the Milesians, are chided by Herodotos for failing to show proper sympathy when Miletos was destroyed in 494.

In sum, while only the small barren islands very near to Miletos fell into Milesian possession, Miletos must have been involved—especially through trade—with other mainland and island states, and it had particularly friendly relations at some point with at least Eretria, Paros, Erythrai, and Sybaris.

As the Greeks traveled further abroad, they became involved in commercial enterprises with the non-Greek powers of the eastern Mediterranean. While the Mycenaeans had been active trade partners of the eastern states, that commerce died with the collapse of their empire.[20] Although Phoenician traders brought back Greek—especially Euboian—wares to Syria and the Cilician coast as early as the second half of the tenth century B.C.E., the Greeks themselves did not arrive in the Levant until the middle of the eighth century, when they appeared not only as traders but also as pirates: in 714/13, Sargon II, along with Phoenician reinforcements, led a great sea battle against the Greek pirates.[21] Greek merchants established themselves in ethnic quarters of existing cities, such as Al-Mina, Bassit, Ingirra (Anchiale), Tarsos, and Shuksu. Their home cities are generally unknown: the only clue consists in the pottery remains, but that evidence is not clear, since, for example, Euboian ware need not be carried on Euboian ships. In the Near Eastern texts, the Greeks were consistently labeled collectively with the term *Yawan*, the Akkadian form of *Ionian*. This designation is not helpful in differentiating between Greeks from

19. Bradeen 1947, 234–35 nn. 53 and 57.
20. Kochavi (1992) discusses the Mycenaean trade with the Levant in the second millennium, as well as enumerating the many trade commodities, items that were still sought when Greek trade resumed with the East.
21. Greek goods have not been found in Palestine before ca. 800 and remain rare in the late seventh century: see Haider 1996, esp. 113–15. For Greeks in the Levant, see Haider 1996; Braun 1982b. For the possibility of a land trade route through Asia Minor conducted by Aramaic speakers in the eighth century, see Röllig 1992.

separate cities, but it does indicate that the eastern Greeks made up a significant proportion of the contingent: even today, *Yunani* is the word used to refer to Greeks in the Turkish, Arabic, and Persian languages.

Typically many Greeks in the Levant were engaged in crafts manufacturing and trade, especially in metals, both worked and unworked: copper from Cyprus, tin from Mesopotamia, jewelry, and both gold and silver plate. Another desirable item was glass, and Phoenicia was also famous for its dye works, from which the Greeks presumably imported cloth (although probably not so much Miletos, which had its own cloth industry). The Greeks offered in exchange chiefly slaves, as well as other goods: Ezekiel (27:13) mentions both slaves and bronze cauldrons. The most important result of this intercourse was the Greek alphabet: it is usually thought that Greek merchants in these cities first learned and then converted the Phoenician alphabet for use with the Greek language, thus ending the Dark Ages and returning literacy to the Greek world.[22]

Among those who were not merchants, the Greeks are most frequently mentioned, often together with the Carians, as mercenaries in the armies of the kings. For example, in 605 when Nebuchadrezzar annihilated Necho's Egyptian army at Carchemish, there is literary and pottery evidence to indicate that Greeks served as mercenaries on both sides, and it is also probable that Greeks served under Josiah in Judea.[23] Because our sources are Near Eastern and the various Greeks are not distinguished in them, it is difficult to establish a specific role for the Milesians or indeed to guarantee their presence in the Levant at all. Miletos was certainly an importer of Eastern trade goods, although only at a late date: the first oriental imports appear at Miletos in the sixth century, mainly ivory and bronze items of North Syrian manufacture.[24] There is no certainty that the goods were carried to Miletos by Milesian, rather than other Greek or Phoenician, vessels, but it seems likely that the leading city in Ionia, famous later as a merchant power, should be involved in trade dominated by Ionians.

In Egypt, too, the Ionians played the leading role in reestablishing

---

22. For an example of this standard view, see Jeffery 1990; however, new theories are abounding. In particular, Woodard (1997) offers a variant theory, in which Greek writing is developed on Cyprus by scribes who were accustomed to writing Greek in the Cypriot syllabary. A completely different view is offered by B. Powell (1991), who argues that a single Euboian adapter worked with a Phoenician informant ca. 800 B.C.E. to establish a prototype of the Greek alphabet for recording hexameter verse.

23. Wiseman 1991, 230; Mitchell 1991, 387.

24. Weickert et al. 1957, 126–32; Röhlig 1933, 48.

contact after the collapse of the Mycenaean trade networks. Here the Greeks arrived in the middle seventh century:[25] no pottery dated to LH III C has been found, and the first post–Bronze Age sign of a Greek presence does not come until the reign of Psammitichos I (r. 664–610). According to Herodotos (2.152), Psammitichos employed a group of sea raiders from Ionia and Caria to work for him as mercenaries, helping him dispose of the eleven enemies arrayed against him. He then granted the soldiers land at Bubastis, on the Pelusian mouth of the Nile, which was called simply the Camps *(stratopeda)*, and this was the beginning of Greek intercourse among the Egyptians (cf. D.S. 1.67). Strabo (17.1.18) tells a similar story but names the Milesians in particular, saying that while Psammitichos reigned, they landed on the Bolbitine mouth of the Nile and fortified a settlement called the Milesion Teichos (Wall of the Milesians). It is tempting to try to connect these two stories, but geography does not allow it. Bubastis is on the Pelusian mouth, which is the far eastern branch of the delta, while the site of Milesion Teichos is to the west, on the Bolbitine mouth (just east of the Kanopic mouth and the future site of Alexandria). In part because no likely candidate for Milesion Teichos has ever been found, some scholars doubt Strabo's entire account, believing it to be based on a much later tradition of Milesian preeminence in Egypt that was not historically grounded.

Nevertheless, the presence of Greek mercenaries is well established in garrisons or forts throughout many sites in Egypt, and the numbers are impressive. Thirty thousand such Ionian and Carian mercenaries headquartered at Saïs were employed by Apries in the first half of the sixth century (Hdt. 2.163). The ruins at Daphnai (Tell Defenneh) can be dated by the pottery remains—mostly from eastern Greece—to the late seventh century and include a fort that housed twenty thousand men. Memphis has Greek remains from the late seventh century, although Herodotos (2.154) says that Amasis moved the Greeks there in the sixth. Certainly we can conclude that Greek (and Carian) mercenaries were busy in Egypt from the middle of the seventh century, and Milesians quite likely stood among their ranks.

After the mercenaries came traders, drawn no doubt by the appeal of Egyptian grain and luxury goods, but, on arrival, they found that access to Egyptian markets was strictly limited. Colonization was not an option.

---

25. For Greeks in Egypt, especially in Naukratis, see Möller 2000; Bowden 1996; Braun 1982a; Boardman 1980, 118–33; Austin 1970.

The pharaoh refused to allow the establishment of normal Greek poleis in his land. The Greeks did not spread out and establish trading enclaves in many Egyptian cities, as they had done in the Near East. Instead, the pharaoh forced all Greeks, regardless of their home city, to settle together. Naukratis, the one true Greek trading center in all of Egypt, was established on the east bank of the Kanopic mouth of the Nile, 65 km. southwest of the future city of Alexandria. It was the sole port in Egypt to which Greek merchants were allowed to sail, and the commerce emanating from it was closely regulated by the Egyptian pharaoh. Among other things, the Greeks there were denied the right to intermarry with the Egyptians, a privilege enjoyed by the mercenaries, who were encouraged to do so to keep up a steady supply of soldiers for the royal army.

The origin of Naukratis is murky: we know neither when it was founded nor by whom, but the story always seems to return to the Milesians. Strabo says, χρόνῳ δ' ἀναπλεύσαντες εἰς τὸν Σαϊτικὸν νομὸν καταναυμαχήσαντες 'Ινάρων πόλιν ἔκτισαν Ναύκρατιν οὐ πολὺ τῆς Σχεδίας ὕπερθεν [But in time, sailing out to the Saïtic district, they [the Milesians] defeated Inaros in a sea battle and founded the city of Naukratis not far above Schedia] (17.1.18). We do not know who Inaros was, but this tradition that the Milesians founded Naukratis becomes an often repeated statement in later antiquity, probably based on Miletos's subsequent reputation for colonial foundations. However, it is completely unsupported by the archaeological evidence and what we know about the later city, so it is almost certainly false.[26]

Herodotos does not confirm the Milesian foundation of Naukratis (2.178.1–3).

φιλέλλην δὲ γενόμενος ὁ Ἄμασις ἄλλα τε ἐς Ἑλλήνων μετεξετέρους ἀπεδέξατο καὶ δὴ καὶ τοῖσι ἀπικνευμένοισι ἐς Αἴγυπτον ἔδωκε Ναύκρατιν πόλιν ἐνοικῆσαι, τοῖσι δὲ μὴ βουλομένοισι

---

26. In Roman times, Naukratis used the Milesian calendar and perhaps Milesian laws, but Bowden thinks this adoption was later and that the story of the Milesian foundation arose as justification for this adoption or as a consequence of it: see Bowden 1996, 24–28; Austin 1970, 23; Möller 2000. The foundation story first occurs in Strabo, but this story has certain reminiscences of Thucydides' account of the start of the Egyptian revolt in 463 B.C.E. (1.104) and may be ultimately derived from it. Strabo's story recurs in the thalassocracy list of Diodoros Sikilos (7.11); the Sch. Theok. 17.98; Euseb. 88b (Helm), with the date 749; and Steph. Byz. s.v. Ναύκρατις. Drijvers (1999), however, embraces Strabo's story and uses it to argue that the Milesian share of Naukratis was only obtained by force.

αὐτῶν ἐνοικέειν αὐτοῦ δὲ ναυτιλλομένοισι ἔδωκε χώρους ἐνι-
δρύσασθαι βωμοὺς καὶ τεμένεα θεοῖσι. [2] τὸ μέν νυν μέγιστον
αὐτῶν τέμενος καὶ ὀνομαστότατον ἐὸν καὶ χρησιμώτατον, καλ-
εύμενον δὲ Ἑλλήνιον, αἵδε πόλιές εἰσι αἱ ἱδρυμέναι κοινῇ,
Ἰώνων μὲν Χίος καὶ Τέως καὶ Φώκαια καὶ Κλαζομεναί, Δωρι-
έων δὲ Ῥόδος καὶ Κνίδος καὶ Ἁλικαρνησσὸς καὶ Φάσηλις,
Αἰολέων δὲ ἡ Μυτιληναίων μούνη. [3] τούτων μέν ἐστι τοῦτο τὸ
τέμενος, καὶ προστάτας τοῦ ἐμπορίου αὗται αἱ πόλιές εἰσι αἱ
παρέχουσαι· ὅσαι δὲ ἄλλαι πόλιες μεταποιεῦνται, οὐδέν σφι
μετεὸν μεταποιεῦνται. χωρὶς δὲ Αἰγινῆται ἐπὶ ἑωυτῶν ἱδρύσαντο τέμενος Διός, καὶ ἄλλο Σάμιοι Ἥρης καὶ Μιλήσιοι
Ἀπόλλωνος.

[Since Amasis liked the Greeks, he performed many services for
them and especially to those who came to Egypt he gave the city
Naukratis to inhabit, and to those sea travelers who did not wish to
settle there permanently he gave land to erect altars and precinct to
the gods. [2] Now the greatest sanctuary of these, the most famous
and the most wealthy, was called the Hellenion. It was erected by
the following people working together: of the Ionians, Chios, Teos,
Phokaia, and Klazomenai, of the Dorians, Rhodes, Knidos, Halikarnassos, and Phaselis, and of the Aiolians only Mytilene. [3] This
sanctuary belongs to these cities, and they are the ones who appoint
the officers in charge of the port. And whatever other cities claim a
share in this, they do so illegally. But the Aiginetans by themselves
built a sanctuary of Zeus separate from the rest, and also the
Samians built one for Hera and the Milesians for Apollo.]

While not attributing the foundation to any one Greek city, Herodotos
does include the Milesians among the inhabitants, and he offers a time
reference, the reign of Amasis I, 570–526. But this date is too late for the
earliest pottery remnants, Corinthian and Attic sherds from the last quarter of the seventh century. Instead, the suggestion is often made that the
site was originally occupied under Psammitichos yet somehow reorganized by Amasis.

The excavation at Naukratis has confirmed three of the four sanctuaries that Herodotos mentions. The Milesian Temple of Apollo dates to the
early sixth century, as probably does the Samian Temple of Hera next to
it, although the evidence there is too sparse for certainty. The Hellenion

was later, just after 570, coinciding with the reign of Amasis. Two other temples have also been found: one to Aphrodite (possibly erected by the Chians, based on the abundance of Chian pottery there) also dates to the early sixth century, while a sanctuary for the Dioskouroi has too few remains left for accurate dating.

From the fact that it was one of only three states to erect its own sanctuary, one might surmise that Miletos enjoyed a favored status, but the evidence is confusing. Herodotos says that those cities who shared in the Hellenion appointed the officers in charge of the port and thus, presumably, had control over Naukratis, excluding from power the Samians, Milesians, and Aeginetans. It has been suggested that the founding of the Hellenion represents a political unification of a previously fragmented Greek settlement. Another view states that the newer arrivals may have joined together against the older powers, a view perhaps confirmed by the fact that the Hellenion dates to a period later than that of the other temples. Or perhaps Herodotos was mistaken or misinformed and the officers were not chosen from such a limited group. Given the evidence available to us, it is impossible to draw a satisfactory conclusion.[27]

Other Milesian evidence besides the Temple of Apollo has been discovered at Naukratis.[28] Möller attributes the Middle Wild Goat–style sherds to a Milesian origin, as well as some of the Fikellura vases from the sixth century, bird bowls, and Ionian bowls.[29] The Greeks sent olive oil and wine to Egypt, much of it for local Greek consumption, although the olive oil was superior to Egyptian castor and sesame oil and so may have been valued by the Egyptians. The Milesians probably exported furniture and wool products as well. Finally, large hoards of Greek silver, including both ingots and coins, have been found in Egypt and the Levant, suggesting that the Greeks paid for many of their purchases in cash, although the mistreatment of the coins suggests that the Egyptians did not prize them for their nominal value but treated them only as bullion. The principal Egyptian commodity available for Milesian import was grain: Bacchylides (fr. 20B14–16 Snell) mentions ships loaded with Egyptian grain in the fifth

---

27. For a summary of the arguments, see Austin 1970, 31–32; Möller 2000, chap. 6. I find it telling that neither Austin nor Möller is confident enough to draw any definite conclusions on the topic.

28. Faience and other Egyptian material thought to come from workshops at Naukratis has recently been found at the Archaic Sanctuary to Aphrodite on Zeytintepe, in Milesian territory. See Hölbl 1999.

29. Möller 2000, chap. 6.

century, and presumably they sailed earlier as well. In general, the Greeks also sought linen for clothing and sails, papyrus, salt, alum for dying, gold and semiprecious stones, incense, animal skins, unguents and perfumes, ebony, ivory, and alabaster.[30]

Thus, in the early Archaic period, Miletos and other Greek cities began to develop commercial relationships both among themselves and with the older civilizations of the eastern Mediterranean. However, that large trade network was not the limit of Greek involvement abroad, for the Ionians and others started very early to establish proper Greek cities in faraway places. A period of colonization began in the Mediterranean and Pontos as early as the middle of the eighth century B.C.E. and lasted for more than two hundred years, serving as a direct stimulus to the prosperity of the Classical Greek world.

Colonization

Although the specific causes for the Archaic colonial expansion continue to be disputed, two main alternatives are postulated. The first holds that the Greek cities were either overcrowded or somehow lacking in resources, so that they were forced by necessity to stretch their skimpy food supply beyond what it could sustain. The problem may have occurred because of a population explosion in the home city or because the availability of resources fell due to drought, famine, or climatic change. According to this scenario, the Greeks colonized especially to get rid of excess people, out of "land hunger" as scholars usually call it. In one variation of this theory, the colonies are also viewed as food producers: the mother city would naturally maintain close ties and a most-favored-nation status with the colonies, so colonies that were located in fertile, grain-producing regions would ship their excess produce back home to the mother city.[31]

---

30. Möller 2000; Ehrhardt 1983, 87–90; Graham 1982a, 134; Boardman 1980, 129; Austin 1970, 35–39; Röhlig 1933, 31–37; Bilabel 1920, 58–59; Dunham 1915, 23–24.

31. Among the many sources on Greek colonization in general, see Tsetskhladze 1998a; Graham 1982a; Graham 1982b; Graham 1983; Boardman 1980; Murray 1980, chap. 7; Danoff 1962, 1056–57; Roebuck 1959. Roebuck (1959, 87–130) summarizes the different motivations and the evidence for them, while Tsetskhladze (1994, 123–26) makes a specifically Milesian argument. Cook 1946 (79), Graham 1982a, and Noonan 1973 typify the arguments for overcrowding. Noonan does not believe that the Black Sea produced sufficient volume of grain to allow for its export until the late sixth or early fifth century B.C.E.

Ever since the fall of the Mycenaeans and the Dark Ages, the Greek world suffered a general scarcity of such metals as tin and copper (the ingredients of bronze) and of gold most of all. Silver was found in a few large deposits in Greece—in Thrace, on Siphnos, and, in the fifth century, in Attika. Iron was more widespread, but even it was lacking at some locations. Without these metals, life could continue only on the most primitive level, without adequate tools and weaponry. Accordingly, the alternative view maintains that the Greeks colonized in regions that offered safe locations near natural resources or on trade routes with native peoples, especially those rich in metals, as well as raw wool, hides, timber, fish, hemp, flax, honey, and probably slaves.[32] Why else would the Greeks bypass good land nearer to home to establish their earliest colonies as far away as the Bay of Naples and the middle of the Black Sea, places that can be seen as the termini of trade routes?[33]

In the end, it is fruitless to look for one exclusive cause of Greek colonization. The motives would have varied according to the situation of the diverse mother cities, over time, and from colonial location to location. One colony may be situated near a friendly native tribe but may itself lack the agricultural land to support even its own population, suggesting that trade should be the motivation for that particular site. Another may have arable land to spare, but little native contact, suggesting an agricultural settlement. A third might exploit other natural resources, either using them locally or by sending them abroad. The conditions in the ancient world are too complex and too little understood to allow for an accurate and convincing reconstruction of the colonial models. At best, we may have enough evidence available for an individual site to

He argues that, instead of being motivated by a need for food in the mother city, the migration was motivated by land hunger. Cawkwell (1992) summarizes the arguments for climatic problems (cf. Camp 1979), at least for the earliest colonies, and argues against the population explosion model.

32. Iron: Aesch. *Prom. Vinct.* 714; Xen. *Anab.* 5.5.1. Silver: Str. 12.3.19. Gold: Str. 11.2.18. Wool and clothing: Pliny *NH* 6.5; Hipponax of Ephesos in Tzetz. *Chil.* 10.348ff. Hides: Str. 11.2.3. Timber: Theoph. *Hist. Plant.* 4.5.5; Str. 11.2.17, 12.3.11–12; Pliny *NH* 16.197. Fish: Arist. *Hist. An.* 8.13.2; Str. 7.6.2, 12.3.19; Hdt. 4.53. Hemp: Hdt. 4.74; Str. 11.2.17. Flax: Hdt. 2.105; Str. 11.2.17; Xen. *Cyn.* 4. Honey and wax: Polyb. 4.38.1ff.

33. For trade as the motivating factor in the north Pontos, see Solovev 1998; Koshelenko and Kuznetsov 1998. Cawkwell (1992, 296) believes that trade may have been a strong motive for later colonies but that the early ones were founded to escape drought and/or famine; however, he does not sufficiently explain the distance to the first few colonies (Pithekousai, Sinope, and Kyzikos).

allow intelligent guesses about its origin and role in the Archaic Greek economy.

The Greek colonization movement was inspired by the first distant expeditions abroad, remembered in such mythological stories as the wanderings of Odysseus, which are sometimes set in Italy and the west, and of Jason and the Argonauts, who sailed into the Black Sea. Sporadic voyages would have opened the eyes of those seafarers to the potential in trade and settlement abroad, leading to a gradual regularization of contact with native peoples all along the Mediterranean and Pontic shores.[34] Beginning in the eighth century, various cities sent out colonies, called *apoikiai*, that were intended to be permanent independent settlements, sometimes with extensive territorial claims. Some thrived and grew over the years to have tens of thousands of inhabitants and even prospered sufficiently to send out secondary foundations, ancillary settlements made by a primary colony to consolidate its agricultural hold over a region or to extend its trading influence.

Each colony, no matter what its nature, was entrusted to an *oikist*, or founder, who was given charge of the operation from start to finish, including establishing the physical layout and autonomous political institutions of the new city. When choosing a specific location, the founder typically looked for a site near native peoples who were amenable to trade. But in the first instance, until friendly relations with the natives could be established, the site had to be defensible. He also sought nearby navigable water with good harbors, to provide ready transportation to and from the site, by river to the native peoples inland and by sea to the rest of Greece. The first settlement in a region was often on an island or peninsula that could be easily defended; it was sometimes later moved to a location with better agricultural or trading potential. Thus, the colonies tended to cluster along coastlines, especially near the mouths of rivers, and close enough to established peoples to profit from trade, but not so close as to provoke a unified military response that the colony could not withstand.[35]

The individual colonies reflected the diversity of circumstances in which they were founded. Some based their economy on farming, fishing, and the general exploitation of other raw materials in the region. Others were primarily oriented toward the exchange of goods and raw materials

---

34. Malkin 1998; Graham 1990.
35. Murray 1980, 100–119.

with the native peoples: as such, they were known as *emporia*. Although modern scholars sometimes try to differentiate between *emporion* and *apoikia* as technical terms, the Greek writers—Herodotos especially— make no clear distinction between the two: nearly all *emporia* were independent poleis in their own right, although it was possible to designate as an *emporion* the port district of a city or a trading post without formal autonomy. One must conclude that the appellation *emporion* meant that the location was heavily involved in trade but said nothing about its political status and did not preclude another economic base for the settlement as well, such as agriculture or fishing. If the colony had its chief base in agriculture, it was more commonly called an *apoikia*.[36]

The Greeks concentrated their colonial settlements in three main areas: Magna Graecia (Italy below Naples) and Sicily; the north Aegean region, including the Chalkidike; and the northeast corner of the Mediterranean, including the Hellespont, Propontis, Bosporos, and Pontos.[37] In the first region, the Greeks found they could gain valuable arable land while also establishing trade routes with the Etruscans and across to Spain and inland Europe. In the second, the Thracians were fierce adversaries whose bellicose customs and migratory habits threatened the stability of the north Aegean colonies, but the well-watered plains, dense forests, and rich mines were well worth the risk.[38] Finally, the Propontic and Pontic regions offered many resources both in food and in metals, and they were inhabited by many native, often nomadic societies that, though sometimes hostile, had much to offer the Greeks in trade.[39]

The colonizing movement swept through Archaic Greece. Some cities sent out only a handful of colonies: Sparta founded only one colony of any importance, Taras (modern Tarento) in southern Italy.[40] Others settled a dozen or more cities, led by the pioneering ventures of the Euboian cities, Eretria and Chalkis, which founded the first confirmed colonies in the

36. Bresson and Rouillard 1993; Hansen 1997a, 1997b; Hind 1997. Danoff (1962, 1050–57) is a spokesman for an older theory of colonization as a lengthy process with distinct stages, from first contact, to trading post, to colony; however, this theory is not now generally accepted.

37. Of course, there were colonies elsewhere (the Adriatic, Libya, and the Mediterranean coast of France and Spain), but they were fewer in number.

38. Mihailov 1991. Graham (1978) makes the argument that the relatively late date for the Parian colonization of the very desirable island Thasos (ca. 650) was due to the strength of the native Thracians and their Phoenician backing.

39. Sulimirski and Taylor 1991; Mellink 1991b; Graham 1971, 40–41; Danoff 1962; Roebuck 1959, 42–60.

40. Malkin 1994.

middle of the eighth century, at Pithekousai and Kyme in the Bay of Naples, and then followed with others in both the west and the north. They were rivaled by Corinth, the master of the isthmus and so a dominant sea power that established, among others, Syracuse (mid–eighth century), soon to become the preeminent city on Sicily, and Potidaia on the Chalkidike (mid–seventh century). Another leading colonizer, Megara, founded Megara Hyblaia on Sicily (728 B.C.E.) and many cities in the Propontis and Bosporos, including the very successful sites of Chalkedon and Byzantion (later Constantinople), built on either side of the mouth of the Bosporos in the early to middle part of the seventh century.

The most successful mother city, the one most renowned for the number and prosperity of its colonies, was Miletos.[41] Strabo says (14.1.6):

πολλὰ δὲ τῆς πόλεως ἔργα ταύτης, μέγιστον δὲ τὸ πλῆθος τῶν ἀποικιῶν· ὅ τε γὰρ Εὔξεινος πόντος ὑπὸ τούτων συνῴκισται πᾶς καὶ ἡ Προποντὶς καὶ ἄλλοι πλείους τόποι.

[The deeds of this city are many, but the greatest one is the number of its colonies. For the Black Sea has been entirely colonized by them, as well as the Propontis and a good many other regions.]

Pseudo-Skymnos (GGM 1.225, lines 734–37) adds that the Milesians were able by their colonization efforts to change the name of the Pontos from "Inhospitable" (Axeinos) to "Hospitable" (Euxeinos). Even under the Roman Empire, the Milesians themselves continued to brag about their colonizing prowess in inscriptional prescripts from the second century C.E., calling themselves Ἡ πρώτη τῆς Ἰωνίας ᾠκισμένη καὶ μητρόπολις πολλῶν καὶ μεγάλων πόλεων ἔν τε τῷ Πόντῳ καὶ τῇ Αἰγύπτῳ καὶ πολλαχοῦ τῆς οἰκουμένης Μιλησίων πόλις [the city of Miletos, the first to inhabit Ionia, and the mother city of many great cities on the Pontos and in Egypt and in many places].[42]

Without a doubt, Miletos colonized far more cities than did any other Greek polis. Ancient sources put the number of Milesian colonies as high as ninety. Modern scholars, using archaeological evidence as well as the

---

41. For Milesian trade and colonization in particular, the main sources are Röhlig 1933, Bilabel 1920, 9–153; Ehrhardt 1983. Roebuck (1959) discusses Ionian trade.

42. This text is found or restored formulaically in the lacunae of prescripts of *Milet* 1.7 #233–36, 239, 240 (= CIG 2878), erected under the emperors Antoninus Pius, Marcus Aurelius, Commodus, and Septimius Severus.

literary references, have made lower estimates, ranging from thirty to forty-five Milesian colonies.⁴³ More cities will be added to that list in years to come, when archaeological efforts in the Propontic and Pontic regions are expanded. Meanwhile, even if we accept the conservative numbers and count only the primary settlements, the fact remains that Miletos established a significant proportion of the Greek colonies: approximately one-fifth of all known Greek colonies between 800 and 500 B.C.E. and, astonishingly, more than one-half of the colonies in the northeast. No other mother city exerts that kind of domination in an area of Greek colonization.⁴⁴

While Pithekousai is generally regarded to be the earliest Archaic Greek colony, being founded before ca. 750–725, Miletos is credited in the literary record with two colonies in the same era: Kyzikos and Sinope.⁴⁵ These foundations are problematic, however, both because of their extreme antiquity and because these cities are given not one but two foundation dates in the extant literature. Eusebius (88b and 93b Helm) gives both 756 and 679 as foundation dates for Kyzikos. He dates Sinope to 631 (96b Helm), but then he dates Sinope's colony, Trapezous, to 756 (1.80e Schoene [Armen.]), implying that Sinope had to have had an original foundation date even earlier.⁴⁶ Pseudo-Skymnos (*GGM* 1.236, lines 941–52 = 986–97 Diller [source of text]) would seem to confirm this double foundation.

(Σινώπη πόλις) - - - - - ἐπώνυμος
Ἀμαζόνων τῶν πλησιοχώρων ⟨ἀπὸ⟩ μιᾶς,
ἥν ποτε μὲν ᾤκουν ἐγγενεῖς ὄντες Σύροι,
μετὰ ταῦτα δ', ὡς λέγουσιν, Ἑλλήνων ὅσοι
ἐπ' Ἀμαζόνων διέβησαν, Αὐτόλυκός τε καὶ
σὺν Δηιλέοντι Φλόγιος, ὄντες Θετταλοί·

---

43. Sen. *Helv.* 7 (75 colonies); Pliny *NH* 5.112 (90); Graham 1982a, 160–62 (30); Ehrhardt 1983, 96 and passim (40 primary and 30 secondary); Bilabel 1920, 13–60 (45). See the appendix at the end of this volume.

44. The numbers I use here are from Graham 1982a, 160–62. Miletos colonized thirty out of fifty-one colonies in the northeast. With the four known secondary settlements in his charts, the figure reaches 69 percent. The next most prolific colonizer, Chalkis, settled nine colonies in the west and seven in the north Aegean, totaling 12 percent of all known Greek colonization and 37.5 percent of the colonization of the west.

45. For early Greek colonization and precolonial contacts, see Graham 1990.

46. Trapezous as colony of Sinope: Xen. *Anab.* 4.8.22; D.S. 14.30.3; Arr. *Peripl. Eux.* 1 = *GGM* 1.370, para. 1; Steph. Byz. s.v.; Eust. Dion. *Per.* 687.

ἔπειτα ⟨δ'⟩ Ἄβρων τῷ γένει Μιλήσιος,
ὑπὸ Κιμμερίων οὗτος ⟨δ'⟩ ἀναιρεῖσθαι δοκεῖ·
μετὰ Κιμμερίους Κῷος πάλιν δὲ Κρητίνης
οἱ γενόμενοι φυγάδες ⟨τε⟩ τῶν Μιλησίων.
οὗτοι συνοικίζουσι δ' αὐτὴν ἡνίκα
ὁ Κιμμερίων κατέδραμε τὴν Ἀσίαν στρατός.

[Next comes Sinope, . . . a city that is named for an Amazon, of whom there were many in that land. At one point, the wellborn Syrians occupied it, and afterward, as they say, some Greeks who had fought against the Amazons, Autolykos and Phlogios with Deileon, Thessalian men. Then came Habrondas, a Milesian by race. It seems that he was killed by Kimmerians. But after the Kimmerians came Koos and Kretines, who were exiles from among the Milesians. These men colonized the city, when the army of Kimmerians overran Asia.]

Many scholars dismiss as fiction the earlier dates, reasoning, first, that excavators have not yet found any material in the Pontos that can be securely dated to the eighth century B.C.E. and, second, that the Greeks were incapable of sailing up the Bosporos before ca. 700. The first reason is a classic *argumentum ex silentio* that cannot be taken as the last word but instead must be seen as a *terminus ante quem*: we can be sure that there is nothing earlier that has not yet been found, especially since the sites in question are by no means excavated thoroughly. In contrast, the written sources have proven themselves generally reliable and should not be discarded cavalierly, without positive counterevidence.[47] The second argument is based on prevailing wind and current conditions blowing from the Pontos out to the Aegean Sea.[48] However, modern wind tables show that

47. Graham 1958, esp. 38–39; Graham 1971, 38; Cook 1946; *PECS* 473–74, 842. Cf. Tsetskhladze 1994, 118; 1998a. According to Graham (1990, 52), Trapezous has never been dug at all, while the excavations at Sinope have been "too sporadic to create any confidence that the earliest material is known." At Olbia/Berezan, the best excavated of the Milesian colonies, the foundation date of 647 (Eus. 95b Helm) is supported by archaeological finds: Vinogradov and Kryzickij (1995, 127) report the discovery of a sherd from Berezan from the second quarter of the seventh century and others from Olbia from the second half of that century. Cf. Solovev 1998. For the reliability of literary dates, see Lazarov 1998 (western Pontos); Ivantchik 1998 (Sinope, but only discussing the second foundation date).
48. Carpenter 1948. For discussion of the question of eighth-century colonization, see Graham 1990, 52–54; Graham 1982a, 118–19, 123; Graham 1958; Ehrhardt 1983, 41–42,

southerly winds blow often enough during the sailing season—in some months up to one-third of the days—to allow sailing ships to make the run up through the Bosporos. In addition, countercurrents and eddies could be utilized, as they continue to be today, and boats could also be towed from land.[49] Thus, the arguments against the early foundation of Sinope and Kyzikos are not definitive, and the eighth-century dates for both should be seen as possibilities, awaiting further confirmation or disproval. Meanwhile, we can conclude that the Milesians joined the Greek colonization movement from a very early date, perhaps its very start: at the same time as the Euboians were extending their interests to Italy, according to the literary dates, the Milesians were also active in the northeast.

The sheer number of Milesian colonies suggests that the desire for trade, more than any other factor, must have acted as the stimulus for their foundation. Certainly, one cannot plausibly argue that a city that sent out forty-five or more colonies was trying solely to relieve overcrowding: indeed, it is likely that Miletos had to recruit volunteers from elsewhere in the Greek world to fill out its colonial contingents. The fact that the first colonies were far distant supports this idea as well: nine subsequent Milesian colonies are located closer to Miletos than is Kyzikos, while Sinope is halfway into the Black Sea. Finally, the interdependency between colonization and trade is demonstrated by the famed prosperity and luxurious living of the Milesians.

It is important to recognize that grain may have been one of the items that was traded back to the mother city. The earliest explicit account of grain ships sailing out of the Black Sea dates to Xerxes' invasion of Greece in 480, as reported by Herodotos (7.146).[50] Elsewhere in Herod-

---

49–50; Boardman 1980, 240ff.; Drews 1976. Contra Carpenter, see esp. Labaree 1957; Graham 1958. See also Danoff 1962, 1053–54; Tsetskhladze 1994; Hind 1994, 482.

49. In the *Anaplus Bospori,* written in the second century C.E., Dionysios of Byzantium (pp. 22–23 Güngerich [2d ed.]) describes ships sailing upstream and others hugging the shore to avoid the strong current. See Graham 1958, 30.

The theory against the Greeks in the Black Sea in the eighth century relies on the idea that the first big oared ships, *pentekonters,* were invented ca. 700, but Thucydides says (1.13.3–14.2) that triremes were invented then and that pentekonters were the normal warships used by the Greeks until shortly before the Persian Wars. To make their theory work, scholars have assumed that Thucydides confuses the two ship types.

50. Noonan (1973) uses the lack of earlier literary accounts as one piece of evidence against the earlier export of grain from the Pontos. However, it is difficult to know what earlier accounts he would seek, since Homer is too early, Hesiod writes about a different part of the world, and the other Archaic writers are few and writing on diverse topics. In short, an *argumentum ex silentio* is not compelling.

otos (1.14–22, esp. 17), earlier shipments may be implied. The Lydians, he relates, plundered Milesian territory for twelve straight years, destroying the crops. The story is set in the reign of Kings Sadyattes and Alyattes, ca. 617–605, and if it is to be trusted, we must believe that before 600 B.C.E. the Milesians had a source of grain abroad. Herodotos clearly states that the Lydians stole the Milesian crops for twelve straight years but understood the futility of besieging the city in the normal way, since the Milesians had the ability to import goods by sea. Even granting the possibility of exaggeration in this story, one cannot throw it out wholesale. It is reasonable to assume that Miletos suffered a lengthy siege and, as a result, looked to its colonies in the Propontis and Pontos for a portion of its grain supply, even if those colonies had not been founded specifically as sources of grain. The grain shipments may have continued through the sixth century as well, as the Milesians converted more and more of their labor force to manufacturing. It is also possible that imported grain enabled Milesian farmers to turn to lucrative cash crops, such as wool, olives, and grapes, since the city was certainly heavily involved both in the cloth industry and in the manufacture of pottery, which is not usually exported empty. Like Athens in the fifth century, the Milesians may have found it more profitable to import a certain amount of grain, not because they could not grow it themselves, but because they could labor more profitably in other ventures while relying on their fleet and colonies to fulfill the food needs of the growing populace.[51]

We must conclude that both the causes and the benefits of colonization were numerous. While some colonies may have been sent out as grain producers for the mother city, this was probably a later phenomenon. It is very likely that many of the earlier Milesian colonies were sent out to exploit the natural resources and to establish commercial contacts with native peoples. Because the colonists rarely entered completely uninhabited regions, a colony was of little use unless or until it could establish a viable economic relationship with the non-Greek populations of the hinterland, guaranteeing the colony a steady supply of raw materials in barter for the worked goods coming in from the colony, the mother city, and beyond.

Immediately to the south of the Propontis and Pontos, Anatolia was

---

51. Moles (1996, 260–61) notes that the Lydian invasions of Milesian territory are intended as an allusion to the Spartan invasions of Attika in the early years of the Peloponnesian War, but Moles still does not question the veracity of the original account.

inhabited by a number of different native peoples.[52] Besides the autochthonous people, called Doliones, who were present in small number, especially near the colony Kyzikos, the native peoples can be divided roughly into the larger groupings of (from west to east) Mysians, Phrygians, Bithynians, and Paphlagonians, followed by the remnants of the Hittite Empire and Assyrians (in the region later known simply as Cappadocia Pontica, or simply, the Pontus). These peoples are generally thought to be of Thracian descent, speaking Anatolian dialects of Indo-European, although the Phrygian language more closely resembles Greek. Most lived in small tribal units that were livestock-based and seminomadic, practicing some agriculture but migrating as necessary. They lived in such close proximity to each other that they were difficult to distinguish (Str. 12.4.4). The Phrygians were the exception: they were the most urbanized and organized of these peoples, possessing what can legitimately be called an empire. Their zenith lasted from the twelfth century to the ninth, and their downfall came with the destruction of their capital city, Gordion, shortly after the reign of their famous king Midas (born ca. 760 or 755 B.C.E.). Control of much of Asia Minor then fell into the hands of the Lydian Empire, ruled from Sardis by the kings Gyges, Ardys, Sadyattes, Alyattes, and Kroisos. In 547, that empire fell in turn to the rising Achaimenid family of Persia, led by Cyrus the Great.[53]

Disruption between these empires was caused by the influx of other Thracian peoples from above the Black Sea, peoples called Skythians and Kimmerians. According to Herodotos (1.103–6; 4.1 and passim), the Skythians followed the Kimmerians into Asia toward the end of the seventh century and occupied the land, plundering and looting, for twenty-eight years before returning north. Today we know that this picture may not be entirely accurate.[54] There is already evidence of some Skythians or Kimmerians in Asia as early as the eighth century, and they stayed there much longer than twenty-eight years, although Herodotos is correct in describing the destruction they wrought. In the early seventh century, the Kimmerians pillaged Gordion, thus destroying the Phrygian Empire, and they sacked Sardis as well. They invaded Asia

---

52. One of the best ancient sources devoted to the native peoples of Anatolia and the surrounding regions is book 12 of Strabo's *Geography;* cf. Xenophon's *Anabasis.* For modern sources, see the many articles in *CAH* 3².2, including Mellink 1991b.

53. Herodotos relates much of these events in his book 1. See also Mellink 1991a; Graham 1971; Hasluck 1910.

54. See esp. Jacobson 1995, 29–51.

Minor and made attacks on the Lydians and Assyrians before they were
beaten back by Alyattes of Lydia in 626 or 637 (Hdt. 1.15) and by
Ashurbanipal of Assyria in ca. 625 or 635. Herodotos says (1.16) they
were driven out of Asia Minor, but small pockets survived in Cilicia,
Cappadocia, and Iran.[55]

The Skythians north of the Propontis and Pontos were more stable,
although still often seminomadic. Descended from the Bronze Age cultures of the Asian steppe, they occupied the Eurasian region from Mongo-
lia to Thrace. They were self-sufficient master horsemen who depended
for their livelihood on herds of cattle, sheep, goats, horses, and, in some
places, yaks and Bactrian camels. By the term *Skythian*, however, we
usually mean the subclass of Skytho-Siberians who entered the Pontic
regions before the seventh century in two contemporaneous waves, one
from the east and south, rounding the Caspian Sea in a counterclockwise
direction, and another from the north. Historically they are subdivided
into the Farming Skythians, the Nomadic Skythians, and the Royal
Skythians.[56] They always lived side by side with numerous other native
peoples, as can be seen in Herodotos's lengthy description of the peoples
living north of the Pontos (4.17–35). Besides the different Skythians, he
discusses Kallipidai, Alizones, Neuroi, Androphagoi ("Man-Eaters"),
and Melanchlainoi ("Black Cloaks").

In general, the process of colonization was peaceful.[57] Miletos was not
an imperial power, nor did it have the military might to forcibly subjugate
the native peoples, some of whom, like the Skythians, were quite formid-
able. Instead, the Milesians relied more on nurturing trade relations with
the native peoples than on seizing land from them. Some colonies—
Milesian or otherwise—may have been located on the site of a pre-Greek
settlement, but only where the native peoples were thinly populated, and
archaeologists are finding evidence that might be taken to indicate that
the Greek colonists were mixed with non-Greek elements.[58] Certainly one

55. Skythians and Kimmerians: Jacobson 1995; Ivantchik 1993; Sulimirski and Taylor
1991, 555–60; Mihailov 1991; Graham 1971, 39–40. Phrygians and Lydians: Mellink
1991b.
56. This distinction is at least as old as Herodotos (4.17–35). On Skythian culture, see
Hdt. 4.59–80; Jacobson 1995; Sulimirski and Taylor 1991, 578–83.
57. Fol 1996, 7; Danov 1990. Cf. Röhlig 1933, 16–17.
58. The argument for a strong non-Greek presence based on the discovery of Skythian
pottery sherds within the city wall (Jacobson 1995, 43–44, 47, 49) is problematic. Pottery
remains tell us more about trade than about the composition of the population and
cultural dominance. In the city of Olbia, Vinogradov and Kryzickij (1995) have discovered

must see that the colonies were fundamentally Greek cities, with Greek
personal names, offices, architecture, and cults, but it is also clear that the
colonists and native peoples entered early on into mutually beneficial
trade relationships that lasted for centuries to come.

The success of Miletos's colonization movement can be seen in the
sheer number and extent of the colonies: five are known today in the
region west of the Propontis, ten along the south shore of the Propontis,
nine more on the south shore of the Pontos, three on the east coast, five
on the west, and as many as ten along the north. The Lesbians, Phokaians, Teians, and Athenians competed with the Milesians for a foothold
in the Hellespont and Thracian Chersonese, a region desirable both for its
trade and tariff potential and for its adequate, but not overabundant,
agricultural land. The Milesians took control of the south littoral of the
Propontis, while the Megarians dominated to the east and north.[59] The
Black Sea was entirely Milesian as far as we can tell, with sixteen to
twenty primary colonies and six to ten secondary ones ringing its shore.[60]
This fact indicates that Miletos must have had very good relations with
the Megarians, since Megara controlled the Bosporos, the only way into
and out of the Black Sea.[61]

The Milesian monopoly on the Black Sea lasted from the foundation
of Sinope in the mid–eighth century until the middle of the sixth century,
when three non-Milesian cities were founded in succession. First, Megara
settled Heraklea Pontika ca. 560 on the stretch of the south shore between the Thracian Bosporos and the Milesian colony Tieion. About fifty
years later, the Megarians acted with their colonies, Byzantion and
Chalkedon, to establish Mesembria across the bay north of Apollonia
Pontika (near modern Burgas, Bulgaria). In addition, Teos founded
Phanagoria ca. 545 in rivalry to Kepoi and Hermonassa, on the east shore

---

house remains that they attribute to native inhabitants: this argument for a mixed population is much stronger, but the evidence is extremely limited at the present time. The best
argument is based on a mixture of Greek and native nomenclature, such as we find at
Tanais (*PECS* 877).

59. The Megarians founded Astakos (modern Izmit) in 711 on the easternmost arm of
the Propontis (it may also have been a later settlement from Chalkedon); Chalkedon on the
Asian side of the mouth of the Bosporos in 676 or 685; Selymbria on the north shore before
668 B.C.E.; and Byzantion on the European side of the Bosporos in 659 or 668. See Graham
1982a, 119–21, 160–62.

60. The most extensive source for the Black Sea in general, including geography, flora,
fauna, mineral resources, native peoples, and Greek settlements, is Danoff 1962, which is
especially good for its bibliography up to that date. See also Ehrhardt 1983.

61. Graham 1982a, 124.

of the Kimmerian Bosporos.[62] The Milesian stranglehold was broken, but why? Perhaps the Milesians were rewarding cooperative trading allies by permitting them into their inner sanctuary, or perhaps they had no choice, weakened in part by the Persian takeover of Ionia in the 540s. Whatever the cause, the golden age of Milesian colonization was over. Only a few more settlements would originate from Miletos after 550. Notably, near the end of the sixth century, the Milesian tyrant Histiaios founded Myrkinos in Macedonia, a gift from the Persian king. That colony was not successful, dying along with Aristagoras (Hdt. 5.11–12, 23–24, 126; Thuc. 4.102).

Some general characteristics of Milesian colonization may be offered by way of conclusion. First, with a few exceptions, the Milesians sent their colonies to the Hellespont, Propontis, and Pontos: there were no Milesian colonies in the west, and there was nothing before the late sixth century in the north Aegean. Second, one cannot describe Milesian colonization as occurring in waves or stages, and it is impossible to distinguish between a Propontic and a Pontic phase.[63] Third, while Miletos shared the colonization of the Hellespont and Propontis with other Greek mother cities, Milesian colonies were for the most part located along the south shore, and indeed, Miletos controlled the Asian littoral of the Propontis from where it began to broaden out at the top of the Hellespont at the cities of Kolonai and Paisos through its course east to Kios (north of modern Bursa). Finally, although the Milesians had no colonies on the Bosporos proper, from the first foundation at Sinope before 756 until the middle of the sixth century, Miletos had a complete monopoly on Black Sea colonization: until ca. 560 B.C.E., no Greeks except Milesians were known to have colonized the Black Sea. Thus, Miletos was undeniably the greatest of all Greek mother cities. Its widespread colonies not only provided trade and economic prosperity but, in the crisis years to come, would play a significant role in reviving and repopulating Miletos in the first decades of the Classical era.

---

62. Burstein 1976 (Herakleia Pontika); Tsetskhladze 1997, 51–55 (Phanagoria). Of all the Milesian colonies for which we have dated evidence, only Tomis is dated later, ca. 500–475 B.C.E., but I would expect that earlier material will be found when the excavation, which is now quite sparse, is expanded.

63. According to Ehrhardt (1983, 250), Milesian colonization paused from ca. 680 to ca. 650 B.C.E., probably because of the invasion of the Kimmerians into Asia Minor: cf. Carpenter 1948; Labaree 1957. Graham (1987) disputes this theory as being artificially imposed by Ehrhardt based on an *argumentum ex silentio*.

The Milesian Intellectuals

Before Periklean Athens, before the Library and Museum of Alexandria, Miletos stood as the foremost intellectual center of the Greek world. Because of the paucity of literary sources from the Archaic period, we know surprisingly little about the individuals involved; we have only a handful of names and a small number of fragments of their works. But what survives is enough to establish that Miletos was the birthplace of some of the leading thinkers of the age, including poets, philosophers, and geographers. The city was the natural location for such intellectual achievement, because of its economic dominance. Its far-flung trading ventures led to contacts with a wide variety of peoples and cultures. The Milesians were in close association not only with the Hellenic cities on the mainland and both the eastern and western Mediterranean but also with the Carians, Lykians, Lydians, and Persians of Asia Minor; the Thrakians and Skythians in the north; the Egyptians in the south; the Syrians and Phoenicians of Asia; and countless other small groups of native peoples that inhabited the environs of the various colonies. This cultural exposure opened the Milesians' eyes to new opinions and perspectives, and they began to investigate and challenge the world around them in ways hitherto unknown. In addition, the prosperity that came with trade provided surplus and luxury, key ingredients to any intellectual movement: only in an environment of affluence can a society afford to allow a highly talented segment of its population to devote their lives to erudition.

The final characteristic that made sixth-century Miletos fertile ground for the growth of new schools of thought was its strong literary tradition in epic and gnomic poetry. The earliest known Milesian poet, Arktinos, was one of the contributors to some of the earliest Greek literature, the poetry referred to today as the Epic Cycle.[64] This collection consisted of a number of epic poems, composed in a Homeric vein and designed to fill in the parts of the story of the Trojan War that the *Iliad* and the *Odyssey* had passed over as well as other great conflicts of the Heroic Age, such as the Seven against Thebes. Because in antiquity the poems were sometimes associated with Homer himself, most of the actual poets have been forgotten; those we do know are recalled merely as names, like Arktinos of Miletos. However, the poems themselves were very fashionable and commonly read through the Classical era; afterward they fell into such a state

---

64. Bernabé *PEG* 1.65–71, 86–92; Davies 1989.

of unpopularity that very little remains of any of the dozens of poems of the Epic Cycle.

Arktinos probably composed his hexameters in the late seventh century, yet, as is so often the case, only brief *testimonia* survive to the present day. His name is associated with two works. The *Sack of Troy* ('Ιλίου πέρσις), in two books, was about the ruse of the Trojan horse and the destruction of the city. It is little known and may not be correctly attributed to him (Paus. 10.25.5). However, the *Aithiopis* (Αἰθιοπίς), in five books, almost certainly belongs to him. It continued Homer's *Iliad*, focusing on the deeds of Achilles, including his victory over the Amazon Penthesilaia, his slaying of Thersites for insulting Penthesileia's corpse, his absolution for this bloodguilt by Odysseus, and his slaying of Memnon, an Ethiopian prince. The work ends with Achilles' death at the hands of Paris and Apollo, and his funeral.[65]

Nothing more is known about Arktinos, but another early poet of Miletos, Phokylides (fl. before 650), was quite famous in antiquity as a poet of gnomic hexameter verses addressed to a nameless companion.[66] Only 39 lines of Phokylides' work are extant, most as isolated individual verses or couplets; one passage of eight lines survives. An interesting characteristic of this poetry is that the phrase καὶ τόδε Φωκυλίδεω [This too is a saying of Phokylides] recurs four times in our limited collection of fragments. Apparently it was used every few lines to separate the axioms. The wording is evidently meant not so much to reserve credit for the work as to lend authority to each of the individual precepts.[67] Yet, despite Phokylides' apparent expertise, the ancients knew nothing about his life. The surviving poems are gnomic sayings, advising on topics like the best life (one spent in agriculture), debts, and looking to the gods for success. In general, the poet recommends a moderate course, and as a result, he enjoyed a reputation as one of the best representatives of the genre of wisdom poetry, a position he shared with Hesiod and Theognis. Isokrates (2.43) mentions all three in the same context when he excoriates the failure of humans to follow the good models that are set for them.[68]

---

65. Davies 1989, 74–79 (*Sack of Troy*), 53–61 (*Aithiopis*).

66. West 1978a, 1978b. For the surviving fragments, see Diehl *Anth. Lyr. Graec.* $1^3.57$–60; Bergk *PLG* 2.445–49. Several later moralizing poems are attributed to him as well, but they were clearly written by an Alexandrian Jew from the turn of the millennium. They are attributed to Ps.-Phokylides and collected by van der Horst (1978).

67. West (1978a, 164–65) attributes this feature to oriental influence.

68. Cf. Dio Chrys. 2.5; Ath. 632d; Cyril. *Patrol.* 76.841d.

Just as Phokylides was highly influential in the field of gnomic poetry, so Timotheos was a crucial figure in fifth-century music and poetry, and he serves as an example of the continuing literary tradition at Miletos into the Classical era.[69] Reputed to be a friend of Euripides, Timotheos was a great innovator famous for combining the dithyramb with nomes. The dithyramb was usually performed in honor of Dionysos by a male chorus dancing to flute music, while the nome was a solo piece sung to Apollo and accompanied by the lyre. According to Clement of Alexandria (*Strom.* 1.16, 51 St.; cf. Pherek. fr. 155.19ff. Kassel and Austin), Timotheos was the first poet to employ a chorus in a citharodic nome.

One example of Timotheos's work has been preserved for us by the desert sand: in 1902, in a grave at Abusir in Lower Egypt, archaeologists discovered a copy of Timotheos's *Persika* (*P. Berol.* 9865). The nome was probably performed in the last decade of the fifth century and may have had a prologue written by Euripides (Satyr. *Vita Eur.* fr. 39, col. 22). The papyrus itself dates from the fourth century B.C.E. and is now recognized as the oldest extant Greek manuscript.[70] The 240 surviving verses recount the story of the Battle of Salamis in a series of separate scenes and mostly from the Persian point of view. The poem also includes an author's address to the audience, defending his musical innovations, such as the use of an eleven-stringed lyre. The language is passionate during the battle scenes and rather obscure elsewhere: Timotheos anticipates the Hellenistic predilection to impress the audience by piling up little-known words and lengthy periphrases.

Thus, Miletos had several poets of note in the Archaic and Classical periods. This literary tradition at Miletos combined with economic affluence and foreign experiences to produce the setting for the creation of rational thinking in the West: Miletos was the birthplace of Greek philosophy and science. Three of the most influential pre-Socratics lived there, and their fame is so great that even today many may know the name *Miletos* solely for its association with Thales, Anaximander, and Anaximenes. These philosophers represent the transition in thought from myth to reason.[71] The first step of this process was to reject the personification of natural forces into gods—something intrinsic to the Greek

69. Janssen 1984; Page *PMG* 399–418, frs. 777–804.

70. Editio princeps: Wilamowitz-Moellendorff 1903b.

71. Every handbook on the history of philosophy will contain a section on the pre-Socratics. The material offered here is based most closely on Kirk, Raven, and Schofield 1983, 1–75, and Barnes 1979, 3–5. See also Emlyn-Jones 1980, 94–132; Hussey 1995.

worldview—while at the same time maintaining certain elements of the tradition in which that personification took place. The Milesian philosophers abandoned the deified natural forces seen in works like Hesiod's *Theogony*, yet they embraced the genealogical structure of those works: each of these three Milesians developed a system of nature around a single primary material that brought forth all other things.[72] They did not renounce the supernatural entirely, since the search for first elements was in a sense the search for divinity. Instead, they were empiricists who abandoned unargued dogma in favor of reason, a crucial beginning for those trying to systematize the world around them.

Traditionally, Thales is not only the oldest of the Milesian philosophers but also the first known Greek philosopher. Simplicius (*Phys.* 23.29 Diels) says that he had many predecessors but that he αὐτὸς δὲ πολὺ διενεγκὼν ἐκείνων ὡς ἀποκρύψαι πάντας τοὺς πρὸ αὐτοῦ [so far surpassed them as to blot out all who came before him].[73] Since no genuine works of Thales have survived—if, indeed, he ever wrote any—what we know about him comes to us through the medium of other authors and is necessarily colored by their views.[74] He is portrayed as a man who consorted with kings and leading politicians but was so absentminded that, while studying the stars above him, he fell into a hole in the ground (Pl. *Tht.* 174a).

Certainly, many of the stories that survive about Thales seem to have more in common with fable than reality. He was the oldest of the legendary Seven Wise Men of the ancient world (Pl. *Prt.* 343a). According to Herodotos (1.75), when Kroisos was fighting the Persians, Thales is supposed to have built a ford across the river Halys by diverting the water from its original course into two new, shallower river beds. In another, probably equally fictional story, Herodotos says (1.170) that Thales

---

72. Their monist systems were probably not as specific as our sources might lead us to believe. Barnes (1979, 39–42) argues that the pre-Socratics themselves made statements like "Everything is from X" and that others, chiefly Aristotle, reexpressed the statements in the form "There is some single stuff that is the material principle of everything." However, the original statement is much more ambiguous, and its interpretation need not imply monism exactly.

73. Trans. Kirk, Raven, and Schofield 1983, #81. For Thales in general, see Kirk, Raven, and Schofield 1983, 76–99; Barnes 1979, 5–13; Guthrie 1962, 45–72; DK 11.

74. According to the *Suda* (s.v. Θαλῆς), he wrote epic verse about his astrological findings. Simplicius (*Phys.* 23.29 Diels) says that he left only a nautical star-guide (ναυτικὴ ἀστρολογία), although Diogenes Laertes (1.23) doubts even that but mentions that some believe that he wrote *On the Solstice* (Περὶ τροπῆς) and *On the Equinox* (Περὶ Ἰσημερίας).

served as a political advisor when the Ionians cities were being attacked by the Persian general Harpagos. Finally, Aristotle (*Pol.* 1.1259a9–18) tells a tale—probably a folktale—that reflects Thales' economic savvy: during one winter when Thales observed from the stars that the olive crop would be very good, he used this information to corner the market in olive presses and realize a great profit, in order to prove ὅτι ῥᾴδιόν ἐστι πλουτεῖν τοῖς φιλοσόφοις, ἂν βούλωνται, ἀλλ᾽ οὐ τοῦτ᾽ ἐστὶ περὶ ὃ σπουδάζουσιν [that it was quite easy for wise men to become rich if they wished, but this is something they are not concerned about] (Arist. *Pol.* 1.1259a17–18).

The same astronomical skills that Thales exhibits in this story are used to determine a floruit date for him: he probably lived in the early to middle sixth century, because, according to Herodotos (1.74) and others, during a war between the Lydians and the Medes, Thales predicted a solar eclipse that astronomers have now dated to May 28, 585. While some scholars doubt that he could have managed this feat, Kirk and Raven defend the prediction. They admit that he did not understand the true cause of eclipses, but since he had access to Babylonian tables of astronomical observations going back to 721 B.C.E., he could have made his prediction based solely on empirical observation, although he could not have named the exact day of the event. According to other sources, Thales also discovered the cycle of solstices, and he defined the constellation Ursa Minor and pointed out its navigational usefulness (presumably because it includes the Pole Star, Polaris), although it is hard to believe that this latter idea is original with him.[75]

Although Thales was an engineer and astronomer, he is most renowned as the first natural philosopher. According to Aristotle (*Meta.* 1.983b6–24):

τῶν δὴ πρῶτον φιλοσοφησάντων οἱ πλεῖστοι τὰς ἐν ὕλης εἴδει μόνας ᾠήθησαν ἀρχὰς εἶναι πάντων· . . . δεῖ γὰρ εἶναί τινα φύσιν ἢ μίαν ἢ πλείους μιᾶς ἐξ ὧν γίγνεται τἆλλα σῳζομένης ἐκείνης. τὸ μέντοι πλῆθος καὶ τὸ εἶδος τῆς τοιαύτης ἀρχῆς οὐ τὸ αὐτὸ πάντες λέγουσιν, ἀλλὰ Θαλῆς μὲν ὁ τῆς τοιαύτης ἀρχηγὸς φιλοσοφίας ὕδωρ εἶναί φησιν (διὸ καὶ τὴν γῆν ἐφ᾽ ὕδατος ἀπεφαίνετο εἶναι), λαβὼν ἴσως τὴν ὑπόληψιν ταύτην ἐκ τοῦ πάντων ὁρᾶν τὴν τροφὴν ὑγρὰν οὖσαν . . .

---

75. Cf. D.L. 1.23; Dercyllides *ap.* Theon Smyrn., p. 198.14 Hiller; Kallim. *Iam.* 1.52 (fr. 191 Pfeiffer). See Kirk, Raven, and Schofield 1983, 81–84.

[Most of the first philosophers thought that principles in the form
of matter were the principles of all things; . . . for there must be
some natural substance, either one or more than one, from which
the other things come-into-being, while it is preserved. Over the
number, however, and the form of this kind of principle they do not
all agree; but Thales, the founder of this type of philosophy, says
that it is water (and therefore declared that the earth is on water),
perhaps taking this supposition from seeing the nature of all things
to be moist . . .]⁷⁶

According to this account, Thales taught that everything is made of water
and the earth floats in it.⁷⁷ He may have been influenced in this philosophy
by Near Eastern and Egyptian cosmologies, but his theory represents the
first nonmythological answer to the question of the origin and makeup of
the universe in the Greek world. One material was chosen as the first
principle, probably because unity is simpler than plurality, and water was
selected, perhaps because it is essential to life.

Thus Thales is credited with inventing the natural philosophy for
which Miletos would become famous, but his own accomplishments are
uncertain and probably distorted by Aristotle and his successors as they
sought to establish a neat progression in theory from Thales' first principle of water through the ideas of his most immediate successors.
Anaximander and Anaximenes both grasped the concept of a first principle, but they transformed it to fit their own theories.

Slightly younger than Thales and possibly his student, Anaximander
brought the history of Greek philosophy into existence when he first com-
mitted his ideas to writing and created a new literary genre about nature
(περὶ φύσεως), extending his innovation so far as to write in prose for the
very first time.⁷⁸ Because of the fabulous nature of the stories about Thales,
Anaximander often stands as the first substantiated thinker in natural
philosophy and so the landmark figure in spreading the influence of that

76. Kirk, Raven, and Schofield 1983, #85. This and the other philosophical texts and
translations in this chapter are taken directly from Kirk, Raven, and Schofield 1983, as
indicated.
77. Cf. Arist. Cael. 294a28–31. See Barnes 1979, 5–13; Kirk, Raven, and Schofield
1983, 88–98.
78. Kahn 1960, 6–7. For Anaximander, see Kahn 1960; Barnes 1979, 19–37; Kirk,
Raven, and Schofield 1983, 100–142. It is difficult to reconcile Anaximander's apparent
use of prose with the unanimous later tradition that Hekataios and his colleagues—the
logographers—were the pioneers in this field.

school abroad. Unfortunately, the sum total of Anaximander's own words that survive consists of one short citation in a later author who was himself working not from the original but from an intermediary source: Simplicius (*Phys.* 24.13 = 12a9 DK), a sixth-century C.E. Neoplatonist, derived his account from Theophrastos, a successor of Aristotle, who worked from the original text of Anaximander.

τῶν δὲ ἓν καὶ κινούμενον καὶ ἄπειρον λεγόντων Ἀναξίμανδρος μὲν Πραξιάδου Μιλήσιος Θαλοῦ γενόμενος διάδοχος καὶ μαθητὴς ἀρχήν τε καὶ στοιχεῖον εἴρηκε τῶν ὄντων τὸ ἄπειρον, πρῶτος τοῦτο τοὔνομα κομίσας τῆς ἀρχῆς. λέγει δ' αὐτὴν μήτε ὕδωρ μήτε ἄλλο τι τῶν καλουμένων εἶναι στοιχείων, ἀλλ' ἑτέραν τινὰ φύσιν ἄπειρον, ἐξ ἧς ἅπαντας γίνεσθαι τοὺς οὐρανοὺς καὶ τοὺς ἐν αὐτοῖς κόσμους. ἐξ ὧν δὲ ἡ γένεσίς ἐστι τοῖς οὖσι, καὶ τὴν φθορὰν εἰς ταῦτα γίνεσθαι κατὰ τὸ χρεών· διδόναι γὰρ αὐτὰ δίκην καὶ τίσιν ἀλλήλοις τῆς ἀδικίας κατὰ τὴν τοῦ χρόνου τάξιν, ποιητικωτέροις οὕτως ὀνόμασιν αὐτὰ λέγων.

[Of those who say that it is one, moving, and infinite, Anaximander, son of Praxiades, a Milesian, the successor and pupil of Thales, said that the principle and element of existing things was the *apeiron* [indefinite, *or* infinite], being the first to introduce this name of the material principle. He says that it is neither water nor any other of the so-called elements, but some other *apeiron* nature, from which come into being all the heavens and the worlds in them. And the source of coming-to-be for existing things is that into which destruction, too, happens "according to necessity; for they pay penalty and retribution to each other for their injustice according to the assessment of Time," as he describes it in these rather poetical terms.][79]

The key to Anaximander's philosophy is the *apeiron,* "infinite" or, more properly (because the concept of infinity probably did not yet exist), "without boundary" or "enormously vast." It is the origin of all things, and it surrounds them. It is unlimited and eternal, indestructible and ungenerated. Most important of all, it is distinct from all of the

---

79. Kirk, Raven, and Schofield 1983, #101a = 12a9 DK. Cf. Hippolytos *Ref.* 1.6.1–2 = 12a11 DK; Ps.-Plut. *Strom.* 2 = 12a10 DK.

other elemental things, such as earth, air, fire, and water. It is that from which these opposites arise and combine to create the things of the earth and into which they degenerate at their destruction. In his system, there is no waste in physical change, because "all change in the developed world takes place between the same original quantity of separate, opposed substances."[80]

Although his greatest impact lay in his definition of the first principle, Anaximander's thought ranged over a wide variety of topics, from cosmology to meteorology and from zoology to geography. For example, not only did he give a model for the universe, as Thales had done before him, but he was the first to offer a theory of human origins. He thought that the earth was a wide cylinder suspended, according to Aristotle (*Cael.* 2.295b10–296a3), by cosmic symmetry, situated in the middle of rings of the heavenly bodies; that humans live on its upper surface and perhaps on the lower, as Antipodes; that it was originally completely wet but has gradually become dried out over time because of the sun and winds and will eventually dry up completely; that the life-forms on the earth—including humans—have their origin as fishlike creatures in the moistness. Finally, Anaximander is credited with drawing the first map of the inhabited earth. He was certainly influenced by Babylonian models, but characteristically he applied strict mathematical proportions to the subdivisions of a perfectly circular earth.[81]

The impact of Anaximander's philosophy can hardly by overstated. According to Charles Kahn, Anaximander's rational outlook

asserted itself with the total force of a volcanic eruption, and the ensuing flood of speculation soon spread from Miletus across the length and breadth of the lands in which Greek was spoken.

He later adds,

All later Greek formulas for the cosmos must accordingly be understood as developments or modifications of the Milesian view, and in so far as our own conception of the laws of nature is derived from that of Greece, its origins can be traced back to Anaximander.[82]

---

80. Kirk, Raven, and Schofield 1983, 115.
81. See esp. Kirk, Raven, and Schofield 1983, 133–42; Kahn 1960, esp. 75–118 passim (for the map see 81–85).
82. Kahn 1960, 7, 199.

Anaximander established the questions that all later philosophers, from the ancient Greeks to the modern day, had to answer. They must approve or contest Anaximander's teachings; they could never simply ignore him.

Anaximenes was a younger contemporary, of Anaximander, sometimes said to be his student.[83] Aristotle says very little about him,[84] but according to Diogenes (5.42), Theophrastos wrote a special monograph on him, from which much of our surviving information is probably derived. Diogenes (2.3 = Kirk, Raven, and Schofield 1983, #138) himself tells us nearly everything that we know about Anaximenes' life, while at the same time summarizing his accomplishments.

'Αναξιμένης Εὐρυστράτου Μιλήσιος ἤκουσεν 'Αναξιμάνδρου, ἔνιοι δὲ καὶ Παρμενίδου φασὶν ἀκοῦσαι αὐτόν. οὗτος ἀρχὴν ἀέρα εἶπε καὶ τὸ ἄπειρον. κινεῖσθαι δὲ τὰ ἄστρα οὐχ ὑπὸ γῆν ἀλλὰ περὶ γῆν. κέχρηταί τε λέξει 'Ιάδι ἁπλῇ καὶ ἀπερίττῳ. καὶ γεγένηται μέν, καθά φησιν 'Απολλόδωρος, περὶ τὴν Σάρδεων ἅλωσιν, ἐτελεύτησε δὲ τῇ ἑξηκοστῇ τρίτῃ ὀλυμπιάδι.

[Anaximenes son of Eurystratus, of Miletus, was a pupil of Anaximander; some say he was also a pupil of Parmenides. He said that the material principle was air and the infinite; and that the stars move, not under the earth, but round it. He used simple and economical Ionic speech. He was active, according to what Apollodorus says, around the time of the capture of Sardis, and died in the 63rd Olympiad [528–525 B.C.E.].]

Diogenes' dates may be inaccurate: he may, for example, be confusing the Persian sack of Sardis in 546/5 with the Ionian sack in 498, or he may be extrapolating from a simple statement like "Anaximenes was a younger contemporary of Anaximander" (cf. Theophr. in Simp. *Phys.* 24.26 Diels). We can say with confidence only that his floruit fell in the second half of the sixth century.

Like Anaximander, Anaximenes chiefly discussed cosmology and meteorology. He is sometimes maligned by modern scholars for a lack of originality; he was certainly very much indebted to his predecessor. Barnes defends him from this charge, arguing, first, that Anaximenes'

---

83. For Anaximenes in general, see Kirk, Raven, and Schofield 1983, 143–62; Barnes 1979, 38–44; Guthrie 1962, 115–40.

84. Three passages in all: *Meta.* 1.984a5–10; *Cael.* 2.294b13–23; *Meteor.* 2.365b6–20.

two innovations were great improvements on Anaximander's system and, second, that "Anaximenes was the more thorough, the more systematic, the more rigorous, and the more scientifically inclined of the two men."[85] Anaximenes' principal modification of Anaximander's theory was that Anaximenes made the first principle air, probably something like "divine breath." According to Anaximenes, that air changed by condensation and rarefication to form the basic elements—earth, air, fire, water, stone, cloud, and wind—which in turn combined in different ways to form the things of the earth: by condensation, air became first water and then, with more condensation, earth, and finally stone, while by rarefication it became atmospheric air and, eventually, fire. Anaximenes' second important contribution was a modification of Anaximander's cosmology so that the thin disk of the earth, instead of being suspended in a cosmic balance, rested on a cushion of air. The heavenly bodies were created by a rarefication into fire and moved around the earth, ὡσπερεὶ περὶ τὴν ἡμετέραν κεφαλὴν στρέφεται τὸ πιλίον [just as . . . a felt cap turns round our head] (Hippol. *Ref.* 1.7.6 = Kirk, Raven, and Schofield 1983, #156). This cosmology became the standard fifth-century Ionian view, to which later figures had to react.[86]

After the Milesian philosophers, the idea of monism was either abandoned or greatly modified by the later Ionian thinkers. They became more concerned with problems of the arrangement, rather than the material, of things. Still, they are deeply indebted to Thales, Anaximander, and Anaximenes for freeing them from the chains of mythological interpretations and introducing them to an empirical approach to natural philosophy.

After Anaximenes, the center of Greek philosophy moved elsewhere in Ionia and west to Sicily, but another intellectual movement developed at Miletos in the late sixth century, a movement that was to have significant influence on the Greek literature of the fifth century and beyond. The earliest known prose writers, called logographers, hailed from Miletos, and their innovations set the stage for Herodotos's invention of the genre of history.

Logography was a creation of the Ionian Greeks.[87] The word *logos* is used in contrast to *epos* to show that these men wrote in prose, not meter, so in the broadest sense, a logographer was any prose writer. However, it

85. Barnes 1979, 38–39.
86. Kirk, Raven, and Schofield 1983, 162.
87. Pearson 1939, chap. 1.

is the modern convention to use this term only to refer to a particular class of writers, rendered literally as "storytellers," who wrote in the sixth and fifth centuries. Their works included chronicles of city foundations, annals of particular cities, histories and customs of non-Greek nations, and geographic handbooks. They often used official city records as source material, while at the same time exercising a good deal of license in making the accounts more interesting. They were also heavily influenced by Homer and the epic poets rather than the empirical spirit of the pre-Socratics, so they made no sharp distinction between myth and history. Their writing was fairly primitive and unadorned, which is not surprising considering that they were pioneering prose style.

Kadmos, Dionysios, and Hekataios were all early prose writers from Miletos. Kadmos and Dionysios are shadowy figures: we have very little information about them and no substantial fragments. Kadmos, son of Pandion, is named among the earliest prose writers by a number of ancient authors.[88] He is a contemporary of Hekataios, which puts his floruit in the last part of the sixth century, and he is supposed to have written a story, in four books, of the foundation of Miletos and all of Ionia.[89] Dionysios was his contemporary, although our information about him is quite late, chiefly from the *Suda* (where he is anachronistically called a *historikos*).[90] Six works are attributed to him: the *Events after Dareios* (Τὰ μετὰ Δαρεῖον), in five books; the *Description of the Inhabited World* (Περιήγεσις οἰκουμένης); the *Persika,* in the Ionic dialect; the *Troika,* in three books; the *Mythika;* and the *Historical Cycle* (Κύκλος ἱστορικός). It is doubtful that he authored all of these; von Fritz thinks that he probably wrote only the *Persika* (a feat corroborated by several scholiasts) and perhaps the *Events after Dareios.*

While the importance of neither Kadmos nor Dionysios can be established definitively, it is probably not an exaggeration to say that Hekataios was the most significant and influential of all the sixth-century logographers.[91] He was a prominent advisor to Aristagoras during the Ionian Revolt, according to Herodotos (5.36, 124), although that role

---

88. Dion. Hal. *de Thuc.* 23; Str. 1.2.6 (alongside Hekataios); Joseph. *Ap.* 1.13; *Suda* s.v. Κάδμος ὁ Μιλήσιος and Κάδμος Πανδίονος ; Clem. Al. *Strom.* 6.26.8; *FGH* 489; von Fritz 1967, 2:54–55.

89. It is likely that the tradition about that he wrote about "all of Ionia" is directly derived from his father's name, *Pandion,* and is false.

90. S.v. Διονύσιος Μιλήσιος = *FGH* 687; von Fritz 1967, 1:415, 2:78.

91. *FGH* 1; Fornara 1983b, chap. 1, esp. pp. 4–12; Drews 1973, chap. 1; Tozer 1971, 70–74; von Fritz 1967, vol. 1, chap. 3; Pearson 1939, 25–108; Jacoby 1912.

may be fictionalized.[92] He is also credited with writing two works, one on myth and the other on geography, and he is the earliest confirmed prose writer in both of those fields.

Hekataios's text on myth was written in four books, of which we have three titles: *Genealogia* (Γενεηλογία), *Heroologia* (Ἡρωολογία), and *Histories* (Ἱστορία). Only thirty-five fragments survive. Of special interest is Hekataios's introductory statement there (*FGH* 1 F 1 = Demet. *Eloc.* 12).

Ἑκαταῖος Μιλήσιος ὧδε μυθεῖται· τάδε γράφω ὥς μοι δοκεῖ ἀληθέα εἶναι· οἱ γὰρ Ἑλλήνων λόγοι πολλοί τε καὶ γελοῖοι, ὡς ἐμοὶ φαίνονται, εἰσίν.

[Hekataios the Milesian tells these stories. And I write these things as they seem to me to be true, for the tales of the Greeks are many and laughable, as it seems to me.]

According to the fashion followed later by Herodotos and Thucydides, Hekataios identifies himself in his very first words in the text. He also sets out part of his purpose: to write the things that he thinks are true. Like the pre-Socratics, he intended to apply a rational explanation to the myths that he treated and thus to avoid λόγοι γελοῖοι. This approach was of course a great departure from that of the poetic writers of the past.[93]

Hekataios's real fame came from his invention of the genre of geography: his second work was the first systematic geography of the known world, called the *Periegesis* (Περιήγησις) or the *Periodos Ges* (Περίοδος Γῆς), from which three hundred fragments survive. His method was to offer descriptions of different cities and peoples in order as they are passed by the traveler; later geographers usually restricted themselves to the coastal sites (writing *periploi*, or "voyages around"), but Hekataios seems to have gone inland in places as well. For each locale, he offered a brief description of the people's customs, marvelous events, foundation

92. Also, according to Diodoros Sikulos (10.25.4), he was sent by the Ionians as an ambassador to Artaphernes. S. West (1991) argues that most, if not all, of Herodotos's portrayal of Hekataios is fanciful, based on the "wise adviser" motif, first identified by Lattimore (1939). For more on Hekataios's putative actions during the revolt, see chap. 4.

93. Pearson (1939, 97–98) argues that Hekataios was going to offer a single version instead of giving a lot of conflicting stories, as Herodotos would do.

or origin, and any part that place might have played in legend. We cannot be certain about the order in which he worked, but the custom among his successors was to start at the Pillars of Herakles and work clockwise around the coast, eastward along the European coast of the Mediterranean, into the Propontis and Pontos, down through Asia Minor and the Levant, and westward across northern Africa.

Hekataios is also famous for his map. Although Anaximander is credited with making the first Greek map, Hekataios is supposed to have improved it. Agathemeros, a very late geographer, wrote (*GGM* 2.471, 1.1):

Ἀναξίμανδρος ὁ Μιλήσιος ἀκουστὴς Θαλέω πρῶτος ἐτόλμησε τὴν οἰκουμένην ἐν πίνακι γράψαι· μεθ᾽ ὃν Ἑκαταῖος ὁ Μιλήσιος ἀνὴρ πολυπλανὴς διηκρίβωσεν, ὥστε θαυμασθῆναι τὸ πρᾶγμα.

[Anaximander the Milesian, a student of Thales, first dared to draw the inhabited world on a tablet. After him, Hekataios the Milesian, a well-traveled man, corrected it, so that it became a thing to be marveled at.]⁹⁴

We usually associate Hekataios's name with the famous map mentioned by Herodotos in his story of the Ionian Revolt (5.49–50). Anaxagoras, the leader of the revolt, tried to enlist Spartan aid by showing them the map, which included many wealthy countries near Ionia for Sparta to plunder: he came ἔχων χάλκεον πίνακα ἐν τῷ γῆς ἁπάσης περίοδος ἐνετέτμητο καὶ θάλασσά τε πᾶσα καὶ ποταμοὶ πάντες [holding a bronze tablet on which were engraved the circuit of the earth and all the seas and all the rivers] (5.49.1). Elsewhere, Herodotos mocks the design of the earth in these early maps, because οἳ Ὠκεανόν τε ῥέοντα γράφουσι πέριξ τὴν γῆν, ἐοῦσαν κυκλοτερέα ὡς ἀπὸ τόρνου, καὶ τὴν Ἀσίην τῇ Εὐρώπῃ ποιεύντων ἴσην [they draw the Ocean flowing around the earth in a perfect circle as if drawn by a compass, and they make Asia equal in size to Europe] (4.36.2; cf. 4.42.1.). Assuming that Herodotos is criticizing Hekataios and his followers, we can conclude that for Hekataios, theory was more important than accuracy. His map was symmetrical, a perfect circle with two equal continents, Europe and Asia (including Africa).

94. Cf. Str. 1.1.11.

Hekataios's influence was considerable. Not only did he inaugurate the study of systematic geography and offer the world a detailed (if idealized) map, but he was the first securely attested logographer. By employing prose writing to examine the past, he and his successors established a genre that would in the next century provide the groundwork for the formal study of history launched by Herodotos and Thucydides. What distinguishes the historians from the Milesian more than anything else is content: Hekataios did not hesitate to write about mythological heroes and gods as if they were real, while the historians would begin to apply a higher standard of credibility to their work. Yet they could not have made the great leap to *historia* without the small steps taken first by the logographers in seeking to rationalize the past and committing their thoughts to prose.

Because the literary survivals from the Archaic period are few and fragmentary, we cannot fully appreciate the accomplishments of these intellectuals leaders, but even without lengthy texts, the bare facts of their accomplishments speak loudly. Continuing the older literary tradition, Miletos produced a poet whose works are ranked alongside those of Hesiod and Theognis. At the same time, Milesians were at the forefront of intellectual innovation, creating the study of philosophy by developing an empirical approach to nature and to systematizing the cosmos, an approach based on monism, without mythological references and personified deities. Finally, the Milesians invented mapmaking, geography, and probably logography as well, setting the stage for the birth of history. No other Archaic Greek city can approach—much less match—these achievements.

3

The Archaic City

Miletos stood as an independent city for more than four centuries, from the time of its refoundation by the Ionians, ca. 1050 B.C.E., until at least the reign of the Lydian king Kroisos in the middle of the sixth century. We know little about the organization of the polis in the early years in the Dark Ages: the unanimous traditions of the later city have it ruled by a Neleid monarchy immediately after its foundation, but there is no corroborating evidence that might clarify the situation. By the time it entered the historical record in the Archaic period, the city was run by an oligarchy. That government can be explicated in some detail: it had an eponymous *prytanis* and suffered civil strife early on, but it eventually settled into a stability that enabled Miletos to become the successful mother city and trade center and establish itself as a paradigm of luxury.

As long as it remained free, Miletos prospered and grew. Even during the early decades of contact with a developing imperial power next door, Miletos was strong enough to fend off the prolonged Lydian aggression that began as early as the second quarter of the seventh century and persisted intermittently until nearly 600 B.C.E. As that attack intensified, however, the military crisis provided the opportunity for one man, Thrasyboulos, to take over the Milesian government toward the end of the century and set himself up as a tyrant. He defended the city well, protecting it from a siege by using the seaborne resources it had developed over the years. Finally, Thrasyboulos was able to draw the Lydians into a treaty with favorable terms. We do not know how long he remained in power, but when the tyranny eventually ended, Miletos reverted to its former oligarchy for about fifty years.

The end of Milesian independence probably came in the middle of the sixth century, when Kroisos took over the Lydian throne, ca. 560, and subjected all of Ionia. There is evidence that Miletos lost its favored status and owed both tribute and troops to its new master. But Kroisos's reign was short-lived: Cyrus the Great of Persia conquered the Lydians ca. 547. He then turned his attention to Ionia. Again, Miletos occupied an exceptional position: it was the only Ionian city to retain the same treaty terms as it had under Kroisos. But with the Persian mastery came a new government for the city, for Persia either allowed or imposed an unpopular tyranny on the Milesians. That tyranny survived for possibly as much as forty years before the abuse of power led the Milesian people to the extreme, eventually fatal step of rebelling from Persia to free itself from the tyranny of one of its own leading men.

Early Archaic Offices

According to all of the mythical accounts examined in chapter 1, Miletos was originally ruled by a monarchy, controlled by the same Neleid family that pioneered the settlement of Ionia. Since no credible records survive from the first few centuries of Ionian Miletos, it is impossible to say whether these myths are accurate in portraying traditional hereditary monarchs *(basileis)*. Typically, by the time the Greek alphabet appears in the eighth century B.C.E. and certainly by the time the literary record becomes abundant, nearly every Greek city-state has strong memories of an early chieftainship or kingship that had eventually been replaced by some kind of oligarchy. In most cases, it is difficult to determine whether those memories, recorded centuries after the fact, reflect a historical situation.

Currently, historians are entangled in debate over the characteristics of those Dark Age kings, a debate that may prove insoluble due to lack of evidence. The Dark Ages not only were a time of great poverty and cultural decline but were also characterized by a near complete illiteracy in the Greek world: the Linear B writing of Mycenaean society was lost, and the alphabet was not yet adapted for Greek use (the Cypriot script may have survived). Other physical remains disclose little that is pertinent to understanding political matters. Dark Age settlements typically leave little trace in the archaeological record, and such evidence as is left by an impoverished and illiterate society can scarcely offer concrete data about such institutions.

The only evidence usually available for the evaluation of Dark Age kingship is subsequent literary sources, ranging from Homer and Hesiod to much later accounts, such as that of Nicolaus of Damascus, a contemporary of Augustus, and even late antique lexicographers. Most scholars of the Dark Ages have recourse to the epics of Homer, because of their status among the earliest surviving works of Greek literature, but those poems are extremely problematic as historical sources.[1] Not only were the Homeric texts composed as literature and not history, but the prevailing view is that they represent a chronological amalgam. Some elements are derived from the eighth century, others date to Mycenaean times, and the majority falls somewhere in between. It is very difficult to isolate an item of Homeric evidence and determine its level of accuracy about a given place and time with any kind of confidence. As a result, the arguments about Dark Age kingship as based on Homer are very tenuous, and it is improbable that a scholarly consensus will ever be reached.

Generally speaking, there are currently three schools of thought about the political structures of Dark Age Greece, which may be summarized in very broad terms. According to one theory, Dark Age monarchy was, as the myths report, both institutionalized and hereditary. Such kings had extensive personal power based on the legitimacy of the office instead of the ability of the man, who ruled by virtue of his inherited right.[2] The second view holds that society was governed not by hereditary kings but by aristocrats, big men or chiefs, who constantly struggled to perpetuate their power, which was itself obtained only locally and only by virtue of their personal ability and the strength of their followers.[3] Finally, a compromise explanation is that Dark Age kings were originally local chiefs, as in the second theory, but the system developed over time so that eventually one paramount chief rose to take control over the others in the region. Ultimately, that king set up a formal system of power sharing through short-term magistracies and collegial boards, and the monarchy itself faded out of use.[4] Each of these theories has attractive elements, and each can be refined according to various nuances. But in the end, the information available is insufficient for the task of clarification, and the power and status of Dark Age kings must remain an open question.

At Miletos, as elsewhere, the monarchy is attested only in myths, so its character and even existence is dubious: all that can be said with confidence is that a vigorous, persistent later memory places Neleid kings at

---

1. The secondary sources on Homer are too extensive to attempt a comprehensive offering. I mention only Page 1959; Finley 1977; van Wees 1992. Raaflaub 1998a offers a review of the scholarship.
2. Van Wees 1992; Carlier 1984.
3. Stahl 1987, 150–55; Drews 1983; Quiller 1981.
4. Donlan 1989.

Miletos in the Dark Ages.[5] However, the reality at the beginning of the historical era is that nearly every Greek city-state was ruled by some kind of oligarchy, and this circumstance is consistent with all of the other evidence about Archaic Miletos as well.

Archaic oligarchy can often be characterized as a government in which citizenship, the franchise, and access to offices were confined to a group ranging in size from tens to several thousands and were often determined according to wealth and family line.[6] The functions that may have once been held by kings were fulfilled by various magistrates—generals, judges, legislators, and priests. The oligarchy often ruled as a council (boule), a strong deliberative body that assiduously limited the actions of the assembly of all citizens (the *ekklesia* or demos).[7]

At Miletos, some of the elements of the earliest oligarchy are witnessed in the mythic accounts of the downfall of the Neleid monarchy, but unlike the monarchical stories, these elements can be examined in the light of more secure evidence. The first part of this story is preserved in a passage already discussed in chapter 2: according to Konon (*FGH* 26 F 44), the Neleid cousins Leodamas and Phitres solved their quarrel over the throne by each commanding a war against a Milesian enemy. The victor, Leodamas, became king. Nicolaus of Damascus (*FGH* 90 F 52) continues the story of the violence between the house of Leodamas and the house of Amphitres, which led to the downfall of the monarchy and the extermination of the Neleid clan. Phitres, or Amphitres (surely the two names must refer to the same individual), was not content with his loss and resorted to violence. He killed Leodamas, and αὐτὸς δὲ μετὰ τῶν αὑτοῦ στασιωτῶν τὴν πόλιν κατελάβετο καὶ τύραννος ἐγένετο ἰσχὺν προύχων Μιλησίων [together with the members of his faction, Amphitres seized the city and became tyrant over the Milesians by force]. The sons of Leodamas fled to nearby Assessos. With the aid of certain sacred objects, they were able to put the army of Amphitres to flight. Then Ἀμφιτρὴν δ᾽ οἱ Λεωδάμαντος

---

5. In addition to the specific Neleids named here, Parthenios (*Er. Path.* 14) mentions Phobios, and Polyainos (8.35) names Phrygios.

6. Rhodes 1972. In his discussion of Greek constitutions (*Pol.* 3.1279a22–1280a6), Aristotle was able to say that for practical purposes oligarchy was really the rule of the rich.

7. By way of contrast, a democracy, such as the one employed in Athens in the fifth century, was a nonrepresentative, direct rule by the adult male citizens of a city through their right to attend, speak before, and vote in the assembly meetings. At Athens at least, the deliberative power of the assembly was significantly enlarged at the expense of the council, which became a kind of secretarial body that prepared and amended legislation according to the demands of the assembly. See Ostwald 1986.

παῖδες κτείνουσι, καὶ ὁ πόλεμος καὶ ἡ τυραννὶς ἐπέπαυτο Μιλησίοις [the sons of Leodamas killed Amphitres and ended both the war and the tyranny among the Milesians]. In this second generation of familial strife, the sons of Leodamas regained their rightful position.

However, the matter was not settled there, as Nicolaus says (*FGH* 90 F 53).

ὅτι Ἐπιμένης μετὰ ταῦτα αἰσυμνήτης ὑπὸ τοῦ δήμου χειρο-
τονεῖται λαβὼν ἐξουσίαν κτείνειν οὓς βούλεται. καὶ ὃς τῶν μὲν
παίδων Ἀμφιτρῆτος οὐδενὸς οἷός τ᾽ ἦν ἐγκρατὴς γενέσθαι (ὑπε-
ξῆλθον γὰρ παραχρῆμα δείσαντες), τὰ δὲ ὄντα αὐτοῖς ἐδήμευσεν
καὶ ἀργύριον ἐκήρυξεν, εἴ τις αὐτοὺς κτείνειεν. τῶν δὲ κοινωνῶν
τοῦ φόνου τρεῖς ἀπέκτεινε, τοῖς δὲ ἄλλοις φυγὴν προεῖπεν· οἱ δὲ
ᾤχοντο. οἱ μὲν δὴ Νηλεῖδαι κατελύθησαν ὧδε.

[Afterward, when Epimenes was elected *aisymnetes* by the people, on taking power he killed whomever he wished. But since he was not able to overpower the sons of Amphitres (they had immediately fled out of fear), he confiscated their property and announced that there would be a reward for anyone who would kill them. He executed three of their accomplices in the murder and ordered the others to be exiled, and some fled. In this way the Neleids were destroyed.]

The sons of Leodamas are dropped from the account: perhaps they perished in the struggle. At any rate, power shifted to an elected office, the *aisymnetes,* a position that would become prominent in historical times.

In examining the historical implications of this myth, we must distinguish carefully between actual offices attested in earliest antiquity and anachronistic references to later institutions of government. It is likely that this passage is affected by such anachronism in Nicolaus's use of the terms *tyrant* and *tyranny.* The root of these words is probably Lydian, and the first extant attestation in the Greek language occurs in a poem of Archilochos from the seventh century B.C.E. (fr. 22 Diehl). From that time until the first century B.C.E., when Nicolaus was composing his work, the word *tyranny* was used with a number of different meanings[8] that can be roughly divided into two uses, each with a technically defined subset.

---

8. Parker 1998; Libero 1996; Barceló 1993; Berve 1967; Andrewes 1956.

Tyranny was used originally as a synonym for *monarchy*. It had no pejorative connotations and could even be used as a compliment. More specifically, tyranny as it occurred in the so-called Age of Tyrants in the seventh and sixth centuries B.C.E. was a subdivision of monarchy, defined by the illegal seizure of power from the ruling government, regardless of whether the ensuing rule was evil or enlightened. This definition is the one ancient historians are usually thinking of when they use the word *tyrant*. The second category of meanings is strictly derogatory: *tyranny* was used to indicate a hated rule characterized by violence and lawlessness. This second meaning became so common as time passed that it too developed a subset: by the fourth century, philosophers employed the term to indicate an evil rule by one man, regardless of its constitutional basis, and this last usage determines the meaning of the word still today. In any case, there is no indication that *tyrant* was ever a formal title.

These events described by Nicolaus—if they occurred at all—must have taken place in the tenth or ninth century B.C.E., long before the age of writing, before the Greeks adopted the word *tyrannos* from the Lydian tongue, and before the Age of Tyrants permanently established the pejorative connotations of it. Thus, Nicolaus's choice of words represents no ancient tradition reflecting Dark Age terminology. Rather, mindful of Amphitres' usurpation and violent rule, and writing under the influence of the philosophical definition, Nicolaus simply applied the word that most aptly fit the situation. The passage should not be considered to be evidence of the political appellations in use in the last days of the Neleids. We have no way of knowing what contemporaries may have called a man in Amphitres' position, whether *basileus, tyrannos,* or something else altogether.

Another anachronism lies behind the name of the successor of the Neleids, Epimenes. This rare personal name recalls an office found in many Greek states, the *epimenios*. The name of this office means literally "a man for the month" or "a monthly official" and was applied most basically to one charged with carrying out certain monthly duties, such as sacrifices. In Archaic and Classical Greece, we find the title attached to men fulfilling an array of sociopolitical functions, including priests, magistrates, and private individuals with sacred duties. Despite the literal meaning of the title, *epimenioi* served terms of various length, ranging from a day to a year depending on the city.[9]

---

9. Hesychius (s.v. ἱεροποιοί) associates them with *hieropoioi* ("those who managed sacred rites"). Szanto (1909) presents evidence from Smyrna, Istropolis, Bargelia in Caria,

The myth of Epimenes is particularly suggestive because, in Classical times, Miletos also had officials of this name. *Epimenioi* are attested in the famous Banishment Decree of the fifth century B.C.E. (*Milet* 1.6 #187). This controversial decree, in which a small group of men is exiled from the city, is discussed in detail in chapter 6, but some of the conclusions drawn there are apt here: first, the decree probably dates to ca. 450 B.C.E. or soon before; second, it represents the action of an oligarchic government; and third, the *epimenioi* mentioned in it (line 5) made up a collegial board with a limited term of office.[10] Presumably they constitute the board empowered to execute the provisions of the decree. Thus, in the fifth century, *epimenioi* were important political officials with executive responsibilities for the city. It is likely that they served as a presiding committee in the assembly, the oligarchic equivalent of the Athenian-style *prytaneis* that were put in place in the fifth century.

It is possible, then, that Nicolaus's story about the rule by Epimenes—if it is not entirely a late invention—may represent a Milesian tradition of the *epimenios* as an important Archaic office as well. In fact, some scholars assume the existence of Archaic *epimenioi* with a prominent position in the community. These officials, it is concluded from their early duties in charge of the monthly sacrifices, became the leaders of the assembly, perhaps when the monthly sacrifices began to coincide with the assembly meetings.[11] However, the corroborating evidence for this view is not convincing: the earliest direct support for Milesian *epimenioi* is the aforementioned Banishment Decree from the mid–fifth century, and the history of Milesian politics is not such that much faith can be put in a presumption of continuity of institutions. Lacking hard evidence from Archaic Miletos itself, confirmation has been sought in the institutions of its colonies, and Kios and Istros may indeed have had eponymous *epimenioi*.[12] But this evidence is in no way informative about early conditions in the mother

---

Delphi, Amorgos, Nesos on Lesbos, Ilion, Kios, Samos, Methymna, and elsewhere. Ehrhardt (1983, 212) adds Kolophon, Minoa, Mylasa, and Lampsakos.

10. Piérart 1969, 365, 370–76, followed by Fornara 1983b, #66; Tod 1946, #35.

11. Ehrhardt 1983, 210–13.

12. Kios: Le Bas and Waddinton #1141.1–3 = *CIG* 3723; #1140.1–3 = Tod 1946, #149 [post-360 B.C.E.]; #1143.9–10. The *epimenios* is listed in the prescripts of the decrees, indicating that he may be an eponym. Unfortunately, only the last inscription has the word preserved in its entirety (ἐπιμηνιεύσαντα); in the first one, it is nearly entirely restored ([Ἐπιμηνεύο]ν[τ]ος), and the second has only the last four letters (- víoυ). See Ehrhardt 1983, 196 n. 1133. Istros: *SEG* 24 (1969) 1095.1–2 (third or second century B.C.E.). See Ehrhardt 1983, 211 n. 1301.

city, for, unfortunately, these colonial *epimenioi* are attested only in inscriptions from the fourth century and later. The supposition that the office of *epimenios* dates back to the early days of colonization and was transferred from the mother city is weak; only two colonies offer this evidence, and an argument based on the assumption of institutional inertia—here lasting several hundred years—can secure no more conviction in the case of the colonies than with Miletos. We can say nothing confidently about the functioning, or even the existence, of the *epimenios* at Miletos before the fifth century: the occurrence of the personal name may only represent a retrojection of the office into earlier times.

We are better informed about the institution through which Nicolaus of Damascus claims that Epimenes carried out his reign of terror, the *aisymnetes*.[13] The *aisymnetes* is clearly established as an Archaic office. The men holding this post, later called the *stephanephoroi,* "crown-wearers," became the eponyms of the city (annual officials who gave their name to the year for the purpose of reckoning dates), and lists of their names inscribed on white marble have been found preserved in the sanctuary of Apollo Delphinios (*Milet* 1.3 #122–29). The lists are titled, Οἵδε μολπῶν ἠσύμνησαν or ἠισύμνησαν [Those of the Molpoi who acted as *aisymnetes*] or Στεφανηφόροι οἱ καὶ αἰσυμνῆται [Crown-Wearers and *aisymnetai*]. Unfortunately for the credibility of Nicolaus's evidence, the lists begin only near the end of the Archaic period, in the second half of the sixth century.

At the most basic level, the *aisymnetes* is a priest of Apollo: there existed at Miletos a corporation of sacred officials, the Molpoi of Apollo Delphinios, at whose head stood a board of men called the *aisymnetes* of the Molpoi and his five *prosetairoi,* "companions." This arrangement is witnessed by the so-called Molpoi Decree (*Milet* 1.3 #133), which can be dated to 450/49 by the *aisymnetes* lists (*Milet* 1.3 #122.i.78).

It records a decision of the Molpoi (ἔδοξα μολποῖσιν, line 4) regulating several cult functions, including the great annual procession to the Temple of Apollo at Didyma. Elsewhere I discuss this decree in the context of Milesian religious institutions (chap. 5), but its political implications are also of importance, although their interpretation is problematic. The first editor of the Molpoi Decree proposed that the *aisymnetes* was not merely the city's eponym and that he and the other Molpoi presided

---

13. Nordin 1905; Wilamowitz-Moellendorff 1914, 74–79; Poland 1935; de Sanctis 1931; Busolt and Swoboda 1920, 1:373–74; Luria 1928; Luria 1963; Hegyi 1977; Romer 1982.

over or even constituted the deliberative body in early Classical Miletos. According to this interpretation, the Molpoi Decree reflects the governmental organization of the Milesian oligarchy.[14] This idea has taken root and spread widely. Nonetheless, it rests on no firm evidence and should be discarded.

Because of the importance of this issue, I will examine at some length the arguments in favor of assuming wide political powers for the *aisymnetes* and Molpoi. It is best to begin with what was taken to be direct evidence that they led the oligarchy. First, proponents of this idea take as evidence the story of Epimenes and the end of the Neleids as related by Nicolaus of Damascus, quoted earlier in this chapter. In that story, Epimenes takes his place in the narrative on his election as *aisymnetes,* and this mention is taken as proof positive that the *aisymnetes* was chief officer of the Archaic state. However, the tale of Epimenes surely belongs to the realm of myth. It is found in the context of details—for example, the sudden appearance of Phrygians under divine instructions to help the sons of Leodamas; and their routing the partisans of Amphitres through fear of the god—which seriously undermines its credibility as a historical source. Moreover, we have already seen that Nicolaus of Damascus uses the term *tyrannos* anachronistically. It is safest to assume that he has done the same with *aisymnetes,* knowing that there was an eponymous official of that name in Miletos in his own time, and perhaps also influenced by Aristotle's definition of an *aisymnetes* as an elected tyranny (*Pol.* 3.1284a31–b4).

Second, the proponents of this theory argue that since the *aisymnetes* was eponymous, he must have had significant political powers. Unfortunately, there is no evidence that the *aisymnetes* was the eponym of the city before the beginning of the lists in the second half of the sixth century. In fact, as we shall see shortly, there is a more likely candidate for the position.

Third, an Athenian decree called the Athenian Regulations for Miletos (*IG* 1³ 21) has been brought forward as evidence. The decree, which dates to the middle of the fifth century, deals with the relationship between Miletos and the Athenian Empire. The inscription is fragmentary, but the appearance of the letters προσετ[. . .] in line 6 would indicate a political role played by the *prosetairoi,* confirming the traditional theory. However, a more recent examination of the inscription, which included removal of the fragment of the stone from the plaster reconstruction, has

14. Wilamowitz-Moellendorff 1904 (editio princeps); Wilamowitz-Moellendorff 1914, 74–79; Luria 1928; Luria 1963; Poland 1935.

disclosed the trace not of a tau but of a rho (or possibly a kappa), so that the fragment now reads προσερ[. . .].[15] Restoration to *prosetairoi* is clearly eliminated, and the evidence of this inscription can be removed from the discussion of this problem.

Besides the Molpoi Decree itself, all other epigraphical mentions— very few in number—of the Molpoi at Miletos date from after the establishment of an Athenian-style democracy in the middle of the fifth century, under which government the Molpoi can be expected to have had no deliberative powers. Among these inscriptions, several refer to the Molpoi in connection with the adjudication of citizenship rights. According to these inscriptions from the late third century B.C.E., prosecution can be made among the Molpoi in cases of complaints against unlawful claims of citizen rights (εἶναι αὐτὸν ὑπεύθυνον πῆι τε ἐμ μολποῖς ἐνστάσει καὶ / τῆι δικῆι τῆς ξενίας κατὰ τοὺς νόμους [he shall be liable for prosecution among the Molpoi and in the court of foreigners according to the laws]).[16] This function, it is claimed, must be a remnant of a much wider jurisdiction held by the Molpoi and *aisymnetes* in the days of the oligarchy. However, the improper assumption of citizen rights had religious implications, since the participation of false citizens in certain rites and cults would be sacrilegious. Thus, the matter judged "among the Molpoi" might be strictly religious in nature and the juridical powers of the board need never have been extensive.[17] In addition, the particular role of the Molpoi as priests of Apollo Delphinios may be at issue here, since this priesthood is tied to the ephebic ritual and citizenship in many states, including Miletos.[18]

The only other direct evidence that the supporters of this theory have brought to bear is that the Molpoi Decree attests the tribes to which the *aisymnetes* and the *prosetairoi* belong. Since the tribes were a basic civic division, it is assumed that their presence in the prescript of this inscription is consistent with a governmental function for the Molpoi. However, an analogy for this usage might be seen in the post-Kleisthenic constitution at Athens, where each citizen was expected to identify himself according to his deme: such identification did not imply that he held political office but merely indicated that he was a citizen, as evidenced by the fact of the demotic. Similarly, the presence of tribal names on the Molpoi

15. Bradeen and McGregor 1973, 39.
16. *Milet* 1.3 #143.32; cf. 146.41, 150.65, etc.
17. De Sanctis 1976, 466.
18. Graf 1979, 7; Bielohlawek 1927.

Decree need not indicate anything more than the basic principle of inclusion in the body politic of the Milesian state. Clearly, since the more important evidence has been shown to be dubious, the possible implications of the mention of the tribes is too weak a supposition to bear the whole weight of the theory that the *aisymnetes* was politically powerful.

There is also indirect evidence about the *aisymnetes,* since the office was not restricted to Miletos, but the other occurrences are so varied that they offer very little help in interpreting the duties of the official at Miletos. Homer uses the word to designate noblemen who are singled out as stewards of the games (*Od.* 8.258–60).[19] The colonial evidence, from Olbia and Sinope, is too fragmentary to be informative.[20] Among other cities, the evidence from Ephesos and Kyme is perhaps the most significant, because it pertains to the Archaic period. According to a very late source, the *Suda* (tenth century C.E., s.v. Ἀρίσταρχος), an Athenian named Aristarchos was said to have been appointed *aisymnetes* at Ephesos for a term of five years in the mid–sixth century B.C.E. The purpose of this extraordinary commission granted to an outsider is not preserved, but it was probably some kind of specific political task or reform. At Kyme, the *aisymnetai* were the leaders of an Archaic oligarchy of one hundred men, and according to Aristotle (fr. 524 Rose), the word itself became synonymous for *archon*. The city of Teos also presents evidence of an *aisymnetes* with significant authority, this time of a judicial character. Here, by the fifth century, the *aisymnetes* was a standing official, a judge whose power included inflicting the death penalty.[21]

---

19. Cf. *Il.* 24.347–48. A third occurrence, at *Il.* 11.303, has *Aisymnos* as a personal name.

20. At Olbia, an eponymous priest of Apollo appears in Hellenistic times (*IOlb.* 26, 30), and a college of Molpoi occurs in the Classical era (*IOlb.* 55, 56, 57, 167). Ehrhardt (1983, 198–99, esp. n. 1175; 202) argues that the *aisymnetes* may have been the eponymous official; however, this interpretation relies on a lacuna in *IOlb.* 58, which is restored by F. Graf (1974, 210ff.) on the basis of the reading of the Milesian Molpoi Decree. The editors of the inscriptions have restored it thus: [Μο]λ[ποί?] με ἀνέθεσσαν Ἀπόλλωνι Δ[ε]λφινίωι ἐπὶ Διονυ[σο]δώρο τô Ληναίο Μολπ[αγόρεω ἄρχον]τος στεφ[ανηφόρο? . . .] Ἑκατ . . . Graf fills the lacuna beginning μολπ differently: μολπ[ῶν αἰσυμνῶν]τος. Graf's restoration is not strong enough to be taken alone as positive evidence for an eponymous *aisymnetes*. At Sinope, the *aisymnetes* is mentioned on two temple amphoras, but no date is given for them. Grakov (*AIKSP* [1968] 100–101, *non vidi*, cited in Ehrhardt 1983, 196 n. 1140) calls this office the eponym.

21. Ephesos: Hegyi 1977, 7; Sakellariou 1958, 124, 133–34. Sakellariou thinks he reorganized the tribes and expanded Ephesian territory, but there is no evidence to go on. Teos: Hegyi 1977, 8; Busolt and Swoboda 1920, 1:373; Dittenberger 1960, #38. Naxos also had two *aisymnetai,* but in Hellenistic times (Dittenberger 1960, #955.1).

Relevant to the politically powerful role of *aisymnetai* in Ephesos, Kyme, and Teos is a general definition of the office laid down by Aristotle in book 3 of the *Politics* (1285a31–b4).

ἕτερον δ' ὅπερ ἦν ἐν τοῖς ἀρχαίοις Ἕλλησιν, οὓς καλοῦσιν αἰσυμνήτας. ἔστι δὲ τοῦθ' ὡς ἁπλῶς εἰπεῖν αἱρετὴ τυραννίς, διαφέρουσα δὲ πῆς βαρβαρικῆς οὐ τῷ μὴ κατὰ νόμον ἀλλὰ τῷ μὴ πάτριος εἶναι μόνον. ἦρχον δ' οἱ μὲν διὰ βίου τὴν ἀρχὴν ταύτην, οἱ δὲ μέχρι τινῶν ὡρισμένων χρόνων ἢ πράξεων, . . . αὗται μὲν οὖν εἰσί τε καὶ ἦσαν διὰ μὲν τὸ δεσποτικαὶ εἶναι τυραννικαί, διὰ δὲ τὸ αἱρεταὶ καὶ ἑκόντων βασιλικαί·

[Another [monarchy] is that which existed among the ancient Greeks, the type of rulers called *aisymnetai*. This is, to put it simply, an elective tyranny, and it differs from the monarchy that exists among barbarians not in governing without the guidance of law but only in not being hereditary. Some holders of this type of monarchy ruled for life, others until certain fixed limits of time or until certain undertakings were ended. . . . These monarchies therefore now and in the past are of the nature of tyrannies because they are autocratic, but they are of the nature of kingships because they are elective and rule over willing subjects.]

This Aristotelian definition of *aisymnetes* is startling, but we cannot accept Aristotle's words at face value. The meaning of *aisymnetes* as an elective tyranny recalls strongly the story of Epimenes with which I started this discussion, but it contradicts both the situation in Archaic Kyme, where the office was part of a ruling oligarchy, and what we know to have been the case at Miletos in Aristotle's own day, when the *aisymnetes* existed as eponym but the city was ruled by a democracy. Instead of offering an observation of historical fact, Aristotle seems to be indulging his penchant for overprecise definition, assigning to the *aisymnetes* a significance originating in his own mind, which the historical situation did not support.[22]

While offering examples of politically powerful *aisymnetai*, the comparative evidence is so diverse as scarcely to constitute a proper ana-

---

22. Romer 1982; Newman 1887, 3:267–69; Busolt and Swoboda 1920, 1:374; Luria 1963.

logue.[23] In addition, none of these cases provide a true parallel to the Milesian situation, because at Miletos the *aisymnetes* is identified primarily by his relationship to the religious body of which he is part: he is the *aisymnetes* of the Molpoi, not of the Milesians. The priestly office of the *aisymnetes* is telling. Wilamowitz, the originator of the theory in question, points out that an oligarchy ruled by a board of priests would be a constitutional arrangement unique in Greece: "Es ist wohl das erste Mal, dass wir die Regierung statt an einen Rat an einen gottesdienstlichen Verein übergehen sehen."[24] Another scholar thinks that it is practically a general rule that *eponimie sacerdotali* [priestly eponyms] had no significant political authority in Greek cities.[25] A careful evaluation of the sources suggests that we limit the *aisymnetes* to his attested religious function and look elsewhere for the presiding officers of the Archaic oligarchy.

Before the *aisymnetes* gained the status of eponym, this function probably was carried out by the Archaic *prytanis*. This oligarchic magistrate—the title means "president" or "manager"—must not be confused with the democratic official that appears with the same title in Miletos after the Athenian-sponsored reforms of the mid–fifth century. The oligarchic *prytanis* is witnessed by an inscriptional dedication to Hekate, written in boustrophedon, probably from the sixth century but possibly earlier (*Milet* 1.3 #129).

$$\dots\dots 12 \dots\dots$$
$$\leftarrow \quad \text{Εὀθρασ} \dots\dots$$
$$\rightarrow \quad \text{..Λεωδάμας}$$

---

23. The linguistic origin of the word *aisymnetes* is unknown, although an assortment of theories abound, in which the word is variously proposed to be pre-Doric, brought over in the migration, probably from the name of a local god (Busolt and Swoboda 1920, 1:1 374; Glotz 1928, 105); Greek, derived from αἶσα ("destiny" or "decree") + ὕμνος, "hymn," or from αἶσα + μνήμη, "memory" (Luria 1963; *Etym. Magn.*); or Anatolian (Chantraine 1968, 1:39–40; Frisk 1960, 46; Hegyi 1977, 9–10).

24. "It is probably the first time that we see the government pass not to a council but to a sacred college" (Wilamowitz-Moellendorf 1914, 77).

25. De Sanctis 1976, 468: "... la eponimia del sacerdote di Zeus dimostra che il sacerdote Zeus non avera politicamente nessuna autorità. Ritengo che in generale ciò possa applicarsi quasi sempre alle eponimie sacerdotali delle πόλεις greche e, a maggior ragione che per tutte le altre πόλεις, per i motivi che vedemmo, alla eponimia di Mileto" [... the eponymous status of the priest of Zeus demonstrates that the priest of Zeus did not have any political authority. I think that in general this may be applied almost always to the sacred eponyms of the Greek cities and, with more reason than for all the other Greek cities, for reasons that we have seen, to the eponym of Miletos].

←   Ὀνάξο πϱυτ[α-]
→   νεύοντες ἀ-
←   νέθεσαν τῆ
→   κάτηι

[[. . .],
Eothras[es, son of . . .],
[. . .] Leodamas,
son of Onaxos, pryt[a]-
neis, dedicated this
to Hekate.]

This fragmentary dedication preserves the names of two *prytaneis* and has room for at least one more. It is possible that the stone was considerably larger than the piece extant and that the inscription contained six names in all, one from each tribe. At any rate, this inscription offers proof that the office was collegial.

Most scholars have assumed that each year, one of the *prytaneis* was the eponym in Archaic Miletos.[26] In this instance, comparative evidence is very informative, because it is remarkably consistent. Eponymous *prytaneis* prevail in the Greek world in general and in Ionia in particular, where we find them as the Classical era in Chios, Phokaia, Lebedos, and the Panionion and as early as the Hellenistic era in Teos, Kolophon, Ephesos, Priene, and Magnesia on the Maiandros. None of this evidence gives us direct information about an Archaic eponymous *prytanis*. Miletos is the only Ionian city known to have had one that early, although the office existed in the Archaic era in the Lesbian cities of Mytilene, Tenedos, and Eresos and in some Doric cities, where it occurs very early and very rarely.[27]

---

26. Ehrhardt 1983, 192–203; Gschnitzer 1973, 733–34; Busolt and Swoboda 1920, 1:505, 509.

27. Gschnitzer 1973, 733–36; cf. Ehrhardt 1983, 193. The presence of the eponymous *prytanis* in the colonies and its significance for the situation in the mother city is more a theoretical conclusion than a matter of evidence. Ehrhardt (1983, 200–201, 222) proposes that it was restricted to the colonies in the Propontis. Because Ehrhardt divides Milesian colonization into separate Propontic and Pontic phases, such a distribution would mean that Miletos's *prytanis* had forfeited his eponymous position by the mid–seventh century, when the colonization of the Propontis ended and that of the Pontos began. However, this view fails to win conviction on two counts. First, Ehrhardt's strict division between the colonization of these two regions is dubious (Graham 1987). Second, the actual evidence from the Propontis is so meager as to be evanescent. For example, Dittenberger (1960, #4

Little is known about the role of this office in Miletos, but it is provocative that this scanty information recalls the tradition about Epimenes, for it seems that the office of *prytanis*, not that of *aisymnetes*, was a suitable vehicle for the attainment of monarchical power. In a discussion of tyranny, Aristotle says (*Pol.* 5.1305a15–19):

ἐγίγνοντο δὲ τυραννίδες πρότερον μᾶλλον ἢ νῦν καὶ διὰ τὸ μεγάλας ἀρχὰς ἐγχειρίζεσθαί τισιν, ὥσπερ ἐν Μιλήτῳ ἐκ τῆς πρυτανείας πολλῶν γὰρ ἦν καὶ μεγάλων κύριος ὁ πρύτανις.

[And tyrannies used to occur in former times more than they do now, because the important offices were entrusted to certain men, as at Miletos, where a tyranny rose out of a prytany (for the *prytanis* had control of many important matters).]

Archaic Miletos had several tyrants, and Aristotle could be referring to any one of these. We are left with Aristotle's testimony and one Archaic dedication, as well as much comparative evidence from surrounding cities, as evidence for the oligarchic prytany at Miletos. From this evidence, we can accept that the *prytanis* was a powerful collegial office and that one *prytanis* gave his name to each Milesian year.[28]

Tyranny and Oligarchy

Miletos is known to have experienced two separate episodes of tyranny, that of Thrasyboulos and that of Histiaios and Aristagoras. Unusually for Archaic Miletos, the chronology of both these episodes can be fixed in reasonably limited bounds. Thrasyboulos was a guest-friend of Periander, the tyrant of Corinth from ca. 627 to 587, and is best known to posterity

---

n. 2; cf. Ehrhardt 1983, 195; Hanell 1946, 81; Werner 1955, 435) thinks the *prytanis* was the original eponym at Kyzikos, but there is no evidence offered for this view. In its stead, Bilabel (1920, 128) postulates an eponymous priest, while Mordtmann (1980, 96) thinks that the eponym was probably an archon. From the mid–fourth century through Roman times, when we do have evidence, Kyzikos has an eponymous Hipparch (Ehrhardt 1983, 253 esp. n. 1121).

28. Ehrhardt (1983, 212) has a theory that the prytany was already established at Miletos in the seventh century, in time to be transferred to three of the colonies. Cf. Gehrke 1980, 25. Piérart (1969; 1979, 440) agrees with an early date for the office but thinks that it developed independently and as a democratic office in Kios, Istros, and Odessos.

for his successful resistance to the expanding power of Lydia under King
Alyattes. The date of Alyattes' attacks is fairly well established: he ruled
from ca. 610 to 560, and the wars with Miletos were early in his reign,
with peace being concluded ca. 605. The second clearly attested occurrence of tyranny came in the last years of the Archaic period. Herodotos
reports a speech given by Histiaios, the tyrant of Miletos, on behalf of
his overlord, Dareios of Persia. This scene is part of the Great King's
Skythian expedition and so dates to ca. 513. This period of tyranny lasted
until 499, when Histiaios's successor, Aristagoras, claimed to have set
aside his tyranny at the start of the Ionian Revolt.

The tyranny of Thrasyboulos and the later one under the Persian hegemony are important for the historian, since they provide
fixed points, both chronologically and politically, around which the
other Archaic evidence must be made to fit. This other evidence primarily concerns civil strife, or stasis, since the extant ancient sources give
three accounts of the involvement of the oligarchy in civil war before
500 B.C.E.

Athenaios (12.523f–524b) cites Herakleides of Pontos (11.5) for
the most brutal of these stories.

Ἡρακλείδης δ' ὁ Ποντικὸς ἐν δευτέρῳ περὶ Δικαιοσύνης φησίν· ἡ
Μιλησίων πόλις περιπέπτωκεν ἀτυχίαις διὰ τρυφὴν βίου καὶ
πολιτικὰς ἔχθρας· οἳ τὸ ἐπιεικὲς οὐκ ἀγαπῶντες ἐκ ῥιζῶν ἀνεῖλον
τοὺς ἐχθρούς. [524] στασιαζόντων γὰρ τῶν τὰς οὐσίας ἐχόντων
καὶ τῶν δημοτῶν, οὓς ἐκεῖνοι Γέργιθας ἐκάλουν, πρῶτον μὲν
κρατήσας ὁ δῆμος καὶ τοὺς πλουσίους ἐκβαλὼν καὶ τὰ τέκνα τῶν
φυγόντων εἰς ἁλωνίας συναγαγών, βουσὶ συνηλοίησαν καὶ παρα-
νομωτάτῳ θανάτῳ διέφθειραν. τοιγάρτοι πάλιν οἱ πλούσιοι
κρατήσαντες ἅπαντας ὧν κύριοι κατέστησαν μετὰ τῶν τέκνων
κατεπίττωσαν. ὧν καιομένων φασὶν ἄλλα τε πολλὰ γενέσθαι
τέρατα καὶ ἐλαίαν ἱερὰν αὐτομάτην ἀναφθῆναι. διόπερ ὁ θεὸς
ἐπὶ πολὺν χρόνον ἀπήλαυνεν αὐτοὺς τοῦ μαντείου καὶ ἐπε-
ρωτώντων διὰ τίνα αἰτίαν ἀπελαύνονται εἶπεν·

καί μοι Γεργίθων τε φόνος μέλει ἀπτολεμίστων
πισσήρων τε μόρος καὶ δένδρεον αἰεὶ ἀθαλλές.

[Herakleides of Pontos, in the second book of his work *On Justice*,
says [Voss 41]: "The city of the Milesians fell upon disasters

through luxury of living and civil animosities; for, not content with reasonable moderation, they destroyed their enemies root and branch. The men of prosperity were at strife with the populace, whom they called Gergithes, and at first the populace got the upper hand, and after they had ejected the rich from the city, they gathered the children of the exiles on the threshing floors and trod them to death with oxen, destroying them with a most outrageous death. Therefore the rich, again getting the upper hand, tarred and burned to death all whom they could get a hold of, along with their children. While they were burning, among many other portents that are said to have arisen, a sacred olive tree burst into flames spontaneously. Hence the god for a long time repelled them from his oracle, and when they asked for what reason, he said, 'I too am mindful of the slaughter meted out to the most unwarlike Gergithes, of the doom of those who were covered with pitch, and of the tree that no longer blooms.' "]

As evidence for Milesian stasis, this story is dubious on several counts. First, the oracle that the passage presents is almost certainly not genuine. In his comprehensive study, Joseph Fontenrose has cataloged extant Delphic and Didymaean oracles.[29] He finds that those likely to be genuine are quite rare and share certain distinctive characteristics: they were uttered during the lifetime of the person recording them, they were formatted as unambiguous simple commands or sanctions, and the content was confined principally to religious subjects, especially the prescription of cult acts. Fontenrose also analyzes those oracles allegedly uttered in historical times but recorded by someone living after the utterance (called "quasi-historical" oracles). Most such oracles—often elaborately obscure predictions about the future—are so unlike historical oracles in form and content that they are untrustworthy and not to be considered authentic. The Gergithes oracle belongs in this category, and we must assume that these words were never given in response to the Milesians by the god at Didyma.[30]

Moreover, comparative study shows that the oracle as reported by Athenaios is not complete. Fontenrose has identified several classes of

---

29. Fontenrose 1978, 1988.
30. Fontenrose 1978, 11–57, Didymaean oracle #3; 1988, #36. Parke and Wormell (1956, #130) locate the stasis in the oracle with the civil strife of the fifth century and, since Didyma was not functioning at that time, identify it as a Delphic oracle.

quasi-historical oracles, of which the Gergithes oracle belongs to the "offended god pattern," but it does not contain all the elements of an oracular story of this class.

> The oracular tales of this kind show the following pattern. (1) Someone offends a god by desecrating his temple or altar or by leaving the dead unburied. (2) The god sends plague, famine, other calamity, or an ominous sign to the offender's city or land. (3) The people seek an oracle, which directs recompense or restitution of some kind (or, as in Q123, rejects the oracle-seekers). (4) The offending people either make amends or come to grief.[31]

In all, Fontenrose collects twelve such Delphic oracles.[32] Eleven offer a means of recompense to the people, while the twelfth (Q123, mentioned in the preceding quote) is a rejection of the Sybarites and a prophesy of their utter destruction, which we know occurred in 510 B.C.E. The Gergithes oracle contains the offense and the ominous sign, but in contrast to the established pattern, it does not offer the possibility of recompense, the prophesy of doom, or the subsequent fate of the Milesians. We may therefore conclude that Athenaios truncated both the oracle and the narrative in which it was embedded.[33]

Furthermore, if proper attention is paid to the context in which this passage is recorded, it is not difficult to conjecture plausibly how the passage must have continued. As in the case of the Sybarites, the god rejects the approach of the Milesians. Athenaios and his source, Herakleides Pontikos, present Miletos and Sybaris as examples of the misfortune that arises when excessive luxury leads to wickedness. Both the Sybarites and the Milesians spill the blood of their enemies in a way that offends the gods. In view of the similarities between the two stories, it is likely that they ended in the same fashion, with Miletos's sack by the Persians paralleling Sybaris's destruction by the Krotoniates. This conclu-

---

31. Fontenrose 1978, 77.

32. Fontenrose 1978, 76–77 esp. n. 35. He does not include the Gergithes oracle in this group, because he considers it to be Didymaean.

33. Athenaios commonly abridges his stories, due in part to the conversational nature of his essay. Here the truncation is especially apparent, for the reasons noted in the text as well as the fact that he goes on immediately from the text of the oracle to a quote from Klearchos about Milesian luxury. Then, without finishing the story of Miletos, he is distracted by the Klearchos story and moves immediately into another Klearchos story about the luxury of the Skythians.

sion would serve the interests of justice and make both authors' points: Athenaios is interested in the corrupting power of luxury (τρυφή), which leads to misfortune (ἀτυχία), while Herakleides includes the stories in his work *On Justice* (Περὶ δικαιοσύνης), which requires that the Milesians be punished for their crimes. Thus, Herakleides and Athenaios must have intended the narrative of the Gergithes oracle to be set in the context of the destruction of Miletos in 494 B.C.E. If we accept the account as genuine—which we probably should not—we must seek the setting for the stasis immediately before the Ionian Revolt.

The character of the narrative framework surrounding the Gergithes oracle constitutes the second principal objection to accepting this passage as reliable evidence for Milesian civil war. The narrative patently stands as an exegesis of the oracle itself. It is of course possible that the exegesis of a fictitious oracle may contain information useful to the historian, but material of this sort must be handled with great care and skepticism. In the present case, it appears quite possible that the exegesis was derived directly from the oracle. From the excerpts of Herakleides contained in Athenaios, we can see that by the fourth century B.C.E., a story of a certain type—luxurious self-indulgence leading to civil strife (and perhaps divine anger) resulting in destruction—had become associated with the fall of cities.[34] Assuming this story type as a pattern and given the connection of the Gergithes oracle with the sack of Miletos, the exegesis of this oracle contains almost no independently attested element that could not be made up from the language of the oracle itself, supplemented by the imagination of the exegete. For example, φόνος (slaughter) and μόρος (doom) might easily bring to mind the stasis of the typical story, and the fact that the Gergithes are given the attribute ἀπτολεμίστοι (most unwarlike) might lead to the supposition that they comprised a nonaristocratic element of the civil strife, the demos. The only important feature of the story not at least implicit in the words of the oracle is the murder of the children of the rich on the threshing floors. However, we have seen that the evidence collected by Fontenrose indicates that the

---

34. Athenaios's stories about Samos (12.525f–526a), Sybaris (12.520a–522a), and Miletos all fit this pattern and are all derived from Herakleides. A fourth city, Kolophon (12.526c) proceeds along the same lines, but Athenaios cites Theopompos and Diogenes of Babylon as his sources there. Athenaios uses a variation on the same pattern (luxury, offended god, destruction), without necessarily involving civil strife, in his accounts of Tarentum (12.522d–f, from Klearchos) and Iapygia (12.522f–523b; no attribution given). Magnesia is destroyed because of its luxury, with no mention of an offended god (12.525c, from Kallinos and Archilochos).

oracle as preserved is truncated. It is possible that the language of the missing lines provided the genesis for that gory detail.

In any case, it would be extremely naive to give credence to the story surrounding the Gergithes oracle based on the presence of the detailed description of the crimes of the Milesians. In connection with the destruction of Sybaris, at least three different versions of the sin that provoked divine wrath were in circulation: Phylarchos (Ath. 12.521d–e = *FGH* 81 F 45) attributes the god's anger to the murder of thirty Krotoniate ambassadors, who were then left unburied; Aelian (*VH* 3.43) reports that the Sybarites murdered a suppliant citharode at Hera's altar; and Herakleides (Ath. 12.521e–f) identifies the victims as the supporters of the former tyrant Telys, who were murdered on altars of the gods. Such heinous actions are stock elements in a typical story. In addition, the story of Milesian misfortune (*atuchia*) that accompanies the Gergithes oracle is manifestly incompatible with the more reliable evidence of Herodotos on the stasis at Miletos with which the story is usually associated: in Herodotos's account, instead of leading directly to the destruction of the city, the stasis was brought to a peaceful end in a settlement that inaugurated a period of great prosperity. In view of these considerations, the narrative framework of the Gergithes oracle is probably of as little historical value as the oracle itself.

Nevertheless, it is necessary to take a closer look at one of the details from the story, since the scholarship on Miletos almost universally accepts this tale at face value. In particular, historians try to use this account to establish the nature of the parties involved in the stasis. The focus of the argument is the strange name *Gergithes*. This term, which the rich used for their enemies, is said to derive from the village Gergis and region Gergithia or Gergithion in the Troad, extending south to the area of Aiolian Kyme.[35] Based on the assumption that the Gergithes were an indigenous people like the prehistoric Leleges, some historians would argue for a class division and stasis along racial lines. On this interpretation, the upper-class *plousioi* are Greeks, while the Gergithes are the native peoples, probably Carians, who toil among the lower classes and artisans at Miletos.[36] However, this view is not tenable, for we have seen

---

35. Hdt. 5.122, 7.43; Str. 13.1.70.616, 13.1.19.589. See Sakellariou 1958, 368; Bürchner 1912.

36. Halliday 1928, 146; How and Wells 1912; Stein 1894; Wilamowitz-Moellendorff 1914, 74. On a possible linguistic link between the words *Carian* and *Gergithes*, see Faraguna 1995, 43–46. Zgusta (1984, 138 paragraphs 202–5) says that it is unproven but tempting to

in chapter 1 that there is no firm evidence for any significant population of native Carians at Miletos at any time since the Ionian Migration. Moreover, mention of the Gergithes in Archaic Miletos is further cause to be suspicious of Herakleides's story. The homeland of this people is more than 250 kilometers distant, and there is no other evidence to put them at Miletos.[37]

Furthermore, the home of the Gergithes is closely associated with the legendary Hellespontine Sibyl.[38] The village of Gergis itself claims to be her birthplace (Lactant. 1.6) and/or burial place (Phlegon *FGH* 257 F 2; cf. Paus. 10.12). This connection points to the possibility that the Gergithes oracle originated in that place as a sibylline pronouncement. It could have been picked up and transmitted from there by a chresmologue wandering through Asia Minor, and it could have been eventually associated with the Oracle at Didyma in order to garner prestige.[39] Such change of attribution was fairly common according to Fontenrose.

There were many oracle collections in the ancient world, both private and public, and there were many oracles that circulated orally. These oracles were variously attributed, and attributions of a single oracle shifted from one reporter to another. Often enough an oracle that one person had attributed to Bakis [a chresmologue] another attributed to the Sibyl and another to the Delphic Apollo.

Once it was affiliated with Didyma, the baleful tone of the Gergithes oracle would have made it easy to connect it with the destruction of Miletos. In any case, until hard evidence of Gergithes at Miletos is produced, their presence at Miletos should be dismissed.

While Herakleides' evidence on this issue is of little use, a second

reconstruct the Greek word Γέργις from the Lykian word *Kheriga,* which is normally translated into Greek as Καρίκας (Carian). Gergithes may thus be a cognate for Carians, but immediately it becomes clear that if this is the case, Gergithes must refer to a much larger area than is conventionally titled Caria, since the name occurs as far north as the Troad and as far south as a personal name in Cilicia. Thus, even if this theory is accepted, the word *Gergithes* is no more specific than the word *Leleges* and cannot be exclusively connected to Miletos.

37. In the Carian mountains east of Miletos, there has been discovered a village called Gerga or Gergakome, which Faraguna (1995, 42–44) uses to argue the presence of Gergithes (i.e., Carians who went by that name) near Miletos. This is a very weak argument, because the village is not in Milesian territory but 60 km. removed into the interior, and because all of the evidence from that site is from Roman times: see Bean 1980, 171–76.

38. Parke 1985b, 179; 1992, 31, 51–52.

39. Fontenrose 1978, chap. 5, with quote at p. 165.

account of the stasis at Miletos, reported by Plutarch, is of some value, though it also presents difficulties in its details. In his *Quaestiones Graecae,* Plutarch writes (32.298c–d):

'Τίνες οἱ ἀειναῦται παρὰ Μιλησίοις;' τῶν περὶ Θόαντα καὶ Δαμασήνορα τυράννων καταλυθέντων ἑταιρεῖαι δύο τὴν πόλιν κατέ-
σχον, ὧν ἡ μὲν ἐκαλεῖτο Πλουτίς, ἡ δὲ Χειρομάχα. κρατήσαντες
οὖν οἱ δυνατοὶ καὶ τὰ πράγματα περιστήσαντες εἰς τὴν ἑταιρ-
είαν, ἐβουλεύοντο περὶ τῶν μεγίστων ἐμβαίνοντες εἰς τὰ πλοῖα
καὶ πόρρω τῆς γῆς ἐπανάγοντες· κυρώσαντες δὲ πὴν γνώμην
κατέπλεον, καὶ διὰ τοῦτ' ἀειναῦται προσηγορεύθησαν.

[Who are the perpetual sailors among the Milesians? After the tyrants around Thoas and Damasenor had been overthrown, two parties held the city, one called Rich and the other Labor. When the powerful men gained the upper hand and brought control over the government into the hands of their own party, they were accustomed to deliberating about matters of the greatest importance by going aboard ships and putting out to sea far away from the land. When they made their decision, they sailed back, and on account of this, they are called "perpetual sailors."]

As a synonym for the Rich[40] and the powerful men, the meaning of the term *aeinautai* is uncertain. The shipboard meetings of the victorious Rich are clearly an etymological invention by Plutarch or his source to explain a term whose meaning had been lost through the passage of time. We are not in a much better position to interpret the word. Various guesses have been made based on etymologizing no more believable than Plutarch's, equating *aeinautai* with an early form of sea police; with officials in charge of the war fleet, like the *naukraroi* at Athens; or with a nickname for the party of the merchant aristocracy.[41]

---

40. Wyttenbach's emendation of *Ploutis* for the nonsensical manuscript reading Πλοντίς is certainly correct.

41. Sea police: W. Helbig (*non vidi*), cited and rejected by Ormerod 1924, 96 n. 3. War fleet commanders: Wilamowitz-Moellendorff 1906b, 78. Merchant aristocracy: Halliday 1928. One last, rather desperate attempt by Wachsmuth (*non vidi;* cited by Szanto 1894) suggests a derivation from ἀεί + ναύτης = ναιέτης from ναίω, meaning "ever flowing." He then relates this term with the fire of the public hearth, which is never allowed to go out, and his conclusion is that the *aeinautai* are the persons who dwell permanently at the public hearth.

Elsewhere in the Greek world, the only traces of *aeinautai* are found on Euboia, where three inscriptions serve as evidence. The first one, *IG* 12(9) 923 from Chalkis, is broken so badly that we are left merely with a list of names and the word *aeinautai*. A second inscription, from Eretria, records the dedication by *aeinautai* of a herm that dates to the fifth century B.C.E.[42] The third is a dedicatory inscription, *IG* 12(9) 909 from the third century B.C.E., also from Chalkis. The text of this inscription is more extensive than the others. But since the stone is broken vertically nearly down the middle, a great deal of the context is lost. The lacuna has been formulaically completed by the editor.

[- - - τοὺ]ς πρ[ο]σπορευομέ-
[νους· ἀγαθῆι τύχηι· δεδόχθ]αι τῶι κοινῶι ᾿Αεναυ-
[τῶν ἐπαινέσαι - - -]βουλον Διονυσοφάνου
[καὶ στεφανῶσαι δάφ]νης στεφάνωι δικαιοσύ-
[νης ἕνεκα τῆς περὶ τὰ] κοινὰ καὶ φιλοτιμίας· ἀνα-
[γράψαι δὲ τόδε τὸ ψήφ]ισμα εἰστήλην λιθίνην
[καὶ ἀναθεῖναι, ὅπου ἂν δ]όξηι τοῦ ἱεροῦ ἐν καλλί-
[στωι εἶναι· τὸ δ᾿ ἀνάλωμα] ἐναπολογίσασθαι τῷ
[κοινῶι τὸν γραμματέα] ᾿Αρχέμαχον.

[. . . those approaching. [Blessings. It seemed best] to the corporation of the *aeinau*[tai to praise - - -], son of Dionysophanos, [and to crown him] with the crown of [laur]el [on account of his jus]tice [in matters regarding the] corporation and on account of his distinction. [It was also decided that they should] in[scribe this vote] on a stone stele [and erect it in the] sacred precinct [where it would be most] beau[tiful. The secretary] Archemachos will be accountable to the [corporation for the cost].]

Although this text is the best evidence available for the meaning of *aeinautai*, it tells us only that these people formed a corporation, or *koinon*, and that they probably had something to do with the cult of Apollo, as they are rewarding a benefactor with a laurel crown and placing a stele in a temple. The editor of the inscription sheds no new light on the question, merely reiterating the old guess about the *naukraroi*.[43]

---

42. Petrakos 1963.
43. The editor, Hiller von Gaertingen, explains the term *aeinautai* thus (*ad IG* 12(9) 909): "collegii cuiusdam quod continuisse videtur trierarchos, fortasse etiam milites

None of these attempted explanations is convincing, and we must avoid accepting assumptions about Milesian politics that are based on the meaning of a word, *aeinautai*, which was probably known to Plutarch or his source only as the obscure name of a corporation of functionaries: the existence of the *aeinautai* in Euboia shows that Plutarch's explanation at *Quaestiones Graecae* 32 is ad hoc and impossible.

The name of the second faction, *Cheiromacha*, may offer better information about the Archaic political situation, but first we must fix its meaning with the greatest possible precision. The first part of the compound, *cheiro-* (hand) is certain, but *-macha* presents a complication. Most experts connect it, despite its alpha, with *mêch-* (make). In this case, the translation "the Artisans" is perfectly adequate (cf. Eust. 1833.56, 1425.64, 1783.13). A rival view links the word with *mache* (fight) and offers the translation "those who fight with their hands," meaning the weaponless poor.[44] In each case, we are seriously handicapped because we do not know whether the name *Cheiromacha* was applied by that faction to itself or was an appellation given by its enemies. The translation "Hand-Maker Party" may imply lower- or middle-class merchants and artisans; if so, Miletos was involved in true class warfare. Equally, "Hand-Maker" may be a term of disapprobation applied to a faction of prosperous merchants by the landed aristocracy. Other possibilities abound. The translation "Hand-Fighter Party" also suffers from ambiguity. While it could indicate those too poor to serve as hoplites, it could conceivably constitute an insult to the new rich by the established warrior nobility. A faction of the old elite itself, perhaps drawing support from the discontent of the lower classes, cannot be ruled out.

The most intriguing item of information in Plutarch's passage is the mention of the tyrants around Thoas and Damasenor, but it will be better to postpone this discussion until I have introduced the third and final account of Archaic Milesian stasis. This time the source of the story is the history of Herodotos and so has the advantage of being much nearer to the events themselves. Herodotos says (5.28–29):

τοῦτο μὲν γὰρ ἡ Νάξος εὐδαιμονίῃ τῶν νήσων προέφερε, τοῦτο δὲ κατὰ τὸν αὐτὸν χρόνον ἡ Μίλητος αὐτή τε ἑωυτῆς μάλιστα δὴ

---

classiarios e Wilamowitzii coniectura" [of a certain college that seems to contain trierarchs and perhaps even naval soldiers, as Wilamowitz suggested].

44. Ruzé 1985, 163.

τότε ἀκμάσασα καὶ δὴ καὶ τῆς Ἰωνίης ἦν πρόσχημα, κατύπερθε
δὲ τούτων ἐπὶ δύο γενεὰς ἀνδρῶν νοσήσασα ἐς τὰ μάλιστα
στάσι, μέχρι οὗ μιν Πάριοι κατήρτισαν· τούτους γὰρ καταρτ-
ιστῆρας ἐκ πάντων Ἑλλήνων εἵλοντο οἱ Μιλήσιοι. [29.1] κατήλ-
λαξαν δὲ σφεας ὧδε οἱ Πάριοι· ὡς ἀπίκοντο αὐτῶν ἄνδρες οἱ
ἄριστοι ἐς τὴν Μίλητον, ὥρων γὰρ δή σφεας δεινῶς οἰκοφθο-
ρημένους, ἔφασαν αὐτῶν βούλεσθαι διεξελθεῖν τὴν χώρην. ποι-
εῦντες δὲ ταῦτα καὶ διεξιόντες πᾶσαν τὴν Μιλησίην, ὅκως τινὰ
ἴδοιεν ⟨ἐν⟩ ἀνεστηκυίῃ τῇ χώρῃ ἀγρὸν εὖ ἐξεργασμένον, ἀπε-
γράφοντο τὸ οὔνομα τοῦ δεσπότεω τοῦ ἀγροῦ. [29.2] διεξε-
λάσαντες δὲ πᾶσαν τὴν χώρην καὶ σπανίους εὑρόντες τούτους,
ὡς τάχιστα κατέβησαν ἐς τὸ ἄστυ, ἁλίην ποιησάμενοι ἀπέδεξαν
τούτους μὲν τὴν πόλιν νέμειν τῶν εὗρον τοὺς ἀγροὺς εὖ ἐξεργα-
σμένους· δοκέειν γὰρ ἔφασαν καὶ τῶν δημοσίων οὕτω δή σφεας
ἐπιμελήσεσθαι ὥσπερ τῶν σφετέρων· τοὺς δὲ ἄλλους Μιλησίους
τοὺς πρὶν στασιάζοντας τούτων ἔταξαν πείθεσθαι.

[For Naxos was the most prosperous of the islands, while, about
the same time [499 B.C.E.], Miletos itself was at its height and
especially was the ornament of Ionia. Previously Miletos had been
very disturbed by civil strife for two generations, until when the
Parians set it in order. For the Milesians chose them out of all the
Greeks to reform their state. [29] The Parians reconciled them in
the following way. When the best men of them arrived at Miletos,
seeing the terrible economic state of the place, they said that they
wished to travel around in the territory. They did these things and
traveled throughout the Milesian territory. Whenever, in the deso-
late land, they saw a well-tilled field, they wrote down the name of
the owner of the land. And although they traveled all through the
region, they saw a well-tilled field only rarely. As soon as they
returned to the city, they summoned an assembly and appointed to
govern the state those men whose land they found was well tilled,
for they said that they thought that such men would tend to public
matters with the same care that they displayed in their own private
affairs. They ordered the remaining Milesians who were previously
in stasis to obey these men.]

Herodotos adds several new pieces of information. He seems to be relating the end of the stasis, for its settlement is presented as a precondition

of the great prosperity in Miletos at the time of the Ionian Revolt. Significantly, the settlement established a landed oligarchy of limited size: though the rich may have had to share power with farmers of more moderate means, there was little place for artisans and small merchants in the new scheme. Furthermore, this passage supplies additional chronological facts: the stasis lasted "two generations." Based on Herodotos's reckoning at 2.142.2 that one hundred years is approximately three generations, this phrase is traditionally taken to indicate about sixty years of factional strife; however, since Herodotean chronological dating is notoriously indefinite, at best we must conclude that it lasted a rather long time and that Herodotos did not know how long himself or he would have used a more specific number.[45]

Basing their understanding on these passages, most historians today share what has become the predominant view about factional strife at Miletos: at some point in the Archaic past, Miletos moved from the rule of tyrants (Thoas and Damasenor) to a lengthy period of stasis; after half a century or more, the strife was settled by a commission of Parians, who established an oligarchy of the most capable landowners; Miletos then entered its most prosperous period. This picture is perfectly plausible and compares well with the process known to have taken place in other Greek cities in the seventh and sixth centuries, in which the hereditary nobility gave way, often through tyranny, to an oligarchy based more on landholdings and wealth than on hereditary status.[46]

Dating these events at Miletos more precisely in the Archaic era is difficult, since the only named figures, Thoas and Damasenor, appear nowhere else in the extant literature. Because the tyranny of Thrasyboulos (ca. 605) is one of the few fixed points in Archaic Milesian chronology, the choice must be made whether to place the Parion arbitration of stasis before or after Thrasyboulos. Almost without exception, historians opt for the later date: Thrasyboulos, according to this view, is the man who, as Aristotle says, used the power of the prytany as a springboard to tyranny.[47] The tyrants Thoas and Damasenor followed, prob-

45. While the figure of thirty years per generation is sometimes correct, a calculation based on other passages (Hdt. 4.158.1, 1.163.2, 1.95.2) might lead one to accept a generation length of forty years, and scholars who have examined this problem of time reckoning in Herodotos amply demonstrate the futility of fixing the length of a Herodotean generation. See Lateiner 1989, 114–25; Ball 1979; Mitchel 1956.

46. Balcer 1984b, 89; Drews 1972.

47. Hanell 1946, 75–81; Mazzarino 1947, 225–32; Berve 1967, 1:101–2, 2:578–79; Graf 1985, 81; Harris 1971, 29–35; Balcer 1984b; How and Wells 1912. I have only found

ably immediately after Thrasyboulos. Then civil strife broke out and lasted for two generations, until ca. 525, when the Parian arbitration reestablished peaceful government and laid the foundation for great prosperity. This rather precise date for the Parian arbitration is based on the traditionally accepted date for the beginning of the lists of eponymous *aisymnetai*. It is quite probable that the first list begins with some kind of reorganization of the government,[48] and the apparent synchronicity of the new eponym with the Parian-established oligarchy has seemed decisively to favor a post-Thrasyboulan date for the era of stasis. Because of the likely significance of the beginning of the *aisymnetes* list, it is convenient to discuss it in some detail before moving on to examine more closely this traditional chronology.

The date of ca. 525/4 for the beginning of the *aisymnetes* list is by no means as certain as it is usually taken to be. Albert Rehm (*Milet* 1.3.241–53), the original editor of the lists, bases the absolute chronology of the first list on two names. The last name on that list, Asandros, son of Agathon (ii.101), can be dated to 314/3 B.C.E. (D.S. 19.75.1, 19.62.5), while Alexander, son of Philip (ii.81), is Alexander the Great. He could not have taken Miletos before late summer 334, so, Rehm concludes, he must have taken the eponymous office in 334/3, at which time the entire first list up to that point was engraved: all of the names before ca. 333 were copied from a previous edition of the list, re-created from memory, or both.[49]

Several dubious presuppositions underlie this dating and weaken its

Stein (1894, *ad* Hdt. 5.28) and Ehrhardt (1983, 202) favoring an earlier date. Stein does so because he thinks the fall of Thoas and Damasenor marks the end of the Neleid monarchy, which is baseless conjecture. Ehrhardt has a theory that the change in eponym from prytany to *aisymnetes* was probably contemporary to the reordering of the city after the Kimmerian invasion in the mid–seventh century B.C.E. However, his argument does not have sound footing: he asserts that the predominant eponym was a prytany in the colonies of the Propontis and a priest in the colonies of the Pontos, but as the earlier discussion of eponym has demonstrated, the evidence is often lacking or postulated, so the pattern he describes is not sufficiently confirmed.

48. Rehm in *Milet* 1.3.242; cf. Hanell 1946, 80–81.

49. There is no reason to question the reliability of the early names on the list. Cf. the work by Salviat (1984) on the archon lists at Thasos, where he concludes from the numerous names and the complexity of the lists that the Thasians had authentic records to work from clear back to the high sixth century and quite possibly to the colony's beginning in the seventh century. However, Cavaignac (*non vidi*; followed by Herrmann in *Milet* 6.1) makes an argument for dating both Asandros and Alexander a year later, in 313/2 and 333/2, respectively. Following this development and counting backward from Alexander, allotting one year for each name, we arrive at a beginning date of 524/3.

security. The first assumption is that there was an *aisymnetes* at Miletos without interruption for all of the years from ca. 525/4 to 334/3. According to Herodotos (Hdt. 6.18–22.1), Miletos was entirely depopulated in 494 B.C.E., and the archaeological record has confirmed the massive destruction done to the city at that time. Rehm notes that he cannot say that the list is without breaks before the year of Alexander's *aisymnetes* and especially before 479/8 (*Milet* 1.3.242).[50] This is an important observation. Based on Herodotos's testimony and the archaeological record, it is likely that the city of Miletos did not exist as a polity for at least some of the years between 494 and ca. 479. The population had been slaughtered or transplanted to Ampe on the Persian Gulf, and the land was given away to Persians and Carians. Certainly refugees may have begun returning at any time in the intervening years, but when the city was emptied, the government would have ceased to exist, probably until after the refoundation, ca. 479 B.C.E. or shortly afterward. We must postulate that the *aisymnetes* list stretches back as much as another fifteen years. If the adoption of the new eponym does coincide with the Parian arbitration, a date of ca. 540/39 would be more likely.[51]

However, the two events may well not be related at all. A strong argument can be made that a date after the rule of Thrasyboulos for the Milesian stasis and the Parian arbitration is untenable. First, no attempt to set the date of the Parian arbitration in the latter half of the sixth century can neglect the implications of the fact that by the late 540s, Miletos was under direct Persian control. If the establishment of the oligarchy is set according to the traditional starting date of the *aisymnetes*

---

50. The stone is intact, but there are no guarantees that there were not temporal gaps between some of the names, especially as the entire list before Alexander was inscribed at one time. Rehm also points out that the big names of the Ionian Revolt are lacking, an objection that is not troubling if this office is powerless and/or chosen by lot. Cf. Hanell 1946, 75–81.

51. An additional, and probably insoluble, problem is the possibility of suffect officials. Twice on the first list (#122.ii.11, 22), two names are written in smaller characters on the same line, suggesting either a mistake on the part of the stonecutter or that the original official died in office and another was chosen to fill out his term. The question then arises whether it would be necessary to engrave the name of a suffect on a list of eponymous officials. The editor has chosen the former alternative, allotting each name its own year, but the possibility remains open that the list may go back two years less than originally thought. In a variant argument, Cavaignac (*non vidi;* see Herrmann in *Milet* 1.6) suggests that these two years coincide with episodes of unrest or civil strife when two different men held the office, the one casting out the other: column ii, line 11 would coincide with Lysander's coup in 403/2 (Polyain. 7.18.2), while line 22 would accord with problems in 392/1 consequent to the battle with Knidos.

list to ca. 525, one must explain why the Persians allowed a major commercial center under their control to remain in civil war for some fifteen years. If, instead, the date of ca. 540 is preferred, one must explain why the Persians, who were completing their conquest and solidifying their rule, would permit the Milesians to call in the Parians to establish a new government for the city, rather than arranging the matter themselves.[52]

A second objection to the traditional view lies in the short duration of the government established by the Parians, if the arbitration is to be dated in the period ca. 540 to ca. 525. Even granting the precarious assumption that Persian laissez-faire administration overlooked continuing civil war and permitted outside intervention, a date in this range does not fit well with Herodotos's implication that the new oligarchy was enduring enough to bring on prosperity. It would be difficult to impute stability to a government set up at this time, for we know that as early as 513, the date of Dareios's invasion of Skythia, the city is again ruled by a tyrant, who seems to have been in place for some time (Hdt. 4.137–42). The point of this story about the establishment of good government would be very much blunted if that government only lasted less than a decade, from 525 to before 513, and was then overthrown by an unpopular tyranny. Even if we accept that the arbitration occurred in ca. 540, then the oligarchy persisted for only about twenty years, a very short period to merit the emphasis that Herodotos gives it.[53] Because these events—a stasis of two generations, the Parian arbitration, and a period of pronounced and remarkable prosperity—do not fit well into the context of the sixth century, it seems that a date before the tyranny of Thrasyboulos should be preferred.

In his text, Plutarch mentions two men, Thoas and Damasenor, who are commonly assumed to be tyrants, and the tendency of scholars is to place them in the sixth century, squarely in the middle of the great Age of

---

52. Balcer (1984b, 99) uses this point in the opposite manner, arguing that under the Persians, Miletos enjoyed a semiautonomous status. Thus, he says, the fact that the Parians were allowed to arbitrate rather than Persians "indicates a high degree of internal self-determination."

53. Some scholars have sidestepped this problem by assuming that the Parian arbitration set up the tyranny. For example, Mazzarino (1947, 230–32) sees the whole stasis as a struggle for power between two families. However, this interpretation is an impossible reading of Herodotos. Unless we are to dismiss the entire story, perhaps as "a political parable inserted here for some unknown reason" (How and Wells 1912, ad Hdt. 5.28–29), we must accept that the resulting government was an oligarchy and face the problems this fact entails for a sixth-century date for the Milesian stasis.

Tyrants in Archaic Greece. Another look at Plutarch's text shows that he does not call them tyrants,[54] for his genitive absolute actually reads, τῶν περὶ Θόαντα καὶ Δαμασήνορα τυράννων καταλυθέντων [after the tyrants around Thoas and Damasenor had been overthrown]. "Those around the tyrants Thoas and Damasenor" is not at all the same thing as "the tyrants around Thoas and Damasenor." This last phrase is admittedly odd, and scholars have been slow to see its meaning. They have been led astray principally by the common Greek phrase οἱ περί + accusative *nominis proprii*. Our grammars identify a peculiar usage of this phrase. In writers of late Greek, it is said to be used as a periphrasis for the object of the preposition: for example, οἱ περὶ τὸν Ἀλκιβιάδην would mean simply "Alkibiades."[55] Confusion arising from this usage has infected the text of Plutarch as well as its interpretation. This confusion has centered on the presence of the word τυράννων in the genitive. Assuming a periphrasis, we would expect an appositional construction to agree with the accusative object of the preposition rather than with the substantively used definite article. While in his Oxford commentary Halliday suggests that τυράννων be deleted as a gloss, Tischner's Teubner edition of 1935 (reprinted in 1971) emends the offending genitive to the accusative τυράννους. The suggested emendation produces the meaning "after those around the tyrants Thoas and Damasenor had been overthrown," or, understanding a periphrasis, "after the tyrants Thoas and Damasenor had been overthrown." The passage then would refer to the fall from power of the supporters of the two tyrants or of the tyrants themselves.

Plutarch's original text, which is found in all the manuscripts, can and should be retained. Recent scholarship has found that instances of the periphrastic οἱ περί + accusative are much less common than previously supposed and therefore that the periphrastic construction should not be assumed without the strongest contextual support.[56] Furthermore, when the periphrasis is discounted, the resultant phrase, "the tyrants around Thoas and Damasenor," does indeed make clear sense, as the following parallels show. Telling of the fall of King Knopos of Erythrai, Hippias, a historian of the same city, writes (Ath. 6.259b–c):

---

54. Gorman and Gorman 2000. Berve (1967, 1:102) is the most accurate of modern scholars, in that he does not call them tyrants but comments instead: "Eine tyrannengleiche Macht konnten für kurze Zeit Thoas und Damasenor mit ihrer Hetairie gewinnen" [Thoas and Damasenor, along with their backers, could have won a tyrantlike power for a short time].

55. Kühner-Gerth 2.1.270; Schwyzer-Debrunner 2.417; *LSJ* s.v. περὶ C.I.2 (with accusative of persons), "later οἱ π. τινά, periphr. for the person himself" (cf. C.I.3).

56. Dubuisson 1977.

καὶ καταληφθέντος τοῦ ἄστεος ὑπὸ τῶν περὶ τὸν Ὀρτύγην πολλοὶ
μὲν ἀναιροῦνται τῶν τοῦ Κνωποῦ φίλων καὶ ἡ Κλεονίκη μαθοῦσα
φεύγει εἰς Κολοφῶνα. οἱ δὲ περὶ τὸν Ὀρτύγην τύραννοι ἔχοντες
τὴν ἐκ Χίου δύναμιν τοὺς ἐνισταμένους αὐτῶν τοῖς πράγμασι
διέφθειρον καὶ τοὺς νόμους καταλύσαντες αὐτοὶ διεῖπον τὰ κατὰ
τὴν πόλιν ἐντὸς τείχους οὐδένα δεχόμενοι τῶν δημοτῶν·

[When the city had been taken by the followers of Ortyges, many of
the friends of Knopos were killed, and Kleonike, learning this, escaped to Kolophon. Since they had the might of Chios behind them,
the tyrants around Ortyges killed everyone who opposed their actions, and after setting aside the laws, they ran things inside the city
while at the same time allowing none of the people to come within
the walls.]

Here we find the phrase "the tyrants around Ortyges." But to whom do
these words refer? They do not refer, as one might guess, to a tyrant
named Ortyges and his faction—though the plural of *tyrannos* sometimes has this use. In a previous passage, Hippias makes the matter clear.
There Knopos, still on the throne, sets out to Delphi to consult the oracle
because he is worried about his own safety (Ath. 6.259a).

καὶ μετὰ ταῦτα ὁρμήσαντος αὐτοῦ εἰς Δελφοὺς οἱ τὴν βασιλείαν
αὐτοῦ καταλῦσαι βουλόμενοι ἵν᾽ ὀλιγαρχίαν καταστήσωνται,
ἦσαν δ᾽ οὗτοι Ὀρτύγης καὶ Ἷρος καὶ Ἔχαρος, οἳ ἐκαλοῦντο διὰ
τὸ περὶ τὰς θεραπείας εἶναι τῶν ἐπιφανῶν πρόκυνες καὶ
κόλακες.

[And afterward, when he set out for Delphi, with him went the very
men who wanted to get rid of his kingship in order to establish an
oligarchy (these men were Ortyges, Iros, and Echaros, who are
called the lap-dogs and the flatterers, because they attended famous
people).]

Hippias is describing a situation where a king is deposed in favor of an
oligarchy. It is a narrow oligarchy, hostile to both the laws and the demos,
but it is clearly an oligarchy.

This passage shows that we must be careful to distinguish the nuances
of the word *tyrannos*. Here we see that, used in the pejorative sense to
characterize a harsh, selfish, violent rule, the term is not restricted to

monarchy alone but may refer to any number of people. It is especially easy for a democratic tradition to stigmatize a narrow and harsh oligarchy with this name. One need only think of the Thirty Tyrants at Athens.

Plutarch is familiar with this mode of expression, as he shows when he describes the oligarchy at Thebes in the mid–fourth century. Here he refers to the group of men in question as τύραννοι[57] and both οἱ περὶ Λεοντίδαν (*Pel.* 6.2) and οἱ περὶ ᾽Αρχίαν (*Pel.* 9.2). Particularly reminiscent of *Quaestiones Graecae* 32 is *Pelopidas* 6.1: καταδεδουλωμένοις ὑπὸ τῶν περὶ ᾽Αρχίαν καὶ Λεοντίδαν οὐδὲ ἐλπίσαι περιῆν ἀπαλλαγήν τινα τῆς τυραννίδος [[the Thebans], being enslaved to those around Archias and Leontidas, had no hope that they could find any escape from tyranny]. A little earlier, Plutarch revealed the line of thought that led to such a choice of terminology, calling these men ἄνδρες ὀλιγαρχικοὶ καὶ πλούσιοι καὶ μέτριον οὐδὲν φρονοῦντες [oligarchical men, wealthy, and intending nothing moderate] (*Pel.* 5.2). Thus, rulers who recognize no measure, whether they be one or several, can accurately be styled *tyrants:* ἔργῳ μὲν τυράννους, λόγῳ δὲ πολεμάρχους ὄντας [In deed they were tyrants, in name polemarchs] (Plut. *Ages.* 24.1).

Clearly then, τυράννους is an unnecessary emendation to the text of Plutarch, because τυράννων not only gives clear sense and is supported by all of the manuscripts but, considering its rarity compared to οἱ περὶ τῶν τυράννων, is the *lectio difficilior* as well. Plutarch's source is describing not a tyranny at all but a narrow oligarchy like that of Thebes, one that either ruled harshly or is remembered by a hostile tradition. With this point established, we may discount what seemed a strong reason to situate the stasis at Miletos in the sixth century.

In this context, certain chronological implications from Herodotos's recounting of the stasis must also be considered. As mentioned earlier, the context of Herodotos's account of the Parian arbitration is the Milesian-led expedition against Naxos in 499 B.C.E. Herodotos joins the tale to its context with the expression κατύπερθε δὲ τούτων [previous to this] (Hdt. 5.28). The word κατύπερθε normally has the spatial meaning "above." Its temporal use is rare, occurring only one other time in Herodotos, and that passage is equally vague: at 9.64.2, κατύπερθε is used of the common ancestors of Pausanias and Leonidas starting at the great-grandfather (τῶν δὲ κατύπερθέ οἱ προγόνων). Unfortunately, neither

---

57. Plut. *Pel.*, esp. 6 and 9; *Comp. Pel. et Marc.* 1.6; *Ages.* 24.2; *de Gen.* 109.576b, 586d, etc.

passage makes it clear whether the previous time referred to is immediate or distant. The use of κατύπερθε, then, does not rule out either a sixth-century date or one before Thrasyboulos.

Similarly, Herodotos's concern with Miletos's rise from hard times to prosperity does not necessitate a sixth-century date for the episode he relates. Herodotos establishes the reversal of fortune is one of the dominant themes of his *Histories* (1.5.3–4).

τοῦτον σημήνας προβήσομαι ἐς τὸ πρόσω τοῦ λόγου, ὁμοίως σμικρὰ καὶ μεγάλα ἄστεα ἀνθρώπων ἐπεξιών. [4] τὰ γὰρ τὸ πάλαι μεγάλα ἦν, τὰ πολλὰ αὐτῶν σμικρὰ γέγονε, τὰ δὲ ἐπ᾽ ἐμεῦ ἦν μεγάλα, πρότερον ἦν σμικρά. τὴν ἀνθρωπηίην ὦν ἐπιστάμενος εὐδαιμονίην οὐδαμὰ ἐν τὠυτῷ μένουσαν ἐπιμνήσομαι ἀμφοτέρων ὁμοίως.

[Saying this, I will continue further with my story, touching on the small and the great towns of men alike. [4] For many of those that were once great are now small, and those that are in my time great were formerly small. And knowing thus that human prosperity does not remain long in the same place, I will mention both alike.]

Coming as it does in the first pages of his work, this statement is clearly thematic. Furthermore, he would reach back as far as necessary to find evidence to fit his pattern. Witness 1.65.2–66.1, where Kroisos, about to launch his campaign against the Persians (ca. 548), has sent to learn about the value of the Lakedaimonians as possible allies.

[[65.2] τὸ δὲ ἔτι πρότερον τούτων καὶ κακονομώτατοι ἦσαν σχεδὸν πάντων Ἑλλήνων κατά τε σφέας αὐτοὺς καὶ ξείνοισι ἀπρόσμεικτοι. μετέβαλον δὲ ὧδε ἐς εὐνομίην Λυκούργου τῶν Σπαρτιητέων δοκίμου ἀνδρὸς ἐλθόντος ἐς Δελφοὺς ἐπὶ τὸ χρηστήριον, ... [5] ὡς γὰρ ἐπετρόπευσε τάχιστα, μετέστησε τὰ νόμιμα πάντα καὶ ἐφύλαξε ταῦτα μὴ παραβαίνειν.... [66.1] οὕτω μὲν μεταβαλόντες εὐνομήθησαν, ... οἷα δὲ ἔν τε χώρῃ ἀγαθῇ καὶ πλήθεϊ οὐκ ὀλίγων ἀνδρῶν, ἀνά τε ἔδραμον αὐτίκα καὶ εὐθενήθησαν.

[65.2] Still, earlier to these things, they [the Spartans] were the worst governed of nearly all the Greeks, both in their own affairs

and in their unsociable attitude toward strangers. They were transformed into good government as follows: Lykourgos, an excellent
Spartan man, went to Delphi to consult the Oracle, . . . [5] For
immediately after he took up his office, he both changed all the laws
and guarded them so that they would not be broken. . . . [66.1]
Being thus altered, they were well governed, . . . Because of the
good land and the great number of people, they shot up quickly and
flourished.]

The parallel between this passage and the story of the Parion arbitration
are clear and instructive.[58] In both, the focus is on present prosperity and
military potential, prosperity arose out of a troubled past, and prosperity
is brought about by a single fundamental reorganization of the government. Significantly, the two stories are set in an unspecified past time
indicated by a single adverbial phrase (τὸ δὲ ἔτι πρότερον τούτων and
κατύπερθε δὲ τούτων): in the case of the legendary Lykourgos, the temporal setting is clearly several centuries before the embassy sent by
Kroisos. Herodotos found a lengthy interval of time no obstacle to the
juxtaposition of cause and effect, and recognizing Herodotos's narrative
pattern, we see that an earlier date for the Parian arbitration is by no
means excluded by the text.

We can and should redate the Milesian stasis and the Parian arbitration to the period before the tyranny of Thrasyboulos. After the Neleid
monarchy had run its course during the Dark Ages, whether over a few
decades or over a few centuries, a hereditary oligarchy of some sort was
established at Miletos, led by an eponymous prytany. That government
concluded with the harsh rule of those who were colleagues with Thoas
and Damasenor. After them, a long period of unrest followed, during
which prolonged and savage civil strife racked the city, to be settled
eventually by a delegation of Parians, who inaugurated a new oligarchy
whose power rested in the hands not of a hereditary nobility but of a
broader base of landowners.

The dating of these events cannot be fixed with precision, but a likely
time for them is the eighth and seventh centuries B.C.E. Around the
middle of the seventh century, Paros was enjoying a period of prosperity,
as demonstrated by the poetry of Archilochos and the colonization of

---

58. I am indebted to both Richard Billows and Robert Gorman for independently suggesting this parallel.

Thasos. In addition, the resulting Milesian prosperity emphasized by Herodotos correlates well with the great explosion in colonization that Miletos experienced, beginning possibly in the mid–eighth century and really taking off in the final third of the seventh.[59] Thus, the new oligarchy continued stably until the end of the seventh century, when Thrasyboulos emerged as tyrant, perhaps as a direct result of the Lydian threat (he might have used the prytany as a means to absolute power). After his tyranny ended, perhaps with the conclusion of the external threat, the oligarchy would have resumed ruling until ca. 540, when a new government reorganization occurred.[60] This reorganization should probably be associated with the establishment of a new tyranny at Miletos, a form of government that was to last some forty years. Whether one-man rule was initiated by the Persians in their conquest of Ionia, or whether some enterprising Milesian recognized in the Lydian and then Persian presence an opportunity for self-advancement, we cannot know. But it is especially in the context of tyranny that it makes sense to transform the eponymous official from the prytany, a politically powerful office, to a priesthood with no known political powers: a tyrant does not abide rivals, whereas in an oligarchy, the power of the eponym could be considerable.

The External Threat

The government of Miletos faced increasingly difficult challenges as the Archaic period progressed. Earlier, during the Dark Ages, the Anatolian interior was occupied by relatively disorganized peoples who posed little threat to the Ionians, so the contacts that Miletos did have with the interior seem to have been primarily commercial and relatively peaceful. The exception to the pattern, the Phrygians held sway far inland, in

---

59. It is possible that some of the first colonies were sent out as a result of the civil strife and that only after the strife was settled and the economic advantages of the original colonies were demonstrated did the Milesians realize their financial potential and become the great colonizing power.

60. There must have been a return to oligarchy in this period, or else we are left to speculate how Miletos could have been ruled by a tyranny for more than a century (ca. 605–499) without comment in a single extant author. Once the theory of stasis is removed, we are left assuming a traditional oligarchy by default. As a comparison, Thucydides himself (1.13) jumps directly from monarchy to tyranny, and people generally just explain away this leap (e.g., Gomme ad loc.). But Athens gives a well-documented, clear example of aristocratic or oligarchic rule between traditional kings and tyrants.

east-central Asia Minor, and with the rise in the seventh century of the powerful Lydian Empire to the west of the Phrygians, Milesian sovereignty suddenly came under attack. For the rest of the Archaic period, a principal concern of Milesian policy would be to maintain an independent position in the face of the increasing pressure felt from the growing powers of the East.

According to Herodotos, the Milesians faced their first real peril from King Gyges (ca. 680–645), the founder of the Mermnad dynasty in Lydia. He attacked Miletos and Smyrna, presumably unsuccessfully, and captured Kolophon (Hdt. 1.14.4). He may have reached some kind of agreement with the Milesians, because that same Gyges is said to have allowed Miletos to colonize Abydos in his territory on the Troad (Str. 13.1.22). Gyges met his death at the hands of the Kimmerian invaders in Asia Minor, who went on to burn the Lydian capital at Sardis (Hdt. 1.15). His son and successor, Ardys, attacked Miletos and seized nearby Priene. Little is said of Ardys's son, Sadyattes, except that he invaded Miletos regularly. The next king, Alyattes (ca. 610–560), was an active general: he fought the Medes, expelled the Kimmerians, captured Smyrna, attacked Klazomenai, and continued the ancestral war on Miletos (Hdt. 1.16–22). In this latter enterprise, he invaded Milesian territory every year, plundering the trees and crops before retiring. These raids continued for twelve years in all, six under Sadyattes and six under Alyattes.[61]

Herodotos makes the claim that τῆς γὰρ θαλάσσης οἱ Μιλήσιοι ἐπεκράτεον, ὥστε ἐπέδρης μὴ εἶναι ἔργον τῇ στρατιῇ [the Milesians had mastery over the sea, so that a proper siege would be futile for his [Alyattes's] army] (Hdt. 1.17.3). His statement implies that Miletos must have been protected by land as well, a conclusion that is verified by the digs on the south slope of Kalabaktepe. While no part of the sea wall running around the city peninsula dates before the late sixth century, archaeologists have found on the south slope of Kalabaktepe the remains of a fortification wall built shortly after 650 B.C.E. They presume that this land wall must have extended from the east shore through the Lion and Sacred Gates, down to the south slope of Kalabaktepe, and then over to the west coast. This extension from shore to shore cut off the city by land.[62]

---

61. The tradition preserved by Herodotos is open to charges at least of exaggeration, based on the theory that he is using these incidents to allude to events of his own day, when the Lakedaimonians were regularly invading Attika. See Moles 1996; Raaflaub 1987.

62. *Milet* 1.8.116–17; *Milet* 2.3.9–10, 118–20 (where it was thought to be a circuit around Kalabaktepe); esp. Müller-Wiener 1986a, 95–97; Graeve and Senff 1990; Graeve and Senff 1991; Cobet 1997.

According to Herodotos, peace between Miletos and Lydia arose in an odd fashion. During the twelfth year of the invasions, ca. 605 B.C.E., Lydians who were burning crops accidentally set fire to a temple of Athena in the town of Assessos in Milesian territory.[63] Soon afterward, the king fell very sick, and on applying to the Oracle at Delphi for healing, he was refused any answer until he rebuilt Athena's temple. Alyattes decided to sue for a temporary truce, so that he could rebuild the temple without harassment. In a story that bears the marks of a folktale, his heralds were received by the tyrant Thrasyboulos. Although the city was suffering greatly from the annual forays on their local grain supply, Thrasyboulos schemed to have all of the city's supplies brought out to a big public banquet, so that the heralds would see a city at ease, enjoying no great inconvenience from the Lydian raids. When these things were reported back to Alyattes, he was so disheartened that he abandoned his idea of a temporary truce and agreed to a permanent peace. Herodotos reports (1.22.4),

μετὰ δὲ ἥ τε διαλλαγή σφι ἐγένετο ἐπ' ᾧ τε ξείνους ἀλλήλοισι εἶναι καὶ συμμάχους, καὶ δύο τε ἀντὶ ἑνὸς νηοὺς τῇ Ἀθηναίῃ οἰκοδόμησε ὁ Ἀλυάττης ἐν τῇ Ἀσσησῷ, αὐτός τε ἐκ τῆς νούσου ἀνέστη.

[Afterward there was a reconciliation between them on the terms that they would be friends [xeinoi] and allies [symmachoi], and Alyattes built two temples in place of the one in Assessos, and he recovered his health.]

Thus Miletos became a friend and ally on equal footing with the Lydian king. However, this status was not to last under the next Lydian king, Kroisos (ca. 560–546). Herodotos says, πρὸ δὲ τῆς Κροίσου ἀρχῆς πάντες Ἕλληνες ἦσαν ἐλεύθεροι [Before the rule of Kroisos, all the Greeks were free] (Hdt. 1.6.3), but Kroisos took Ionia along with the rest of western Anatolia, by conquest: χρόνου δὲ ἐπιγενομένου καὶ κατεστραμμένων σχεδὸν πάντων τῶν ἐντὸς Ἅλυος ποταμοῦ οἰκημένων· [in the course of time, nearly all the peoples west of the river Halys had been subdued] (Hdt. 1.28). The terms of the subjection are not delineated in our sources, but Ionia certainly owed a financial tribute to its new master (Hdt. 1.6.2, 27.1), and it probably took part in his military levy as

---

63. For physical confirmation of the part of the story dealing with Assessos, see chap. 5.

well.[64] Nothing in Herodotos states directly that Kroisos changed the terms of the existing treaty with Miletos; the historian simply says that Kroisos conquered each Ionian city in turn and forced Ionia to pay tribute. There are no exceptions mentioned, and it is unlikely that the man who conquered all of western Asia would allow a prosperous commercial center in the midst of his holdings to avoid taxation. Miletos must be considered a tribute-paying ally by that time. However, Lydian control of Miletos did not last long: Kroisos soon moved to expand his empire to the east. When he turned against the Persian king, Cyrus, Kroisos could manage only a draw. He returned to Sardis and dispersed his troops for the winter, but Cyrus boldly followed, and the suddenness of his attack led to the capture of Sardis and the conquest of Lydia (ca. 547 B.C.E.).[65]

During his war with Lydia, Cyrus had sought to convince the Ionians to defect to the Persian side. The Ionians were not persuaded—an indication that they did not find Kroisos's rule too onerous or that they feared worse from the Persians—and, as a consequence, they now faced the anger of the Great King (Hdt. 1.76.3). When, after the fall of Sardis, the Ionians sent to Cyrus asking to submit on the same terms as they had received from Kroisos, the Persian refused. Under threat of attack, the cities of Ionia met together at the Panionion to decide their response.

The Ionian League, or the Panionion, apparently created as a reflection of the ethnic and cultural unity of the Ionian people, was a religious association that dated perhaps as early as the ninth century: certainly it was well established by the seventh. The name *Panionion* was also given to its meeting place on Mount Mykale, as described by Herodotos (1.148.1).

τὸ δὲ Πανιώνιόν ἐστι τῆς Μυκάλης χῶρος ἱρός, πρὸς ἄρκτον τετραμμένος, κοινῇ ἐξαραιρημένος ὑπὸ Ἰώνων Ποσειδέωνι Ἑλικωνίῳ· ἡ δὲ Μυκάλη ἐστὶ τῆς ἠπείρου ἄκρη πρὸς ζέφυρον ἄνεμον κατήκουσα Σάμῳ, ἐς τὴν συλλεγόμενοι ἀπὸ τῶν πολίων Ἴωνες ἄγεσκον ὁρτήν, τῇ ἔθεντο οὔνομα Πανιώνια.

[The Panionion is a sacred place on Mount Mykale, on the north slope, chosen in common by the Ionians for Poseidon Helikonios.

---

64. The evidence is ambiguous and may refer instead to mercenary troops. At Hdt. 1.77.4, Kroisos dismisses his army, ὅς ἦν αὐτοῦ ξεινικός. Ξεινικός can mean "allied," as at Thuc. 7.42, but the usual meaning is "mercenary" (*LSJ* s.v. ξενικός meaning 2).

65. Cook 1985, 210–14.

And Mykale is a peninsula of the mainland projecting out to the west toward Samos, and in this place the Ionians from the cities gather and are accustomed to celebrating the festival that is called Panionia.]

The site of the festival was found at Melie in the middle of the twentieth century, about 17 km. south of modern Kusadasi. For this festival, the Prienians probably supplied the priests, but because Samos and Priene fought repeatedly over the site, the festival was moved before the mid-fifth century to a location near Ephesos. The list of members admits some small variation but is usually restricted to these twelve: Miletos, Myous, Priene, Ephesos, Kolophon, Lebedos, Teos, Klazomenai, Phokaia, Samos, Chios, and Erythrai (Hdt. 1.142–48).[66]

The Panionion was not originally a political or military organization: when the Lydians were attacking the cities of Asia Minor, there was no sign of any collective response.[67] Miletos, Kolophon, Priene, and Klazomenai were individually attacked by the predecessors of Kroisos. In the case of Miletos, only Chios came to its aid, and this because Miletos had previously assisted the Chians in a war against Erythrai (Hdt. 1.14.4–22, esp. 1.18.3). Kroisos attacked Ephesos and then each of the Ionian and Aeolian cities individually (Hdt. 1.26.3). The weakness inherent in disunity did not escape Herodotos, who records a conversation among the Ionians in which Thales of Miletos, one of the Seven Sages, suggests that they form a common government at a central location, the city of Teos. Thales probably never proposed this scheme: the speech fits too neatly into the pattern of Herodotean "wise adviser" speeches, which serve the narrative function of giving useful advice that will be disregarded.[68] It does suggest that Herodotos believed that the best course was to unite: they could have experienced a *synoikism* and become a politically unified Ionian state, but this unprecedented step was not appealing to the independent-minded poleis. Nowhere did the Ionians act together until Cyrus refused to give them terms and the Ionians met at the Panionion to

66. *PECS* 671 (site); Str. 8.7.2, 14.1.20; D.S. 15.49.1. Cf. Thuc. 3.104; *IvPriene* #35. Kleiner, Hommel, and Müller-Wiener (1967, 6–9, 91–93) argue that the Ionian League probably existed in some form by the time of the ca. 700 B.C.E. destruction of Melie (Vitr. 4.1; *IvPriene* #37). Cf. Tausend 1992, 90–95; Cook 1962, 803; Roebuck 1959, 9–10; Roebuck 1955; Lenschau 1944; Caspari 1915; Wilamowitz-Moellendorff 1906a.

67. Lateiner 1982, 132–34 (religious); Roebuck 1955, 26 (nonreligious); Caspari 1915 (political).

68. Lattimore 1939; Lang 1968, 29–30; Lang 1984, 55.

decide what to do. Even then, they did not present a united front, because the Milesians did not attend the meeting. Miletos had made a separate peace with the Persians: for unspecified reasons, Cyrus granted to Miletos alone the terms they had enjoyed under Kroisos. Thus, the Milesians were satisfied and refused to take part in the Panionian council (Hdt. 1.141–52). Deeply disadvantaged by the loss of its leading member, the league nevertheless resolved to send envoys to Sparta to beg for military aid, which was never produced.

Despite its efforts, the Panionion was a complete failure as a political or military organization. The cities of Ionia faced Cyrus individually, and each fell in turn. The Persians reduced all of Ionia except Miletos, with its favorable terms, and Teos and Phokaia, whose inhabitants fled rather than be subjugated—the Teians to refound their failed Thracian colony, Abdera, and the Phokaians to the far west (Hdt. 1.161–69).[69] It is reported that the islanders were so afraid that they surrendered as well (Hdt. 1.169.2), but this statement—if accurate—can only refer to the islands immediately off the coast, such as Leros and the other small islands in Milesian territory. The Persians had no fleet to speak of, and large islands like Samos and Chios are unlikely to have felt intimidated into surrendering their freedom without a direct threat.[70] The more distant of the Kyklades were entirely uninvolved.

Although its individual members were defeated, Herodotos tells us that the Ionian League continued to meet (1.170.1). That Cyrus allowed them to do so is the final, conclusive sign that the league was first and foremost religious in nature. Cyrus had a policy of promoting religious institutions in the conquered territories,[71] but he was not likely to tolerate a political organization that might stand as a threat to his mastery of Ionia. Of course, the Ionians probably still used these meetings to talk about the problem posed by the Persians: one story, which may well be false—it features the "wise adviser" motif again—recounts a gathering after the Persian conquest, when Bias of Priene is supposed to have suggested that the only way the Ionians would ever regain their freedom

69. Demand 1990, 34–44.
70. The islanders may not even have participated in the Panionion meetings against Cyrus, since they may not have felt too threatened by this land power. Samos was probably attacked in the 540s, along with the rest of Ionia, but it was not taken until after the death of Polykrates in 522, when the Persians helped Syloson obtain the tyranny there. According to Herodotos (3.149), they handed it over to Syloson after they had swept the island clean of people, in a process like gathering fish into a net. See Shipley 1987, 78–90.
71. Wiesehöfer 1987; Cook 1983, 41.

would be to stage a mass migration of all Ionians to Sicily, a proposal Herodotos praises very highly (Hdt. 1.170.2). However, no remedy was ever taken, and the Panionion remained politically impotent.

As part of the Persian Empire, the Ionian cities, and so also Miletos, were subject to the wishes of the Great King, but in its early days his empire was not well organized. Certainly it seems that Cyrus preferred to rule through his own governors rather than through vassals, although those governors were not necessarily Persian. However, both Cyrus and his immediate successor, Kambyses, were so consumed by nearly unceasing wars of conquest from Thrace to Egypt that they had little time for real administration, leaving the door open for local corruption and opposition. Subsequently, the Persian king Dareios changed all that. He came to the throne through a military coup in 522, and initially he too faced constant war: he boasts about having defeated nineteen enemies and captured nine kings all in the space of a single year. After his famed expedition against the Skythians in ca. 513, Dareios settled down in a period of comparative peace.[72]

At some point in his reign, Dareios reformed the organization of Persian rule; it may have occurred immediately after he took the throne, as Herodotos reports, or as late as 493 B.C.E., when Ionia was reassessed after the Ionian Revolt (Hdt. 6.43).[73] Dareios's reorganization consisted of a redivision of the satrapies, splitting up some and joining together others along traditional ethnic or national lines, and the determination of a fixed tribute based on the productive capacity of the region. He appointed a governor for each satrapy, usually a high Persian official and often a relative of the Great King himself. This satrap was responsible to the king for the payment of the annual tribute, the raising of military levies, the administration of justice, security, and the entertainment of visiting Persian nobility.[74] There was no uniform administrative organization within the various satrapies; rather, each was governed in a way best

---

72. Cook 1983, 41–42 (governors), 56 (Dareios).

73. Even before Dareios, the Persian Empire was split into administrative units called satrapies by the Persians and *archai* by the Greeks, and each satrapy was ruled by a satrap or archon. See Kuhrt 1988, 130–32; Young 1988, 87–91.

74. The allied payment of tribute and military service both date back at least to Kambyses, because on his death, a pretender to the throne declared a three years' remission of military service and tribute (ἀτελείην εἶναι στρατηίης καὶ φόρου ἐπ' ἔτεα τρία), thus earning popularity with all the subjects under his rule except the Persians (Hdt. 3.67.3). For the reorganization in general, see the larger discussions in Cook 1983, 167–82; Cook 1985, 267–77; Petit 1985; Harris 1971, 95–96; Cameron 1973.

fitting to the makeup of its constituency. In western Asia Minor, the satraps generally did not act through lieutenants but rather conducted internal affairs themselves, while garrisons with separate military commanders were often present at important cities and frontier posts.[75] Miletos and the other cities of Ionia were grouped in a satrapy with the Aiolians, Carians, Lykians, Milyans, and Pamphylians. Its seat was at Sardis, which housed a garrison, and in 500 B.C.E. the satrap was Artaphernes, a full brother of Dareios (Hdt. 5.25.1).

Thus Miletos and the rest of the mainland Ionian cities lost their independence in the central decades of the sixth century. They were not destroyed or even significantly damaged at that time, but they did owe both money and troops to the Persian king. Their external affairs were subject to his dictates, and as we shall see, even their internal politics took a turn for the worse as a result of the conquest. Ionia would never again achieve the kind of commercial and intellectual prosperity it had known in the past, and it would never again enjoy political independence. While "Freedom of the Greeks"—meaning the freedom of the Ionians—would become a rallying cry for Greek military operations in the fifth century, especially during the Peloponnesian War, it was never to be. Ionia merely wound up trading one master, Persia, for another, Athens, until, by the end of the fifth century, it found itself firmly ensconced back in Persian hands.

---

75. Xen. *Cyr.* 8.6; Petit 1985; Corsaro 1985 (taxes); Cook 1983, 173, 176 (satraps), 84 (garrisons); Armayor 1978. The two chief sources for the information on satrapies are the Behistun Inscription and Herodotos (3.90–97, 7.61–95).

4

Ionian Revolt and Refoundation

The decades after the Persian conquest were some of the most eventful in Milesian history. Although at first Miletos fared well under Persian control, enjoying the same terms under Dareios as it had under the Lydians, its days of growth and expansion were past. The city's economic opportunities were beginning to be curtailed, with most colonization ending and with its rival powers growing in influence in the Aegean. This was also a time of significant political change for Miletos, as it came to be ruled by tyrants. We cannot say exactly when they arose or whether they were directly established by the Persians. Certainly they received Persian support. In any case, the Milesians and the other Ionians came to resent these tyrants—their own countrymen—so much that they were willing to risk everything to be rid of them. Across Asia Minor, hostility toward the tyrants embroiled the Greeks in a revolt against the Persians that brought catastrophic consequences. Ionia was recaptured and punished by the Persians, and as instigator and leader of the revolt, Miletos was treated most harshly: in 494 the city was completely depopulated and razed to the ground. The setback was monumental, and Miletos would never again be a leading political power, but its return to prosperity was remarkable. Rebuilding their home from the ground up, the Milesians created a city that served as a model of urban planning for the rest of the Greek world for centuries to come.

The Ionian Revolt

Miletos reached its economic peak just before the Persian takeover, but the last half of the sixth century was marked by clear indications that loss of sovereignty was accompanied by a certain decrease in prosperity. There was no sharp economic collapse, but signs reveal that Milesian power was beginning to wane at long last. In the middle of the sixth century, the Milesian monopoly on Black Sea colonization was broken, and Miletos also faced growing rivalry from other Hellenic cities and was cut off from some traditional trade partners. In the late sixth century, Athens especially succeeded in displacing much of the Milesian trade at Naukratis and also to some extent in the northeast, where Attic pottery was becoming quite common. Peisistratos sent the elder Miltiades to take over the Thracian Chersonese (Hdt. 6.34), thus controlling access to the Propontis and cutting further into Milesian trade and dominance. Moreover, at this time, Polykrates, the tyrant of Samos, was exploiting the traditional rivalry with Miletos through piracy, attacking Milesian trade with his fleet (Hdt. 3.39; cf. Ath. 12.540d). Another blow to Milesian commerce was the destruction of Sybaris, Miletos's illustrious trading partner in the west, in 510 (Hdt. 5.44). Thus, in the years after 540, Milesian prosperity was threatened by changing economic circumstances.[1]

During the 540s, the Milesian government also experienced a transformation when the traditional oligarchy was put aside in favor of a tyrant, a situation that was repeated in many of the Ionian Greek cities under the Persian Empire. Persian-backed tyrannies did irreparable harm to the civic life of the poleis in the last half of the sixth century and were probably the most onerous feature of Persian rule. These tyrants might have been directly established by Persian policy; once inaugurated, they were maintained by Persian support. Many of them were harshly despotic, governing more in their own self-interest than for the benefit of their citizens.[2]

The nature of their rule is vividly illustrated by Herodotos (book 4) in the episode of the Istrian Bridge, ca. 513, during Dareios's invasion of

---

1. Georges (2000) argues for increased prosperity of the Ionians in general after the Persian takeover, but his evidence for Miletos specifically (pp. 10–12) is not strong. First, he says that the Milesian acquisition of Myrkinos gave them an inroad into the profitable Thracian silver trade, but he fails to note that the settlement was a failure and that Histiaios was soon recalled. Second, he points out the preeminence of the Milesian colonization movement but neglects to mention that the movement for all intents and purposes ended by the middle of the sixth century. Third, the Milesian possession of Didyma put them in a very favorable position, with which one cannot quarrel. Finally, Georges believes that Miletos was an "independent native dynasty" that payed no tribute to Persia, which is probably not true: Herodotos never specifically mentions Milesian tribute, but Miletos probably began paying tribute under the stricter policies of Kroisos. See chap. 3.

2. Georges 2000, 19–23.

Skythia.[3] The king is said to have gathered for this campaign a large land force along with a fleet provided by the Greeks from Ionia, Aiolia, and the Hellespont (Hdt. 4.83ff.). Dareios entered Skythia by way of a bridge over the Istros (Danube) River, which was assigned to the protection of the Ionians for the next sixty days. When they had waited for the appointed length of time and the king had still not returned, the Greek commanders considered abandoning the bridge and returning home. In the context of this debate, Herodotos first introduces Histiaios, the tyrant of Miletos. Herodotos reports (4.137.2) that Histiaios persuaded his fellow commanders that it was in their best interest to support the Persian king,

λέγοντος ὡς νῦν μὲν διὰ Δαρεῖον ἕκαστος αὐτῶν τυραννεύει πόλιος, τῆς Δαρείου δὲ δυνάμιος καταιρεθείσης οὔτε αὐτὸς Μιλησίων οἷός τε ἔσεσθαι ἄρχειν οὔτε ἄλλον οὐδένα οὐδαμῶν βουλήσεσθαι· γὰρ ἑκάστην τῶν πολίων δημοκρατέεσθαι μᾶλλον ἢ τυραννεύεσθαι.

[saying that at the present each one of them owed his position as tyrant of his city to Dareios, and if the power of Dareios should be destroyed, he himself would be unable to rule Miletos and none of them would be able to rule his own city—for each of the cities would prefer to be ruled democratically than by a tyranny.][4]

Histiaios won over all of the assembled leaders—tyrants like himself—to his point of view, so that when Dareios finally appeared, he was able to recross the Istros to safety. Thus they preserved the king along with their own tyrannies at home.

---

3. All Herodotean accounts—especially the earlier ones—are open to modern charges of embellishment, since he had historiographic goals other than a precise recounting of events. The question of accuracy is often unanswerable. I err on the side of trusting Herodotos, for, if we start doubting reports about fairly recent times that are both detailed and plausible, we find ourselves on a slippery slope, not knowing when and how to stop. See, for example, the discussion later in this chapter about the depopulation of Miletos in 494: when two passages seem to contradict, scholars arbitrarily choose which one to accept, instead of establishing genuine principles by which to judge them or finding a plausible way to retain both accounts.

4. D. Graf (1985, 81) claims this speech is anachronistic, suggesting more the political atmosphere of Herodotos's own time than the events at the Skythian bridge. Cf. Andrewes 1956, 124.

The incident at the bridge demonstrates Herodotos's view of the relationship between the Persian king and the Ionian tyrants: they could not hope to maintain control of their cities if the power of the Persians was broken. Not only did Dareios support them, but he even felt free to set up individual tyrants against the wishes of their own peoples. When Koes of Mytilene, who had suggested that the Ionians be left at the bridge as a rear guard, was asked what reward he desired for his good advice, he replied that he wanted to be made tyrant of Mytilene (Hdt. 5.11). As a result, the government of Mytilene was arbitrarily replaced. Similarly, Dareios installed Syloson to power at Samos in exchange for an earlier favor (Hdt. 3.139–49).

The reasonable conclusion from Herodotos's evidence is that Ionian tyrants at the end of the sixth century were more loyal to the Persian king than to their own cities. Unlike the earlier Greek tyrants who achieved power through factional or popular backing, the Ionian tyrants at the end of the sixth century were chiefly occupied with pleasing the Persians to maintain their own position. This is not to say that all Greek cities under Persian control received tyrants or that all tyrants in those cities were put in place by the Persians. The older view has been that Persia, as part of a sweeping governmental and satrapal reform, had a policy of imposing tyrants on the Ionian cities and perhaps retaining some previously existing tyrants.[5] New studies have argued for a more moderate position: the Persian king supported some tyrants in cities where they already existed and set up some others. But some cities also remained free of tyranny (Ephesos is a conspicuous example), suggesting that the Persian king did not change the government of subject cities arbitrarily.[6] Histiaios's comments at the bridge are in harmony with this revised view. He says not that Dareios made them all tyrants but rather that they were able to maintain their tyrannies only with the backing of the king.[7] Histiaios's words imply that the tyrants faced a great deal of hostility in their own cities. It seems that once the tyrants could rely on the support of the king,

---

5. Balcer (1984b, 208) states the extreme view: the tyrants "did not arise internally but were imposed externally upon the poleis." See also Mazzarino 1947, 244–45; Andrewes 1956, 117, 123; Harris 1971, 96–104; Berve 1967, 1:85; Jeffrey 1976, 219; Tozzi 1978, 121; Gillis 1979, 10; Emlyn-Jones 1980, 33–34; Boffo 1983, 59–61; Burn 1985, 295; Georges 2000.

6. Graf 1985; Austin 1990.

7. Cf. Ure 1922, 268–71. D. Graf (1985, 86) has interpreted the passage poorly when he refers to Herodotos's thesis that "the tyrants in Ionia or elsewhere in Asia were appointees of the new king."

they could and did use their power in their home cities beyond what was tolerable to their people. The dissatisfaction of the Greeks with their rulers is seen clearly in the outbreak and spread of the great rebellion known as the Ionian Revolt.

Paradoxically, the architect of the revolt was another tyrant of Miletos, Aristagoras, son of Molpagoras. When Histiaios went to Thrace to occupy Myrkinos, the town given to him for his good advice at the bridge, he chose his son-in-law and nephew, Aristagoras, to rule Miletos in his stead, giving him the title *epitropos* ("guardian" or "deputy"), although Herodotos usually simply calls him "tyrant" or "king." Aristagoras's position became permanent when Histiaios was recalled to the Persian court to serve as an adviser to the king. According to the story Herodotos tells, he was brought back not because of his qualities as a counselor but rather because of suspicions against his loyalty that were harbored by the Persian general Megabazos.[8] In the narrative as it stands, Histiaios did nothing at Myrkinos that could be viewed as disloyal, yet Megabazos was greatly alarmed by τὸ ποιεύμενον [what he was doing] (Hdt. 5.23.1). Presumably Herodotos means the fortification of Myrkinos, the only specific activity mentioned. Yet this site, on the edge of the Persian domain and in the midst of untamed Thracian tribes, would require fortification. Megabazos may have used concerns about the fortification as a ruse to disguise his objection to Histiaios's very presence in Thrace. Dareios had made Megabazos the Persian commander in the Hellespont and in Thrace (Hdt. 4.143–44, 5.2) before Myrkinos was given to Histiaios (Hdt. 5.11). Megabazos could have seen Histiaios's presence as an encroachment on his own sphere of command by a Greek tyrant who had an overexaggerated sense of his own self-worth.[9]

Megabazos arranged for Histiaios's recall to Susa by complaining to Dareios that it was folly to entrust the wealth and divergent populations of Thrace to a clever Greek (ἀνδρὶ Ἕλληνι δεινῷ τε καὶ σοφῷ, Hdt. 5.23.2) who might well lead Persian subjects against the king in a civil war (οἰκηίῳ πολέμῳ, Hdt. 5.23.3). While emphasizing that Histiaios was a Greek and therefore not to be trusted, Megabazos also suggested that the neighboring peoples would eagerly take Histiaios as their leader and obey his every word (5.23.2). However, Herodotos had just described how the

---

8. Hdt. 5.11, 23–24. Heinlein (1909, 341–44) attempts to redate all these events.

9. For the rivalry between Ionian (esp. Milesian) tyrants and Persian nobles, see Georges 2000, 12–19.

Thracians would, in his opinion, be the strongest people in the world if they could be united but that this unity was impossible, so they would remain forever weak (Hdt. 5.3). Obviously he did not place much stock in the argument that he put into the mouth of Megabazos. Although Histiaios was recalled, it is difficult to believe that Dareios seriously questioned his loyalty. On the contrary, Dareios's trust in Histiaios was demonstrated by the thirteen or more years during which he counseled Dareios as well as by the fact that when Miletos later revolted, Dareios sent the Milesian to help stop the insurrection in Histiaios's own home city, an unthinkably foolish assignment if the king had any doubts about his allegiance.[10]

Miletos was in the hands of Aristagoras when, in 500 B.C.E., a faction of rich Naxian exiles arrived in Miletos and approached the ruler on account of the guest-friendship they held with his kinsman Histiaios. They asked for Aristagoras's help in regaining their city (Hdt. 5.30.1–3), and this request set in motion the chain of events that would lead to rebellion. In reviewing the petition, Aristagoras saw an opportunity for himself, ὁ δὲ ἐπιλεξάμενος ὡς, ἢν δι᾽ αὐτοῦ κατέλθωσι ἐς τὴν πόλιν, ἄρξει τῆς Νάξου [thinking that if they return to their city with his aid, he will rule Naxos] (Hdt. 5.30.3). He must have believed that, in exchange for bringing Naxos under Persian rule, Dareios would put him in control there, perhaps by annexing Naxos to Milesian territory. Consistent with this plan, Aristagoras used the guest-friendship as a pretext for helping the Naxian exiles (σκῆψιν δὲ ποιεύμενος τὴν ξεινίην τὴν Ἱστιαίου, Hdt. 5.30.3) but immediately referred the matter to Persia, knowing that he had insufficient troops to deal with it himself.

Aristagoras approached Artaphernes, the satrap at Sardis, asking for one hundred ships to use against Naxos. He began by describing the wealth of Naxos that Persia stood to gain, adding that he and the exiles would be responsible for the costs of the expedition. Furthermore, he claimed that the rest of the Kyklades would fall to Persia at the same time as Naxos and that, from there, Euboia would be an easy step (Hdt. 5.31). Induced by these arguments, the satrap leaped at the opportunity to please his king: he immediately agreed to the plan, pending the king's approval, and promised to have not one hundred but two hundred ships ready in the

---

10. Some argue that Histiaios's stay in Susa was a "golden cage," designed to keep him out of trouble. However, as an enemy, he would have been both inconsequential in the vastness of the Persian Empire and entirely disposable, but as a friend who offered sage advise, he would have been invaluable.

spring of 499. These were to oppose the eight thousand soldiers and the large fleet possessed by Naxos (Hdt. 5.30.4, 5.31.3–32).

In Herodotos's account, the fleet commanders, Aristagoras and Megabates, a high-ranking Persian, hoped to take Naxos by surprise and avoid a siege. However, the expedition was troubled from the beginning. Aristagoras and Megabates quarreled over the supreme command of the fleet, and when they arrived at Naxos, they found the islanders prepared for their assault. After only four months, they ran out of supplies, and Aristagoras had spent all his money (Hdt. 5.34.3). The expedition failed through lack of resources. Aristagoras panicked. He feared that he would lose his power at Miletos both because he was unable to pay the debt owed to Artaphernes and because he had clashed with a Persian general. Since he was about to lose Persian backing for his power, he took the drastic step of revolting from Persia. Thus, according to Herodotos, the Ionian Revolt took its start from the disappointed personal ambition of Aristagoras, who was in no way motivated by an ideological opposition to the Persian rule of Ionia. He was inspired by self-preservation in the face of a threat to his power caused by his own failure.

Herodotos maintains that, from his place at the court in Susa, Histiaios was a second instigator of the revolt. In addition to mentioning Megabazos's earlier suspicions about Histiaios's loyalty, Herodotos says that Histiaios sent to Aristagoras a slave whose head was tattooed with a message to revolt. This episode has the ring of a folktale, very similar to the tales of the message sent from Harpagos to Cyrus inside a hare (Hdt. 1.23.3–24) and the message sent by Demaratos to Sparta on the wood underneath the wax of some tablets (Hdt. 7.239). Its authenticity must be questioned.[11] Apart from this implausible story, at no time in Herodotos's narrative did Histiaios and Aristagoras act in concert; they were not even reported to be at the same place at the same time. We may conclude that Histiaios was loyal to Persia even after his recall from Myrkinos and had no part in the start of the rebellion.[12] That role belonged entirely to Aristagoras.

Aristagoras knew that to maintain his rule, without Persian backing, he needed to make his rule palatable to the Milesian people. Therefore, he

---

11. Chapman 1972, 559; Heinlein 1909, 346; de Sanctis 1931, 60; Tozzi 1977; Tozzi 1978, 139–41; Foucault 1967.

12. Manville 1977 (rivals); Chapman 1972, 546–63 (loyal); Georges 2000, 28–33 (loyal). Blamire (1959, 142–47) and Evans (1963, 113–18) argue that Histiaios was loyal only up through his recall from Myrkinos.

summoned a meeting with his partisans (5.36.1) to decide how best to achieve popular support. Herodotos mentions only the geographer Hekataios by name, but this group was a political faction, presumably the same group that Aristagoras later convened before fleeing Miletos permanently (5.124–26). First, they agreed with his decision to revolt; Hekataios alone dissented. Next, they sent to seize the commanders of the fleet that had just returned from Naxos. Finally, reports Herodotos (5.37.2), Aristagoras declared open rebellion and, turning to the people of Miletos, instituted an apparent change in government.

καὶ πρῶτα μὲν λόγῳ μετεὶς τὴν τυραννίδα ἰσονομίην ἐποίεε τῇ Μιλήτῳ, ὡς ἂν ἑκόντες αὐτῷ οἱ Μιλήσιοι συναπισταίατο.

[And first, after putting aside the tyranny at least in word, he set up *isonomia* so that the Milesians would be willing to revolt with him.]

The precise meaning of *isonomia* here is difficult to evaluate. Some scholars equate it with democracy;[13] however, the term itself is probably being used anachronistically and may mean that Aristagoras simply opened the way to political power to a larger number of his fellow citizens. It may represent not an actual democracy but rather a slogan designed to win over popular support. No doubt Aristagoras intended to hold onto the reins of power despite the change. He only gave up his rule λόγῳ, "in word" or "allegedly."[14]

Aristagoras's declaration of *isonomia* indicates that he recognized the unpopularity of tyranny. More than a decade earlier, Histiaios had argued that if given a chance, the Ionian cities would all democratize.[15] Now Aristagoras gave them that opportunity when he used his faction to capture the tyrants who led the naval contingents against Naxos (Hdt. 5.37.1). Many commanders were captured. Most were allowed to leave their cities, but Koes of Mytilene was stoned to death by his own people (Hdt. 5.37.2). By freeing the cities of their tyrants, Aristagoras enabled them to establish new governments. Thus, the rebellion against Persia could in no way be separated from the revolutions that broke out through-

---

13. Vlastos 1953, 337; Hansen 1986.
14. Cf. Hdt. 8.68γ, 1.59.3.
15. The term *isonomia* may here represent an anachronism: they were seeking not necessarily a true democracy but rather a widening of power.

out Ionia: it was primarily the behavior of the tyrants and only second-arily the overlordship of Persia itself that the people found offensive.[16]

Once underway, the Ionian Revolt proved momentous, lasting more than five years and encompassing most of western Anatolia, including both Greek and barbarian in the uprising. Although Herodotos nowhere records a complete catalog of cities in the Ionian Revolt, he mentions in the course of his narrative many allies: the Ionian cities of Ephesos (5.100), Samos (5.112.1), Klazomenai (5.123), Priene, Myous, Teos, Chios, Erythrai, and Phokaia (6.8), as well as "the Ionian cities on the mainland" (6.31.2); Byzantion (6.33.2), Dardanos, Abydos, Perkote, Lampsakos, and Paisos on the Hellespont (5.117); Aiolians on Lesbos (6.8) and at Mytilene in particular (5.37), on Tenedos (6.31.2), at Kyme (5.37, 123), and in the Troad (5.122.2); native Gergithes near Troy; Mylasa and Termera (5.37); Kaunos (5.103.2); Kios in Mysia (5.122.1); much of Caria (5.103.2); and all of Cyprus except Amathos (5.104.1).

At the beginning of the revolt, Aristagoras went on an embassy, seek-ing allies also from mainland Greece (Hdt. 5.38–97). He stopped first at Sparta, the most powerful Greek city, which was known for its anti-tyrannical efforts (Hdt. 5.49.3; Thuc. 1.18). Aristagoras's petition was rejected there because it involved sending the Lakedaimonian army too far abroad. He then brought his case to Athens, the second most powerful city (Hdt. 5.97), where his appeal resulted in the promise of twenty ships. For Herodotos, the importance of the embassy lay in this small success. He portrays the Athenian involvement in the Ionian Revolt as the cause of the later Persian invasions of the mainland (Hdt. 5.97.3, 5.105),[17] which is the major theme of his *Histories:* αὗται δὲ αἱ νέες ἀρχὴ κακῶν ἐγένοντο Ἕλλησί τε καὶ βαρβάροισι [these ships were the beginning of evils for both the Greeks and the barbarians] (Hdt. 5.97.3). Finally, Eretria sent five ships to Miletos in return for the service rendered by Miletos during the Lelantine War centuries earlier (Hdt. 5.99.1).

---

16. Georges 2000. Georges suggests that the Ionians wished not to fight Persia but only to rid themselves of the tyrants. Aristagoras drummed up support over in Athens and Eretria as a way of forcing the Ionian hand and starting the conflict. Berve (1967, 1:118; cf. 104) believes that the tyrants were not unpopular, because they were restrained by Persia and because the Ionians were not politically ambitious. Rather, he argues, the people revolted to remove Persian limitations on Ionian commerce. Cf. Hegyi 1966, 292–94; Tozzi 1978, 116–18, 123–25; Murray 1988, 477–79.

17. He does this despite the story that Dareios's interest in Greece dated back to the beginning of his reign (Hdt. 3.137). Cf. Hdt. 6.48–49, 8.22.2. For the Ionian Revolt, see Murray 1988; Tozzi 1978; Meiggs 1972, 23–41.

Herodotos is sparing in his details about the campaigns of the rebellion, and his chronology of events is sketchy at best.[18] A surprise attack in the first year of campaigning resulted in the burning of Sardis and a great victory for the rebellion. It was followed by a battle on Cyprus, which was won on the sea by the Ionians but on land by the Persians. Meanwhile, on the mainland, a counteroffensive led by Dareios's three sons-in-law resulted in the crushing of the Carian resistance and the accompanying Milesian allies. Finally, the Persians decided to move against Miletos, the home of the revolt, and they prepared for an all-out sea battle against the entire allied fleet off the island of Lade in 494 B.C.E.

Whenever a number of states are cooperating against a common enemy, some measure of organization must be present, and in this instance, there are several reasons to believe that much of the joint effort of the rebels was organized through the Panionion. First, Herodotos repeatedly refers to the forces arrayed against Persia as "the Ionians" (Hdt. 5.100, 101.3, 102.2, and passim), and at the defense of Cyprus, the allies reported that they had received their orders not from Aristagoras but from τὸ κοινὸν τῶν Ἰώνων [the common council of the Ionians] (Hdt. 5.109.3).[19] Second, when the allies were preparing for the Battle of Lade, the Ionians sent representatives to the meeting of the Panionion at Melie to debate strategy for opposing the Persians (Hdt. 6.7). Third, with the exception of Aiolian Lesbos, the only allies present at Lade were members of the Ionian League: Miletos, Priene, Myous, Teos, Chios, Erythrai, Phokaia, and Samos (Hdt. 6.8). Finally, the coinage issued by the Ionians at that time was a well-marked, homogeneous series of electrum staters, all issued on the Milesian standard and all bearing an incuse square divided into four squares on the reverse and marked on the obverse with the symbols of various cities. By reverting from silver to electrum and by returning to a Milesian standard, the Ionians were proclaiming a kind of independence, returning to the coining methods they had practiced before the coming of Persia.[20]

None of these four factors—the nomenclature, the meeting at Melie,

18. How and Wells 1912, *ad* 5.33; Macan 1895, app. 5; Stein 1894, *ad* 5.33; Grundy 1901, 84–141.

19. Busolt 1893, 2:1283 n. 3 (uses of the word *koinon* in Greek politics).

20. Gardner 1908, 119–22; Gardner 1911; Gardner 1913; Gardner 1918, 92–100; Caspari 1915, 178–83; Seltman 1933, 86–89; Nenci 1962; Meiggs 1972, 441–42 n. 25; Kraay 1976, 20–40; Carradice and Price 1988, 33. Graf (1985, 85 esp. n. 22) minimizes the association of the coinage with the revolt.

the array of forces at Lade, or the uniform series of staters—makes good sense except in the context of a military operation that was being decided by a council made up from the members of the Ionian League. Therefore, we must conclude that at the very least, from the time of the Cypriot campaign, which may have occurred a year or more after the siege of Sardis (Hdt. 5.109.3), until the Battle of Lade, the Ionian League acted for the first and only time in its known history as an organized and competent military unit.

The role of Miletos in that league is more tenuously understood. For example, on one occasion after a number of allied losses, when Persia invaded Caria, the Carians were aided not by "the Ionians" but by Μιλήσιοί τε καὶ οἱ τούτων σύμμαχοι [the Milesians and their allies] (Hdt. 5.120). This phrase is reminiscent of the designations for the Peloponnesian League (Λακεδαιμόνιοί τε καὶ οἱ σύμμαχοι, Hdt. 8.142.4; cf. 7.157.1) and the later Delian League (οἱ Ἀθηναῖοι καὶ οἱ ξύμμαχοι, Thuc. 3.90.3 and passim), leading to the question of whether Miletos may have played a hegemonial role in the Ionian League. Certainly the prominence of Miletos was recognized by the allies, who followed the lead of Aristagoras in starting the rebellion and accepted his appointees for commanders in the initial campaign (Hdt. 5.99), and also by the Persians, who made Miletos the ultimate object of their attack. But the formal role of Miletos is less certain.

Miletos is not known to have possessed any prerogatives of a league hegemon.[21] Although the common foreign policy of opposition to Persia was instigated by Miletos, one cannot claim that it was dictated by that city. We know nothing about a Milesian role in summoning, chairing, or voting in league congresses, only the bare fact that the league met annually to celebrate a religious festival, the Panionia. Miletos did not monopolize military command. Aristagoras appointed the commanders for the initial expedition (Hdt. 5.99.2), but at the Battle of Lade, the allies as a whole elected the commander, and he was a Phokaian (Hdt. 6.11–12). In this decision, the Milesians had no greater influence over the voting than had the other Ionians. Finally, the Ionian League met to decide general strategy, both when they sent their navy to Cyprus (Hdt. 5.109.3) and when they decided to face the Persians at Lade (Hdt. 6.7).

21. Cf. the Peloponnesian League (Ste. Croix 1972, 108–12; Larsen 1932; Larsen 1933; Larsen 1934; Hammond 1967, 166–68, 195) and the Delian League (Hammond 1967, 256–58; Meiggs 1972; Schuller 1974; Powell 1988, 1–58).

Thus, there is no extant tradition of a hegemonial structure in the Ionian League, and the scanty information that Herodotos offers indicates quite the opposite: the alliance was made up of autonomous states, all equally empowered. Herodotos's one reference to "the Milesians and their allies," made during his discussion of the Carian expedition, must be taken to mean that only the Milesians and a few others went to Caria, since this campaign occurred at a time when the Ionian forces had dispersed after the Cypriot expedition. The specific mention of the Milesians may serve additionally as a rhetorical device to heighten the effect of the slaughter that the Milesians were about to suffer. Herodotos rarely mentions the names of individual cities when narrating the events of the Ionian Revolt. The Milesians only earn this honor here, in the battle for Caria, and this because they suffered so badly: πεσόντων δὲ τῶν πάντων πολλῶν μάλιστα Μιλήσιοι ἐπλήγησαν [while all were defeated, the Milesians were stricken the worst of all] (Hdt. 5.120).

So why was Aristagoras allowed to conduct an embassy to the mainland and appoint the commanders at the start of the revolt? Perhaps the authority came to him, just as to the Phokaian commander at Lade, through a vote of the league congress. When he sought to unite the Ionian cities in opposition to Persia, Aristagoras would have turned naturally to an organization that was already in place and that provided a link between the Greek cities of southern Asia Minor, regardless of the previous nature of that organization. After all, the league had already demonstrated the potential for political action during the Persian conquest, when it voted on sending an embassy to Sparta (Hdt. 1.141–52, 170). If Aristagoras did appeal to the Ionian League to organize the revolt against Persia, it would not be surprising if the league turned over the actual leadership for this venture to Aristagoras. Such an assumption would explain the subsequent actions of Aristagoras: how he was so easily able to stir up rebellion in all Ionia simultaneously; by what authority he ordered generals to be appointed in all the cities while he himself went as envoy to Greece; and why he was allowed to appoint other Milesians (including his own brother) as commanders of the expedition against Sardis despite his own conspicuous absence.[22] (According to Plutarch [*de mal. Her.* 24=861b], the siege of Sardis was undertaken to relieve a Persian siege of Miletos: if this is true, Aristagoras may have been leading the defense of his own city.)

---

22. Murray 1988, 480.

In short, the Ionians had no compelling reason to accept the command of Aristagoras unless he had received that authority officially from their own representatives in the Ionian League. Moreover, since the league was commanding the forces at Cyprus before the flight of Aristagoras from Ionia, it would be simpler to envision that the individual who had started the revolt was cooperating with the body directing it than to assume a tacit transition of power from the individual to the organization in the middle of the rebellion. It is very likely that at the inception of the Ionian Revolt and at the provocation of Aristagoras, the league found the impetus to exercise its newfound authority and military capability in leading the rebellion. Certainly, despite the prominent role played by Aristagoras in sparking the revolt, once the military action began, he disappeared entirely from Herodotos's narrative until he fled to Myrkinos. The date is uncertain; it may have been as early as 497 B.C.E. or as late as 494.[23] The actions at Cyprus and Lade indicate that the Ionian League became the organizing and controlling force behind the Ionian Revolt before the time of the Cypriot campaign and continued in this role until the rebelling forces were destroyed at Lade.

Aristagoras proved to be a fainthearted commander, and when the Carian defeat was coupled with other scattered losses throughout Asia Minor, he decided to flee Miletos. The direct cause of his flight is not certain, especially since Hekataios suggested that he instead fortify Leros and wait there for an opportunity, ἔπειτα δὲ ἐκ ταύτης ὁρμώμενον κατελεύσεσθαι ἐς τὴν Μίλητον [since starting out from there he might return to Miletos] (Hdt. 5.125). The initial inclination is to interpret this passage to mean that Aristagoras was abandoning Miletos because he was fleeing from the Persian army:[24] Aristagoras saw the Persians recapturing cities and realized that he could not defeat the king, so he was relinquishing the struggle to save himself. However, in this context, the suggestion that he fortify Leros as a base from which to retake Miletos makes no sense. It would be unrealistic for Aristagoras to consider that he and a small group of supporters could maintain a fort on the small offshore island, much less use it as a base from which to retake Miletos from the Persians. An alternate interpretation is that Aristagoras was in

---

23. Murray 1988, 485.

24. How and Wells 1912, ad loc. Georges (2000, 28–33) argues that Aristagoras fled when Histiaios showed up acting as the king's agent responsible for bringing the instigators of the rebellion to justice.

fact fleeing from the factional strife of his own people.[25] Certainly, he was the man who started all this trouble for Ionia, and one could imagine that he wished to flee Miletos to avoid Ionian rancor, anticipating that he would be—or perhaps he already was being—blamed for the defeat. Yet even then, the purpose of removing to a base on Leros still remains unclear. If Aristagoras planned to retake Miletos from another faction, it would have to be done quickly, before the Ionian Revolt was completely smashed and the city was in the hands of the Persians. But then Aristagoras would still have to face the larger struggle of the rebellion against Persia. Neither of these explanations usually offered is plausible: Leros was contemplated neither as a base from which to fight the Persians nor as a springboard for an assault and recapture of Miletos.

Perhaps the most plausible possibility is that Hekataios planned for Aristagoras to occupy Leros as a base from which he could betray the city to the Persians and thus regain their favor.[26] Herodotos (6.5.1) makes it clear that Aristagoras had lost his popularity: when Histiaios, the original tyrant of Miletos, attempted to return to the city after Aristagoras's departure, he was abruptly rebuffed.

οἱ δὲ Μιλήσιοι ἄσμενοι ἀπαλλαχθέντες καὶ Ἀρισταγόρεω οὐδαμῶς πρόθυμοι ἦσαν ἄλλον τύραννον δέκεσθαι ἐς τὴν χώρην, οἷά τε ἐλευθερίης γευσάμενοι.

[The Milesians, being glad to have also gotten rid of Aristagoras, were in no way eager to receive another tyrant into their land once they had gotten a taste of freedom.]

In any case, Aristagoras wisely realized the futility of fortifying Leros and instead fled to Myrkinos.[27]

The war continued for some time after the escape of Aristagoras and the rejection of Histiaios, and things continued to go poorly for the Greek cities. In all, they lost battles in Cyprus, the Hellespont and Propontis,

---

25. Macan 1895, ad loc.; de Sanctis 1931, 70–71. Murray (1988, 485) writes, "This plan of establishing a nearby base makes no sense as a response to danger from Persian attack but is typical of those exiled for internal political reasons."

26. Suggested by Graham in private conversation.

27. He was successful in obtaining control of Myrkinos but was killed while besieging a nearby town. Histiaios later fled to the same region after the Battle of Lade: he attempted to take control of Thasos, without success (Hdt. 6.28).

Caria, and several places in Aiolia and Ionia. Finally, in 494 B.C.E., the Persians set out against Miletos itself (Hdt. 6.6). By disregarding the other cities and concentrating their forces against Miletos, the Persians demonstrated that they viewed Miletos as the heart of the rebellion and that they believed that by taking that city, they would crush the entire revolt at one stroke. At the Panionion, the allies decided to meet the Persians on the sea, leaving the Milesians to defend their own city against the land army (Hdt. 6.7). The sea battle was lost due to Samian treachery, and much of the Ionian fleet fled in panic (Hdt. 6.13–17).

After Lade, the Persians immediately turned against the city of Miletos itself. Using saps and machines, the Persians besieged this metropolis probably for some months before capturing it in 494 B.C.E. Herodotos (6.19.3–20) reports that the Persian treatment was brutal.

[19.3] . . . ὅτε γε ἄνδρες μὲν οἱ πλεῦνες ἐκτείνοντο ὑπὸ τῶν Περσέων ἐόντων κομητέων, γυναῖκες δὲ καὶ τέκνα ἐν ἀνδραπόδων λόγῳ ἐγίνοντο, ἱρὸν δὲ τὸ ἐν Διδύμοισι, ὁ νηός τε καὶ τὸ χρηστήριον, συληθέντα ἐνεπίμπρατο. . . . [20] ἐνθεῦτεν οἱ ζωγρηθέντες τῶν Μιλησίων ἤγοντο ἐς Σοῦσα. βασιλεὺς δέ σφεας Δαρεῖος κακὸν οὐδὲν ἄλλο ποιήσας κατοίκισε ἐπὶ τῇ Ἐρυθρῇ καλεομένῃ θαλάσσῃ, ἐν Ἄμπῃ πόλι, παρ' ἣν Τίγρης ποταμὸς παραρρέων ἐς θάλασσαν ἐξίει. τῆς δὲ Μιλησίων χώρης αὐτοὶ μὲν οἱ Πέρσαι εἶχον τὰ περὶ τὴν πόλιν καὶ τὸ πεδίον, τὰ δὲ ὑπεράκρια ἔδοσαν Καρσὶ Πηδασεῦσι ἐκτῆσθαι.

[[19.3] . . . Most of the men were killed by the long-haired Persians, and the women and children were made into slaves. The sanctuary at Didyma—both the temple and the Oracle—was plundered and burned. . . . [20] Then the survivors of the Milesians were taken to Susa. But King Dareios did no further evil to them; rather, he settled them on what is called the Red Sea, in the city of Ampe, near which the Tigris River flows as it empties into the sea. Of the Milesian land, the Persians themselves took possession of the areas around the city and the plain, while they gave the heights [of Stephania] to the Carians from Pedasa to have as their own.]

Herodotos's account here is introduced by an oracle about the destruction of the city. He quotes (6.19.2; Fontenrose 1978, Q134):

καὶ τότε δή, Μίλητε, κακῶν ἐπιμήχανε ἔργων,
πολλοῖσιν δεῖπνόν τε καὶ ἀγλαὰ δῶρα γενήσῃ,
σαὶ δ' ἄλοχοι πολλοῖσι πόδας νίψουσι κομήταις,
νηοῦ δ' ἡμετέρου Διδύμοις ἄλλοισι μελήσει.

[And then, Miletos, contriver of evil deeds,
you will be a feast for many and a shining gift,
your wives will wash the feet of many long-haired men,
and my temple at Didyma will be a care to others.]

Thus, it would seem, the prediction of the oracle—which is itself almost certainly false[28]—dictated the details that Herodotos records. Herodotos concentrates on the depopulation of the site and the destruction of the Oracle, while failing to mention the extensive damage done to the city itself. Definitive proof that it was burned and razed is evident everywhere in the ruins. The best example is the older Temple of Athena, which was damaged, but not totally destroyed, by the fire: it was toppled by the plundering, described by the excavator as malicious rather than systematic.[29]

Before Lade, the Persians had threatened to burn the houses and temples of the Ionians in revolt, enslave them, castrate their sons, abduct their daughters, and give their land to others (Hdt. 6.9.4); at Miletos, they fulfilled their promises. When the Persians captured the other Ionian towns in the next year, their cruelty was only slightly abated. They burned the towns, complete with their temples, but they castrated only the most handsome boys and abducted only the prettiest girls (Hdt. 6.31). The land was not given away, and the adult inhabitants were left unmolested. This treatment stands in contrast to the fate of Miletos, starkly emphasized by Herodotos: Μίλητος μέν νυν Μιλησίων ἠρήμωτο [But now Miletos was emptied of Milesians] (Hdt. 6.22.1).

The Ionian Revolt had started through the efforts of one Greek tyrant to maintain his grasp on power, but the insurrection spread widely due to the hatred many cities felt for their Persian-backed tyrants. The deposed rulers fled to their Persian master and worked for the reconquest of the

---

28. Fontenrose 1978, 170–71.
29. Mallwitz 1968, 120–24. Cf. *Milet* 1.8.54–58, 72, 121; Weickert et al. 1957, 114; Mellink 1961, 47–48. Hammond (1998; contra Parke 1985a) theorizes that the destruction of Branchidai was done not by Dareios in 494 but by Xerxes in 479. If this is the case, Herodotos passed without warning from the events of 494 to 479 and then back again, which seems very unlikely.

Greek cities, but the efforts of Aiakes of Samos led those islanders to desert at the critical Battle of Lade (Hdt. 6.9–10, 13). We must understand in this context the action of Mardonios, who was sent by Dareios to be the military commander in Asia Minor and Thrace. Reaching Ionia, he carried out an amazing feat: τοὺς γὰρ τυράννους τῶν Ἰώνων καταπαύσας πάντας ὁ Μαρδόνιος δημοκρατίας κατίστα ἐς τὰς πόλιας [For, deposing all the tyrants of the Ionians, Mardonios set up democracies in the cities] (Hdt. 6.43.3). This one achievement of the Ionian Revolt endured: the people had revolted against their tyrants, and now Persia was remedying this cause for discontent. But the Milesians could not enjoy the change, since they did not survive the revolt as a political unit.

Refoundation

The Persians invaded Greece twice, in 490 and in 480, and were twice beaten back. After a Hellenic naval victory at Salamis in 480, the Greek fleet was emboldened to sail east to Delos and thence to Asia. According to Herodotos, on the very day that the Hellenic army wiped out the Persians at Plataia in 479, the fleet, dominated by the Athenians but commanded by a Spartan, landed on Mt. Mykale and engaged the Persians there (Hdt. 9.97ff.). Before this battle, the Persians were worried about the loyalty of the Ionian Greeks in their midst, so, according to Herodotos, they disarmed the Samians and ordered certain Milesians who were present to the rear, ostensibly to guard the mountain passes but actually to get away from a position in which they could harm the Persian cause. The battle joined, and eventually the tide swung in favor of the Greeks. As the Persians fled, their initial design to get the Ionians out of the way backfired because the Milesians led them down the wrong paths, back into the fighting, and finally set against them openly (Hdt. 9.104).

After the Battle of Mykale, the city of Miletos rejoined the historical record, appearing regularly in the literature of the fifth century, in the Athenian tribute lists, and in a flurry of building activity on the city site. Miletos returned to relative prosperity so quickly in the fifth century that many scholars assume that the city never really lost all of its population, and they cite the presence of the Milesians in the Persian army at Mykale as the evidence for their position.[30] In other words, one passage in Herodotos,

---

30. Berve 1967, 1:105–6; Tozzi 1978, 205. Berve's argument is also based on the absence of any indication of a gap in the *aisymnetes* list. Cf. Graham 1992, 69–72; *Milet*

about the Battle of Mykale, is used to reject another passage, about the depopulation of Miletos.

It is better to accept the accuracy of both passages. It is impossible to use archaeological data to prove that a city was not inhabited for such a short period of time, because the lack of physical evidence can never be conclusive, but one may at least note a complete absence of any building or sherd on the city peninsula of Miletos that can be accurately dated to the years between 494 and 479 B.C.E. At the same time, the physical evidence can testify to the actual destruction of the site: a layer of ash and debris has been found at the appropriate level throughout the city. Moreover, Herodotos dwells at length on the depopulation of the city, describing it in detail and strongly emphasizing it both by comparing it to Sybaris, another luxurious city famous for its utter destruction, and by including the story about Phrynichos and his ill-fated play. To argue that Herodotos is simply wrong here or grossly exaggerating about an event from his own lifetime that would have been familiar to his audience is to cast doubt on the reliability of his entire work. The story is entirely plausible when seen in light of the Persian treatment of the other Ionian cities that were held less accountable for the revolt: Miletos was made an example. It is also entirely consistent with a long-standing Near Eastern policy of resettlement: the king would occasionally cause the population of an entire city to migrate to a distant part of the empire. The purposes for this policy varied but certainly included the desire to resettle a fertile area depopulated by other events, the need to fortify weak border areas, and the need to break up local power bases and so eliminate potential rivals.[31] Miletos was destroyed and its inhabitants resettled to remove potential troublemakers from the region of Ionia while at the same time dispensing a lesson to the other Persian subjects.

The people returning to the site settled first in the highest and safest location, the hill of Kalabaktepe, south of the city proper. New buildings were erected on layers of Persian debris used to terrace two plateaus with considerable care and at great expense, indicating that the people who

1.3.241–42. Another theory, that the inhabitants of Miletos were not restored until at least the mid–fifth century (Wilamowitz-Moellendorff 1914, 81; Mayer 1932, 1633–35), has been disproved by archaeological finds.

31. Ambaglio (1975) concludes that deportations in Herodotos were never done to exterminate the inhabitants but rather to tear them from their own land, break up political unity, and eliminate the possibility of rebellion. The deportees were allowed to maintain relative autonomy, along with their customs and language.

did this work probably intended it to be their permanent home. But soon, presumably after the Battle of Mykale, it became apparent that the city was safe from invasion and that many more citizens were being gathered than had been expected, enough to reestablish the city on its former scale. The one small hill could not house such a city, no matter how thoroughly it was terraced, so the citizens mapped out a new city on the peninsula to the north. Heavy construction took place in the second quarter of the fifth century, and at about the midcentury mark, once the initial streets and homes were put in place, the settlement on Kalabaktepe was permanently abandoned.[32]

The restored city was culturally indistinguished from the original, proving that the new settlers had Milesian roots. Thus, the potential sources for the settlers were very few. Some would have come from the Milesian refugees who escaped the Battle of Lade and the destruction of Miletos (Hdt. 6.22.3). Others may have been Milesians who made their way back from Ampe. (Either of these groups could have supplied the small army contingent at the Battle of Mykale.) However, while these refugees undoubtedly contributed to the refoundation of the city, it is unlikely that their total number was large enough to explain the magnitude of the restored city.

The likely source for many of the new Milesians must have been the citizens of the many colonies of the Pontos and Propontis, which could have provided any number of settlers with the same ancestry and heritage as the original Milesians. Evidence for this source of citizens may be contained in certain Milesian inscriptions from the fourth century that record treaties with several colonies. The first, a treaty with Olbia that is dated before 323 and possibly in 330, is discussed thoroughly by Graham.[33]

τάδε πάτρια ᾿Ολβιοπολίταις καὶ Μιλησ[ί-]
οις· τὸμ Μιλήσιον ἐν ᾿Ολβίη(ι) πόλει ὡς ᾿Ολ-
βιοπολίτην θύειν ἐπὶ τῶν αὐτῶμ βω-
μῶν καὶ εἰς τὰ ἱερὰ τὰ αὐτὰ φοιτᾶν τὰ
δημόσια κατὰ τὰ αὐτὰ καὶ ᾿Ολβιοπολί-   5
τας· εἶναι δὲ καὶ ἀτελείας Μιλησίοις καθάσσα καὶ πρότερον ἦσαν· ἐὰν δὲ θέληι

---

32. Graeve 1986a, 42–43; Kerschner 1995, 218.
33. *Milet* 1.3 #136 = Tod 1946, #195; Graham 1983, chap. 6; Ehrhardt 1983, 233–41. The translation given here is from Graham 1983, 100.

148   *Miletos, the Ornament of Ionia*

τιμουχιῶμ μετέχειν, ἐπὶ βουλὴν ἐπίτω
καὶ ἀπογραφεὶς μετεχέτω καὶ ἔστω
ἐντελής, καθότι καὶ οἱ ἄλλοι πολῖται   10
εἰσίν· εἶναι δὲ καὶ προεδρίαγ καὶ εἰσκη-
ρύσσεσθαι εἰς τοὺς ἀγῶνας καὶ ἐπα-
ρᾶσθαι ταῖς τριακάσιγ, καθάσσα καὶ
ἐμ Μιλήτωι ἐπαρῶνται· ἐὰν δέ τι συμβό-
λαιον ἦ(ι) τῶι Μιλησίωι ἐν Ὀλβίαι, ἰσχέτω δί-   15
κηγ καὶ ὑπεχέτω ἐμ πένθ᾽ ἡμέραις ἐπὶ
τοῦ δημοτικοῦ δικαστηρίου· εἶναι δὲ
[ἀ]τελεῖς πάντας Μιλησίους, πλὴν ὅσοι
ἐν ἄλλη(ι) πόλει πολιτεύονται καὶ ἀρχείω(μ)
μετέχουσιγ καὶ δικαστηρίων. κατὰ ταῦ-   20
τὰ δὲ καὶ Ὀλβιοπολίτας ἐμ Μιλήτωι ἀτε-
λεῖς εἶναι, καὶ τὰ ἄλλα κατὰ τὸν αὐτὸν
τρόπον Ὀλβιοπολίταις ἐμ Μιλήτωι ὑπάρ-
χειγ καθότι καὶ Μιλησίοις ἐν Ὀλβίη(ι) πόλει.

[The following are traditional arrangements for the Olbiopolitans and Milesians. That the Milesian in the city of Olbia sacrifice like an Olbiopolitan on the same altars, and partake [5] in the same public cults under the same conditions as the Olbiopolitans. That the Milesian have exemption from taxation as it was formerly. That, if he wish to become eligible for office, he is to come before the Council and be entered on the rolls and be liable to [10] taxation as other citizens are. That they (i.e. the Milesians) have the right of privileged seats at public gatherings, of being announced at athletic contests and of praying at the festival of the *triakades,* as they pray at Miletus. And that, if the Milesian have a law suit [15] arising from a legal contract, the case shall be tried within five days at the public court. That all Milesians be exempt from taxation except those who in another city exercise citizenship, [20] hold magistracies and take part in the courts. That, on the same terms, the Olbiopolitan be exempt from taxes, and the other arrangements apply in the same way to the Olbiopolitan in Miletus as to the Milesians in the city of Olbia.]

This inscription establishes equal citizenship, or *isopoliteia,* between the two cities Miletos and Olbia. Citizens from either city could go to the other and enjoy a privileged status: exemption from taxation, the right to sacrifice in the public cults, special seats at public gatherings, and the right to argue lawsuits in the public court that was reserved for citizens. In addition, any citizen of one city who wanted to obtain full citizenship in the other—especially eligibility for public office—needed only to declare himself liable to taxation. This relationship was very unusual, for while it was common for mother cities to reserve the right to send later settlers to a colony as full citizens, the colonists' right of return was usually strictly limited.

Its abrupt beginning establishes that this decree is a restatement of "traditional arrangements" [τάδε πάτρια]. Generally, scholars feel that this relationship must have been in effect in the past and then lapsed for some reason before it was reestablished in this treaty. Graham says: "It may be assumed that the treaty was necessary because these arrangements had been in abeyance. The most obvious reason for this would be the Persian control of Miletus."[34] Since Miletos was in Persian hands from ca. 540 to 479 and again from 412 to 334, the earlier treaty must have dated either to the fifth century or to before 540. Graham thinks it dates most probably to the second half of the fifth century, after Miletos had returned to prosperity, or to the early sixth century, before the Persian conquest of Ionia.

However, another period should be considered as a more likely date for the original treaty of *isopoliteia*. Immediately after the Battle of Mykale, when the city of Miletos was being refounded, it was natural for the returning Milesian refugees to look to the colonies for additional settlers. A means of persuading the citizens of the colonies—many of them prosperous cities—to move to the ruins of Miletos needed to be found. Perhaps the Milesians opened up the citizenship to people from the colonies who wanted to return to the mother city. Parallels for this action exist. In the clearest one, Teos was abandoned to the Persians but resettled around the second half of the sixth century by settlers from its colony Abdera. Afterward, the two cities may have been very closely linked, sharing not just *isopoliteia* but *sympoliteia* (one unified government for the two).[35] Graham gives other examples both of possible mother cities being refounded by colonies (Sybaris, Skidros, Posidonia) and of cities besides Miletos that were destroyed in one account but

---

34. Graham 1983, 105.
35. Demand 1990, 39–43; Graham 1992, esp. 53, 69–70.

appear again as functioning polities fairly soon afterward (Eretria, Kamarina, Priene). He argues for the colonies as a major source for settlers at Miletos, but he does not directly connect the treaties of *isopoliteia* to this incident.

My interpretation would be weak if Miletos shared *isopoliteia* with just one colony, because one city, no matter how prosperous, was not likely to provide the thousands of settlers needed for Classical Miletos. However, this *isopoliteia* existed with Kyzikos as well. A decree from Miletos (*Milet* 1.3 #137) that is dated to the same time as the treaty with Olbia, before 323 B.C.E., is more abrupt but comes to much the same terms. The inscription breaks off after only sixteen lines, but after a sudden beginning consisting only of a listing of the people who are vouching for the treaty, the surviving body of the text reads:

> . . . τὰς μὲν πόλεις φίλας εἶ-
> ναι ἐς τὸν ἅπαντα χρόνον
> κατὰ τὰ πάτρια· εἶναι δὲ τὸν
> Κυζικηνὸν ἐμ Μιλήτωι Μι-
> λήσιον καὶ τὸν Μιλήσιον ἐν   15
> Κυζίκωι Κυζικηνόν, καθότ[ι]
> [καὶ πρότερον ἦσαν -----]

[. . . the cities be friends for all time according to the traditional arrangements, and the Kyzikene at Miletos [15] be Milesian and the Milesian at Kyzikos by Kyzikene, just as [it was formerly][36]. . .

Again there is a bald beginning and a reference to traditional arrangements. These are followed by the clear statement of *isopoliteia*: any citizen of the one city who comes to the other may be a citizen there.

We must keep in mind that what we know about Milesian *isopoliteia* depends on the chance survival of later inscriptions. We have two treaties that are clearly examples of this relationship. Another inscription containing a treaty with Istros may have included similar provisions, but the text is too broken for certainty.[37] One between Miletos and Kios from ca. 228 B.C.E. (*Milet* 1.3 #141) also contains some elements of *isopoliteia,* and the fact that Miletos and Amisos issued the same coinage in the third

---

36. The restoration is formulaic (cf. line 7 of the treaty with Olbia).
37. Lambrino 1927–32, 398; restored by Robert (1928, 171–72) as a treaty of *isopoliteia.*

century might be a sign of such a relationship there.[38] If two or three such inscriptions survive, many more may have been lost; certainly the original decrees have not been found. That only Miletos out of all the Greek mother cities had such a treaty with several colonies is more than just coincidence. These treaties of *isopoliteia* may serve as the most important witness to the source of the new population of fifth-century Miletos: any colonist who would return to the mother city would be given full citizenship in exchange for his participation in the rebuilding of Miletos.

The Orthogonal Plan

The city that rose again from the ashes of the Persian destruction was a splendid achievement, for fifth-century Miletos was the first to exhibit a systematic and total application of urban planning.[39] The entire city peninsula, far beyond the limited extent of the original resettlement, was divided into uniform, right-angled blocks by straight streets that enclosed but did not radiate from the public markets and buildings. The Archaic remains had been laid out without a uniform orientation—some portions were orthogonal, but one cannot speak of a plan that encompassed the entire Archaic city—as were the buildings in the temporary settlement on Kalabaktepe, but even the earliest shrines built after the destruction of the city were oriented according to the new street alignment, which guarantees that the orthogonal city plan did not grow up gradually but was utilized from the start by the people resettling Miletos. Immediately after 479 B.C.E., before any construction was done except on Kalabaktepe, the peninsula north of the Sacred Gate and the later Hellenistic cross wall was completely surveyed, and the lines of partition were laid down. Deviations from the orthogonal grid were scarcely tolerated, and no Archaic remains that survived the destruction of the city were reused in conflict with the new system.

The peninsula was divided into two main districts. The northern district encompassed both the North Hill and the Theater Hill and extended through the city's center on the Lion Bay, where open space was left for the main agora of the city, the North Market, and where the majority

---

38. Ehrhardt 1983, 235, 238.
39. Standard works on ancient city planning are Haverfield 1913; Gerkan 1924a; Castagnoli 1971; Martin 1974; Ward-Perkins 1974; Owens 1991.

of public buildings eventually found their homes. The orientation of the streets there was probably determined by the Archaic remains on the Theater Hill, in the area west of the Bouleuterion, and by the remains of the Delphinion, for in these areas many of the Archaic walls corresponded exactly to the fifth-century constructions: the orientation of the buildings on the Theater Hill remained the same from Archaic times until the Middle Ages, and some Archaic walls were reused in the fifth century.[40] In the southern district, which included everything below the later South and West Markets, some of the Archaic house walls east of the Temple of Athena also corresponded to the new Classical buildings. One may conclude that the area around the temple may have determined the size and shape of the blocks, whereas the correspondence of walls decreases further west of the temple, where Classical remains are rare.[41]

The street arrangement on the peninsula (which is 2 km. long) has been investigated several times in this century. When Gerkan drew up his original plan of Miletos—which included both the Classical and the Hellenistic constructions—he recognized the two main districts and saw that the relationship between the two was slightly askew. In the north, the two hills had approximately the same orientations and small and somewhat variable city blocks, all about 29 m. wide, but ranging between about 18 and 33 m. deep. The southern district had a slightly different orientation and had blocks nearly double in size, about 35 × 44 m. The streets throughout Gerkan's plan were less than 5 m. wide.[42] This whole scheme was reevaluated by Hoepfner and Schwandner,[43] who widened the streets, especially three main avenues, and doubled the size of Gerkan's blocks in the north. In their plan, the blocks in the north and south have approximately the same area, although with different dimensions (north 29.4 × 52.92 m. [5:9]; south 35.33 × 44.1 m. [4:5]). Neither of these plans is entirely satisfactory, however, and a third, more accurate depiction of the city grid is being developed by Berthold Weber on the basis of recent measurements from the site.[44]

The success of the grid can be seen in the allocation of space to public buildings, for those constructions that were to be larger than a city block

---

40. Kleiner 1961; Mellink 1962, 185–88; Mellink 1984, 454; Pfrommer 1985, 40–46.

41. *Milet* 1.8.82–83; Kleiner 1960, 40–41; Mellink 1961, 47–48; Mellink 1974, 114.

42. Gerkan reconstructed the presumed city blocks in his plan (*Milet* 2.3 fig. 1). This is the plan that appears everywhere in discussions of Milesian city planning.

43. Hoepfner and Schwander 1994, 17–22.

44. Forthcoming in Weber's *Milet* volume on the *Heroa*.

were not allowed to alter or significantly deform the grid. Instead, they were assigned areas whose dimensions were multiples of a city block together with the streets between them. The building thought to be the Prytaneion corresponds perfectly to two of Gerkan's city blocks, while the North Market occupies six. The Delphinion originally occupied two blocks but was later expanded to four. Despite the grandeur of its construction, the fifth-century Temple of Athena and its *temenos* were allotted only one block in the southern section of the city. Oddly enough, the temple was slightly out of alignment with the prevailing orientation. The excavators have generally assumed that this anomaly was probably due to the scarcity of nearby roads and buildings from which to orient the temple,[45] but when this phenomenon is compared to the asymmetrical arrangement of the Archaic altars in the Delphinion, it seems possible that the religious significance of the precise locations took precedence over the demands for orthogonal exactitude.

It is remarkable that the new inhabitants were able to plan so effectively for the future of Miletos. A glance at Gerkan's map of the Hellenistic city demonstrates their success in creating uniformity over the whole peninsula. When the rebuilding first began, the city occupied only a fraction of the peninsula. But the orthogonal plan accommodated the growth of the city through Hellenistic times, and in the second century B.C.E., it was still following the plan laid out in the fifth century. Miletos is one of the most successful examples of city planning known to us from the Greek world.

We now know that the plan utilized so brilliantly at Miletos probably had it roots in the regular, but not necessarily orthogonal, city plan that developed in various places throughout the Archaic Greek world, especially in the course of the Greek colonization movement of the seventh and sixth centuries B.C.E.[46] In sending out at least one colony a year for two centuries, the Greeks would have naturally learned the most convenient way to make a settlement: they laid down streets and divided the

---

45. *Milet* 1.6.89.

46. Gerkan 1924a, 30–37; cf. Martin 1951, 350. Some scholars attribute the development of the plan to Egypt, where an axial arrangement of temples has been found at Kahun (nineteenth century B.C.E.) and Tell-el-Amarna (fourteenth century B.C.E.), or to Asia: see Nissen 1877, 583 (Egypt or Babylon); Haverfield 1913 (Asia); Lavedan and Hugueney 1966; Castagnoli 1971, 105–6; Owens 1991. But there is no evidence for any large-scale implementation of the plan in Egypt or the East and equally no reason to think that the Greeks were not imaginative enough to have thought of it themselves. For a summary of the scholarship, see Castagnoli 1971, 2–7.

land for allotment with an eye toward its best use, whether residential, commercial, religious, or political. Gradually they planned more at the start to avoid later difficulties, and colonies began to resemble orthogonal cities to a greater degree.

Examples of partially planned cities can be found in most parts of the Greek world, but the evidence tends to be slim. In the colonies in the Propontis and Pontos, where we might hope to see the development of the Milesian plan, excavations are not very extensive, and certainly no entire city was founded on the principle of regularity: the city most thoroughly excavated, Olbia, is disappointing in that it shows no sign of planning.[47] On the mainland itself, only Halieis on the Argolid had a regular city plan in the fourth century, which seems to have descended from a similar plan in the sixth and fifth centuries.[48] The situation is slightly better in Asia Minor and the Aegean, with evidence of planning found at Smyrna (end of eighth century), Emporion on Chios (eighth and seventh centuries), and Thasos (mid–sixth century).[49] The best place to see the development of Greek city planning is in the colonies of Sicily and Magna Graecia, where the numerous excavations have demonstrated that many cities displayed such plans at an early date: examples are Megara Hyblaia (eighth century), Naxos (ca. 700 B.C.E.), the acropolis at Selinos (mid–sixth century or fourth century), and a section of Syracuse (mid–sixth century), as well as Agrigentum, Metapontum, Kamarina, Himera, Kroton, Poseidonia, and elsewhere in the Classical Era.[50] For the most part, the Archaic cities did not exhibit the signs of a rigid imposition of a preconceived plan; rather, they developed in an orderly fashion, but only gradually, with the order imposed in part because the inhabitants

47. Martin 1974, 301–7 (Pontic colonies). Castagnoli (1971, 10) says that Olbia did show signs of planning already in the sixth century, but this view is disputed by the excavators. According to Vinogradov and Kryzickij (1995, 29), "Es soll betont werden, daß in dieser Zeit [6. Jh. v. Chr.], übrigens wie auch später, Olbia kein einheitliches reguläres rechteckiges Planungssystem hatte" [It should be emphasized that at this time [in the sixth century B.C.E.], and moreover later as well, Olbia had no uniform, regular, right-angled system of planning].

48. Boyd and Rudolph 1978; Rudolph 1984.

49. Cook 1958/59 (Smyrna); Cook 1962, 70–72 (Smyrna); Martin 1974, 289–91 (Smyrna and Emporion), 331 (Smyrna); Martin 1978 (Thasos).

50. In general: Castagnoli 1971, 10–12, 128–30; Martin 1974, 309–29; Asheri 1975, 7–9; Graham 1982a, 103–13; Graham 1982b; Owens 1991, 30–50. Megara Hyblaia: Vallet 1973 (esp. 85 fig. 2); Vallet, Villard, and Auberson 1976, 1983. Selinos: Martin 1975; Martin 1977; Theodorescu 1975; Owens 1991, 44–46 (Owens thinks the plan dates to the fourth century). Metapontum: Martin 1972/73, 354–55. Himera: Adriani et al. 1970; Belvedere 1976.

mostly abandoned curved houses and built rectilinear structures that shared a common wall with their neighbor. Only in the fourth century were both creativity and the conditions of the terrain subordinated to the demands of orthogonality.[51]

Most cities could only adopt planning gradually, when specific neighborhoods where being annexed for the first time or else rebuilt after a calamity, but in the case of Miletos, the complete destruction of the Archaic city allowed for a full-scale imposition of planning on the entire city site. The planners adhered completely to the strictest orthogonal grid of parallel and perpendicular streets, regardless of the terrain, resulting in city blocks that were of nearly equal size in each section. The Milesian devotion to form, uniting theory and function, became the standard expression of the orthogonal plan in the fifth and early fourth centuries. It was born of the availability of an open site, the practical need for land division, the social and political considerations inherent in the foundation of a city, and philosophical speculations on the makeup of the ideal city.[52]

Hippodamos

Miletos was the first completely planned city in the Greek world. In subsequent years, this style of orthogonal planning became known as Hippodamian, after Hippodamos, the Milesian architect who popularized it.[53] This identification became so automatic that scholars since the Renaissance have erroneously associated the invention of the orthogonal city plan with him. But Hippodamos lived in the fifth century and can hardly have been responsible for a plan that archaeological evidence has reliably dated back to at least the eighth century B.C.E. The origin of this scholarly misunderstanding may be traced to several passages from Aristotle's *Politics*. In book 7 (1330b21–31), Aristotle refers to the "Hippodamian method" of laying out streets in an orderly quincunx. Then, in

---

51. Owens 1991, 30–50.
52. Martin 1974, 331–32.
53. Arist. *Pol.* 7.1330b21–31. The argument posed here is condensed from Gorman 1995. Modern discussions of Hippodamos are Hermann 1841; Erdmann 1884; Castagnoli 1971, 65–72; Fabricius 1913; Gerkan 1924b; McCredie 1971; Wycherley 1973, 17–18; Martin 1974, 15–16, 103–6; Ward-Perkins 1974, 14–17; Burns 1976; Szidat 1980; Falciai 1982; Triebel-Schubert and Muss 1983/84; Owens 1991, 51–73 passim; Kostof 1991, esp. 105.

book 2, during a discussion of earlier theoretical models of the ideal state, the philosopher discusses Hippodamos himself (1267b22–30).

Ἱππόδαμος δὲ Εὐρυφῶντος Μιλήσιος, ὃς καὶ τὴν τῶν πόλεων διαίρεσιν εὗρε καὶ τὸν Πειραιᾶ κατέτεμεν, γενόμενος καὶ περὶ τὸν ἄλλον βίον περιττότερος διὰ φιλοτιμίαν οὕτως ὥστε δοκεῖν ἐνίοις ζῆν περιεργότερον τριχῶν τε πλήθει καὶ κόσμῳ πολυτελεῖ, ἔτι δὲ ἐσθῆτος εὐτελοῦς μὲν ἀλεεινῆς δέ, οὐκ ἐν τῷ χειμῶνι μόνον ἀλλὰ καὶ περὶ τοὺς θερινοὺς χρόνους, λόγιος δὲ καὶ περὶ τὴν ὅλην φύσιν εἶναι βουλόμενος. πρῶτος τῶν μὴ πολιτευομένων ἐνεχείρησέ τι περὶ πολιτείας εἰπεῖν τῆς ἀρίστης.

[Hippodamos, the son of Euryphon, and a Milesian, who both invented the division of cities and cut out the Peiraios, was in the rest of his life very extraordinary because of his love of reputation, so that to some people he seemed to live his life very elaborately, wearing his hair long and arranged in a costly manner, while his clothes were of cheap material that was nevertheless warm, which he wore both in the winter and in the summer alike. He wanted to be knowledgeable about nature in general. First among those who were not statesmen, he tried to speak about the best state.]

In the phrase ὃς καὶ τὴν τῶν πόλεων διαίρεσιν εὗρε, translated literally as "who also invented the division of cities," scholars have found the evidence that seems to establish that Aristotle considered Hippodamos to be the inventor of regular city planning. No one disputes the literal translation, but because the precise meaning of the word *diairesis,* "division," is unclear, there is a tendency among scholars to elaborate on it in order to guide their readers to what they feel to be the correct interpretation. Often this interpretation necessarily involves city planning, and many editions translate this phrase along some variation of "the division of cities into streets or quarters."[54]

Such an interpretation of Aristotle's passage was understandable before this century, when archaeology was in its infancy, but no such excuse exists for the scholarship that has been written in the last thirty years especially, in the time since archaeological evidence has proven that this

54. Newman 1887; Jowett 1905; McKeon 1941; Aubonnet 1960; Stahr 1839; Fabricius 1913.

interpretation must be wrong. Instead of acknowledging that a misunderstanding has taken place, many scholars still cling to the old interpretation but in a modified form. For example, one hypothesis is that Aristotle did not mean that Hippodamos invented city planning per se but rather that he invented a modification of city planning involving an alternation of major and minor streets. Another credits Hippodamos with the introduction of "a specific system of planning which differed in both detail and overall design from contemporary practice," principally by using the "clear demarcation of these [sc. land-use] areas by wide arterial roads."[55] Such efforts are misdirected. They aim at explaining what seems to be a mistake on Aristotle's part, when in fact the mistake lies not with Aristotle but with his interpreters and translators.

The context of the *Politics* makes it quite clear that Aristotle is not thinking about the actual physical layout of cities and that by *diairesis* he means the division of people into classes and of land into types.[56] The purpose of book 2 of the *Politics* is to discuss theoretical and actual models of the ideal state, beginning with the question of how a state should share or divide its basic goods (2.1260b36–40), the topic that forms the basic framework for the following discussion. Aristotle recognizes two possible states, one in which the citizens share everything and another in which they share only certain things. He discusses first Plato's ideal state, which is an example of Aristotle's first alternative (*Pol.* 2.1261a5–8), and then two other ideal states, which are variations of the second alternative. The first of these two models was preferred by Phaleas of Chalkedon, who was the first to suggest the distribution of equal lots of land to be held privately, to prevent discord among the citizens (*Pol.* 2.1266a38–40). The last model is that pioneered by Hippodamos, in which the people are divided into classes and the land is divided among them. Aristotle says (*Pol.* 2.1267b30–37):

κατεσκεύαζε δὲ τὴν πόλιν τῷ πλήθει μὲν μυριάνδρον, εἰς τρία δὲ
μέρη διῃρημένην· ἐποίει γὰρ ἓν μὲν μέρος τεχνίτας, ἓν δὲ

---

55. Owens 1991, 60–61; cf. McCredie 1971 (alternating streets). Owens's discussion of Hippodamos (51–61) is probably the best work in English to date, but he tends to overgeneralize.

56. A few scholars do employ the philosophical translation without refuting the others, but this is by no means the rule. Millon (1803) has offered the following: "est inventeur de la division des Etats par ordres de citoyens" [He is the inventor of the division of the state into orders of citizens]. Ward-Perkins (1974, 14, 16) likewise translates, "he invented the division of cities by classes."

γεωργούς, τρίτον δὲ τὸ προπολεμοῦν καὶ τὰ ὅπλα ἔχον. διήρει δ᾽ εἰς τρία μέρη τὴν χώρην, τὴν μὲν ἱερὰν τὴν δὲ δημοσίαν τὴν δ᾽ ἰδίαν·ὅθεν μὲν τὰ νομιζόμενα ποιήσουσι πρὸς τοὺς θεούς, ἱεράν, ἀφ᾽ ὧν δ᾽ οἱ προπολεμοῦντες βιώσονται, κοινήν, τὴν δὲ τῶν γεωργῶν ἰδίαν.

[And he furnished his city with ten thousand men, divided into three classes; for he made one class craftsmen, another farmers, and the third to defend the city and carry arms. And he divided the land into three parts: sacred, public, and private. The sacred land provided for the rites that they made for the gods, the commonly held land was that from which the warriors took their living, and the private land was owned by the farmers.[57]]

The repetition of διαιρέω is significant. When Hippodamos divided (διῃρημένην) his people into classes (repeated at *Pol.* 2.1268a16) and divided (διῄρει) his land into types, he was in fact making a division of the city (διαίρεσιν). The immediate context makes it clear that this division, as Aristotle describes it, is what Aristotle meant by τὴν τῶν πόλεων διαίρεσιν. There need be no implication that the division of land and people was accompanied by an actual physical division by streets in the layout of the ideal city, although such physical division was not excluded.[58]

To take *diairesis* to mean "city planning" would seriously damage the organization of Aristotle's essay, since Aristotle introduces his discussion of the other theoretical communities by linking them to his overall theme of how property should be shared. To interpret τὴν τῶν πόλεων διαίρεσιν as is traditionally done destroys this link: no other phrase in this passage (*Pol.* 2.1267b22–30) can be understood to introduce the topic of Hippodamos's theory. In this way, the general structure of book 2 of the *Politics* as well as the immediate context of the passage in question supports the theoretical interpretation of *diairesis*. Aristotle says not that Hippodamos invented "the division of cities into streets/

---

57. Hippodamos also divided the laws and legal verdicts into three (Arist. *Pol.* 2.1267b37–1269a12).

58. Burns (1976, 416–17) realizes that in the immediate context of the discussion of Hippodamos, *diairesis* is explained by the subsequent paragraphs, but he fails to identify the importance of the larger organizational pattern of book 2, which is much more important in determining the absolute meaning of Aristotle's statement that Hippodamos invented the division of cities.

quarters" but rather that he was the first to theorize about the divisions of people and land within a city.[59]

According to the ancient sources, Hippodamos held three vocations or avocations.[60] He was first a theoretician. Next he was a meteorologist, a profession that might also be reflected in Aristotle's statement "He wanted to be knowledgeable about nature in general," for meteorology in antiquity meant literally "the study of things aloft" but was used in reference both to astrological phenomena and to earth science in general, like earthquakes and storms.[61] Finally, Hippodamos's source of renown was as a city planner, or what the sources call an architect.[62] In this capacity he is regularly associated with four different cities: Miletos, the Peiraios, Thourioi, and Rhodes. We have already discussed how Miletos was regularly planned in the second quarter of the fifth century. The date for the work at the Peiraios is uncertain: it may have been conducted by Themistokles ca. 480 B.C.E. but should probably be connected with the innovations of Perikles at about the midcentury mark. Thourioi was founded in 444/3 B.C.E. and Rhodes in 408/7 B.C.E. Obviously, if we are to accept that Hippodamos was in charge of planning all four of these cities, we run into a chronological obstacle that must be resolved: his career must have spanned seventy years, an unlikely figure.

Nearly every extant source says that Hippodamos was a Milesian, but not a single one says that he was responsible for the layout of Miletos. However, because he has been held up as the inventor of city planning for so long, many scholars believe that he must have planned Miletos, the first known completely orthogonal city. As a consequence, it is assumed that Hippodamos must have been born before ca. 510, in order for him to have been deeply involved in the refoundation of Miletos from the start.[63] According to this theory, he would be a mature adult at the time of the Battle of Mykale, which immediately preceded the resettlement of Miletos. To be the driving intellectual force behind the new city plan, he needed to be at least thirty years old: the entire plan was conceived before the rebuilding commenced, and the Milesians were not likely to entrust their entire future

---

59. Gorman 1995 traces the erroneous idea to its origin with Piero Vettori in 1576.

60. In addition to Aristotle, see Harp. s.v. Ἱπποδάμεια (= Ps.-Dem. 49.22); Hesych. s.v. Ἱπποδάμου νέμεσις; Phot. s.vv. Ἱπποδάμεια and Ἱπποδάμου νέμεσις; Andok. de Myst. 45; Xen. Hell. 2.4.11; Anec. Gr. 1.266.28 Bekker (s.v. Ἱπποδάμεια ἀγορά); Suda s.v. Ἱπποδάμεια.

61. Gilbert 1907.

62. About architects, see Coulton 1977.

63. Gerkan 1924a, 42–61; Gerkan 1924b; Martin 1974, 103–6; Szidat 1980.

to an unproven youth. In addition, that he seems to have been in charge of the work at the Peiraios would indicate that he had both experience and reputation in city planning. However, a necessary corollary of this theory is that Hippodamos could not possibly have planned Rhodes, because to do so he would have had to have lived to be more than one hundred.

This theory rests on the assumption that Hippodamos had to be in charge of planning Miletos. However, once the idea that Hippodamos actually invented city planning is discarded, there remains no evidence that he planned his home city or even, for that matter, that he was involved in its refoundation. The sources merely say that he was a Milesian. It is plausible that Hippodamos was a young architect who was concerned with, but not in charge of, the rebuilding of Miletos at some time after 479 B.C.E. Building on the peninsula continued for more than a century before the city expanded to fill the space that had been plotted out for it, so Hippodamos could have been born ca. 490 or even later and still have participated in the construction. Since he was already an accomplished architect by the 450s, when he was hired by Perikles to lay out the Peiraios, where better could he have learned his trade than in the rebuilding of his own home?

It was at the Peiraios that Hippodamos won real fame, for there an agora was named after him. The layout of that port city is not altogether clear today, because the excavations have been severely curtailed by the modern city that occupies the site.[64] Individual streets have been excavated in small pieces only, not along their entire length. However, the archaeological finds confirm a pattern that is, on the whole, orthogonal, although the street orientation changes many times, particularly in response to the topography of the site. The width of the streets also varies, but not enough is known to identify a regular scheme of alternating widths. Finally, a series of boundary markers have been discovered at the Peiraios, which seem to have separated districts of the city and to have delineated areas for public or private use.[65]

It is difficult to date the layout of the Peiraios, in part because of the limited access archaeologists possess, but also because the historical situation of the fifth century B.C.E. allows for several possibilities. Themistokles was responsible for the selection and fortification of the Peiraios as the port of Athens in the wake of Xerxes' invasion of Greece

---

64. Eickstedt 1991, esp. fig. 1; Hoepfner and Schwandner 1994, 22–50, esp. fig. 14.

65. Judeich 1931; Garland 1987; Eickstedt 1991. On the boundary stones, see Hill 1932; McCredie 1971, 96–98; Garland 1987, 225–26; Lewis 1990, esp. 250–51.

(Thuc. 1.93), which has caused some scholars to date Hippodamos's layout of the city to that time.[66] However, it is equally likely that Themistokles was only responsible for the construction of the walls and the fleet, which were credited to him directly by Thucydides (even then, because of the haste involved in their preparation, the walls were only built up to half the desired height [Thuc. 1.93.5]). Instead, the thorough, time-consuming planning of the Peiraios was probably another of the undertakings in the building program of Perikles in the middle of the century, which also included the building of the long walls from Athens to the Peiraios.[67] This latter date may be indicated by the style of lettering on the boundary markers and dramatically increases the feasibility of Hippodamos's involvement at Thourioi and, especially, Rhodes.

Thourioi was another fifth-century orthogonal city, originally founded in 444/3 as a Panhellenic undertaking settled under the guiding hand of Perikles. He designated two Athenians as founders but sent along the Sophist Protagoras of Abdera to establish the laws.[68] Presumably Hippodamos was included to lay out the city, though we possess no statement that explicitly connects him to the plan. This assumption is commonly made both because it explains Hippodamos's participation in the colony and because it is consistent with the resulting layout of the city. Although the excavation of the site has yielded few solid results,[69] Diodoros (12.10.7) gives a description of the layout of the city that included a network of major and minor streets similar to the one at the Peiraios, although we know too little to determine whether zoning was employed as well.

Rhodes was the last city to be associated with Hippodamos. Strabo mentions the connection, saying, ἡ δὲ νῦν πόλις [Rhodes] ἐκτίσθη κατὰ τὰ Πελοποννησιακὰ ὑπὸ τοῦ αὐτοῦ ἀρχιτέκτονος, ὥς φασιν, ὑφ' οὗ καὶ ὁ Πειραιεύς [the present city was founded during the Peloponnesian War by the same architect, as they say, who did the Peiraios] (14.2.9). Although he is not mentioned by name, this passage must refer to Hippodamos. Those scholars who think that Hippodamos planned Miletos choose to disregard this statement, saying that Hippodamos, if still alive, would be a very old man by the year of Rhodes's foundation, 408/7 B.C.E. Some even read the phrase ὥς φασιν, "as they say," to mean that Strabo himself did

66. Martin 1974, 104.

67. Wycherley 1964; Burns 1976, 427; Owens 1991, 55–56.

68. D.L. 9.8.10. The historian Herodotos also went along, according to the *Suda* s.v. Ἡρόδοτος. For an account of the foundation, see D.S. 12.10–11. See also Ehrenberg 1948.

69. Rainey 1964; Foti 1964; Kondis 1958.

not believe the story,[70] but this interpretation is not corroborated by a study of Strabo's use of the term elsewhere in his work. Nowhere does he dispute a fact reported as ὡς φασιν; instead, Strabo uses this phrase to indicate that he has a source for a particular fact, here probably the local inhabitants of Rhodes. A great deal of public evidence for the role of Hippodamos at Rhodes would have been preserved in Strabo's time in the form of inscriptions recording decrees and honors granted at the time of the founding of the city.[71] If Hippodamos was only a young man at the planning of Miletos, he could have been born as late as the 480s and still have been old enough to plan the Peiraios in the 450s or early 440s. In this scenario, he could have been in his seventies or even eighties at the time of the foundation of Rhodes in 408/7—certainly an advanced age, but not at all impossible. Thus, Strabo's evidence should be accepted.

Rhodes is the only city credited to Hippodamos in antiquity that has been well excavated in modern times. The ruins there have revealed a fine example of an orthogonal city, oriented only two or three degrees off of the compass.[72] The rectangular division of the city by streets, terraces, canals, and support walls was based on the organization of the city into large quadrants, 201 m. on a side (= one stade). These were further divided into four squares, which were in turn divided into six parts, 50 × 33 m. Among the long north-south streets, every third street was a major thoroughfare, significantly wider than the others (some were as wide as 16 m., as opposed to 5.15 m. for the smaller streets). The combination of the street plan with the symmetrical terraces produced an impressive theaterlike effect (D.S. 9.45.3, 20.83.2). Thus, again we see the characteristic alternation of major and minor streets that was very common in the next two centuries of Greek town planning.

Hippodamos was an architect, famous for laying out the streets of the Peiraios, Thourioi, and Rhodes by employing an orthogonal plan that was coming to full fruition in the Greek world after long centuries of development, a system that came to bear his name. Aristotle's reference to this "newer method of building" as the "Hippodamian method" (*Politics* 7.1330b21–31) can be understood in the context of the notoriety of Hippodamos's work, in the Peiraios especially, and the popularity of the orthogonal plan in the cities of Greece. Hippodamos used a variation of the strict orthogonal plan, at least in Thourioi and Rhodes (alternating

---

70. Gerkan 1924a, 48; Gerkan 1924b, 9; Martin 1974, 104.
71. Wycherley 1964.
72. Kondis 1958, pl. III; Konstantinopolis 1970, 52–55 and fig. 1; Konstantinopolis 1989, 198ff.; Hoepfner and Schwandner 1994, 51–67.

wider, more important streets with narrower roads or alleys and perhaps instituting zoning of districts by use), but we should not seek to identify him with the invention of any given plan. Aristotle never said that Hippodamos invented city planning or even one of its variations; he merely said that Hippodamos was the first man to articulate the theoretical division of land and people in the ideal state.

When Persian-backed tyrants took over Miletos in the last decades of the fifth century, that change in government represented the first step toward the downfall of the city. In overthrowing the tyranny, the Milesians found themselves leading a futile war against a vastly superior opponent, and they paid a high price for their leadership: their city was destroyed, and the population was killed or displaced. It was nothing less than a catastrophe for the greatest city in Ionia. Yet the Milesians returned and rebuilt. They not only supplanted the former scale of the city but improved on its design, creating a city that became a showcase of orthogonal planning for the entire Greek world. From this new beginning in the second quarter of the fifth century, the planned city went from being an isolated innovation to being an example of the best and most popular way to lay out a city in Classical and Hellenistic Greece.[73]

In the fifth century, the planners were mostly interested in form: in 414, Aristophanes caricatured a town planner who wanted to build a perfectly round city (*Av.* 995–1009). As planning gradually evolved and cities experimented with variations of the rigid gridded theme, the result went beyond the regular plan to culminate in a design that impresses with its grandeur. The layout of the city of Pergamon under the Attalids is a preeminent example of this. It occupied a steep hillside mounted by a very narrow main road (5 m. wide) that wound from the main gate at the base up to the theater on the acropolis, passing through a complex of temples, gymnasia, markets, and various other public buildings on its route. The effect was sensational: "It combined monumental architecture within a monumentally conceived layout, and at the same time fully exploited the difficulties of the terrain to produce one of the most impressive and visually spectacular cities of the ancient world."[74] Thus, the refoundation of the city of Miletos marked a turning point for the science of urban planning in the Greek world.

73. Owens 1991, 30–93.
74. Owens 1991, 88.

5

Archaeology and Cult

The image of Archaic Miletos that is presented by the literary sources is that of a highly prosperous and populous city that dominated Ionia economically and culturally. The physical remains of the city that have been discovered thus far are entirely consistent with that image: they show a city that fills the entire peninsula from the Lion Bay down to Kalabaktepe, with a necropolis further to the south.[1] It is partially orthogonal but fundamentally random, reflecting gradual growth over the centuries. Then, in all areas of the city, archaeologists have identified an unmistakable layer of ash and destruction conforming to the Persian destruction of Miletos in 494 B.C.E.: virtually nothing was left standing as the Persians exacted their vengeance for the Ionian Revolt. On top of the burn layer, the Milesians rebuilt their city with a systematic plan and on a more modest scale than the Archaic settlement, for it was only in the fourth century and following that the Milesians reoccupied the entire city peninsula.

The ruins from the Archaic and Classical eras are difficult to excavate for two main reasons. First, since the Hellenistic and Roman city continued to prosper, the Milesians built many magnificent structures—a theater, a stadium, markets, baths, and basilicas—all of which damaged the underlying strata during their construction and, with their very presence, continue to protect the older ruins from the archaeologist's shovel. Second, the groundwater problem at Miletos is considerable. Most trenches dug below the Hellenistic level require the expediency of pumps, but even they cannot always remove the water faster than it can seep back in, so such a procedure often becomes an exercise in frustration. Thus, the majority of the accessible ruins at Miletos are later than the scope of this work.

---

1. Archaic ceramic, sculpture, architectural remains, and other artwork found in various areas of the city are discussed in Hommell 1967; Graeve 1986b; Dupont 1986; Koenigs 1986; Voigtländer 1986b; Pfrommer 1986; Schwarz 1989.

Where archaeologists have persisted either in excavating around or through later buildings, where there were no later structures, or where archaeologists could overcome the groundwater problem, archaeological efforts have been rewarded with evidence about the city before 400 B.C.E. The Lion Bay and the southern plain offer little more than hints in that regard. However, on locations with raised elevations (e.g., Kalabaktepe, the Stadium Hill and the Theater Hill, and some sites outside the city proper), the Archaic remains are substantial. Within the city, a small area near the Temple of Athena has been thoroughly drained to investigate the Bronze Age layers, and the Archaic remnants were happily revealed at the same time.

The City Wall

A survey of the city site may begin with the Archaic ring wall.[2] I have already mentioned the seventh-century wall that cut off the peninsula by land in the face of the Lydian attacks. Late in the sixth century, that southern wall was expanded into a circuit wall that enclosed the entire city: anomalies found in recent geomagnetic surveys indicate the course of the Archaic wall from the hill to the area near the Sacred Gate, and archaeologists have unearthed indications of the southern end of this wall. However, when they tried to dig out a trench near the Sacred Gate, they were defeated by the groundwater problem: once they reached the Hellenistic layers, the groundwater poured in faster than the pumps could clear it out, and they found only two sherds of Late Geometric pottery before they abandoned the effort.[3] Elsewhere in the city, small remnants of the Archaic city wall have been found along the edge of the Theater Hill and the Lion Harbor and under the Byzantine Church just north of the South Market. A larger segment—perhaps a tower base—was built into the front wall of the theater building and is clearly visible today. These scanty remains are enough to indicate that by the end of the sixth century, the peninsula was ringed by a fortification circuit, although the remaining course of the wall must be filled in tentatively. The earliest

---

2. *Milet* 1.8.26–38, 116–17; *Milet* 2.3.9–11, 51–52, 91ff., 118–20 (where it was thought to be a circuit around Kalabaktepe and an isolated tower on the Theater Hill); Kleiner 1961; Kleiner 1966, 18–21; Kleiner 1968, 23–32; Müller-Wiener 1986a; Stümpel 1997; Schneider 1997; Cobet 1997.

3. Schneider 1997; Stümpel 1997; Graeve 1997, 111–12; Schröder et al. 1995.

stratum of the Sacred Gate is Classical, but it probably had an Archaic antecedent. The bearing of the wall from Kalabaktepe to the west coast is unknown: the North Hill may not have been enclosed, since remnants of a city wall there have been dated to the Archaic Period but probably actually belong to the fourth-century wall.[4] One must conclude that up to ca. 110 hectares (270 acres) of Archaic Miletos was enclosed by a fortification wall.[5]

This archaeological evidence agrees with the written record. The Lydians, coming by land in the seventh century, would have encountered only a partial land wall along the southern limit of the city, at Kalabaktepe, but after the Milesians were subjugated to the Persians in the mid–sixth century, they extended their wall to include the shores: they must have felt threatened by sea powers, presumably Samos most of all. Certainly, when the Persians attacked Miletos in 494, they came up against a completely walled city, since they had to employ a combination of naval superiority with both sapping and siege engines to win the day. Thus, Miletos was walled at the very end of the Archaic period. After a siege—we do not know how long it lasted—the Persians captured Miletos and destroyed it. The circuit wall was destroyed along with the rest of the city, and there is no sign that Milesians rebuilt it when they refounded the city.

Considering the devastation that they had just suffered and the fact that the Persian problem was far from being solved, this absence must be considered odd. Since they did not even stack together a makeshift wall out of the debris of the Archaic city, as the Athenians did after 480, we must look for the reason in the changed circumstances of the fifth century. Thucydides makes a universal statement that Ionia was unwalled in 427 B.C.E. (ἀτειχίστου γὰρ οὔσης τῆς Ἰωνίας, 3.33.2). While not everywhere accurate, this statement reflects the Persian damage done to the cities in the reconquest of Ionia as well as the systematic dismantling of any remaining fortifications, almost certainly as part of Athenian imperial policy in the fifth century, imposing sanctions on rebellious and potentially rebellious allies in Asia, as at Samos in 440.[6] Since the

---

4. North Wall: Müller-Wiener and Voigtländer 1980, 37–38 (Archaic). Müller-Wiener and Weber 1985, 17 (Classical); Mellink 1984; Müller-Wiener 1986a, 96 (Archaic). Archaeologists have found a Hellenistic temple on the point of the hill, but there is no indication of a Classical or Archaic precursor: see Müller-Wiener 1981b.

5. The total area should be reduced if the North Hill is excluded. Compare the area of Athens, with 225 hectares. See Müller-Wiener 1986a, 98.

6. Thuc. 1.117; Meiggs 1972, 149–50.

Milesian walls had already been demolished, the policy would have had the effect of discouraging or even forbidding the construction of a new wall until the situation had changed so that either the Athenians saw the wisdom of such a wall or else the Milesians did not feel constrained by Athenian regulations. Only after the Milesians rebelled against the Athenians in 412, departing permanently from the Athenian Empire, were they able to construct some kind of fortification, and even that was initially just a hurried, provisional structure.

Cults at Miletos

Apollo Delphinios was the patron god of Miletos and so played a vital role in civic affairs. His priests, the Molpoi ("Singers"), provided the eponymous official of the city after about 540 B.C.E., and his emblem, the lion, served as the symbol and coin type of Miletos. Electrum staters from as early as ca. 575 B.C.E. feature either a recumbent lion or two lions' heads back-to-back.[7] In addition, Apollo was the patron of the great Oracle at Didyma, which was controlled by the Milesians.

The sanctuary of Apollo, called the Delphinion, was located in the heart of the city, at the southeast base of the Lion Harbor and northeast of the North Market. The oldest remains date to the sixth century, but there must have been a cult earlier. Indirect evidence indicates an early date before colonization, since Apollo Delphinios was worshiped in nearly every Milesian colony and so must have existed in the mother city. The shrine of Delphinios was not a temple proper but rather a sanctuary containing an altar of Apollo and a cluster of five smaller, cylinder-shaped altars (*bomoi*) for other deities, three of which are inscribed.

Like that of the rest of the city, the destruction of the Delphinion by the Persians is indicated by an ash layer. Its importance to civic life is demonstrated by the fact that it was swiftly rebuilt after the reoccupation: it was the only certain construction on the Lion Harbor in the first half of the fifth century, about 29 × 50 m., occupying a pair of city blocks. The first

---

7. Cahn 1950; Ehrhardt 1983, 132; Kraay 1976, 23–26, 37, 258 (coinage); Kraay and Hirmer 1966, #588, #591 [PCG 1.7] (staters). A tetradrachm from Classical Miletos features an obverse with the laureate head of Apollo and a reverse with a lion with its head reverted, looking at a star (Kraay 1976, #934), a type that became a common symbol for Miletos (Mørkholm 1991, #262 = *SNG* 978; #568 = *SNG* 988; #571 = *SNG* 987).

layout probably had two walls of porous stone, built of reused Archaic material on a thin gneiss foundation and lying opposite each other on the north and south. Benches along the inner sides were converted to stoas by the mid–fourth century. That building was replaced during Alexander's lifetime, more than doubled in area (61 × 50 m.) and enclosed by a three-sided hall (the fourth side was added later) whose superstructure was covered by inscriptions of state documents. Despite these additions, the basic character of the sanctuary remained unchanged: it was an archive, a shrine, and the embarkation point for the annual procession down the Sacred Way, which started immediately outside the Delphinion, and south to Didyma.[8]

Apollo's epithet caused some confusion in antiquity, since the ancient Greeks believed that the name *Delphinios* was derived from the Greek word meaning "dolphin" (δελφίς) and so that Apollo was a dolphin-god.[9] This derivation is explicitly stated in one of the earliest works of Greek literature, the *Homeric Hymn to Apollo* (lines 400–496), perhaps as early as the eighth century B.C.E. and certainly antedating the mid-sixth century. In it, the anonymous poet tells the story of the foundation of the Oracle of Apollo at Delphi by a shipload of Cretans from Knossos who were led to the site by Apollo in the guise of a dolphin. This story records an extremely early attempt to explain the etymology of both Delphi and Delphinios by making Apollo the dolphin-god.

This traditional derivation has been challenged recently and should be dismissed as a false etymology, parallel to the incorrect derivation in the same poem of *Pythia* from πύθειν, "to rot."[10] Apollo's connection with the sea is not justified. Many of Delphinios's cult sites are not on the sea, and there is no element in his worship that particularly links the god to water: no early cult statue and nothing in his festivals connect him with a dolphin, and he has no particular tie to sea journeys or colonial founda-tions. Instead, in four of the best-known sites of his worship—Miletos, Olbia, Athens, and Crete—the cult of Apollo Delphinios is characterized by its connection to the state government.

Apollo Delphinios was worshiped in many other locations in the

---

8. *Milet* 1.3. esp. 408; *Milet* 1.6.88–89; Aly 1911, 1–5; Gerkan 1924a, 40; Gerkan 1940; Gerkan 1950; Mellink 1974, 114 (ash); Hommel 1975; Mitchell and McNicoll 1978/79, 63–64; Koenigs 1986.

9. According to an older theory, he was a Chalkidian god of sea travel. See Wernicke 1896, 47.

10. Graf 1979.

Greek world by a very early date,[11] and many times that worship is closely tied to questions of citizenship. At Athens and on Crete, the Delphinion is linked with the ephebic oath and ritual that admitted young adult men (ephebes) into full citizenship status. In Archaic Dreros on Crete, Apollo Delphinios is mentioned along with the other main civic deities in the ephebic oath (*Inscr. Cret.* I.ix.1C.124ff.). The Cretan poet Rhianos (fr. 68 Powell) placed under the god's protection a youth making a hair offering, another ritual that marked the change from boy to man. At Athens, female citizens swore an oath at the Delphinion that the son born to them had been begot by a full citizen, thereby assuring that the child would also be a full citizen (Ps.-Dem. 40.11, 39.2; Isok. *Or.* 12.9). In Hellenistic Miletos, the questionable exercise of citizen rights had to be examined before the Molpoi and a state court (*Milet* 1.3.319 #143.31–37, 331 #146.41–46, etc.). Thus, at Athens, Crete, and Miletos, Apollo Delphinios was especially tied to issues of admittance into membership in the state.

The Delphinion is also consistently identified with state government. At Knossos, the Delphinion housed proxeny decrees and treaties with other states. At Dreros, many state laws were inscribed there, and at Hyrtakina, the guests of honor of the city dined at a common hearth in the Delphinion (*Inscr. Cret.* II.xv.2.17). At Miletos, besides providing both protection as patron of the city and a priest to serve as eponym, Apollo Delphinios safeguarded the state archives: epigraphic finds there include an Archaic sacrifice calendar, lists of the eponymous officials, and hundreds of inscriptions spanning centuries, including treaties, *anagraphai* conferring citizenship or proxeny, and other state decrees. In Roman times, the Molpoi took part in the official state cult of the Roman people and Roma.[12] As at Miletos, Apollo Delphinios was the patron god of Olbia in the Classical era (although apparently Apollo Ietros, "Healer," had taken precedence in the Archaic time), and the *aisymnetes* of the Molpoi may also have been the eponymous official. A *temenos* north of the agora was the Delphinion and served as the state archives.[13] We must therefore conclude that it was one of

---

11. Wernicke (1896, 47–48) lists Aigina, Athens, Chalkis, Chios, Harbor of Oropos, Knossos (as Delphidios), Krisa, Massalia, Megara, Miletos, Olbia, Olus, Sparta, and Thera. F. Graf (1979, 3–4) adds Erythrai, Hermonassa, Aigiale on Amorgos, Nisyros, Dreros, and Larissa. Attestations go back to the seventh century at least in Miletos, Phokaia (because of Massalia), Olus, Thera, Aigina, and Dreros.

12. Sokolowski 1955, #49B.26–37.

13. Vinogradov 1981, 20–22; Graf 1974; Graf 1979, 8–9 esp. nn. 69–73; Vinogradov and Kryzickij 1995, 109–11.

the chief universal obligations of Apollo Delphinios to shelter and protect official state documents.

Delphinios may have been a pre-Dorian god who had a Minoan or Mycenaean predecessor on Crete. The meaning of the name *Delphinios* is unknown, since it is non-Greek, probably a holdover of earlier worship. The presence in the earliest Greek literature of the false etymology that links Apollo with dolphins and the sea indicates that the origin of the cult title had become obscure by a very early date. Moreover, the worship of Delphinios was clearly bound up with the ephebic ritual and with the central institutions of certain states, including—in addition to the ones already discussed—Thera, Aigina, Chios, and Erythrai. Thus, at Miletos the cult may have belonged to the first Milesian settlers in Submycenaean or in Early Protogeometric times, perhaps brought from Athens in the Ionian Migration.

Judging from the consistency of the colonial evidence, Apollo was probably worshiped in Archaic Miletos under many different epithets, including *Lykeios* (wolf), *Ietros* (Healer), and *Thargelios* (Master of the festival Thargelia). Other names that may also have been old include *Thyios* (Inspired), which is known only for Miletos and only through Hesychius (s.v. Θύϊος· Ἀπόλλων ἐν Μιλήτῳ), and *Ulios*, attributed to the Milesians and the Delians by Strabo (14.1.6), who derives it from οὔλειν, which means "to be healthy," signifying Apollo as healer (cf. *Suda* s.v. οὔλιος). Yet another epithet, *Hebdomaios* (God of the Seventh), is implied both by the festival Hebdomaia mentioned in lines 6 and 21 of the Molpoi Decree and by a curious bone plaque from Olbia.[14]

Greek sanctuaries were often communal locations for the worship of more than one god, and Apollo was especially generous about sharing his space in Miletos. His twin sister, Artemis, had her own Archaic altar in the Delphinion there (*Milet* 1.3.276 #131), probably with the matching epithet *Delphinia*, while at Didyma Artemis was the second most venerated deity, usually worshiped under the epithet *Pythia*. She had an Archaic *temenos* at Didyma from the seventh century, complete with an altar, rock basin, and spring, and a dedication from the sixth century found near the northwest corner of the Temple of Apollo reads: "to [Arte]mis [--- and Ap]ollo."[15] In addition, Artemis had her own *temenoi*:

---

14. See the discussion of oracles later in this chapter. For a full review of the individual epithets and the colonial evidence for them, see Ehrhardt 1983, 130–47.

15. Rehm 1958, #17: [Ἀρτέ]μιδι[----καὶ Ἀπ]όλλω[νι]. The lacuna is surely restored correctly. Fontenrose (1988, 122) postulates that *Pytheia* may have filled in the remainder

a probable sanctuary stood by the southern cross wall at Miletos; and as *Kithone* (Goddess of the Tunic), she had a short-lived fifth-century temple on the East Terrace of Kalabaktepe that is referred to by Kallimachos in his *Hymn to Artemis* (3.225–27). In other evidence, she is portrayed with Leto in a sixth-century votive statue and with Hekate, KUROTROPHOS (?), Leto, and Apollo in a fourth-century dedicatory relief. After the resettlement of the city, her cult was continued: an inscription of regulations dated to 380/79 concerns benefits to her priestess, and a gold stater from the second or first century B.C.E. features her head on the obverse and a standing lion with its head reverted, looking at a star, on the reverse.[16]

The cults of other deities are witnessed in inscriptional evidence stored in the archive of the Delphinion. One of the earliest attested cultic inscriptions that survives is a sacrifice calendar, carved on a block of white marble, .54 × 2.26 m., discovered built into the foundation on the south side of the Delphinion, although this was not its original location or use: it was probably an orthostat from the oldest wall. It was carved in boustrophedon, with straight lines carved between the rows and three vertical dots between each word or phase. Based on the letter shapes, the excavator judges that this stone was inscribed shortly before 500 B.C.E., and because the writing breaks off on one edge, the inscription must have continued onto an adjacent stone or stones, now lost.[17]

The inscription (*Milet* 1.3 #31a) reads:

πϱ]οδόϱπια δίδοται Δ. . . . . . . ΣΙΝ δύ[ο γ]υλλ[οί ----
-----] σπονδαί διφάσια [μ]ελίχματα δύο γυλλοί ἐστεθμ-
ένοι ξύλα ⁚ δωδεκάτηι ἐς βασιλέως δίδοται Διο[νυσι--
-----]λαμπάδα ἄλφιτα ἀλέατα τυϱὸν ἀγνόν μέλι δαι-

---

of the lacuna, although there is no attestation for that title before 280 B.C.E. The goddess was also worshiped at Didyma as *Lykeia* in the third century B.C.E. and possibly as *Phosphoros*. Most of the epithets of Artemis that occur in the colonies cannot be securely traced to Miletos, although they may well have occurred there as well.

16. Southern sanctuary: Graeve 1973/74; Graeve 1975b; Kleine 1979. Kalabaktepe: *Milet* 1.8.16–17; Kerschner 1995, 218–20; Kerschner and Senff 1997 (corrects the dating to the fifth century). Statue of Leto and Artemis: Hadzisteliou-Price 1971, #VI.14. Fourth-century relief: Hadzisteliou-Price 1971, #V.8. Regulations: Sokolowski 1955, #45. There also survive fragments of a decree concerning Artemis Skiris from before 228/7 B.C.E. (Sokolowski 1955, #47) and another regulating the cult of Artemis from the end of the first century B.C.E. (Sokolowski 1955, #51 = *Milet* 1.7 #202). Stater: Jenkins 1972, #688/689 = PCG 44.11. Didyma: Fontenrose 1988, 122–23; Rehm 1958, #120, #29.15–19.

17. Stones #31b and #31c are probably the continuation, but only small parts of them are readable: two lines on #31b and one or two letters on each of six lines on #31c.

δα μαλλόν σπονδήν μελίχματα σκόροδα τῆς [----   5   ←
-- τρίτηι ἐπ]ὶ δέκα Ἥρηι Ἀνθέηι οἷς λευκὴ ἔγκυαρ λευκῶι ἀν-   →
αβεβαμένη χοῦς τῆ ἱερῆι δίδοται καὶ ξύλων ὀ[----   ← → ↓
---- ἡ]μιέκτο ἐς τὸ ἱερέως δίδοται χοῦς ξύλα κἀπί βωμὸ-   →
ν ἀμφορεὺς οἶνο ∴ τετράδι ἐπὶ δέκα ΔΙΝΟΣΙΩΙ [----   ←
-----]ι οἷς ἄρσην ἐκτεὺς πυρῶν ἐκτεὺς κριθέων ἔκτη οἶ-   10   →
νο ξύλα μέλι ἄλειφα ∴ Λεύκωι οἷς ἄρσην ἀργῆι[----   ←
-----]τηι ἱσταμένο ἐορτὴ κηρύσσεται Ἀπόλλωνος Δελφιν-   →

[[1] An early dinner is given . . . [including] two cubes (?) . . [2] .
drink offerings, soothing things of two kinds, two wreathed cubes
(?), [3](and) wooden things. On the twelfth day, he gives to the
house of the king, (and) to Dio[nysos] . [4] . . torches, barley, wheat
groats, holy cheese, honey, a pine-wood torch, [5] wool, a drink
offering, soothing things, garlands of . . [6] . [On the thir]teenth a
white sheep that has been impregnated by a white ram is given to
Hera of the Blooms [7], a measure is given, and the . . . of wood . .
[8] . of a half of a sixth to the house of the priest is given, a measure,
wood, and on the altar [9] an amphora of wine. On the fourteenth
day, DINOSIOI (?) . . [10] . a male sheep, a sixth [bushel] of wheat,
a sixth of barley, a sixth of wine, [11] wood, honey, (and) oil. To
Leukos, a male sheep with a shining . . [12] . is set up on the sixth,
and a feast of Apollo Delphin[ios] will be announced . . .]

The calendar mentions festivals from two consecutive spring months,
but the problems in interpreting it are manifold, beginning with the difficulty in simply rendering the words. For example, among the offerings
are *gulloi* (lines 1–2), which Hesychios describes as stone cubes (s.v.
γυλλός· κύβος ἢ τετράγωνος λίθος; but also s.v. γυλλοί· στολμοί). However, his explanation has not pleased many scholars—the use of stone
cubes in this religious context seems very odd—and so various suggestions have been made to explain them, including wicker baskets and
wreaths.[18] In addition, the agent in this decree is omitted, although it may
have been the Molpoi or other officials acting on behalf of the city.
Besides Apollo Delphinios, four other deities are mentioned in the course
of this decree: Dionysios on line 3;[19] Di Nosioi (Zeus Notios or Nosios)

18. *Milet* 1.3.164.
19. Wilamowitz-Moellendorff (1914, 99–100) suggests filling the lacuna with the name
Dioskuroi (Δ[ιοσκόροι]σιν), but this emendation is rejected by Ehrhardt (1983, 187 n.
1078) and Herrmann (*Milet* 6.1 #31a).

on line 9; Hera Antheia ("Flowering") on line 6, a goddess of the spring-time also known from Argos (Paus. 2.221); and Leukos on line 11.

Dionysos is especially well attested, since archaeologists have un-earthed a shrine dedicated to him ca. 150 m. southwest of the Delphinion (40 m. west of the possible Prytaneion). Discovered under the Christian Basilica of St. Michael, this shrine had seven different building phases. Phase I, from the late (?) sixth century, consisted of the remains of a simple building, about 5.2 m. wide and at least 5 m. long, with a founda-tion made of round, unworked fieldstone, a superstructure of clay bricks, and a tiled roof. After a clearly demarcated destruction layer between the Archaic and Classical building phases, the new shrine (phase II) was built in the second quarter of the fifth century on the site of the old one. A very small building (its inside walls measured 2.5–2.8 × 2.5 m.), it had four sides but was not rectangular. The building was probably made of mud-bricks and had an altar of heaped-up ash inside it. It was destroyed by fire late in the fifth century but then immediately rebuilt.[20]

Although no particular temple or sanctuary has been found for him, Zeus was unquestionably worshiped throughout Milesian history. *Notios,* however, is a rare epithet: it is unknown elsewhere in the Greek world but recurs in another Archaic inscription from Miletos, a one-word dedica-tion, Νόσιε (*Milet* 1.3 #186). The epithet may be derived from νόσος (disease) and refer to Zeus as healer, or—less likely—from νόστος (home-coming). Zeus also appears portrayed with Leto in a sixth-century statue of two seated figures from Didyma, and one of the Archaic altars in the Delphinion is dedicated to Zeus Soter ("Savior"), the protector of cities. His cult occurs in many of the colonies, including Olbia, where he shared a place in the central *temenos* with Athena, and at Didyma, where Zeus Soter was particularly important, possessing a sanctuary in Apollo's *temenos* and, by Hellenistic times, a festival called the Boegia.[21]

---

20. Archaic: Mellink 1974, 123; Müller-Wiener 1977, 145–37; Müller-Wiener 1977/78b, 95–96; Müller-Wiener 1988d, 289; Müller-Wiener 1988a, 35; Mitchell and McNicoll 1978/79, 63–64; Müller-Wiener and Voigtländer 1980, 29. Destruction: Mellink 1974, 114; Müller-Wiener 1977, 135–37; Müller-Wiener 1977/78b, 95; Müller-Wiener 1988a, 35–36; Müller-Wiener and Voigtländer 1980, 29. Classical: Mellink 1974, 123; Müller-Wiener 1977, 135–37; Müller-Wiener 1977/78b, 96; Müller-Wiener 1988d, 289; Müller-Wiener 1988a, 35–36; Real 1977/78; Müller-Wiener and Voigtländer 1980, 29. The shrine was made into a full-fledged temple with a cult image of the god in the third century B.C.E. See Müller-Wiener 1977/78b, 97–99. For an inscription regulating the cult of Dionysos at Miletos from 276/75 B.C.E., see Sokolowski 1955, #48.

21. With Leto: Naumann and Tuchelt 1963/64, 57–62. Altar: *Milet* 1.3 #130 (*Soter* is a common epithet, especially at Didyma and Olbia). Treaty of *isopoliteia* with Herakleia:

Zeus's usual consort at Miletos is not Hera, whose only appearance at Miletos and the colonies is in this Sacrifice Calendar (and then with the rare epithet *Antheia*). Instead, Hera must have been considered a minor springtime deity, while Leto took pride of place as a goddess more appropriate to Miletos, since she was the mother of Apollo and Artemis. In addition to the Archaic statue of Leto and Zeus, she appears with Artemis in the aforementioned votive statue from the southeast portion of the theater, also from the sixth century, as well as the fourth-century dedicatory relief mentioned already.[22]

Leukos, the last god mentioned in the Sacrifice Calendar, is essentially unknown. The word *leukos* itself means "white" or "shining," and the only precedent in the Greek world for it as a divine epithet is at Tanagra, where the people worshiped Leukos Hermes (Sch. Lykoph. 679). The original editor dismisses this interpretation out of hand, suggesting other possibilities: a hero from Crete; a light daimon; a nymph known from Delos; or Arge, the mother of Dionysos. However, it is difficult to see how this reference could stand for a female divinity, since in this context, with the masculine ending and a male sacrificial sheep, the deity is certainly himself masculine. Instead, a fairly appealing suggestion has been made that he should be connected with the Panhellenic hero Achilles, since the most celebrated site for the worship of Achilles was the Island of Leuke, 50 km. southeast of the Istros River delta.[23] Perhaps, then, *Leukos* was occasionally used in antiquity as an epithet for Achilles.

Certainly Achilles was worshiped at Olbia since at least the sixth century as a chthonic deity and a protector of fertility in nature. Oddly enough, the cult of Achilles seems to be concentrated along the north

---

Milet 1.3 #150.21–22; Ehrhardt 1983, 155–58; Hasluck 1910, 225–26; Vinogradov and Kryzickij 1995, 112. Boegia: Kallim. 229 Pf.; Fontenrose 1988, 135–44. It is possible that Zeus-Ammon was worshiped in the first half of the sixth century on Zeytintepe, but that identification is not secure: see the discussion of Aphrodite later in this chapter.

22. Ehrhardt 1983, 156, 159 esp. n. 721 (Hera), 158–60 (Leto). Since evidence for the worship of Leto has not been found at Olbia, where the excavation is well advanced, but since it has been found at Istros from the fourth century, the likely conclusion is that Leto was a relatively late addition at Miletos, arriving in the sixth century, and that she reached Istros separately.

23. *Milet* 1.3.165; Ehrhardt 1983, 180. Achilles: Hedreen 1991; Hommel 1980; Hind 1996. Leuke: Demetrius in Ps.-Skym. *GGM* 1.228, lines 786–92 = 783-89 Diller; Lykoph. 188–89; Anon. *Peripl. Eux.* 64 = *GGM* 1.419; Paus. 3.19.11. One fifth-century inscription from the site reads, Γλαῦκος με ἀνέθηκεν Ἀχιλλῆι Λευκῆ μεδέοντι παί<ε>ς Ποσιδήο [Glaukos, son of Posideios, dedicated me to Achilles, master of Leuke] (Hedreen 1991, 319 n. 42 = *SEG* 30 [1980] #869).

coast of the Pontos, at Olbia, in Megarian Chersonesos, and is perhaps reflected in the name of the town Achilleion on the Asian shore of the Kimmerian Bosporos (Str. 7.4.5, 11.2.6.). However, it is unattested on the southern or western littorals of the Pontos. Perhaps the cult originated among the Skythians and was transferred from the colonies to the mother city, where the only other evidence for him is a reference in Athenaios (2.43D) to a spring of Achilles at Miletos.[24]

The Molpoi Decree and the Procession to Didyma

Another important religious inscription found in the Delphinion is a very long and difficult text called the Molpoi Decree (*Milet* 1.3 #133), which has already been discussed in chapter 3 for its political importance. Relating to the Festival of Apollo Hebdomaios in the month Taureon, the decree gives instructions for two of the most important events in the annual life of the city: it provides for the beginning of the new year and the formal inauguration of the new *aisymnetes* of the Molpoi, and it recounts the sacrifices and procedures that must be followed during the great annual procession in honor of Apollo that began at the Delphinion at Miletos and crossed by land to the Temple of Apollo at Didyma.

Because of its length, I break the decree into appropriate subheadings for discussion.[25]

Prescript (lines 1–6)

ἐπὶ Φιλτέω τὸ Διονυσίο μολπῶν αἰσυμνῶντος, προσέταιροι
 ἦσαν Οἰνώ-
πων Ἀγαμήδης Ἀριστοκράτεος, Ὁπλήθων Λύκος Κλέαντος,
Βίων Ἀπολλοδώρο, Βωρ(έ)ων Κρηθεὺς Ἑρμώνακτος, Θράσων Ἀν-
τιλέοντος. ἔδοξε μολποῖσιν τὰ ὄργια ἀναγράψαντας θεῖναι ἐς
[5] τὸ ἱερὸν καὶ χρῆσθαι τούτοισιν. καὶ οὕτωι τάδε γραφθέντα ἐτέ-
θη.

---

24. Vinogradov and Kryzickij 1995, 117–18 (Olbia); Hedreen 1991 (Skythian origin); Farnell 1921, 286–87; Hommel 1980; Ehrhardt 1983, 179–80.
25. The editio princeps was published by Wilamowitz-Moellendorff (1904), and for the most part Rehm (*Milet* 1.3 #133) agrees with him. The Greek text offered here is from Rehm. Cf. Herrmann in *Milet* 1.6; Sokolowski 1955, 129–30.

[[1] When Philteos, the son of Dionysios, was the *aisymnetes* of the Molpoi, and from the tribe Oino[2]pes, Agamedes, the son of Aristokrates, and from the tribe [H]opletes, Lykos, the son of Klean, [3] and Bion, the son of Apollodoros, and from the tribe Boreos, Kretheus, the son of Ermonax, and Thrason, the son of An[4]tileon were the companions [*prosetairoi*]. It seemed best to the Molpoi that the rites be engraved and placed in [5] the sanctuary and be performed in the following way. And thus they were engraved and placed [6] there.]

Inauguration of New Aisymnetes *(lines 6–18)*

Ἑβδομαίοισι˙ τῆι ογδωι απολεικαιτα ἱερὰ ἢ σπλάγχνα σπείσοσι
    μολπῶν
αἰσυμνήτης˙ ὁ δὲ αἰσυμνήτης καὶ <ο> προσεταίρος
    προσαιρεῖται, ὅταν οἱ
κρητῆρες πάντες σπεσθέωσι καὶ παιωνίσωσιν˙ τῆ δὲ ἐνάτη ((καὶ
    ἀπὸ
τῆς ὀσφύος καὶ τῆς πεμπάδος, ἢν ἴσχοσιν στεφανηφόροι,
[10] τούτων προλαγχάνει τὰ ἰσέα ὁ νέος.)) ἄρχονται θύειν τὰ
    ἱερῆα
αρχο ἀπὸ τούτων Ἀπόλλωνι Δελφινίωι˙ καὶ κρητῆρες κιρνέαται
    κατό-
περ ἐμμολπῶ(ν) καὶ παιὼν γίνεται, ὁ δὲ ἐξιὼν αἰσυμνήτης ἀπὸ
    τῶν ἡμίσε-
ων θύει Ἱστίηι ((καὶ κρητῆρας σπενδέτω αὐτὸς καὶ
    παιωνιζέτω))˙ τῆι δεκά-
τηι ἀμιλλητήρια, καὶ δίδοται ἀπὸ μολπῶν δύο ἱερῆια τοῖσι
    στεφανηφό-
[15] ροισιν τέληα, καὶ ἔρδεται Ἀπόλλωνι Δελφινίων, καὶ
    ἀμιλλῶνται οἱ στε-
φανηφόροι οἵ τε νέοι καὶ οι ερεω καὶ οἶνον πίνοσι τὸμ μολπῶν,
    καὶ κρητῆρες
σπένδονται κατόπερ ἐμμολπῶ(ν)˙ ὁ δὲ ἐξιὼν αἰσυμνήτης
    παρέχει ἅπερ ὁ
Ὀνιτάδης καὶ λαγχάνει ἅπερ ὁ Ὀνιτάδης.

[At the festival of the Hebdomaia, on the eighth day the *aisymnetes* of the Molpoi . . . [provides?] both the sacrifices or the viscerals for the people pouring libations.

[7] The *aisymnetes* and the *prosetairos* select [others] [or "the *aisymnetes* chooses the *prosetairoi*"], when [8] all the kraters have been poured and they have chanted the paean. And on the ninth day ((and from [9] the loins and fifth part, which the *stephanephoroi* receive, [10] and the new man possesses things equal to these)), they begin to sacrifice the victims [11] from those things [? αρχο] to Apollo Delphinios. And the kraters are mixed just as [12] is done among the Molpoi and the paean is sung, and the *aisymnetes* leaving office [13] sacrifices to Hestia from the halves ((and let him himself pour the libation from the kraters and sing the paean)); on the tenth day, [14] there are contests, and two perfect victims are given from the Molpoi to the *stephanephoroi* [15] and sacrificed to Apollo Delphinios. And the *stephanephoroi* compete, [16] both the new ones and [οι ερεω], and they drink the wine of the Molpoi, and [17] the libation is poured from the kraters just as [is done] among the Molpoi. The outgoing *aisymnetes* provides the things like those of [18] Onitadai and takes for his portion just as the Onitadai do.]

Procession to Didyma (lines 18–31)

ὅταν στεφανηφόροι ἴωσιν ἐς
Δίδυμα, ἡ πόλις διδοῖ ἑκατόνβην τρία ἱερήια τέλεια· τούτων ἕν θῆλυ, ἕν
[20] δὲ ἐνορχές· ἐς μολπ(ῶ)ν ἡ πόλις διδοῖ Ταργηλίοισιν
ἱερ(ῆι)ον τέλειον καὶ Μεταγε[ι]-
τνίοισιν ἱερ(ῆι)ον τέλειον, Ἐβδομαίοισιν δὲ δύο τέλεια καὶ χὸν τὸμ παλαιὸν ὁ[ρ-]
τῆς ἑκάστης· τούτοισι τοῖς ἱεροῖσιν ὁ βασιλεὺς παρίσταται, λαγχάνει δὲ
οὐδὲν πλῆον τῶν ἄλλων μολπῶν. ((καὶ ἄρχονται οἱ στεφανηφόροι Ταυρεῶ-
νος θύειν Ἀπόλλωνι Δελφινίωι ἀπὸ τῶν ἀριστερῶν ἀπαρξάμενοι, καὶ κρητη-
[25] ρίσας τέσσερας)). καὶ γυλλοὶ φέρονται δύο, καὶ τίθεται παρ' Ἑκάτην τὴν πρόσθεν
πυλέων ἐστεμμένος καὶ ἀκρήτω κατασπένδετε, ὁ δ' ἕτερος ἐς Δίδυμα ἐπὶ
θύρας τίθεται· ταῦτα δὲ ποιήσαντες ἔρχονται τὴν ὁδὸγ τὴν πλατεῖαν μέχρι

ἄκρο, ἀπ' ἄκρο δὲ διὰ δρυμὸ· καὶ παιωνίζεται πρῶτον παρ'
Ἑκάτη τῇ πρόσθεν πυ-
λέων, παρὰ Δυνάμει, εἶτεν ἐπὶ λειμῶνι ἐπ' ἄκρο παρὰ νύφαια',
εἶτεν παρ' Ἑρμῇ Ἐν-
[30]κελάδο, παρὰ Φυλίωι, κατὰ Κεραιίτην, παρὰ Χαρέω
ἀνδριᾶσιν, ἔρδεται δὲ τῶι παν-
θύωι ἔτει παρὰ Κεραιίτηι δαρτόν, παρὰ Φυλίωι δὲ θύα θύεται
πάντ' ἔτεα.

[Whenever the *stephanephoroi* go to [19] Didyma, the city gives as
a hekatomb three perfect victims, one of which is to be female and
another [20] uncastrated. And the city gives to the house of the
Molpoi a perfect victim at the Targelia and a perfect victim at the
Metagei[21]tnia, and on the Hebdomaia two perfect victims, and
an old measure at [22] each festival. The king is present at these
sacrifices, and he receives [23] no more than the other Molpoi.
((And the *stephanephoroi* begin in Taureon [24] to sacrifice to
Apollo Delphinios offering the first fruits from the left [or "with
their left hands"?], and [25] mixing four kraters)). Two stone cubes
are brought in, one of which is placed before the sanctuary of
Hekate before the [26] Gates; wreathed; pour it unmixed. The
other is placed on [27] the doors to Didyma. And after doing these
things, they follow the flat road as far as [28] the heights and from
the heights through the woods. And the paean is sung, first before
Hekate before the [29] Gates, then before the sanctuary of Dynamis, then in the meadow on the heights before the nymphs, then
before the shrine of Hermes with the Loud Voice [? *Enkelados*],
[30] before the Tribesman [*Phylios*], opposite the Horned One
[*Keraiites*], before the statues of Chares. Sacrifices are made in the
year of all offerings [31] before the Horned One, an animal that
must be skinned [? δαρτόν], and before the Tribesman, sacrifices
are burned every year.]

Duties and Rights of the Onitadai (lines 31–40)
Ὀνιτά
δηισι πάρεξις κεράμο σιδήρο χαλκὸ ξύλων ὕδατος κύκλων
δαίδος ῥιπῶν

κρέα ἐπιδιαιρ ἐν φαλαγκτηρίων δεσμῶν τοῖς ἱερήιοισιν ((παρὰ στεφανηφόρος
λύχνον καὶ ἄλειφα)) · ὄπτησις σπλάγχνων, κρεῶν ἔψησις, τῆς ὀσφύος καὶ
[35] τῆς πεμπάδος, ἣν στεφανηφόροι ἴσχοσιν, ἔψησις καὶ διαίρεσις, καὶ μοίρης λάξις. ((ἐπιπέσσεν τὰ ἔλατρα ἐξ ἡμεδίμνο τὠπόλλωνι πλακόντινα, τῆι Ἐκά-
τηι δὲ χωρίς)). γίνεται Ὀνιτάδηισιν ἀπὸ μολπῶν ὀσφύες πᾶσαι ἐκτὸς ὧν οἱ
στεφανηφόροι ἴσχοσιν, δέρματα πάντα, θυαλήματα τρία ἀπ᾽ ἱερήο ἑκάστο, ((θύ-
ων τὰ περιγινόμενα, οἶνον τὸν ἐν τῶι κρητῆρι περιγινόμενον)), πεμπὰς τῆς ἠ-
[40] μέρης·

[The Onitadai receive [32] a provision of clay, of iron, of bronze, of wood, of water, of dishes, of a pine torch, and of wicker [33] to divide anew the meat, of wooden blocks, of fetters for the sacrificial animals. ((Next to the *stephanephoros* [34] lamps and oil.)) The roasting of the entrails, the boiling of the meat, of the loins, and [35] of the fifth part, which the *stephanephoroi* receive, the boiling and the cutting up, and the allotment of a portion. [36] ((He cooks flat cakes of half mina to Apollo and to [37] Hekate separately)). All of the loins go to the Onitadai from the Molpoi apart from those that the [38] *stephanephoroi* receive, all of the skins, three burnt offerings from each victim, ((the [39] remaining parts of the sacrifices, and the wine that is left in the krater)), a fifth [40] on the day.]

Miscellaneous Additions (lines 40–45)

((ὅτι ἂν τούτων μὴ ποιῶσιν Ὀνιτάδαι, ἔαδε μολποῖσιν ἐπὶ Χαροπίνο, στεφανηφόρος ἀπὸ τῶν Ἰστιήιων παρέχεν. ὅτι δ᾽ ἂν Ὀνιτάδαι χρηίζωσιν, ἔαδε μολποῖ-
σι στεφανηφόροισιν ἐπιτετράφθαι.))
(((τῶι κήρυκι ἀτελείη ἐμμολπῶ(ν) πάντων καὶ λάξις οπλάγχνων ἀπὸ θυῶν ἑκασ-

τέων καὶ οἶνο φορὴ ἐς τὰ ψυκτήρια τέλεσι τοῖσ᾽ ἑωυτô, ὁ δ᾽
οἶνος ἀπὸ μολπῶ(ν) γίνεται.)))
[45] (((τῶι ὠιδῶι δεῖπνον παρέχει ὁ ἱερ(ε)ως, ἄριστον δὲ
ὠισυμνήτης.)))

[(((Whatever of these things the Onitadai do not do, it pleases the
Molpoi in the year of Charopinos, [41] the *stephanephoros* should
do from the things of Hestia. And whatever the Onitadai are lacking, it pleases the Molpoi [42] to entrust it to the *stephanephoroi*.))
[43] (((An exemption from all things from among the Molpoi for
the herald and a portion of the entrails from each of the sacrifices
[44] and the transport of the wine in the psykters at his own cost,
and the wine is provided by the Molpoi.))) [45] (((And the priest
provides the feast to the singer, and the *aisymnetes* provides the
breakfast.))))]

Considering its length, this document is remarkably intact, but it is
maddeningly difficult because of the circumstances of its engraving. It is
actually a series of decrees and amendments on the same subject that have
been put together and reengraved over a span of centuries. While the
stone was carved ca. 100 B.C.E., it is a copy of the decree from 450/49,
when Philteos was the eponym of Miletos. However, line 40 is an amend-
ment passed in the year Charopinos was the *aisymnetes*, 479/8. This fact
indicates that the original decree must have been previous even to that.
Some other smaller sections were added between 479/8 and 450/49 and
also subsequent to the year of Philteos but before the year of the engraving. Hence Rehm makes the following proposal for dating the parts of the
decree:[26]

Pre-479/78	Lines 6–7, 11–22, 25–35
479/78	Lines 40–42
Interim 1	Lines 13, 33–34, 38–39
450/49	Lines 1–6; reengraving

---

26. *Milet* 1.3.277–79.

Interim 2   Lines 8–10, 23–25, 36–37, 43–45
Ca. 100   Reengraving of the whole

By the time of the final engraving, parts of the earlier stone must have been obscure to the engraver, either because of damage to the stone or because it contained arcane words or phrases that were meaningless by the first century. As a result, some sections—particularly lines 6–7, 11, 16, and 24–25—deteriorate into gibberish.

The inscription is divided into four main parts, of which the first is the prescript, lines 1–6, listing the *aisymnetes* of the Molpoi and his companions. It is a normal feature of every Milesian decree (post–ca. 540) to list the *aisymnetes* in the prescript as a way of dating the decree, in this case to 450/49 B.C.E. The list of companions is more curious: they are not necessary for dating, so we must ask why they are here. Probably they are included because this decree is about the annual change to a new board of companions, although it is possible that they are listed because they are part of the organization deciding this decree. Together the six officials named represent three of the six Archaic Milesian tribes, indicating that this decree predates the democratic reorganization of the mid–fifth century (the presence of only three tribes may mean that the six tribes alternated years in office, with three tribes represented among the *prosetairoi* each year, although the fact that three tribes are listed may be entirely coincidental). Finally, we learn that the decree was to be engraved and erected in the Delphinion at Miletos.

Lines 6–18 record the inauguration of the new *aisymnetes* and his board of companions. The dates are the eighth, ninth, and tenth days of the month of Taureon (line 23), which begins with the spring equinox, during the Festival of Apollo Hebdomaios. On the eighth day, after sacrifices and libations, a selection takes place. Lines 6–7 are difficult to read, but apparently the *aisymnetes* has already been designated; by what means is unknown. Line 7 may read that the *aisymnetes* chooses the *prosetairoi* or that the *aisymnetes* and the *prosetairoi* choose something or someone else: the grammar is impossible to decipher. Then libations are poured and the sacred paean is sung. On the following day, there are more sacrifices, songs, and libations, this time dedicated specifically to Apollo Delphinios. The outgoing *aisymnetes* makes sacrifices to Hestia, the goddess who protects the public hearth. Then he sings a paean and pours a libation. On the tenth day, there are more sacrifices and also contests. Here a distinction is made between *stephanephoroi,* Molpoi, and Onitadai. Since we know that the *aisymnetes* is one of the Molpoi and that he is also called *stephanephoros* (the *aisymnetes* lists were interchangeably called *stephanephoros* lists), the category of Molpoi seems to subsume the *stephanephoroi*. Also, the outgoing *aisymnetes* offers sacrifices "like those of the Onitadai and takes for his portion just as the Onitadai do" (lines 17–18), implying that he is rejoining their midst. It is likely that the term *stephanephoroi* represents those of the Molpoi who are in office at a given time, while the Onitadai are those of the Molpoi who are not.[27]

The procession to Didyma is recorded in lines 18–31. As is not uncommon in Greek religion, Miletos had an annual procession from one sanctuary to another. At Athens, for example, there was an annual procession to Eleusis for the Great Mysteries. In the case of Miletos, the procession began at the Delphinion and marched along the Sacred Way to the Temple of Apollo at Didyma. This parade was not part of the Hebdomaia proper but followed immediately afterward and was a complicated festival in its own right, and this decree details some of the stops along the route, at which other lesser deities were worshiped.

First, provision is made for the city's contribution: this procession is run by the *stephanephoroi* of the Molpoi, but it is a public festival representing the city as a whole, so it is vital to the continued well-being of Miletos that the procession be conducted properly. A comparison is made to the city's contribution at other festivals of Apollo, the Targelia, the Metageitnia, and the Hebdomaia. At this last festival, the city gives a larger donation: three perfect victims, one of which must be female and another of which must be an uncastrated male. The male victim is presumably intended for Apollo himself, either at the Delphinion or at Didyma, but the female victim must be sacrificed to a female goddess—probably Hekate, whose importance we will see, or perhaps Artemis, Apollo's twin sister, who was also worshiped at Didyma. The third victim is curiously unspecified. Another stipulation of this subsection is that the king (*basileus*) is to be present at these sacrifices. Miletos had long since disposed of its monarchy, so this figure is not political. While some have tried to associate him with Zeus Basileus, the context makes it fairly certain that this individual is a human being,

---

27. Wilamowitz-Moellendorff (1904), followed by Rehm in *Milet* 1.3. Robertson (1987) connects the Onitadai with the cult of the Kabeiroi, which he believes is Carian. He then concludes that this inscription demonstrates a conscious effort on the part of the Milesian people to conciliate and include Carians from Assessos in the life and rituals of the city.

probably the city's own chief priest or representative, like the Archon Basileus in Athens.[28] He is a member of the Molpoi or at least is treated as such for the purposes of this ceremony (lines 22–23).

After the *stephanephoroi* sacrifice to Apollo Delphinios (lines 23–24), the actual procession begins. They start their march down the wide Sacred Way, which leads south to the later South Market and then crosses over to the west and south, eventually reaching the portal in the center of the southern cross wall, called the Sacred Gate. According to the decree (line 25) they bring with them two *gulloi,* which are set up, one at the gateway itself and the other at some altar or shrine immediately outside the city wall that was sacred to Hekate before the Gates (Ἐκάτη τῇ πρόσθεν πυλέων), probably the same deity as Hekate Propylaia, a common gatekeeper in Greek cities.

This goddess, sometimes seen as an alternative incarnation of Artemis, was worshiped from Archaic through at least Hellenistic times at Miletos. At the Delphinion, one of the three inscribed Archaic altars is dedicated to her by a group of *prytaneis* (quoted in chap. 3). She also received two Archaic votive statues with dedications at Didyma. Her worship is attested in the fourth century by a dedicatory relief of a group of deities, mentioned earlier.[29] The Molpoi Decree marks her importance in the fifth century: libations are offered to her, and wreaths are somehow involved. A paean is sung. Then the group proceeds up the valley road to the heights, through some woods and a meadow, and on down to Didyma.

Along the route to Didyma, a number of mostly obscure shrines are visited, and a paean is sung before them: besides Hekate, the inscription mentions Dynamis, nymphs, Hermes Enkelados, Phylios, Keraiites, and Chares. The nymphs could be almost any of the lesser female nature deities, while Hermes is well known as one of the twelve Olympians, although the epithet *Enkelados* is obscure (it may mean something like "with a Loud Voice").[30] The cult of Dynamis also occurs in a fifth-century inscription from Teios (Dittenberger 1960, #38.32), but with no

---

28. Wilamowitz-Moellendorff 1904.

29. Altar: *Milet* 1.3 #129. Votive statues: Rehm 1958, #10, #16; Tuchelt 1973, 84. Relief: Hadzisteliou-Price 1971, #V.8.

30. Ehrhardt 1983, 171 esp. n. 857; he next appears in a decree marking provisions for the endowment of a school from 200/199 B.C.E., where he is named repeatedly, usually in conjunction with Apollo and the Muses.

more information about it. Phylios ("the Tribesman") is probably a local hero. A collection of large seated statues, known as the Chares Group, has been found near Didyma and identified by a fourth-century inscription (*Milet* 1.2 #8c = *IG* 1³.3): apparently this is a case of a votive offering that came to have its own heroic cult attached to it.[31] Finally, Keraiites ("the Horned One") is explained in a strange reference to Kallimachos: τόπος Μιλήτου ἀπὸ τοῦ τὸν Ἀπόλλωνα κέρατα τοῦ ἄρρενος τράγου ἀμελγομένου ὑπ' αὐτοῦ πῆξαι ἐκεῖ, ὡς Καλλίμαχος ἐν Ἰάμβοις [a place at Miletos named from the fact that there Apollo himself constructed horns taken from a male goat who has been milked as Kallimachos says in the *Iambi*] (fr. 217 Pf.). At this shrine, constructed out of horns by Apollo himself, and also before the statue of Phylios, sacrifices are made.

Several other shrines from the Sacred Way do not appear in this procession but are attested elsewhere in the Milesian record and so should be noted here. The local hero Neleus is said by Pausanias (7.2.6) to have had a tomb on the left side of the road to Didyma, not far from the city gates, and he would have been worshiped at his tomb as founder. There was a temple of Branchos, the eponymous founder of the race of Branchidai, at Didyma.[32] An unnamed sanctuary has been recently found on the Sacred Way midway between Miletos and Didyma. It is thought by its excavator to belong to an aristocratic Milesian family. Built ca. 530 B.C.E., it was destroyed in the fifth century, probably in the Persian destruction, and never rebuilt.[33]

The instructions in the Molpoi Decree do not extend to the activities at Didyma. Instead, the third section deals with the duties and rights of the Onitadai (lines 31–40). Much of this section seems to consist of various additions, clarifying the original parts of the decree and sorting out some of the specific duties at the occasion of a sacrifice. The Onitadai receive a

---

31. Fontenrose 1988, 166.

32. Neleos: Ehrhardt 1983, 182–83. Branchos: Varro in Lactant. 3.479, 8.198; Stat. *Theb.* 8.198; Quint. Smyrn. 1.283; Fontenrose 1988, 164–65.

33. Tuchelt (1988; 1989, 209–17; 1991a, 40–50; 1991b, 91–94), thinks that its destruction should be linked to civil strife at Miletos and the expulsion of certain aristocratic families (as per theories described in my chap. 6). However, only a small portion of the city of Miletos was immediately rebuilt after its destruction, while the rest grew up gradually. A sanctuary of questionable importance and short duration (less than forty years old), located at a distance from the city, may not have been deemed worthy of reconstruction, especially if its founding family was seriously damaged, impoverished, or even wiped out during the Persian Wars.

number of provisions: clay, iron, bronze, wood, water, dishes, a torch, wick, wooden blocks, and fetters for the victim. The *stephanephoros* provides oil and lamps. The meat is roasted and divided between the *stephanephoroi* and the Onitadai, and small flat cakes are baked for Hekate and Apollo. Finally, the last few lines (40–45) contain miscellaneous provisions, all later additions to the decree. There is a provision stipulating that if the Onitadai fail in their responsibilities, the Molpoi should endeavor to fulfill them. Financial difficulties of the Onitadai are also given to the Molpoi and *stephanephoroi* to solve. Then a portion of meat and wine is set aside for the herald and for the singer.

In sum, the Molpoi Decree gives evidence for the beginning of the new year at Miletos, marked by the inauguration of the new board of *stephanephoroi* at the Festival of Apollo Hebdomaios. It also records the details of the great annual procession to Didyma, during which special emphasis is placed on both Apollo and Hekate. Another goddess who is mentioned with some prominence is Hestia, a civic goddess who protects the city by guarding the sacred fire at the public hearth. On line 13, in an Archaic section of the Molpoi Decree, the outgoing *aisymnetes* makes sacrifices first to Apollo and then to her; she is mentioned again on line 41 in a context that is not very clear but that seems to imply that the cult of Hestia is supposed to supply materials for the festival if the Onitadai are unable to do so. The connection made here between Hestia and Apollo Delphinios reinforces the theory that Delphinios is a civic cult. In addition, the cult of Hestia at Miletos was probably tied in part to the custom of obtaining sacred fire from the Prytaneion in the mother city for use in the colonies.[34]

Didyma

The procession ended at Didyma (modern Yenihisar), without question one of the foremost religious centers in the entire Greek world, famous for an Oracle of Apollo that was second in importance only to that of Delphi. The site was within the territory of Miletos, but in the Archaic period the Oracle was administered by a family of priests called the Branchidai and so dominated by them that, before the Classical era, the site was commonly referred to simply as the Branchidai, using the feminine article, while

---

34. Hestia: Ehrhardt 1983, 175–76. Sacred fire: Malkin 1987, 114–34.

references to the priestly family used the masculine.[35] The Oracle was surrounded by a *temenos,* the border between the sacred and profane demarcating the area of asylum. Within this perimeter was part of a sacred grove of laurel trees, Apollo's great temple, and also many lesser sanctuaries or altars, including those of Artemis Pythia and of Zeus Soter ("Savior"), Angelos ("Messenger"), and Phosporos ("Light-Bringer"). In time it also came to enclose a small village, statues, public buildings, shops, baths, porticoes, and stone benches—amenities for the temple attendants and visitors. But these constructions would never be very important; Didyma was not a town but a religious sanctuary.[36]

The myths of the foundation of the cult site and Oracle are many and varied, indicating that it occurred so early as to be unknown to the Greeks. Pausanias (7.2.6) says that the sanctuary and Oracle date to before the Ionian settlements in Asia Minor, hence to the eleventh century or earlier. In his support, both the names *Didyma* and *Branchidai* are not apparently Greek, and their strangeness has spawned many of the myths as aetiological explanations of the names. For example, in one story (Konon *FGH* 26 F 1.xxxiii), a pregnant woman saw a vision in which the Sun (Apollo) entered her mouth and exited her womb. Since the god passed through her throat, she named her child Branchos, which means "hoarseness" or "sore throat," and he became the founder of the priestly family. Likewise, the ancients have tried to find something doubled about the site to explain the name *Didyma,* "twin," in Greek. While Apollo and Artemis were themselves twins, the sanctuary is predominantly his. There are not two temples, two hills, or two of anything else important. Instead, the name *Didyma* is almost certainly Carian, with a suffix cognate to those in such place-names as Idyma and Sidyma.[37]

---

35. An alternate theory, held chiefly by Tuchelt (1988, 1996) is that Didyma was an independent political unit in the Archaic era. This is refuted by Ehrhardt 1998.

36. Fontenrose 1988, 30–31 (physical layout of the village). Fontenrose and Parke (1985b), as well as the various archaeological reports by Tuchelt (esp. 1973, 1991a, 1996), are the sources for all of the discussion of Didyma that follows except where I have noted otherwise. Following normal scholarly usage, *Oracle* (capitalized) refers to the sacred place, while *oracle* (lowercase) is used to refer to individual pronouncements.

There is speculation whether the village buildings were inside the actual *temenos* or just outside it. Strabo (14.1.5) says that they were inside, but Fontenrose (1988, 30–31) discusses the ambiguity inherent in that statement, based on the exact meaning of *sekos* (enclosure).

37. For other accounts of pre-Ionian Didyma, see Paus. 5.13.11; Parthen. 1; D.L. 8.5; *Orph. Arg.* 152–53; Quint. Smyrn. 1.283; Stat. *Theb.* 3.478–79, 8.198–200; Lykoph. 1378–81; Tzetz. *Chil.* 13.110–16; Fontenrose 1988, 3–6; Parke 1985b, 2–10. Parke

Modern opinions about the origin of the site are nearly as varied. Some scholars believe that Pausanias's witness for a pre-Greek sanctuary must be accepted as true, while others question it as unlikely.[38] Unfortunately, there is no real evidence on which a decision can be based. Part of the scholarly uncertainty can be attributed to the problem that no consensus has arisen about the time and place of the origin of the cult of Apollo. While it probably developed among the Dorian Greeks, another widespread theory advocates a source for the god Apollo in Lykia in Asia Minor, not Greece. If the latter is the case, one may argue that the cult arrived in Ionia long before it made its way over to the mainland.[39] However, if Apollo is Greek, the name must have reached Miletos with the Greeks, but it may have assimilated with a preexisting native cult. Thus, regarding the origin of Didyma, we can say only that the sanctuary was extremely old and its name Carian. Perhaps the Milesians borrowed the place-name and established the cult of Apollo there, perhaps they adopted a previous cult but developed the Oracle, or maybe they adopted both cult and Oracle. We simply do not know.

The antiquity and significance of this sacred place is witnessed by anecdotal evidence in Herodotos. From him we learn that the Egyptian pharaoh Necho dedicated to Branchidai the clothing he wore when he defeated Gaza in Syria in 608 (2.159.3). A half century later, Kroisos, the king of Lydia, both consulted the Oracle and enriched its sanctuary with gifts as many and as fine as the ones he gave to Delphi (1.46.2, 1.92.2; cf. 5.36.3). Also in the middle of the sixth century, the Aiolic city Kyme consulted the Oracle about surrendering the refugee Paktyes to his pursuer (1.157.3–1.159.4). If Herodotos's stories are genuine, the Oracle of Didyma was already famous in the seventh and sixth centuries and was consulted by Greeks beyond Ionia, Lydians, and even Egyptians.

Any visitor to Didyma today—as in antiquity—is profoundly struck by the enormity of the structure standing there. It is a Hellenistic construction from the late fourth century, with a foundation measuring 118 × 60 m.,[40] making it the third largest temple of its time: only the Heraion of Samos and the Artemision of Ephesos—one of the Seven Wonders of the Ancient World—were larger. On top of the foundation was a dipteral

---

(1985b, 5 n. 3) lists scholarship suggesting the additional possibility that *Didyma* is actually *Dindyma*, the name of several mountains in western Asia Minor.

38. Parke 1985b, 2 (true); Fontenrose 1988, 6 (unlikely).

39. Lykia: Wilamowitz-Moellendorff 1903a. Dorian: Burkert 1975; 1994, 49–51.

40. Fontenrose 1988, 34–41; Voigtländer 1986a, 1–29 (with models).

Ionic colonnade with a total of 120 columns, 12 of which filled the *pronaos* (foretemple) in three rows of four. Each column was 19.7 m. high to the capital and ca. 2 m. in diameter. Only three are left standing today; an earthquake in 1493 knocked down all the others.[41] Inside was the *adyton* (innermost sanctuary, literally "not to be entered"), an unroofed area, 54 × 22.33 m., that was cut off from the eyes of the exterior world by an encircling wall that was designed to extend as much as 28 m. above the ground level but was never completely finished. At the west end of the *adyton* was the *naiskos* (little temple), which was the shrine proper, a small marble building (14.2 × 8.5 m.) with four Ionic columns across the front, 7 m. high. This building was the "house" of the god and sheltered an Archaic bronze statue of Apollo. Just outside it to the northeast was the sacred spring.

Underneath this impressive Hellenistic structure, archaeologists have found evidence of earlier buildings on the site. In addition to isolated sherds from the eighth century and earlier, there was an eighth- or seventh-century wall of sun-dried bricks, nearly one meter thick and enclosing an oblong area about 10.2 × 9.3 m. This wall was an outer enclosure, marking the sacred space and enclosing an altar and the spring, but not a temple building. The oldest temple proper, a small *naiskos,* was erected in the late seventh century, with an *adyton* wall surrounding it on at least three sides and a portico to the south made of mud-brick walls with wooden columns.[42]

The largest and most memorable Archaic structure was built a century later.

About the middle of the sixth century construction was begun upon the second temple, a large structure about as long as the Parthenon [in Athens] and somewhat wider. It had a double row of columns on all sides, a pronaos that contained eight or twelve columns, and an hypaethral (unroofed) adyton that was more than twice as large as the whole first temple. In the western part of the adyton was situated a naiskos (whether this was the original or a new naiskos is uncertain). This structure is known to scholars as the archaic temple . . .[43]

41. Fontenrose 1988, 24.
42. Parke 1985b, 23–24; Fontenrose 1988, 9.
43. Fontenrose 1988, 9.

The outer dimensions of the sixth-century temple are not precisely known, but the *adyton* was 33 × 19 m., running east to west. Various reconstructions of the upper temple have been proposed, including one with the same basic design as the Hellenistic temple, but the details are not self-evident.[44] According to Pausanias (5.13.11), the temple had an ashen altar founded by Herakles; to the east of the temple, archaeologists have found a circular limestone base almost 8 m. across that is usually taken to be that altar.

One of the most remarkable features of the Archaic temple was its cult statue. It was cast in bronze by the sculptor Kanachos (Paus. 2.10.5, 9.10.2; Pliny *NH* 34.8.75), probably only slightly larger than life-size. It can be reconstructed on the basis of its representation on coin types and reliefs.

> Evidently it was one of the latest examples of the original Kouros type: a nude male figure symmetrically posed facing forwards with the left leg advanced. The left arm holding the traditional bow was somewhat lowered, the right arm was stretched forward at a right angle to the body and supported on the palm the figure of a stag.[45]

We do not know any details about the oracular procedure, or mantic session, that was employed by the Branchidai in the Archaic period, but presumably it was similar to the one used later about which we are well informed.[46] After propitiatory sacrifices, the consultant entered the *pronaos* and presented his petition, probably in written form. It is likely that the consultant never entered the *adyton* but rather waited above while the priest and assistants went within. The priest (or the consultant) asked the question loudly, so that the priestess, waiting below, could hear it, for while the whole procedure was presided over by the priest, the god's breath actually fell on the priestess, who had been fasting for the last three days. She listened to the question while dipping her feet or the hem of her mantle in the sacred spring. She breathed in vapor that arose from the ground to receive the god and pronounced his oracle. Probably the priest or a scribe wrote down her words, which were then delivered to the consultant.

---

44. Fontenrose 1988, 31–34.
45. Parke 1985b, 26.
46. Porph. *Ep. ad Aneb.* 14; Iambl. *Myst.* 3.11; Fontenrose 1988, 78–85.

According to the study done by Fontenrose, very few of the oracles can be taken as genuine, and those were usually simple confirmation of decisions already made, chiefly about religious matters.[47] He lists only five that he believes are probably genuine that come from the Archaic period. The first three are derived from inscriptions found in Milesian territory. The earliest (*Milet* 1.3 #178 = Fontenrose R1), found in the Delphinion and dating from the first half of the sixth century, is very vague, reading simply:

[---ἀπ]/ομυθέομ[αι· τ]ῆ[ι]αρ---/---τεως τῆι προτέρηι / νυκτὶ εἶπον. καὶ [τῶι μὲν πειθομέ/νωι λῶιον καὶ ἄ]μεινον ἔσται, τῶι / δὲ μὴ πειθομένω[ι τοὐναντίον.]

[. . . I dissuade . . . on the previous night I said. And it will be better [and preferable for him who obeys, but the contrary] for him who disobeys.[48]

Equally ambiguous is the second, from the same era but found this time at Didyma (Rehm 1958, #11 = Fontenrose R2).

---σοι[σι?] / ληιστοί· θε[ò/ς] δὲ ἔπεν· Δίκ/αιον ποιεῖν / ὡς πατέρας.

[. . . plunderable? And the god said, "It is just to do as your fathers."]

Without knowing the context, we can garner very little from the responses. However, the third oracle, also from the Delphinion (*Milet* 1.3 #132a = Fontenrose R3), dates to fifty years later and is a little clearer because it gives a specific reference.

[περ]ὶ τὠρακλέ[ος ----]   →
[--- θεòς ἔπεν· γυν-   ←

---

47. Fontenrose 1978, 1988. There are many pre-Classical oracles that Fontenrose considers to be doubtful or not genuine, usually recorded much later in a literary text. Among the most famous are the Gergithes oracle (Herakl. fr. 50, discussed in chap. 3), Kroisos's test of the Oracles (Hdt. 1.46.2–48.1), and the Kymaian request about surrendering Pakytes (Hdt. 1.158.1ff.).

48. For this and the next two oracles, I am following Fontenrose's translations, given in his catalog of responses (1988, 179–244).

[α]ἶϰας ἐς τὦραϰ[λέος ---]　→
[---]λαχάνων: [ο]ὖ [β-　←
ϱ]ῶσις: γυναι [-----]　→
[----]ων: ἔσιν　←
[γ]υνὴ [-------]　→

[On Herakles' [sanctuary?], the god said, "Women may not enter . . ."]

This oracle, along with the story of the ashen altar (Paus. 5.13.11), demonstrates that the Milesians worshiped the Panhellenic hero Herakles.[49]

The other two Archaic oracles that are probably genuine are preserved in literary accounts, so their exact wording is lost. They both pertain to Milesian colonization, and the second is cultic in nature. It was common practice in the Greek world for a mother city to consult an Oracle before setting out to found a new colony: it was necessary to receive the god's sanction to guarantee the success of the colony. In the following oracle, one can envision a setting wherein the Milesians desired to refound the lost colony at Kyzikos, ca. 675 B.C.E. They consulted the Oracle and received a favorable response. Aristides says (*Or.* 16.237 Jebb = 1.383 Dind. = Fontenrose R34):

πεπύσθαι δέ τινα ἤδη ϰαὶ τῶν ἐν Ὑπερβορέοις οἶμαι τὸν περὶ Κυζίϰου χρησμὸν ϰαὶ τὸν μάρτυρα τῆς εὐδαιμονίας τῇ πόλει, ὃς ταῖς μὲν ἄλλαις πόλεσιν ἐξηγητής ἐστιν, τῇ δὲ πόλει ταύτῃ ϰαὶ ἀρχηγέτης. τὰς μὲν γὰρ ἄλλας πόλεις διὰ τῶν οἰϰιστῶν ᾤϰισεν οὓς ἀπέστειλεν ἑϰαστόσε, ταύτης δὲ ἐϰ τοῦ εὐθέος αὐτὸς γέγονεν οἰϰιστής, ὥστε πῶς οὐϰ εὐδαίμων Κύζιϰος ἀπὸ τοιαύτης τε ἀρχῆς ἀρξαμένη εἰς τοσοῦτόν τε ἄμα [τὸν] οἰϰιστὴν ϰαὶ μάρτυρα ἀναφέρουσα;

[I think that even anyone of those who live among the Hyperboreans [i.e., someone totally uninformed] has heard about the oracle concerning Kyzikos and witness of the prosperity of that city, which is advisor to the other cities and founder even of this city. For he founded the other cities through [human] founders whom he sent out each time, but of this city he himself was founder openly, so that how

---

49. Ehrhardt 1983, 180–82.

can Kyzikos not be happy, begun from such a beginning, and attributed to one who is at the same time so great a founder and a witness?]

Here Apollo is not just the god who inspired the foundation but the
actual founder (*oikist*) of Kyzikos and the driving force behind the resulting Milesian colonization ("advisor to the other cities").

Also at Kyzikos, the god directed the citizens (or the colonists) to erect
a sacred stone in the sanctuary of Athena Iasonia (Ap. Rhod. *Arg.* 1.958–
60 = Fontenrose R35).

. . . .ἀτὰρ κεῖνόν γε θεοπροπίαις Ἑκάτοιο
Νηλείδαι μετόπισθεν Ἰάονες ἱδρύσαντο
ἱερόν, ἥ θέμις ἦεν, Ἰησονίης ἐν Ἀθήνης.

[. . . however that sacred stone the Ionian Neleids later dedicated, as
instructed by the oracles of Hekatos, in the sanctuary of Athena
Iasonia.]

Although Apollonios wrote in the third century B.C.E., Fontenrose thinks
this response is "very likely authentic," perhaps even directing the first
foundation of the cult of Athena Iasonia.

Recently a new inscription has been found in the colony Olbia and
dated ca. 525 B.C.E.[50] In separate texts on a bone plaque, we find the
number seven (ΕΕΠΤΑ) and the phrases ΑΠΟΛΛΩΝΙ / ΔΙΔΥΜ /
ΜΙΛΗΣΙΩΙ [To Apollo of Didyma the Milesian] and ΜΗΤΡΟΛ
ΟΛΒΟΦΟΡΟΣ / ΝΙΚΗΦΟΡΟΣ ΒΟΡΕΩ / ΔΙΔΥΜ [Bearer of luck
from the metropolis (?) / Bearer of victory of the North / Didyma]. The
number seven is often associated with Apollo: the Hebdomaia (Festival
of the Seventh) was a celebration involving sacrifices made to him on
the seventh day of every month, and *Hebdomagetes* (Leader of the
Seventh) was a common epithet for him. The word *olbos* (luck) is a
reference to Olbia, just as *Boreas* (North) refers to *Borysthenes,* the
earlier name for Berezan.

Accompanying these phrases is a very odd text, which Burkert takes as
an oracle from Didyma.

---

50. Ehrhardt 1987, 116–17; Burkert 1994 (I have used his texts and translations);
Dubois 1996, 146–54; Onyshkevych 1998, 70–152. The editio princeps was done in
Russian by A. S. Rusjaeva.

Ἑπτά—λύκος ἀσθενής
Ἑβδομήκοντα—λέων δεινός
Ἑπτ(α)κόσιοι—τοξοφόρος, φίλι(ο)ς δωρεῆ(ι). δυνάμ(ι)
   ἰητῆ(ρ)ος
Ἑπτακι(σ)χίλι(οι)—δελφὶς φρόνιμος
Εἰρήνη Ὀλβίη(ι) πόλι
Μακαρίζω ἐκεί(νην)
Μέμνημαι Λητο(ῖ)

[7—wolf without strength.
77—terrible lion.
777—bowbearer, friendly with his gift, with the power of a healer.
7777—wise dolphin.
Peace to the Blessed City [i.e., Olbia].
I pronounce her to be happy.
I bear remembrance to Leto.]

All of the characteristics listed are typical of Apollo. The wolf is a re-minder of the epithet *Lykaios,* while the lion is a common symbol at Delos and on Milesian coinage. The mention of him as "bowbearer" is an obvious reference to his patronage of archery, just as the mention of Leto refers to his parentage. The reference to him as "healer" points out his support of the medical profession and the worship of him under the epithet *Ietros.* The dolphin refers to the false etymology, frequent in antiquity, for his name *Delphinios.* Seven is the number most associated with him, as we have already seen, but the numerical progression makes interpretation of this inscription mysterious and difficult: it is almost certainly a "rhetorical number" (cf. Polyain. 8.33; Plut. *Mor.* 245d33). The two leading suggestions are that the numbers refer to the growing number of colonists at Olbia or to temporal stages in the development of the colony.[51] However, Burkert's identification of this inscription as an oracle is problematic, since the text does not fit the pattern established by Fontenrose: while it obviously pertains to religious matters, it does not contain any instruction or confirmation that can be taken as an answer to a question. Instead, it has been suggested that the plaque may be either a membership token or a hymn or prayer to Apollo Hebdomaia, related to or a precursor of the Orphic cult.[52]

---

51. Burkert 1994, 55–59.
52. Ehrhardt 1987, 116–17; Dubois 1996, 146–54; Onyshkevych 1998, 70–152.

The Oracle fell silent when Miletos was sacked in 494 B.C.E., and Didyma fell with it: ἱρὸν δὲ τὸ ἐν Διδύμοισι, ὁ νηός τε καὶ τὸ χρηστήριον, συληθέντα ἐνεπίμπρατο [the sanctuary at Didyma, both the temple building and the Oracle, was plundered and burned] (Hdt. 6.19.3).[53] Evidence of the looting has been discovered in this century at the Persian capital of Susa, where archaeologists have found a curious huge bronze knucklebone (Rehm 1958, #7) .23 × .37 × .21 m. in size and weighing 98 kg. (nearly 200 pounds). It has a handle on one end and is inscribed with a dedication to Apollo. Because of the Ionic script, the letterforms, and the proper names used in the dedication, it has been concluded that this knucklebone was one of a pair (the other was connected by a chain to the handle) that was dedicated in the first half of the sixth century to Apollo at Didyma and stolen by the army of Dareios.[54] As a result of the sack, the sacred spring ceased to flow and the Oracle lapsed for the whole of the Classical period. Some cult practices seem to have continued, however, since the Molpoi Decree from the mid–fifth century records the continuation of the annual procession from the Delphinion at Miletos to Didyma. Also, archaeologists have found several fifth-century altars and a small *naiskos* at Didyma, indicating that some worship continued there.[55]

A full revival had to wait until the coming of Alexander the Great.[56] After he took Miletos in 334, the spring began to flow again and the Oracle was reestablished (Kallis. 124.14j = Str. 17.1.43). The Hellenistic building was begun, mainly through the generosity of Seleukos Nikator, who even recovered the cult statue from the city of Ekbatana, a capital of Media, ca. 300 B.C.E. (Paus. 1.16.3, 8.46.3). Construction continued for centuries and was never completed, but the Oracle began making pronouncements almost immediately. Control over the Oracle should have gone back to the Branchidai, but at the time of the destruction, Dareios transplanted them east to Sogdiana, where they lived in a town called after themselves. According to one story that is almost certainly false, the

---

53. Tuchelt (1988, 1996) and Hammond (1998) dispute the traditional account, that Didyma was sacked by Dareios, and instead delay the destruction until 479/8, when Xerxes was returning from his Hellenic invasion. In this theory, they follow Pausanias (1.16.3, 8.46.3) and Strabo (14.1.5) but disregard the more immediate source, Herodotos.

54. Knucklebones were used as dice, so this dedication may reflect an oracle given by lot, or perhaps the dedicators won a great deal of money by chance. See Parke 1985b, 30–32; Kurke 1999, 283–95.

55. Fontenrose 1988, 14.

56. Günther 1971.

priests betrayed the temple to the Persians and reaped this resettlement as a reward. However, it is certain that when he arrived at Sogdiana, Alexander the Great ordered the entire line—man, woman, and child—to be murdered.[57] The Oracle was placed under the direct control of the Milesian state. The site was hereafter called Didyma, not Branchidai, and a *prophetes,* or presiding priest, was chosen each year, assisted by treasurers and a board of overseers.

Didyma was a tremendously important Panhellenic center. Control over it gave the Milesians considerable honor and prestige, and the various cults of Apollo at Miletos gained all that much more distinction as a result of their connection with Didyma. This was especially true of Delphinios, whose special connection was noted through the annual procession from the one sanctuary to the other. Thus the famous oracular shrine was inextricably linked to the worship of the patron of Miletos on the Lion Harbor.

The City and Kalabaktepe

The area around the Lion Harbor was erroneously judged by early archaeologists to have been unoccupied in the Archaic era. As that notion was disproved by later excavation, a new theory emerged in which it was occupied, but only as a peripheral attachment to the more important Theater Harbor. Finally, after a century of excavation, the evidence is clear both that the area around the Lion Harbor was occupied throughout the Archaic period and also that it was a vital city center in the Classical era—far more important than the area around the Temple of Athena—and that it may have been so for the Archaic city as well. At that time, while the Theater Harbor housed only the Temple of Athena and some commercial and residential buildings, the Lion Harbor was home to at least two major shrines, a marketplace, houses, and perhaps a government building.

West across the Sacred Way from the Delphinion, the Milesians con-

---

57. Kallis. 124.14j in Str. 17.1.43, 11.11.4, 14.1.5; Curt. *Alex.* 7.5.28–35; Plut. *Mor.* 557b; *Suda* s.v. Βραγχίδαι (B514); Fontenrose 1988, 12–13; Parke 1985b, 34–41; Hammond 1998; Ehrhardt 1998. There is much discussion about his motivation, ranging from his desire to make an example out of them to ward off potential disruptions among the native peoples to his patronage of some of the other Milesian families who did not want to yield their position back to the Branchidai.

structed the North Marketplace (ca. 5,000 sq. m.), the oldest known agora in Miletos. Although poorly excavated, there is some indication that it was used in pre-Classical times. An inscription known as the Banishment Decree (*Milet* 1.6 #187) was found in the northwest corner of the agora. The inscription began on a stele, which has been lost, but overflows onto the base, which is preserved. Since its prescript is missing, we cannot date it precisely from the eponymous *aisymnetes*, but the style of the letterforms indicates an origin in the first half of the fifth century. The fact of the overflow shows that what we have preserved is probably not the end of the original decree but a fifth-century addition to an Archaic decree.[58] This conclusion is confirmed by the alignment of the stone in the marketplace: the Classical city was aligned orthogonally, yet this stone sat askew, which may be taken to indicate both that it predated the Classical boundaries of the market and that the market itself had a sixth-century predecessor on the same location.

The buildings around the agora were for the most part later, and we can only guess about Archaic antecedents. The marble harbor stoa dates to the fourth century, as does the square building of unknown purpose attached to the south edge of it. A rectangular building on the southwest corner of the marketplace was built with strong walls of gneiss and porous stone and stood in place by the mid–fourth century, if not the late fifth century. It may have served as the early Prytaneion, a building for meetings and meals of the presidency of the Assembly. This conclusion is based on its symmetrical layout as well as its proximity to the North Marketplace and to the second century B.C.E. Council House, or Bouleuterion, located slightly south of the marketplace. However, only half of the building has been excavated, and the objects found inside it, which would serve as important clues to its function, have not been published.[59]

Directly south of the possible Prytaneion and west of the Bouleuterion is an area rich in remains, both public and private in nature. The Archaic buildings tend to be small rectangular houses, with walls made of small flat stones. The fifth-century houses that were built on top of the destruction layer often used the same walls, indicating the orderliness of the

---

58. A much more extensive discussion of this decree, including arguments about its length and date, can be found in chap. 6.

59. *Milet* 1.6.87–91. Miller (1978, 231) reserves judgment on the function of this building. Perhaps it was constructed as part of the shift to democracy in the mid–fifth century?

building arrangement in this region. However, the crowded houses of the sixth century give way to much more loosely spaced construction in the fifth, demonstrating a significant depopulation of the district, as we would expect after the catastrophe of 494. No large religious sanctuaries have been unearthed to date except the Shrine of Dionysos. Nevertheless, the cultic significance of the area can be shown by the broken terracotta statuettes of a goddess (perhaps Demeter?), the head of a bearded god (Zeus?), and another of a youthful god (Priapos?). This entire area, particularly near the Shrine of Dionysos, was rich in Attic red-figure pottery of the second half of the fifth century, more so than anywhere else in Miletos.[60]

The finds west of the Bouleuterion are not spectacular: there are no major building projects or momentous inscriptions but instead one shrine, some houses, and sherds. But these remains demonstrate that the Lion Bay was not only in use during the sixth century, both for residential and for religious purposes, but densely populated.[61] It is impossible to guess what archaeologists will find in the future, but it would certainly be odd if this area was heavily populated while the port area just to the north lay underutilized. It seems more likely that Archaic and Classical ruins closer to the harbor either have been destroyed by later construction or have not been uncovered because of the challenges of the groundwater problem.

Another residential district has been found to the west on the Theater Hill. The settlement remains from the southern region of the hill were washed away by erosion before even the Hellenistic and Roman construction there, but excavations on the northern area of the plateau have been more informative. The older material—isolated Mycenaean and Geometric sherds—was not found in established layers. However, the excavators discovered postholes that indicate the presence of early Archaic wooden houses, and sixth-century remains of the fortification wall indicate that the hill was part of the area enclosed by the circuit wall. After the destruction, the debris layer was leveled off into a bank of earth 20 cm. thick in

---

60. Archaic: Weickert et al. 1957, 102; Cook and Blackman 1964/65, 50–51; Kleiner and Müller-Wiener 1972, 49–50; Mellink 1980, 511; Voigtländer 1981, 115–21; Müller-Wiener 1986a, 100–103. Text of the inscription: Wiegand 1901, 909–10. Destruction: Kleiner and Müller-Wiener 1972, 50–55, 71; Voigtländer 1981, 115–21. Classical: Kleiner and Müller-Wiener 1972, 49–52, 71; Mellink 1980, 511; Voigtländer 1981, 111–15; Mitchell 1984/85, 86.

61. Kleiner 1960; 1966, 19. Cf. Cook and Blackman 1964/65, 50–51.

preparation for the new buildings. Some of the house walls from the sixth century were arranged in such an orderly fashion that many of them were reused again in the fifth century, when the city was aligned orthogonally. The houses there were mostly rectangular, made of small stones (one was made of larger, coarse stones), and among them were found numerous fifth-century red-figure sherds. Because the new housing was built up in such a dense fashion here, the Theater Hill must have been one of the principal residential areas of the Classical city.[62]

Across the Theater Harbor to the south, excavations on the Stadium Hill have uncovered a particularly thick Archaic level containing walls and household pottery in at least two layers (pre–600 B.C.E. and 600–500 B.C.E.). The destruction affected this district as well, and, while the area on the western tip of the Stadium Hill peninsula (on the far western side of the Temple of Athena) shows almost no signs of reinhabitation in the fifth century, on the Stadium Hill proper and just to its west there was a buildup of walls, fountains, and canals. A high concentration of Classical amphoras indicates that it was a mixed residential and commercial neighborhood, containing more homes than workshops.[63]

In the area of the Temple of Athena, intensive archaeological efforts have rewarded us with some of the clearest finds from the Archaic and Classical city. Like the Mycenaean and Geometric settlements before it, the Archaic city expanded over the region south and southwest of the Theater Bay, where the central feature must have been the Temple of Athena. Worship of this goddess reached back into the Dark Ages, since a Late Geometric or Early Archaic shrine was discovered overlapping the Bronze Age fortification wall. The shrine consisted of a building 3.27 m. square with walls only 40 cm. thick, containing an oval of small stones, unsymmetrically oriented. This sanctuary is not positively identified as belonging to Athena, but considering the later use of the same location, it

---

62. Archaic: esp. Kleiner 1961; see also Kleiner 1960, 41; Kleiner 1966, 19; Mellink 1961, 47–48; Mellink 1962, 185–86; Mellink 1989, 123; Cook and Blackman 1964/65, 51; Müller-Wiener and Weber 1985, 17. Destruction: Kleiner 1961, 47; Mellink 1984, 454; Müller-Wiener and Weber 1985, 31–34. Classical: Kleiner 1961, 46–48; Mellink 1962, 185–86; Mellink 1984, 454; Pfrommer 1985, 40–46. Hellenistic house remains on the Theater Hill are rare, and there is no indication of how early that hill was in use as a theater, though it certainly was by Hellenistic times, to which era some of the pieces of the *skene* date. The Romans constructed the massive stone theater visible there today.

63. Kleiner 1960, 39–40; Hommel 1959/60, 40–42; Mellink 1961, 47–48; Mellink 1974, 114, 123; Mellink 1976, 279; Schiering 1979, 77–79. Destruction: Kleiner 1960, 40; Mellink 1974, 114. Reinhabitation: *Milet* 1.8.82–83; Kleiner 1960, 40–41; Mellink 1961, 47–48; Mellink 1974, 114.

was probably an early shrine to her, where the inhabitants celebrated her as a protectress of the walls and city.[64]

By the second half of the seventh century, Athena was venerated in a primitive building that has been identified by simple dedicatory inscriptions, such as Ἀθηναίη εἰμὶ [I belong to Athena].[65] The building was unearthed under the south end of the terrace of the Classical temple and is generally regarded as the predecessor of that temple. Facing east, it was 4.82 m. long with a *pronaos in antis* (columns on the corners of the doorway). On the north and east it rested on a cleared Mycenaean destruction layer, while on the south it was grounded on stone; it had no real foundation, so the walls had to adjust with varying heights. The earliest roof was flat, supported by a series of columns, while the walls were probably of porous stone. After the building was damaged by fire ca. 550 B.C.E., the walls were lined with marble on the inside, and stone paving was laid out to the north and, still later, to the east of the temple. The sanctuary around the temple was fairly small: buildings came to within 5 m. of it in the north and within less than 8 m. on the east.[66]

A wealth of Archaic religious relics have been discovered near the temple. Votive offerings made of bronze, stone, and terracotta have been unearthed mostly to the south and southeast of the older temple, and the continuous range of sherds from Geometric down to black- and red-figure vases testifies to a virtually unbroken occupation in this area.[67] Among the finds were a helmeted terracotta head, probably of Athena, discovered near the *pronaos* and dated to the first half of the sixth century, and a series of bronzes, including a disk 28 cm. in circumference displaying an Asian "Tree of Life" motif. Silver and bronze votive offerings were found in a burned level north of the temple, along with the head of a griffin that had been removed from a cauldron with a tool and thrown away as worthless.[68]

A newer, much larger, marble temple was built on a framework of

64. Hommel 1959/60, 38–40; Mallwitz 1959/60a; Mallwitz 1968, 120–23.

65. Wiegand 1904, 85.

66. The Archaic temple was originally thought to be a provisional temple from the fifth century. Provisional: *Milet* 1.8.70–72; Gerkan 1924a, 38–40; Weickert et al. 1957, 102; Weickert 1958. Seventh-century: Mellink 1963, 161–62; Cook and Blackman 1964/65; Cook and Blackman 1970/71, 45; Kleiner 1966, 17–18; Kleiner 1968, 38–40; Mallwitz 1968, 117–24 (an excellent source).

67. The fifteen years in the fifth century in which the site may have been unoccupied is too brief a period to be reflected by a break in the pottery evidence.

68. *Milet* 1.8.77–78, 82; Gerkan 1924a, 38–40; Mellink 1963, 161–62; Kleiner 1966, 17–18; Kleiner 1968, 38–40; Mallwitz 1968, 122.

gneiss support walls on a terrace that was constructed by leveling off the debris of the earlier temple to a width of 40 m.: there was no digging, so the older remains beneath it were left intact. The temple had a double colonnade in front but was otherwise pseudodipteral, meaning that it had a single row of columns all the way around, but they were spaced far out from the wall, as if they were forming the outermost of two rows; there were probably fourteen columns on the long sides and eight on the short. The *cella* was about 9.2 × 15.8 m., and the structure measured approximately 30 × 18 m. in all. Oddly enough, instead of having the eastern exposure normal to Greek temples and characteristic of the Archaic Temple of Athens, the Classical temple was turned at a ninety-degree angle, facing south.[69]

A recent rethinking of the considerations dating this new marble Temple of Athena has had important consequences. Originally it was thought that this temple was built in the middle of the fifth century.[70] In 1968, Alfred Mallwitz developed a theory whereby the new temple was one of the first and most ambitious construction projects undertaken in the second quarter of the fifth century. According to his explanation, the prominence of the Temple of Athena—the only fifth-century building made out of marble—should be taken as a reflection of the alliance with Athens that started in 479 B.C.E. and continued for more than fifty years.[71] However, W.-D. Niemeier revised this dating in the 1990s when he found that the sherd on which it was based was not actually discovered under the foundation and, stylistically, most closely resembles finds from the late sixth century. According to Niemeier, this temple must have been constructed in the last quarter of the sixth century, as one in a series of magnificent buildings undertaken by the tyrants Histiaios and Aristagoras during an extended program of public works.[72] But Neimeier

---

69. Gerkan (*Milet* 1.8.52–70) reconstructs the Classical temple as a large peripteral podium temple (raised up on a large pedestal and having a single row of columns all the way around spaced at a normal distance from the wall), without precedent in fifth-century Ionia, but Kleiner (1968, 36–38) and Mallwitz (1968, 122–23; 1975, 67–81) reject that model. Likewise, Gerkan dates it to the middle of the fifth century, while Mallwitz dates it more precisely to the second quarter of the century.

70. Gerkan in *Milet* 1.8.52–70. Cf. Mitchell and McNicoll 1978/79, 63–64; Weickert et al. 1957, 116; Hommel 1959/60, 41–42; Mellink 1961, 47–48; Schiering 1968, 156.

71. Mallwitz 1968, 120–24; 1975, 82–89.

72. This program would have included the construction or renovation of the Delphinion, the Temple of Artemis Kithone on the East Terrace of Kalabaktepe, the Temple of Aphrodite on Zeytintepe, the Temple of Athena at Mengerevtepe, and the Altar of Poseidon at Monodendri. See Niemeier 1999; Weber 1999.

does not explain sufficiently what happened to the city block after 494. He implies that it was probably abandoned and that the cult was probably transferred to another location. However, several factors indicate that the city block may have been rebuilt. First, the *temenos* seems to have served as the model for the southern city blocks, an unlikely scenario if the sanctuary was abandoned. Second, the block was left intact until the Hellenistic era, when it was systematically dismantled in favor of neighboring constructions: the entire terrace north of the temple was removed for the building of the West Market; a strip of the west terrace 6 m. wide was cut off in the third century when a house with a courtyard was built next door; the southern terrace was shortened from an unknown extent down to 9 m. in width when the street was widened; and, finally, the eastern terrace was shortened by 2.8 m. to widen the alley. If the temple was moved immediately after 494, why was the block left intact and unoccupied for several centuries and only then dismantled?

It is likely that the two dominant theories should be combined. Niemeier is probably correct in dating the temple to the last quarter of the sixth century, during the building program of the tyrants. Since the plot itself is left intact for several centuries, the temple was probably rebuilt in the fifth century, on a modest scale perhaps and using the same foundation as the Archaic marble temple. It is not so surprising that we have no remains from this putative Classical temple, as the remains of the marble Archaic temple are exceedingly few.[73] Finally, either the shrine was moved to another, as yet unknown location in the city, as Niemeier suggests, or else Mallwitz is correct in viewing the piecemeal destruction of the *temenos* in the Hellenistic era as a reflection of the fall from favor of the patron goddess of the Athenian League. The buildings and streets on all sides were expanded at the expense of the sanctuary, and under the Romans, the temple itself was gradually and systematically dismantled in favor of shops and factories. Today only a few small fragments of the entire superstructure have been found, in wells and debris around the site.[74]

The area around the Temple of Athena was otherwise a commercial district. Archaeologists have uncovered numerous painted amphoras, especially from the Classical era, a blacksmith shop littered with iron slags, and another building displaying a stone anchor. The other buildings in

---

73. Weber 1999.

74. Weickert 1959/60b, 64; Mallwitz 1968, 123; Mallwitz 1975, 70–71, 82–89; Koenigs 1980, 58; Weber 1999.

the area are principally warehouses and workshops measuring roughly
4–5 × 6–10 m. each, haphazardly scattered on all sides of the older
temple. Since the artifacts indicate that the buildings are related to ship-
ping, this area must have served as a shipyard on the Theater Bay.[75]

Away from the central districts, excavation in the area just north of the
Hellenistic cross wall (near the later Round Church) has revealed a district that was inhabited with only short breaks from Geometric—and
even Mycenaean—to Roman times. On top of a debris layer that contains Late Mycenaean, Protogeometric, and Geometric sherds, the earliest Archaic constructions are limestone and porous-stone oval houses
from the eighth and early seventh centuries, followed soon after by rectangular houses oriented from east to west. The houses are dated by pottery
that is thought to include the earliest local Milesian variety of Rhodian
style, and they may have included a shrine, although there are no dedicatory inscriptions to confirm this theory. The buildings are all damaged by
fire both ca. 700 and ca. 650, perhaps corresponding to attacks by the
Kimmerians and/or Lydians, and they were destroyed in the Persian sack.
The Classical settlement seems to have been sparse, which is not unexpected: since there were fewer inhabitants in the fifth century than the
sixth, it would take some time for the settlement to spread so far.[76]

Even further to the southwest is "Hat Hill," or Kalabaktepe, sometimes
claimed to be the acropolis of Miletos.[77] (Strictly speaking, the city has no
acropolis, and during the Byzantine era, this problem was solved by the
construction of the fortress on top of the theater.) Kalabaktepe has two
plateaus, both artificially terraced in antiquity, in part by using the debris
of the Persian destruction. A recent revision of the archaeological evidence
from the hill has transformed our interpretation of its role in Milesian
history: the buildings on top of the East Terrace (formerly called the
Temple Terrace) were for many decades misdated to the Archaic period,[78]
but in 1986 Volkmar von Graeve announced that they belonged instead to

75. *Milet* 1.8.78–80; Kleiner 1960; Kleiner 1968; Kleiner 1969/70; Schiering 1959/60;
Müller-Wiener 1986a, 100–103.

76. Archaic: Mellink 1963, 161–62; Cook and Blackman 1964/65, 51; Graeve 1973/74,
67; Graeve 1975b, 38–39; Kleine 1979, 137–38; Müller-Wiener 1986a, 98; Heilmeyer
1986. Destruction: *Milet* 1.8.39–40; Graeve 1975b, 38. Classical: *Milet* 1.8.39–45; Graeve
1975b, 36–37; Kleine 1979, 138. Kleine (1979, 136–37) thinks this whole area might have
been a cult area functioning together, but there is no proof. Heilmeyer believes it was an
ordinary settlement and perhaps an industrial section.

77. *Milet* 1.8; Kleiner 1960, 41; Mellink 1962, 185–86; Cook and Blackman 1964/65,
51.

78. *Milet* 1.8.8–24, 115–19; Kleiner 1968, 40.

the fifth century and that they were resting on a debris layer 2–3 m. deep from the Persian destruction.[79] Thus, Kalabaktepe as a whole contains not only some of the most extensive Geometric and Archaic finds in the city but also offers heretofore unsuspected clues to the sequence of events that made up the refoundation of Miletos in the fifth century. Excavation on the hill has been especially active in the last fifteen years, divided into three discrete areas: along the fortification wall on the south and west slopes, on the low East Terrace, and on the Summit Terrace.

The south slope of the hill was a residential area. Traces of buildings without stone walls have been dated to the eighth century, and stone houses went up in the first half of the seventh, when the area was terraced. The remains are divided into five building phases: four are Geometric and Archaic, and the last one rests on the debris of the Persian destruction, implying that the area was continuously occupied with nothing more than short breaks from at least the eighth until the fifth century. However, the fifth-century ruins are fairly sparse in this area, and it was abandoned entirely sometime late in that century until the time of the Romans.[80]

In the middle of this Archaic period of habitation, a city wall was erected around the south slope, built in two main phases. The early sections, constructed out of large gneiss blocks with a fill of small blocks, flat stones, and earth, simply cut through the houses in its path. Later this wall was reinforced and extended with gneiss, white limestone, and brown porous stone. The date of the renovation is pretty closely set to the time immediately after 650 B.C.E., since all of the houses from the late seventh century were built parallel to the inner face of the wall, mostly arranged in a linear series of rooms. Two segments of the wall, complete with bastions, are extant today. The surviving western segment is quite small, but the southern is impressive: it is 4 m. thick at its thinnest point, continues for 250 m., and contains three gates. The wall breaks off on the southeast end: it probably extended originally to the tower discovered on a small segment of wall 70 m. to the southeast and then continued on course for the Sacred Gate.[81]

79. Graeve 1986a, 38–43; Graeve 1987; Graeve 1990; Müller-Wiener 1986a, 100–104; 1988a, 32–35; Mellink 1987; Mitchell 1989/90, 103; Brinkmann 1990; Graeve and Senff 1990; Graeve and Senff 1991; Heinrich and Senff 1992; Kerschner 1995; Senff 1995; Senff 1997b; Senff et al. 1997; Kerschner and Senff 1997.
80. Graeve 1987; Graeve and Senff 1990; Graeve and Senff 1991; Heinrich and Senff 1992; Senff 1995; Senff 1997b.
81. *Milet* 1.8.26–37, 2.3.119; Müller-Wiener 1986a, 96–98; Mellink 1991a, 144–45.

Aside from the work done around the piece of fortification wall during the original excavation at the beginning of this century, there has been no large-scale excavation on the west slope. But when a field-worker recently found a piece of carved marble, the archaeologists investigated. They found a small L-shaped cult building with a fireplace, dating from the second half of the seventh century. Evidence of blood and drink offerings suggest that this area may have been dedicated to a chthonic, or underworld, deity, although that identification is by no means certain.[82]

On the hillside, the entire southeast portion of the East Terrace has eroded, washing away down the hill. What remains is covered with a tangle of buildings. The Archaic settlement rested on the gently sloping hillside and was nearly completely destroyed in 494. In the debris layer, archaeologists have found sherds indicating occupation as early as the mid–eighth century, although there are no extant building remains that early. The unfinished nature and exceptionally high quality of the local work—the head of a statue of a man from the last quarter of the sixth century, pieces of unfinished kouroi, finished and unfinished dedicatory reliefs, and broken ceramics—have led Müller-Wiener to posit the existence of one or more workshops here.[83] In the fifth century, the Persian debris was spread systematically over a packing of coarse stones to form a large terrace, and a support wall was erected along the cliff edge on the north and east. The houses built on it—all dating to the fifth century— were nearly all about 4–6 m. long, and most were divided into two rooms. Their arrangement was haphazard, with alleys and water canals dividing the buildings from each other.[84]

On the north edge of the terrace was a fifth-century temple, recently identified as that of Artemis Kithone. It faced south and measured 6.84 × 8.48 m. The marble walls of the temple rested on a foundation measuring ca. 10 × 18 m., made of limestone and gneiss blocks, filled with small limestone chunks and dirt. While nothing survives of the columns or their bases, numerous remnants of the terracotta roof remain, some decorated with lions, gorgons, and lotus blossoms. The archaeologists have reconstructed the temple with a square *cella* and a *pronaos in antis,* very much like the Classical Temple of Athena, which also faced south.[85]

82. Brinkmann 1990; Mellink 1991a, 144–45.
83. Müller-Wiener 1988a, 32–33.
84. *Milet* 1.8.8–15; Graeve 1986a, 41–42; Graeve 1987, 6–9; Müller-Wiener 1988a, 32–33; Mitchell 1989/90, 103; Kerschner 1995, 214–18.
85. *Milet* 1.8.16–26; Kerschner and Senff 1997.

The results of the excavations on the Summit Terrace concur with those on the lower terrace. An extensive layer of Persian debris was spread to form a large terrace, and in that debris were artifacts dating from the Late Geometric to the Late Archaic periods, indicating that the summit was occupied from the eighth century to the sixth. Early in the twentieth century, excavators reported finding house remains from at least two periods (Late Geometric and Archaic), but much of those remains have since eroded away. Recent excavators have uncovered an Archaic wall, a round altar, a dedicatory inscription, and marble debris including parts of a kouros and lamps, all indicating that the Summit Terrace was the location of an Archaic *temenos*. However, after the destruction of the structure in 494, the fifth-century buildings on that location were profane: for some reason, the *temenos* was desanctified.[86] Fifth-century remains are rare, perhaps reflecting the damage of erosion, and as with the lower terrace, the summit seems to have been abandoned at some point in the fifth century.[87]

The Necropolis

For a long time, one of the mysteries of Miletos was the location of the Archaic necropolis: since Greeks only exceptionally buried someone within the city walls, and since Miletos was enclosed by water on three sides, the cemetery must lie south of the city. Indeed, that is where the excavators have found the Mycenaean necropolis, on Degirmentepe, and the Hellenistic one, on Kazartepe. Thus, it is assumed that all of the Hellenistic, Classical, and Archaic graves should be found south or southwest of a line drawn from Kalabaktepe to the Sacred Gate, the approximate course of the city wall.[88] Until recently, archaeologists only knew of one Archaic burial, a great chamber tomb found amid the Hellenistic graves on Kazartepe. It is sometimes called the Tyrant's Tomb because of its size and implied importance; however, because the contents offer no clue as to the identity of the deceased, others prefer to call it the Lion Tomb, after the two identical, life-size statues of lions that marked it. Only the hindquarters of one lion remain (Inv. Sk. 1897), but the other lion (Inv. Sk. 1790) is

---

86. Perhaps this was the Archaic sanctuary of Artemis Kithone and, after the destruction, her temple was moved down to the lower East Terrace?

87. *Milet* 1.8.7–8; Graeve 1990; Senff et al. 1997.

88. Kleiner 1968, 125.

remarkably well preserved, with only the upper left side of its head broken off from the eye up and a crack in its left front leg. The plinth on which it rests measures 1.71 m. long × .66 m. deep × .15 m. high; the lion is another .54 m. high. Both lions were damaged, probably when they were thrown down the hillside from a higher situation.[89]

The tomb they guarded was approached by way of a *dromos* 11 m. long cut into the ground. It led to an entrance chamber 2.5 m. high × 3 m. long × 2.25 m. wide, which was filled with rocks. This chamber in turn led to a tunnel in the hillside, 9.5 m. long and filled with rocks and pottery sherds, probably thrown in as offerings by relatives during the closing of the grave. The burial chamber was 4.1 m. long × 3.34 m. wide × 3.36 m. high, with a saddle roof. The contents were covered with a layer of black debris 4 cm. thick. Beneath it, the excavators found the badly decomposed bones of one adult and a few grave goods: vessels for food (and numerous mussel shells), cups and dishes, a large amphora, a wooden box, two large silver *phialai* (shallow dishes), and pottery sherds. Most date to the seventh century and first half of the sixth, but the few sherds from the second half of the sixth century point to a date for this grave late in that century.

Blind luck has both concealed and partially revealed the rest of the Archaic necropolis. The village of Balat moved in 1955 from its location on the Stadium Hill to its present location, just to the east of Kazartepe. In doing so, it obscured the necropolis. Over the course of several decades, while digging trenches for water pipes, villagers have come across a total of four Archaic sarcophagi clustered in a small area along one village street. None were destroyed or robbed in antiquity, although the first one found was badly damaged during discovery. They are all monolithic sarcophagi containing adult males and—characteristic of East Ionian burial practices from the second half of the sixth century—remarkably few grave goods (principally a couple of finger rings). The contents are undatable, but the style of burial and the sherds found in the fill dirt indicate an origin in the late sixth century.[90]

The presence of the village makes it impossible to excavate the neighboring area, but it likely was the primary cemetery for the city. It lay

89. The intact lion is on display at the Pergamon Museum in Berlin. The grave was unearthed in 1906, but the original excavator, A. von Salis, never published his results. Some comments were made about it in Kleiner 1968 (126–27) and Graeve 1989 (143–44). Recently, the results were fully published by Forbeck and Heres (1997), who quote extensively from Salis's daybooks and catalog the finds.

90. Müller-Wiener 1986a, 104; Müller-Wiener 1988c (sarcophagi); Graeve 1989; Mellink 1989, 122–23; Mitchell 1989/90, 103.

outside the furthest expanse of the city walls, in sandy soil conducive to burials. Also, the Sacred Way would have passed through this district on its way to Didyma, transforming the district into a very desirable location for one's final resting place. Probably the street was lined with monuments, such as the statues of young men and women (kouroi and *kourai*), standing or seated, that have been found often in the excavation of the city and may have been originally erected as graver markers. Other tombs were marked by stelae, like the late Archaic Anthemion Stele (named for the floral design on top of the stele) found in Akköy. Although it is broken badly and its inscription is unreadable from age, it was almost certainly a freestanding funereal monument from the Sacred Way, originally rising nearly 3 m. high.[91] To the casual traveler or to the participants in the annual procession to the Oracle, the monuments of the necropolis astride the Sacred Way stood as a reminder of the praise and piety owed to parents and ancestors, the makers of this extraordinary city.

Sites in the *Chore*

Beyond the city proper and beyond the necropolis, several other sites in Milesian territory exhibit signs of early prominence, especially as religious sanctuaries. They are witnessed by the ancient literature and confirmed by excavation. Didyma has already been discussed in detail, but several other locations can be distinguished, principally as the locations of major sanctuaries in Milesian territory.

Poseidon was the patron god of the Ionian League, so we would expect to find him worshiped at Miletos as well. One of his common epithets in the Hellenic world is *Taureos,* and judging from the month name *Taureon,* he was present at a very early date in Miletos and many of the colonies of the Pontos. Strabo (14.1.3) confirms this early arrival, saying that back during the Ionian Migration, Neleos founded an altar on a cape named for Poseidon. Archaeologists have located an altar dating to the first half of the sixth century at Cape Monodendri, at the extreme southwest corner of the larger Milesian peninsula, 7 km. southwest of Didyma. The altar is made entirely of richly ornamented marble, with a total length of 19 m. and a platform measuring 11.5 × 10 m. In addition, in the city, during an excavation at the Hellenistic Heroon by the West

91. Kleiner 1968, 127 (statues as markers); Graeve 1989, 143 (stele).

Market, just north of the Temple of Athena, there was recently found a stone inscribed with a decree passed by the Milesian democracy late in the fifth century. Although badly broken, the inscription has been interpreted to be a *lex sacra* (cult regulation) concerning the cult of Poseidon Helikonios and possibly another god. In it Poseidon has a priest and a sanctuary but not a temple proper, and certain things are prescribed to be done in the month of Taureon. Possibly the decree refers to the same sanctuary mentioned by Pausanias (7.24.5), who says that the Milesians had an altar dedicated to Poseidon Helikonios—the patron of the Panionion—between Miletos and a spring called Byblis, but this second alter has not been uncovered.[92]

Until very recently, evidence for the worship of Aphrodite at Miletos was only attested in Hellenistic and Roman inscriptions, where she is usually named with the epithet *Agoraia*. Because she was present in Istros and Kepoi in Archaic times and in many other colonies in the Classical era, her cult is assumed to have existed in Archaic Miletos as well. Several literary sources from later centuries refer to just such a cult, especially Theokritos, an Alexandrian poet from the third century B.C.E.[93] He says that somewhere in the Milesian territory, on a hillside between the riverlets Byblis and Hyetis, near the main road, there was a temple of Aphrodite Oikeous. In the excavations beginning 1989, a sanctuary of Aphrodite dating back to the early seventh century was located and partially excavated on the summit of a hill west of Miletos and 1 km. northwest of Kalabaktepe. The site on Zeytintepe has yielded numerous votive items—figurines and inscriptions to Aphrodite and Aphrodite Oikous dating as early as the sixth century—that confirm the identification of this sanctuary with the one mentioned by Theokritos.[94]

A temple area was discovered on the summit, where a plateau was constructed and reconstructed several times in the Archaic and Classical periods by filling in the numerous crevices in the rock with layers of building debris.[95] The oldest debris stratum, located immediately on top

---

92. *Milet* 1.6 (altar); Herrmann 1970 *(lex sacra)*; Ehrhardt 1983, 171–73 (Taureon); Koenigs 1986 (altar).

93. Theokritos 7.115, 28.4; see also Sch. ad loc. Cf. Posidipp. in *Anth. Pal.* 12.131 (Gow and Page 3082–85); Charito 2.2.7.

94. Ehrhardt 1983, 164–66; Gans 1991; Senff 1992; Senff 1997a; Heinz and Senff 1995. Inscriptions with the dedication to Aphrodite include Mil. Inv. Z 90.33.1 (sixth century), Z 90.45.2 (no date given), Z 91.68.15 (Roman), Z 92.83.14 (Archaic), Z 94.127.17 (Archaic?). See Herrmann 1995, 282–88.

95. Gans 1991; Senff 1992; Heinz and Senff 1995; Senff 1997a.

of the rock, is a thick gray layer of ash, limestone, wood coals, large and small bones, animal teeth, and sherds of glass, all dating to the late seventh century. The nature and frequency of these finds indicate that sacrifices were offered here and that the sanctuary had become popular by the late seventh century. A few votive fragments from the beginning of the seventh century demonstrate an even earlier date for the establishment of the sanctuary. In the mid–sixth century, the plateau was enlarged by extending the debris layer. On it, the Milesians built an Ionic temple out of marble, many pieces of which where used as rubble in yet another, later layer of the plateau. This temple was decorated with kouroi and contained many votive offerings made of metal, clay, and other substances. The finds reflect the international character of the sanctuary: they include Cypriot terracotta; Egyptian faience, seals, amulets, and stone statuettes (from workshops at Naukratis and Rhodes especially); Asian bone carvings; a probably Thracian dedication; and Greek ware from Attika, Corinth, Chios, and Lakonia.

The Archaic temple was ruined in the destruction of 494, but in the refoundation of the city, the Milesians leveled off the plateau yet again—an Attic sherd from ca. 500 B.C.E. was found in the debris layer—and rebuilt. The new temple was apparently much like the old one, a marble structure constructed in the Ionic style. A foundation wall 7 m. long dates to this period, as do many remnants of a marble building. The bust of a woman from the second quarter of the fifth century is praised for the extremely high quality of its workmanship.[96]

The Temple of Aphrodite was not the only recent find of great import. In the eastern part of Milesian territory, an archaeological field survey of the entire Milesian peninsula that was conducted in the 1990s by Hans Lohmann has led to an Archaic discovery on the northeast corner of the large plateau called Stephania, on a hill named Mengerevtepe, 7 km. southeast of Miletos and south of the modern road from Söke. There the survey team and later excavators have discovered a town that was settled since the prehistoric period. Sculpture remnants date from the Protogeometric through the Archaic periods, and rubble in the debris layer reveals that the site endured a destruction and subsequent rebuilding in the late seventh century, probably as a result of the Lydian invasions. The town reached its prime in the sixth century B.C.E. and was destroyed and abandoned at the end of that century.

96. Gans 1991, 140; Hölbl 1999.

Thus far, the two most interesting aspects of this settlement are its defensive wall and temple. The wall is a structure 2.2 m. thick and 185 m. long, aligned north-to-south and stretching along the west edge of the settlement. It contained three towers in all. The temple, made in the Ionic style, was located on the south edge of the hill, on a leveled terrace made of late Archaic debris. It was not finished when it was destroyed at the beginning of the fifth century, but a sixth-century boustrophedon inscription indicates that the temple belonged to Athena (τ]ῆι Ἀθη[ναίηι], Mil. Inv. S 92.119).[97]

Because this site includes a temple to Athena and suffered destruction ca. 600 and again ca. 500 B.C.E., excavators identify it with Assessos, a town known from literary sources. According to Herodotos (1.19), when the Lydian king Alyattes attacked Miletos in the last years of the seventh century, he accidentally burned down a temple of Athena at Assessos, in atonement for which he built for her two temples in place of the one.[98] One corner of one temple has thus far been found, but the excavation has been limited: only six trenches have been sunk into the large hillside, so it is still possible that a second temple may be uncovered to confirm our literary notice. In any case, if this identification is correct, the two destruction layers correspond to the burning by Alyattes and the Persian destruction. Apparently the site was abandoned after 494 B.C.E., because Classical and Hellenistic sherds are very rare there; a Byzantine church was later built on the north edge of the plateau.

In summary, a few general conclusions can be drawn from the archaeological remains of Miletos from ca. 1000 to 400 B.C.E. First, one is struck by the indications of continuous habitation throughout this period of time. To be sure, the Submycenaean and Early Geometric city must have been rather small, but over the centuries it grew to an impressive extent, encompassing the entire peninsula and Kalabaktepe. This conclusion is reinforced by the population estimates for the city, which run as much as sixty-four thousand for the sixth-century city, although that number is probably too high. Estimates for the population in the fifth century vary from fifteen to twenty thousand to as little as seventy-five hundred.[99]

97. Senff 1995b; Weber 1995; Lohmann 1995; Herrmann 1995, 288–92 (inscription).
98. Cf. Theopomp. *Philippika FGH* 115 F 123; Steph. Byz. s.v. "Assessos"; Nic. Dam. *FGH* 90 F 52.
99. Sixty-four thousand: Roebuck 1959, 21–23, based on the number of ships launched at Lade. Fifteen to twenty thousand: Hoepfner and Schwandner 1994, 21. The lowest figure

Since this was a period of recovery, we naturally expect a smaller city, and the remains indeed show that it covered the peninsula less widely and less densely as a rule. Miletos was hurt badly by the Persian destruction, but it rebounded with tenacity and determination.

A second unmistakable conclusion is that the Persians inflicted a total destruction on the city in 494. In every location where the excavators have dug down to the appropriate levels, they have found a substantial burn layer between the Archaic and Classical strata. This burn is often confirmed by a terracing of the Archaic debris to form a level foundation for fifth-century construction. While there is not a single artifact that can be securely dated to the years between 494 and 479, the terraces on Kalabaktepe, the newer Temple of Athena, the shrine of Dionysos, some walls west of the Bouleuterion, and a stele from the North Marketplace all fall in the second quarter of the century.[100] Miletos was indeed destroyed, and it was "emptied of Milesians" (Hdt. 6.22.1).

Finally, the general argument can be made that most of the Panhellenic gods were worshiped in both Archaic and Classical Miletos. The consistency of the cults and, especially, the rebuilding of Classical sanctuaries on the sites of their destroyed Archaic predecessors strengthen the overall picture of Miletos as an Ionian city that was reestablished by the same society that inhabited it before the destruction by the Persians. Again, these findings are consistent with the societal findings in general: there is no great division between the Archaic and Classical social institutions of language, calendar, tribes, and religious cults. The Milesians were a discrete people before the destruction of their city, and this fact does not change later. To the best of our knowledge, the society of fifth-century Miletos represents a conscious perpetuation of the culture of the people who inhabited the city immediately before its destruction.

Only a fraction of the city of Miletos has been excavated, and even less has been dug down to the Archaic levels. Thus, we must conclude that we know very little about the physical city in the era of its greatest prosperity, when it was the "ornament of Ionia" (Hdt. 5.28). Yet everything that we do know confirms the literary accounts. Miletos was a great commercial center, a trading power, and a mighty metropolis,

---

is obtained by Pounds (1973, 60; cf. Renfrew 1982, 277) through a crude estimate from the tribute assessment of 425/4 B.C.E., which he calculates was probably based on an equation of one talent of tribute for every 750 citizens.

100. On stylistic grounds, Graeve (1975a) dates the statue of a seated woman to immediately after 479 B.C.E.

swollen with inhabitants who shared in its remarkable opulence. From this height, the city fell into complete disaster, sufficient to wipe it from the face of the earth. But that was not to be. The Milesians returned and rebuilt, and characteristically they did so in a manner that demonstrated their progressive attitude and their confidence in the restoration of their previous prosperity.

6

The Fifth Century

In the late summer or autumn of 478, the year after the Battle of Mykale, the eastern Greeks asked Athens to take them under its protection and form a new league against Persia. Because the appeal was based on kinship, just as Miletos's appeal had been in 499, we know that the Ionian Greeks played a leading role in the formation of this league; certainly after their defection from Persia in the Battle of Mt. Mykale, both Samos and Miletos would have been original members. Thus Athens established the Delian League, a permanent alliance that would grow in the next few decades to encompass most of the coastal and island cities of the Aegean. It pursued campaigns against the Persians, driving them out of Thrace and western Asia Minor and eventually completely out of the Aegean Sea.[1]

Prosperity returned to Miletos and the other cities that had been punished by the Persians, but over the next few decades, it was constrained by the increasingly imperialistic behavior of Athens, whose hegemonial role in the Delian League soon became a despotism that has led the organization to be renamed in modern times "the Athenian Empire." Originally the league's headquarters and treasury were on the island of Delos, but in 454 they were transferred to Athens in a move that stands as an overt symbol of the changed nature of the league. Allies who disagreed with Athenian policy were harshly subdued: their walls were dismantled, their fleets were confiscated, a cash indemnity was leveled against them, and garrisons and Athenian officials were often left behind to ensure future cooperation. The governments of rebellious allies were often converted summarily into democracies: one character in Thucydides is made to say to the Athenian people, νῦν μὲν γὰρ ὑμῖν ὁ δῆμος ἐν πάσαις ταῖς πόλεσιν εὔνους ἐστί [The people in all the cities are well disposed to you] (3.47.2).

---

1. The best sources for the Delian League are Meiggs 1972 and Rhodes 1992.

Revolt and Revolution

Miletos was in many ways a typical Athenian ally. It was originally well pleased with the Athenian presence in the east Aegean, but when freedom proved to be a sham perpetuated by the Athenians while they built up their power and empire, ally after ally revolted and was subdued, until Miletos took its turn. At the middle of the century, Milesian discontent with Athenian interference led to a sequence of events that included internal strife and active revolt from the Delian League. The Athenians responded with characteristic severity, eventually imposing financial and military penalties, as well as establishing new political institutions modeled after the government of Athens. Thus the government of Miletos was transformed into a democracy.

While the fact of this change in constitution is not in question, the scholarship that has dealt with working out its detailed circumstances is most remarkable for the lack of any kind of consensus.[2] Several questions exercise scholars: Was Miletos governed in the first half of the fifth century by oligarchy or by democracy succeeded by oligarchy and then by democracy again? In the middle of that century did Miletos revolt once or twice from the Delian League? And was the democratic government with which Miletos ended the century set up in 450 or ca. 443 or in the 420s? A careful examination of the evidence leads to the conclusion that the refounded city enjoyed its traditional, oligarchic government until civil strife became so bad as to prompt an initial Athenian intervention in favor of the oligarchy in 450/49. However, when the flames of stasis did not cool and led to a revolt from the league, Athens intervened again, this time sometime before 443, severely restricting the autonomy of the Milesian government and forcing that city to abandon its old ways and accept a new democratic government.

The first step in sorting out these events is to establish a *terminus ante quem* for the establishment of the Milesian democracy. Two Milesian *leges sacrae,* taken together, demonstrate that Miletos must have obtained its democracy before it left the Athenian sphere of influence in 412 B.C.E. The first law is concerned with a priestess of Arte-

---

2. A brief list of the work of scholars who have tackled one or more of the major aspects of this problem must include Oliver 1935; Mattingly 1961, 1981; Barron 1962; Fornara 1971; Herrmann 1970; Meiggs 1972; Piérart 1974; Gehrke 1980; Cataldi 1981; Robertson 1987.

mis.³ It was found by the southern cross wall in Miletos and dated by the eponymous official to 380/79. It begins (lines 1–5):

Ἐπὶ Παρ[θ]ενοπαίο, μηνὸς Ἀρτε-
μισιῶνος, Κεκροπὶς ἐπρυτά-
νευεν, Φιλιννῆς Ἡροδότο
ἐπεστάτει, ἔδοξεν τῆι βολῆι
καὶ τῶι δήμωι, Ἡράκλειτος εἶπεν·

[In the year of Parthenopaios, in the month of Artemision, when the tribe Kekropis held the prytany and Philinnes, son of Herodotos, was president. It was decided by the Council and the people, and Herakleitos proposed: . . .]

This law uses Athenian formulae to announce a decision made by the Council and the Assembly, and the Athenian tribal name *Kekropis* is further proof of a change, as the six old Ionian tribes present in Archaic Miletos have been abandoned in favor of the twelve tribes we see in the Hellenistic city, ten of them Athenian in origin.⁴ Though this inscription dates to the first quarter of the fourth century, it provides indirect evidence on the form of the Milesian government in the last years of the fifth century as well, since the Milesians would not have adopted such changes after departing from the Delian League in 412. On the contrary, we can go further and say that the fact that the democracy, complete with its Athenian-style offices and tribes, survived its break with Athens is indication that the democracy was strongly fixed in Miletos by 412 and so was most likely set up considerably earlier.

It is not necessary to rely on such an inference to extend the period of democracy in Miletos back many years before the break with Athens. A second *lex sacra* (Herrmann 1970, 166–67) offers direct evidence of Athenian-style democracy at Miletos already in the 430s. This inscription, concerning the shrine of Poseidon Helikonios and possibly the cult of another deity, also contains an Athenian-style prescript reflecting a democratic government. The decree was first published and thoroughly explained by Herrmann, who says that it is so similar to an Athenian

3. Herrmann 1970, 163ff.; Wiegand 1901, 911 (editio princeps); *SGDI* #5496; Sokolowski 1955, #45.
4. For the twelve new tribes, see Haussoullier 1897; Ehrhardt 1983, 98 n. 9.

decree that we would think it was from Athens if we did not know for a
fact that it came from Miletos.[5]

Although very fragmentary, we can tell that this inscription originally
had a fuller form of the prescript than the previous one, because it includes the name of the secretary between the prytany and the president
(lines 1–5):

[- 10 -]'[-- 12 --]
[- 9 - E]ὐδήμο, Λεωντ[ὶς ἐ-]
[πρυτά]νευεν, Τήλαγ[ρ]ος ἐγρα[μ-]
[μάτευ]εν, Τήμεν[ος] ἐ[πεστ]άτε[.]
[--- 5 ---]ς εἶπεν· . . .

[[. . . E]udemos, when the tribe Leont[is
held the pry]tany, Telag[r]os was the se[cre
tar]y, and Temen[os] was the e[pist]ate[s.
. . .] proposed: . . .]

The naming of the eponymous official as Eudemos presents a choice
between two likely dates for this decree, 437/6 and 404/3 (respectively,
Εὔδημος Ἀριστοδήμο and Εὔδημος Ἡγέμονος, *Milet* 1.3 #122.i.90
and ii.12).[6]

Both internal and external evidence favors the earlier date. Herrmann
states that the style and letterforms in this inscription are consistent with
a date in the second half of the fifth century. He notes a remarkable
similarity between this decree and the Milesian Banishment Decree (*Milet*
1.6 #187), which was erected before 443/2 B.C.E. In addition, the later
date is virtually eliminated by the short-lived oligarchic coup at Miletos
in 404/3 (D.S. 13.104.5–6; Plut. *Lys.* 8.1–3; Polyain. 1.45.1). Yet another clue that a democratic Miletos could have published this decree as
early as 437/6 comes from Thucydides, who says (1.115.2–3) that in
440/39 war broke out between Miletos and Samos over Priene. Athens
sided with the Milesians and some revolutionaries from Samos, over-
whelmed the Samian oligarchy, and established a democracy there. Thus,
the democrats at Athens and the democrats at Samos sided with the

---

5. Herrmann 1970, 168.

6. An additional possibility is 413/2, Ἡγέμων Εὐδήμο, if one accepts Eudemos as the
father of an eponymous official. However, this possibility is rendered unlikely since neither
the secretary nor the president is called by his patronymic.

Milesians against the oligarchs at Samos. While this passage says nothing specific about the form of the Milesian government, its general circumstances are favorable to the assumption that Miletos was democratic in 440/39, so the date 437/6 is the most likely for this inscription.

Since these two democratic *leges sacrae* indicate that the Athenian form of government had been established in Miletos probably by 437/6 (certainly by 412/11), the next step is to examine the evidence for the traditional oligarchy to fix with precision the most likely date for the transition to democracy. The Molpoi Decree from Miletos (*Milet* 1.3 #133) offers a clear *terminus post quem* for that change. In the first four lines (quoted in chap. 5), three of the old oligarchic tribes are mentioned. These tribes are clear indication that at the inscribing of this decree in 450/49 (as dated by the *aisymnetes* lists), the government at Miletos was an oligarchy. Critics can argue that it is possible that the form of the Molpoi Decree might represent the retention—with a conservatism unremarkable in religious matters—of traditional offices, even under a democratic regime. According to this interpretation, the Molpoi Decree would be anachronistic in that it exhibits oligarchic features that, due to some sacred importance, outlived the oligarchy itself.[7] Such an interpretation requires the corroboration of other evidence if it is to be preferred to a more simple and straightforward reading of the inscription, but this view entails a troubling scenario. It requires the transformation of the traditional Milesian oligarchy into a democracy at or soon after the refoundation of Miletos and its entrance into the Delian League, ca. 478. This version of events is very difficult to reconcile with the best literary evidence on the government of Miletos in the first half of the fifth century. To be sure, Herodotos says that at the start of the Ionian Revolt in 499, Anaxagoras, the tyrant at Miletos, laid aside his tyranny and declared *isonomia,* but the resulting democracy—if, indeed, it was one—would not have been able to establish itself as a Milesian tradition in the scant five years of its existence, which were wholly consumed with fighting the Ionian Revolt.

Other support for the anachronistic reading of the Molpoi Decree might be drawn from another possible occasion for the early establishment of a democratic tradition at Miletos. The occasion is offered by the general Mardonios at the end of the Ionian Revolt, when, Herodotos tells us (6.43.3), Mardonios deposed the tyrants and set up democracies in all

---

7. Gehrke 1980, 22–23.

the Ionian cities. To assume that Miletos is included among these cities begs the very serious question of whether a polity of Miletos existed at that time. In any case, the only clear inscriptional evidence on the form of the later Milesian democracy features, as we have seen, Athenian officials and tribes. This fact cannot be reconciled with a Persian establishment of democracy without further complicated and uncorroborated argumentation. Since the *leges sacrae* clearly testify to the fact that democracy at Miletos was organized on the Athenian model, it is most reasonable to assume that it was established under direct Athenian influence. Recognizing this conclusion, it is still possible to claim that the Molpoi Decree of 450/49 was a product of democracy by assuming that the Milesians adopted this form of government after the Battle of Mykale as a kind of vote of thanks and esteem to Athens for freeing Ionia from the Persians. But this scenario, unlike the first two, has not a shred of positive evidence in its favor.

None of these theories is compelling in its own right and in view of the evidence available to support it. In addition, all three possible explanations for an anachronistic reading of the Molpoi Decree face a further, fatal difficulty in the lack of direct evidence for the existence of an oligarchy at Miletos in the middle of the fifth century. In his description of the *Constitution of Athens,* an anonymous writer called Pseudo-Xenophon, or "the Old Oligarch" (because of his bias), probably writing during the early years of the Peloponnesian War,[8] tells us of Athenian involvement in Milesian affairs (Ps.-Xen. *Ath. Pol.* 3.11).

ὁποσάκις δ᾽ ἐπεχείρησαν αἱρεῖσθαι τοὺς βελτίστους, οὐ συνήνε-
γκεν αὐτοῖς, ἀλλ᾽ ἐντὸς ὀλίγου χρόνου ὁ δῆμος ἐδούλευσεν ὁ ἐν
Βοιωτοῖς· τοῦτο δὲ ὅτε Μιλησίων εἵλοντο τοὺς βελτίστους,
ἐντὸς ὀλίγου χρόνου ἀποστάντες τὸν δῆμον κατέκοψαν· τοῦτο
δὲ ὅτε εἵλοντο Λακεδαιμονίους ἀντὶ Μεσσηνίων, ἐντὸς ὀλίγου
χρόνου Λακεδαιμόνιοι καταστρεψάμενοι Μεσσηνίους ἐπολέμ-
ουν Ἀθηναίοις.

[Whenever they [the Athenians] tried their hand at siding with the best men [i.e., the oligarchs], it has not turned out well for themselves. But rather within a short time the people in Boiotia were

---

8. See Mattingly 1997 for the differing views on the date of composition. Mattingly himself narrows the date to 414 B.C.E.

enslaved. And when they sided with the best men of the Milesians, within a short time this class revolted and slaughtered the people. And when they sided with the Lakedaimonians against the Messenians, within a short time the Lakedaimonians subdued the Messenians and made war on the Athenians.]

Clearly an oligarchy ruled in Miletos at some time when it was under Athenian influence, from 479 to 412. To maintain the anachronistic reading of the Molpoi Decree, we must therefore assume two revolutions at Miletos in the middle of the fifth century. In the first, the early Milesian democracy would have been discarded in favor of an oligarchy that was backed by the Athenians. Later, when this oligarchy revolted, it would have been replaced by a democracy, once more under the Athenian aegis. This scenario, based on very little solid evidence, has become over-complicated. The simpler and better interpretation accepts the Molpoi Decree as issued by a religious college during the rule of the ancestral government. This evidence implies that the oligarchy held power in Miletos from the refoundation in 479 or shortly thereafter until at least 450/49, the year of the Molpoi Decree.

The evidence that we have examined so far reveals that the period from 445 to 437/6 is the most likely period for the introduction of Athenian-style democracy in Miletos. The passage of the Old Oligarch already quoted offers clues about the circumstances of that change of government in terms of the details of Athenian intervention on behalf of oligarchy. The Old Oligarch mentions two areas of intervention besides Miletos: Boiotia and Lakedaimonia. According to the chronology established by Buck,[9] the Athenians gained control of Boiotia with the Battle of Oinophyta in 458 B.C.E. (Thuc. 1.108.2–3) and maintained it for about twelve years, until they were defeated by Boiotian exiles at the Battle of Koroneia in 446 (Thuc. 1.113.2–4). During this period of control, the Athenians supported the pro-Athenian contingent in each Boiotian state, which was sometimes, but not always, an oligarchic party. The second reference made by the Old Oligarch is better known. The Messenian revolt occurred in 464 B.C.E. after an earthquake in the Peloponnesos. Kimon led an Athenian contingent in aid of the Spartans, but he was dismissed, and having been thus insulted, the Athenians broke off their alliance with the Spartans and the Hellenic League. Four or ten

---

9. Buck 1970; 1978, 143–54.

years later,[10] the Spartans negotiated an end to the revolt (Thuc. 1.101–103.1), and what is called the First Peloponnesian War between the Athenian and Peloponnesian forces soon began in earnest (Thuc. 1.105ff.).

In sum, the Athenian interventions in Boiotia and Lakedaimonia both occurred around the middle of the century, between 464 and 447. Thus, it is likely that the intervention at Miletos also occurred around the middle of the fifth century. In all three examples, the extent of time between the Athenian favor and its ugly consequences was described as ἐντὸς ὀλίγου χρόνου [within a short time]. In Boiotia and Lakedaimonia, the intervention lasted twelve years or less. Presumably the interval of time at Miletos was in the same range as the other two examples, probably twelve or fewer years and almost certainly not a great deal longer.[11] In addition, that the Athenians backed existing oligarchies where they found them in both Boiotia and Lakedaimonia is significant evidence telling against the view that the Molpoi Decree was the product of a democratic government. Based on the evidence of these parallel examples, the Athenians probably intruded into Milesian affairs somewhere near the middle of the fifth century in support of an existing oligarchy.

In the long run, Athenian intervention was not able to stabilize the traditional government and keep it loyal to Athenian imperial designs in the face of the forces of civil discord. Not only does the Old Oligarch tell

---

10. The manuscript reading is a very difficult problem: see Gomme 1945, 1:302–3 (*ad* 1.103.1), 401–11.

11. Piérart (1969, 385–87) uses this reasoning—mistakenly, I believe—to support the idea that a democracy was established when the city was refounded. His notion is that since the Molpoi Decree shows an oligarchy in 450/49 and since the time between the refoundation of the city and this date was much too long (as much as twenty-nine years) to be described by the Old Oligarch as "a short time," the refounded city must have been governed by a democracy that was later converted into an Athenian-backed oligarchy and then back into a pro-Athenian democracy. However, Piérart is forgetting that in both Boiotia and Lakedaimonia, the Athenians supported oligarchies that existed long before the Athenian intervention. The Oligarch's words "within a short time" describe not the extent of the oligarchic government but the extent of the active Athenian support of that government, presumably in the face of political opposition. With respect to Boiotia, Buck (1970, esp. 222) argues that the oligarchies there were not set up by the Athenians but were preexisting governments utilized by them. In the case of Lakedaimonia, there is no doubt that Athens was supporting the traditional oligarchic government of Sparta in maintaining and preserving the status quo ante bellum. The circumstances of these two other examples support the likelihood that the oligarchy existed at Miletos before the active Athenian intervention mentioned by the Old Oligarch. Moreover, Piérart's theory of an original democracy leads to unnecessary complications because it requires two discrete revolutions in the Milesian government (one from democracy to oligarchy and another, after the revolt mentioned by the Old Oligarch, back to democracy).

us that Miletos suffered from civil stasis during the time of Athenian intervention, but many scholars find independent evidence for that stasis in the Athenian tribute lists. These engraved stelae from Athens record the one-sixtieth of each ally's tribute payment that is given as an offering to the goddess Athena beginning in 454/3, when the treasury was moved from Delos to Athens. In the very first year, the entry for Miletos reads (*ATL* 1.342 #1, column vi, lines 19–22):

Μιλέσιοι
[ἐ]χς Λέρο: HHH
[Μι]λέσιοι
[ἐκ T]ειχιόσσε[ς: . . .]

[The Milesians
from Leros: 300 drachmas
The Milesians
from Teichioussa: . . .]

The Milesians from Leros are paying three talents of tribute,[12] while the amount from the Milesians at Teichioussa is lost. Milesians are completely missing from the next list but reappear without a tribute amount in 452/1 (#3.ii.28) and paying ten talents of tribute in 450/49 (#5.v.18). From the strange fact that Milesians are listed as paying tribute from other places but not from Miletos, the conclusion is usually drawn that Miletos was riven by stasis and revolt in 454/3. The argument is that the government in the city withheld its payment, while loyalists who had fled to Leros and Teichioussa paid their tribute, and that Athens recovered Miletos by the time of its tribute payment in 452/1.[13]

This interpretation was complicated by the discovery of an additional fragment of the first tribute list, published by Meritt in 1972, on which Miletos does occur.[14] Column iii, lines 18–20, now reads:

Νεοπο[. . . . .]
Μιλέ[. . . . .]
Ἀκρ[. . . . . .]ι: HHH

---

12. In Athenian coinage, there are six thousand drachmas in a talent. Since the three hundred drachmas recorded here represent one-sixtieth of the total tribute payment, the total (60 × 300) is eighteen thousand drachmas, or three talents.

13. Dunham 1915, 132–38; Earp 1954; Meiggs 1972, 562–63.

14. Meritt 1972.

[Neopo[. . .]
Mile[. . .]
Akr[. . .]: 300 drachmas]

The restoration of this fragment that Meritt offers in the editio princeps is designed to preserve the theory of a divided polity and revolt at Miletos in 454/3.

Νεοπο[λῖται ἐκ νν]
Μιλέ[το ἐν Λευκôι]
Ἀκϱ[οτεϱίο]ι: ΗΗΗ

[The Neopo[litai from]
Mile[tus on Leukos]
Pro[montor]y: 300 drachmas]

According to Meritt, the Neopolitai on Leukos Promontory would be another group of Milesian loyalists who had fled from Miletos. But this reasoning is circular: the theory of the revolt is based on the absence of Miletos from the first tribute list, while the restoration keeping Miletos off that list is based on the presupposition of a revolt. Meritt's restoration is gratuitous. It may also be an impossible restoration of the stone, since according to another scholar, there were no traces of his long restoration of line 19 evident where they would be expected, on the adjacent fragment of stone, above the letters on line 20.[15] Therefore, the safest way to understand this fragment is to read it as a straightforward entry registering a payment of tribute by the Milesians.

The three separate listings for the Milesians in 454/3 can be interpreted in two ways. Perhaps these listings merely reflect a method of accounting resumed in the years after 427 B.C.E. In that year, the Milesians, Leros, and Teichioussa are again listed individually (#28, lines 15–17), and between the reassessment of 425 and the payment of 416/5, they are named separately but join in a single tribute payment.[16] However, it is possible that the separate listings may indeed be an indication of civil strife among the Milesians. Without further evidence, there can be no

---

15. This discussion is problematic, because it is based on differing readings of the stone, and because the adjacent fragment, stone #2 of the Athenian tribute lists, is now lost. See Piérart 1974.

16. Piérart 1974, 167; *IG* 1³ 71.1.121–22; *ATL* 1 #37, column i, lines 88–90, #39, column i, lines 36–38.

clear choice between the possibilities and therefore no definitive interpretation. The listings neither prove nor disprove civil unrest and revolt in 454/3, so we must look elsewhere for the events related by the Old Oligarch.

The recovery of the city after a revolt is partially attested in *IG* 1³ 21, a decree found in Athens that records regulations for Miletos. A text of this decree has been reconstructed, but the extremely fragmentary nature of the inscription makes the interpretation of the material difficult.[17] The decree begins (lines 1–3):

[Μι]λεσί[οις χσυγ]γρ[αφαί· | ἔδοχσεν] τει βολει κα[ὶ τοι δέμοι· . . .
ca. 6 . . . ὶς ἐπρ]υτάν[ευε, . . . ca. 6 . . . ἐγραμμάτ|ευε, . .
ca. 4 . .]ορ ἐπεστάτε, [Εὔθυνος ἐρχε· τάδε hοι χ]συνγγρα[φὲς
χσυνέγραφσαν· . . .].

[[Agreement for the Mi]lesi[ans.| Resolved] by the Council an[d the people, -8- held the pr]ytan[y, -6?- was secre|tary, -4?-]or presided, [Euthynos was archon. The s]yngra[pheis drew up the motion . . .].]

The dating of the decree presents the first major problem. Normally Attic decrees are dated by the name of the eponymous archon. In this prescript, the name of the archon Euthynos is restored in line 3 by the editors of *IG* 1³, based on the occurrence of that name twice in the decree itself, at lines 61 and 86, but the date of the decree is still disputed because Euthynos's archon year is not certain. Diodoros names the archons of 450/49, 431/0, and 426/5 Euthydemos (12.3.1, 12.38.1, 12.58.1), but we have inscriptional evidence that he was mistaken once: the archon for 426/5 was actually Euthynos.[18] Most scholars, favoring an early date based on internal evidence, such as letterforms, have assumed that Diodoros made the same mistake twice, and, thus, the Athenian Regulations for Miletos are customarily dated to 450/49 B.C.E.[19] Following this

---

17. A translation of the decree without many of the restorations proposed in *IG* can be found in Fornara 1983b, 92–94 #92. The most thorough commentaries are Oliver 1935; Bradeen and McGregor 1973; Cataldi 1981. See also Balcer 1984a.

18. *IG* 1³ 369.5. See also Philochoros *FGH* 328 F 128. Concerning the archon of the year 431/0, see Develin 1989, *ad* 431/0.

19. Beginning with Kirchhoff in *IG* 1 Suppl. (1891) 22a. See also Oliver 1935, 182; Meritt and Wade-Gery 1957, 183; Meritt and Wade-Gery 1963, 100–102; Meiggs 1943,

reasoning, the decree fits nicely into the temporal context we have been discussing. However, it is not sound reasoning to replace the name of the archon in the prescript of a decree based on references to that archonship in unknown contexts in the body of the decree.[20] It is possible that the references are to actions initiated in the same year in which the Athenian Regulations for Miletos were passed, but it may be safer to assume only that the regulations were passed subsequent to the archonship named. On the basis of this argument, 450/49 will serve as the *terminus post quem* for the Athenian Regulations for Miletos.

The content of the decree contains a number of provisions for Athenian intervention in Miletos. After a very brief mention of rites owed to the gods ([ν]ομιζόμενα το[ῖς θεοῖς], line 4), provision is made for the appointment of five Athenian archons to act as a permanent board of political residents at Miletos, as opposed to a temporary board of overseers (*episkopoi*). Lines 8–23 are badly damaged, but key words and phrases survive: "triremes" or "trierarchs" [τριερ-] (10), "troopships" [τον στρατιο[τ]ίδ[ον]] (10), "to furnish arms" [ὅπλα παρέχεσθαι] (11), "to render service" [ὑπερετεν] (12), "four obols" [[τέ]τταρας ὀβο[λὸ]ς] (13), "soldiers" [στρ[α]τιό[τεσι] (15), and "Athens" [ἈΘέ[ν]εσ[ι] (20). This section is sometimes interpreted to be arranging for Milesian military aid to Athens,[21] based on the restorations of Ἀθέναζε at lines 15, 16, and 19. Many scholars prefer to view these lines in reference to the transport and maintenance of the board of archons and a garrison at Miletos. Either interpretation is possible, because the context is completely lost.[22]

The remainder of the decree is preserved in half lines or less. Lines 24–28 are difficult to interpret at all,[23] but lines 28–51 without doubt establish a procedure for two different kinds of trials of Milesians at Athens,

---

25; Meiggs 1963, 24–25; Meiggs 1966, 95 n. 1; Barron 1962; Bradeen and McGregor 1973, 38. Mattingly (1961, 1981; aided by Lawton 1992; 1995, 19–21) attempts to redate this decree to 426/5, but his arguments are unconvincing. The best responses to him are Meiggs 1963, 24–25; Meritt and Wade-Gery 1963, 100–102; and esp. Bradeen and McGregor 1973, 65–70.

20. Fornara 1971; cf. Cataldi 1981, 177; Robertson 1987, 384–86.

21. Oliver 1935, 190–91; Mattingly 1961, 176; Meritt and Wade-Gery 1963, 101.

22. Bradeen and McGregor 1973, 40–41; Cataldi 1981, 180–83.

23. The range of opinion is broad. Oliver (1935) assumes that the clauses limit the anti-Athenian activity by Miletos's representative in the allied assembly. Bradeen and McGregor (1973) think that they might apply to Milesian supporters of a previous revolt who are now subject to trial or, more probably, that they look to the future. Cataldi (1981) thinks they probably apply to the arrangements made in the preceding lines.

although the subject matter of the proceedings is unclear.[24] This section is followed by the provision for restitution and repayment of lost property (lines 51–63).[25] Here the archonship of Euthynos is first attested (line 61). Lines 64–72 refer to an oath, apparently sworn by the Milesians and the Athenians, although its content is unknown.[26] In the middle of this section is mention of the *prytaneis* of the Milesians (line 65). Lines 74–77 provide penalties for transgressions as well as the referral of certain important cases to Athens. Lines 77–86 include provisions for a number of minor points, probably including some of the powers of the five archons.[27] Line 85 mentions a garrison, while line 86 contains the other preserved mention of the archonship of Euthynos.

The provisions made by the Athenian Regulations for Miletos—a board of five Athenian archons at Miletos, significant Athenian intervention in Milesian legal proceedings, a restoration of property, oaths, a garrison, and perhaps a Milesian military obligation to Athens—are typical of the restrictions that the Athenians imposed on the recovery of a rebellious ally, as demonstrated by a handful of similar decrees that have been found. When Euboia was recovered in 446/5 after its revolt, the Athenian Regulations for Chalkis (*IG* 1^3 40)[28] featured mutual oaths between the Athenians and the Chalkidians, with the Athenians swearing to treat Chalkis according to the laws and the Chalkidians swearing loyalty, promising to pay their tribute, and promising to defend the Athenian people. In addition, the decree discusses hostages, the taxpaying status of non-Athenian resident aliens at Chalkis, and an appeal to

---

24. It is generally agreed that the latter cases involve private or commercial matters. The former trials may pertain to tribute (Oliver 1935, 191–95; Meiggs 1943, 25), treason (Bradeen and McGregor 1973, 42–52), or other public crimes (Cataldi 1981, 184–200).

25. Oliver 1935, 196–98; Bradeen and McGregor 1973, 52–57, 64; Cataldi 1981, 166, 200–209. According to the restorations made by Bradeen and McGregor and by Cataldi, a group of people previously exiled from Miletos were taxed illegally before they left the city, and their property was illegally confiscated afterward. Certain other Athenian decrees brought about their return. Now this decree is prohibiting such confiscations in the future and is providing for the return of the money and property that was taken from them by the other party in the stasis. This restoration of wealth is being carried out "according to the decrees made when Euthynos was archon." Thus, according to these interpretations, this decree contains evidence for stasis, both immediately previous to this decree and also previous to the decrees passed in the archonship of Euthynos.

26. Oliver 1935, 189; Bradeen and McGregor 1973, 57–59; Cataldi 1981, 209–10.

27. Bradeen and McGregor 1973, 59–62; Cataldi 1981, 210–13.

28. *ATL* 1 #D17.70–72 = Tod 1946, # 42 = Meiggs and Lewis 1988, #52 = Fornara 1983b, #102. See also Balcer 1978.

Athens of court cases involving capital crimes. The contemporary Athenian Regulations for Eretria (ca. 446/5, *IG* 1³ 39) also features loyalty oaths. The Athenian treaty with Kolophon (ca. 447/6, *IG* 1³ 37) contains another oath and a commission of five men, though not specifically called archons. Finally, the Athenian Regulations for Erythrai (ca. 453/2, *IG* 1³ 14), which establishes the democratic government in that city, contains sacrificial obligations, a garrison commander and a garrison, and loyalty oaths.

Thus, we have evidence for Athens's recovery of Miletos after a revolt, and it would seem reasonable to associate this decree with the episode given by the Old Oligarch. Accordingly, most scholars understand this decree as an Athenian operation stabilizing the oligarchy in the face of civil dissension, an action corresponding to the pro-oligarchic stance depicted by the Old Oligarch.[29] However, this interpretation is based on the supposition that the decree dates to the archonship of Euthynos in 450/49, which we have seen is a questionable assumption.

One argument is that the Athenians are here dealing with an oligarchy because there is no surviving mention of a democratic Council (*Boule*).[30] Due to the extremely fragmentary nature of the inscription, this argument *ex silentio* is not very strong: the *prytaneis* could be acting on behalf of the Council, or in such a fragmentary decree, the word *boule* could easily have fallen in one of the numerous lacunae. In fact, this inscription only preserves positive evidence about the prevailing institutions of government in Miletos at line 65, where mention is made of ηοι πρυτάνες ηοι Μιλεσ[ίον]. Some scholars incorporate these prytanies into the traditional interpretation of this inscription by maintaining that this board may have represented some descendant of the Archaic Milesian prytany.[31] However, it is likely that the eponymous prytany was stripped of its power ca. 540 and replaced with an eponymous *aisymnetes* (see chap. 3). If the office of prytany survived through tyranny and oligarchy, it will have lost much of its significance, whereas here the prytanies are playing an important role in the relationship between the Athenians and the Milesians, as is evidenced by their mention in the middle of the provisions for the swearing of mutual oaths between Athens and Miletos. In contrast, we have already seen Athenian-style prytanies at Miletos in a *lex*

29. Notably Bradeen and McGregor 1973; Meiggs 1972.
30. Meiggs 1972, 563.
31. Ehrhardt 1983, 193–203, 248; Meiggs 1943, 27; Cataldi 1981, 178; Robertson 1987, 386–87.

sacra of the second half of the fifth century, where the prytanies are definitely an institution of democracy.[32] Therefore, it is better to conclude that the prytanies of *IG* 1³ 21 are the democratic officials from the later *leges sacrae* and that this inscription thus represents the state of affairs after the democratic reorganization of the government. We must assume that the mentions of the archonship of Euthonos do not fix the date of this inscription in that year (for on the evidence of the Molpoi Decree, the oligarchy was in place until at least 450) but rather refer to earlier steps taken by Athens to deal with Milesian affairs.[33] That is to say, there were two episodes of Athenian intervention at Miletos, one in 450 B.C.E., which is perhaps, but not necessarily, supported by the Athenian tribute lists of 454/3, and another some time shortly after this date. This theory fits exactly with the events described by the Old Oligarch. The first intervention was a pro-oligarchic action taken in the year of the archonship of Euthynos (450/49), as referred to in this decree, while the second was the action actually represented by this decree, the Athenian Regulations for Miletos. It was the response to the oligarchic revolt and resulted in the establishment of democracy at Miletos.

To fix more precisely the date of this second settlement, we must return to the evidence supplied by the Athenian tribute lists. The total amount of the Milesian tribute is preserved for the first time in 450/49, when the Milesians are paying ten talents (#5, column v, line 18). In the following decade, they appear four times in the extant lists. In 447/6 (#8, column i, line 108) and 442/1 (#13, column 1, line 31), they are listed, but the amount of their payment does not survive. In the year 443/2, their tribute amount is listed and has been reduced to five talents (#12, column i, line 33), where it remains in 440/39 (#15, column ii, line 11).[34] This halving of the tribute payment is a conspicuous indication that the Milesians revolted before 443/2 and were forcefully brought back into the Delian League: when settling an allied revolt, the Athenians would often confiscate the best land, present it to their own citizen-residents, called cleruchs, and reduce the tribute payment accordingly. Comparable

---

32. Herrmann 1970.
33. Cataldi 1981, 206–7; cf. Robertson 1987, 384–90.
34. The next year in which an amount is preserved for the Milesians is 421/0, when the Milesians, Leros, and Teichioussa are listed under one entry as paying ten talents. But this is much later than the period with which we are dealing, and it postdates the great reassessment of 425 B.C.E., which significantly raised the financial obligations of many of the allied cities.

cases from the same decade include Kolophon, the end of whose revolt brought with it an Athenian colony and a tribute reduction from three talents, attested in 452/1, to one and a half talents in 446/5, and Chalkis, which received a tribute reduction from five talents in 448/7 to three talents in 442/1, after the revolt of Euboia.[35]

The revolt of Miletos may have occurred any time after the tribute payment of 450/49, the last sure indication that the Milesians were loyal allies, and probably after the payment of 447/6.[36] Of course, we cannot tell with any exactitude how long the Milesians were able to remain outside the fold of the Delian League, but it is not unreasonable to think that Miletos may have been in revolt for several years, especially if Athens was engaged in events closer to home. Once Athenian attention was turned to Miletos, the revolt could not have survived long. After all, it took the Athenians only nine months to besiege and force into surrender Samos, a city with strong walls and a powerful navy.[37] The Milesians had not yet rebuilt their city walls, lost in the Persian destruction of 494, and were in no position to hold out even that long.

No discussion of the change in government at Miletos is complete without consideration of the famous Banishment Decree,[38] of which the beginning is lost.

> [. . . . . 15 . . . .]σ[. . . . .τ]ὸ[. Ν]υμφαρήτο καὶ Ἀλκι[μον]
> [καὶ Κ]ρεσφόντην [τὸ]<ς> Στρατώνακτος φεύγεν τὴν ἐπ᾽ αἵμ[ατ|ι]
> [φυγὴν] καὶ αὐτὸς [κα]ὶ ἐκγόνος, καὶ ὃς ἄν τινα τούτωγ κατ[α]-
> [κτείνε]ι, ἑκατὸν [στ]ατῆρας αὐτῶι γενέσθαι ἀπὸ τῶν
> 5 [χρημά]των τῶν Νυμ[φαρή]το· τὸς δ᾽ ἐπιμηνίος, ἐπ᾽ ὦν ἂν ἔλθωσ|ιν
> [οἱ κατα]κτείναντες, ἀποδοῦναι τὸ ἀργύριον· ἢν δὲ μή, αὐτὸ|[ς]
> [ὀφε]ίλεν. ἢν δὲ ἡ πόλι[ς ἐ]γκρατ<ή>ς γένηται, κατακτέναι
> [αὐ]τὸς τὸς ἐπιμηνίος [ἐ]π᾽ ὦν ἂν λαφθέωσιν· ἢν δὲ μὴ κατα-

---

35. Kolophon: *IG* 1³ 37 = Meiggs and Lewis 1988, #47 = Fornara 1983b, #99. Chalkis: *IG* 1³ 40 = Meiggs and Lewis 1988, #52 = Fornara 1983b, #103. For these and other cases of the lowering of tribute, see *ATL* 3.298–300.

36. However, we cannot assume, as Barron (1962, 1–2) and Earp (1954) have done, that every absence from the *ATL* must be accounted for by revolt or recalcitrance. In none of the early years is even half of any given list preserved, and only after 443/2 do the lists contain an administrative organization in which "absent from full panel" indicates a true absence of an ally from that list.

37. According to Thucydides (8.76), Samos was so powerful that it very nearly wrestled naval control away from Athens.

38. *Milet* 1.6 #187; Tod 1946, #35; Meiggs and Lewis 1988, #43.

[κτ]είνοσιν, ὀφείλεν ἕ[κ]αστον πεντήκοντα στατῆρας.
10 τὸν δὲ ἐπιμήνιον, ἢν μὴ προθῆι, ἑκατὸν στατῆρας ὀφείλε[ν]
καὶ τὴν ἐσιōσαν ἐπιμηνίην αἰὶ ποιεῖν κατὰ τὸ ψήφισμα·
ἢν δὲ μή, τὴν αὐτὴν θωιὴν ὀφείλεν.

[[-21- the sons of N]ympharetos, and Alki[mos and K]resphontes,
[the] sons of Stratonax, shall suffer bloodguilt [banishment,] both
themselves and their descendants, and whosoever kills any one of
them shall receive one hundred staters from the [5] [assets] of the
family of Nym[phare]tos. The *epimenioi* in office when a claim is
made by the slayers shall pay out the money. If (they do) not, they
themselves shall be liable to pay (for the reward). If the city should
get hold of (the condemned men), they shall be put to death by the
epimenioi in whose term of office they are seized. If they do not put
them to death, they shall each be liable to pay fifty staters. [10] The
(presiding) *epimenios,* if he does not put (the matter) up for decision, shall owe a fine of one hundred staters. Successive boards of
epimenioi shall always proceed according to this decree. Otherwise,
they shall be liable to pay the same penalty.][39]

This decree was discovered in situ in the northwest corner of the North
Market at Miletos in 1905. It was inscribed on a marble block that served
as the base of a stele that has not been found. Since the decree covers
three-quarters of this base and lacks its beginning, it must have started on
the missing stele and overflowed onto the base. This base was sent to
Berlin but is now lost, so confirmation of the reading of the stone must be
based on the photograph published in *Milet* 1.6 and a squeeze of the
stone.[40]

Unquestionably the text of this inscription calls for the banishment or
execution of a number of people, almost certainly for the crime of treason,
and some scholars have argued that it refers to events that occurred in the
aftermath of a democratic revolution against a defeated oligarchy.[41] This

39. The text of the decree is here given from Meiggs and Lewis 1988, #43. The translation is based on Fornara 1983b, #66. Square brackets enclose words that have been
restored, while parentheses contain explanatory additions to the text.
40. Herrmann (1970, 170 n. 1) had access to the squeeze.
41. The treason charge was first argued by Glotz (*CRAI* 1906, 513–16, as summarized
by Meiggs 1972, 562–65; Barron 1962, 3) and has been universally accepted by later
commentators. The theory of a democratic revolution is expounded most fully by Glotz and
by Barron (1962).

line of reasoning begins with a complicated prosopographical argument about the Banishment Decree, in which the names listed are linked to names associated with Neleus, the legendary founder of Ionia.[42] According to this theory, the decree represents a banishment of the Neleid clan, which must have provided the leaders of oligarchic Miletos. Thus, they were banished as part of the revolution against oligarchy noted by the Old Oligarch.[43] This prosopographical argument can be refined even further by identifying as Neleid the names of the *prosetairos* of 450/49 (Kretheus, son of Hermonax, *Milet* 1.6 #187) and the *aisymnetes* of 445/4 (Thrason, son of Antileon, *Milet* 1.3 #122.i.82), who is also the *prosetairos* of 450/49 B.C.E. Accepting the assumption that this decree represents an action of the democracy against the Neleids, the date of the decree can then be fixed after 445/4 B.C.E. An important consideration for this whole argument is the length of the original decree: since the inscription overflows onto the base of the stele, one might conclude that there was only one inscription on the entire stele and that it must have contained very many names. In this case, a date after a democratic revolution might be fitting, because it would be consistent with a thoroughgoing banishment of the oligarchical faction.[44]

While it is impossible to know how many names were included in the Banishment Decree, the idea that this decree represents a democratic revolution is almost certainly wrong for several reasons. First, it would be a careless stonecutter who laid out his inscription so badly that it had to overflow for twelve lines onto the base of the stele. It is more reasonable to conclude that the stele contained an earlier inscription of a similar nature and that the overflow came as a later and fairly brief addition: had that addition been very long, it would have been allocated its own stone.[45] Second, the reward of one hundred staters is to be paid to anyone who kills one of the exiles, but the property of only one family, that of Nympharetos,

---

42. Glotz based this theory in part on an allegorical reading of a story in Nicolaus of Damascus (*FGH* 90 F 53, quoted in chap. 3) about the monarchy and tyranny in Archaic Miletos.

43. Glotz's dating method is flawed, because he sets this revolution contemporary to the events in Boiotia and Messenia but then uses the death of Kimon in 449 B.C.E. as a fairly rigid *terminus ante quem* both for the end of the events in Messenia and for the revolt of the Milesian oligarchy.

44. Barron 1962. However, as Meiggs and Lewis point out (1988, 106), "The evidence barely justifies the conclusion," and Piérart (1969) argues convincingly against this entire prosopographical argument. Also, it would be odd to find a Neleid oligarchy ruling the city still a full five hundred years after its foundation.

45. Glotz 1906a, 519–21; Meiggs 1972, 564–65; Meiggs and Lewis 1988, 106.

is mentioned as the source of those rewards, implying either that the rewards were to be few or that the property was very great.[46] Third, it would be a rare coincidence if, in the long list that is postulated, Nympharetos, whose estate is to supply the rewards, happens to be one of the only four names of exiles extant in our decree. Surely a man thus singled out for his wealth and, one assumes, his prominence must have been a leading man in the oligarchy, and we would expect his name to have occurred much higher in such a lengthy list of the condemned.

The layout of the decree on the stone therefore tells against the claim that the decree banished a large oligarchic class. Another counter-argument can be brought to bear against this theory. The decree charges certain officials, the *epimenioi,* with enforcing its provisions. These officials were almost certainly magistrates of the traditional government who made up a monthly board that presided over the oligarchic assembly and who thus performed a function similar to the democratic prytany.[47] Their function as political officials is corroborated by the political duties assigned them in this decree: they are responsible for the execution of captured exiles (lines 7–8), the payment of rewards (lines 5–6), and the introduction of appropriate motions into some citizen body (lines 10–11). Thus, it is likely that the Banishment Decree represents the action of an oligarchic government and has no connection to any putative democratic revolution at Miletos.

The position of the stone in the North Market further affirms the idea that this inscription was not a democratic decree. The stone was discovered situated below the ground level of the market, which had minimal construction in the fifth century. In addition, the stone was skewed in relationship to the city grid. The misalignment of the stone, its location

---

46. Meiggs and Lewis 1988, 106.

47. Glotz 1906a, 526–27; Piérart 1969, 365, 370–76; Meiggs 1972, 565; Ehrhardt 1983, 210–13; Robertson 1987, 379–83.

The idea that the *epimenioi* made up a collegial board with a limited term of office is derived from Piérart's interpretation of this difficult text (and he is followed, for example, by Fornara in his translation). Piérart interprets the word ἐπιμηνίην to mean "the college of *epimenioi,*" so that line 11 of the Banishment Decree implies that successive colleges are responsible for carrying out the decree. Cf. Meiggs and Lewis 1988, 107.

It is, of course, possible to make the argument that the office of *epimenios* continued at Miletos for a short time after the revolution, while the new government was being organized. In this case, *epimenioi* would not necessarily be oligarchic officials. However, this argument assumes its own premise, that this inscription must be the action of democrats against oligarchs. As we have seen, the only other support for this theory is Barron's prosopographical argument (Barron 1962), which is itself weak.

below the Classical ground level, and the possibility that it contained a previous—that is, Archaic—decree indicate that this stone was erected in Archaic times in an Archaic agora that existed on the site of the later North Market.[48] It would have recorded a banishment enacted by the traditional Milesian oligarchy or by the late Archaic tyranny but certainly not by a democracy. The stone survived the destruction of the city and was allowed to remain standing by the oligarchic government of the second quarter of the fifth century, further indication that it was not antioligarchic. Finally, it was reused in the publication of a similar expulsion decree in the mid–fifth century. Unfortunately, the date of the Banishment Decree within the oligarchic period of government cannot be closely fixed. The physical evidence of the stone itself is inconclusive, because there are very few securely dated inscriptions from this period to which this decree can be compared. The letterforms do suggest a date early in the fifth century, perhaps between 470 and 440, but this is just an educated guess.[49]

To summarize, while much of the evidence presented by the Milesian Banishment Decree is inconclusive and its date cannot be fixed, certain deductions may be made. First, this decree does not represent an action of a democratic government against an oligarchic opposition but rather is likely to be the work of an oligarchic government. Second, the group of people being banished for treason is not large, so this decree cannot be used as evidence of a revolt from Athens, nor does it even necessarily indicate significant civil stasis, since it may represent an action against only a few families. Thus, the Banishment Decree offers no sure evidence about either the civil stasis at Miletos or the revolt from Athens that occurred in the middle of the fifth century B.C.E.

In conclusion, the following chronological sequence of events best explains the diverse and fragmented evidence: The government that rebuilt Miletos and governed it in its first decade after the Ionian Revolt was a traditional oligarchy. In the 450s, civil dissension arose so powerfully that the Milesians might have been physically divided, paying their

---

48. Piérart (1969) is wrong when he says that the Archaic city did not encompass the area around the Lion Bay. See chap. 5.

49. Rehm in *Milet* 1.6.101–4 (early fifth century); Meiggs and Lewis 1988, 107 (between 470 and 440). Herrmann (1970, 170) thinks it could date as late as 450, based on the similarity of style and letterforms between this inscription and the *lex sacra* for Poseidon Helikonios.

tribute both from Miletos and from enclaves at Leros and Teichioussa.[50] The situation became volatile enough that the Athenians were compelled to intervene in 450/49 B.C.E., passing a decree or decrees during the archonship of Euthynos, which were later referred to in the Athenian Regulations for Miletos. These early decrees probably restored the property of the exiles—possibly those Milesians at Leros and Teichioussa—and established a garrison similar to the one the Athenians left at Samos after settling the civil strife there (Thuc. 1.115.3). Whatever else they did, the Athenians favored the oligarchs and left them in power, as the Old Oligarch says. The year 450 is also as likely a date as any for the Banishment Decree, because the circumstances of that year best fit the necessary conditions; that is, after a period of dissension, a group of people were exiled by an oligarchical government for the crime of treason. Perhaps a few families at Miletos had been negotiating for aid from Persia. This would explain the perception of danger that necessitated the Athenian intervention, particularly as Athens was in a vulnerable position at this time. The abysmal failure of the Athenian expedition against Egypt in 454 may have encouraged Persia to put increased pressure on Ionia to return to the Persian Empire. Erythrai revolted at about this time, and Athens, at least in part out of a concern for security, transferred the Delian League's treasury from Delos to Athens. A widespread disaffection in the league forced Athens to spend a few years to consolidate its power.[51] One result was the establishment of cleruchies on Naxos, Euboia, and Andros. Perhaps fearing an imminent revolt in Miletos, Athens stepped in before the fact, to settle the dissension and expel the Medizers.

A short time after the Athenian intervention in 450/49 and the Milesian tribute payment of 447/6, but before the tribute payment of 443/2, the ruling oligarchy attacked the democrats viciously and revolted from Athens. The most likely time was in or after the unrest of 446, when Athens was busy with events nearer to home and so may not have settled

---

50. Tuchelt (1989, 209–17; 1991a, 40–50) has suggested further support for this theory. He believes that a sanctuary recently discovered on the Sacred Way between Miletos and Didyma belonged to a private, aristocratic family and was destroyed in the fifth century during the course of civil dissension in which certain aristocratic families were expelled from Miletos. He has no proof for this assertion, so it is better to assume that the sanctuary was destroyed during the destruction of both Miletos and Didyma by the Persians in 494 B.C.E.

51. Meiggs 1972, 123.

things in Asia Minor immediately. In that year, the defeat at Koroneia forced Athens out of Boiotia, most of Euboia revolted, Megara revolted and cut off the Athenian garrison there (Thuc. 1.114.1), and the Peloponnesians were on the verge of invading Attika (Thuc. 1.113.3–114.1). The revolt of Miletos was settled before the halved tribute payment of 443/2: Miletos was forced back into the Delian League and a democracy was set up. The decree that actually restored Miletos to the Delian League, containing the text of the loyalty oath and detailing the constitutional changes there, is lost, but the Athenian Regulations for Miletos preserve some of the additional conditions and requirements of that settlement.

The Peloponnesian War and Beyond

For the next thirty years, we hear of no actual disputes between the Milesians and the city of Athens, and the few extant mentions of Miletos indicate that it stood as a loyal ally, backed by its Athenian master. For example, when Samos and Miletos quarreled over the territory of Priene in 440/39 (Thuc. 1.115), Athens sided with Miletos and eventually established a democracy at Samos as well. When the Peloponnesian War broke out between Athens and Sparta in 431, the Milesians sent contingents to aid the Athenians in campaigns in 425 against the Corinthian territory and Kythera (Thuc. 4.42, 53) and in 413 against Syracuse (Thuc. 7.57). The stability of this relationship must be due at least in part to the democratic government at Miletos.

But all of the Milesians were not entirely happy with the situation. Many things may have contributed to this dissatisfaction, but the only cause we know of is financial:[52] Athens doubled the tribute in 425 (*IG* 1³ 71) and imposed a 5 percent tax in 413 on all trade goods carried by sea to or from the harbors of the empire (Thuc. 7.28.4). Affecting both the raw materials being imported and the finished products being exported, this tax would have particularly hurt Milesian trade, in a city whose resources were already stretched thin by increased tribute payments. Once it was given a viable opportunity, the city was quick to join in the general rebellion by Ionia in the beginning of the second half of the Peloponnesian War (sometimes called the Decelean War or Ionian War,

---

52. Dunham 1915, 110–11.

413–404 B.C.E.). At that time, in accordance with the advice of the exiled Athenian general Alkibiades, Sparta pursued a policy of building up a navy and depriving the Athenians of the tribute and grain supply from the allies in the Delian League. In 412, as part of this policy, Alkibiades approached some friends of his, leading men in Miletos, who started a revolt of the city: when the Athenians sailed up right behind Alkibiades, the Milesians would not let them into the harbor, and the Athenians were forced to retreat to Lade (Thuc. 8.17.3). Thus Miletos joined Chios, Erythrai, Klazomenai, Teos, Methymna, some Lesbian cities, and other Greek cities in Asia in revolt from Athens (Thuc. 8.14–25). The importance of Miletos can be seen in the immediacy of the Athenian attempt to retake the city, νομίζοντες, εἰ προσαγάγοιντο Μίλητον, ῥᾳδίως ἂν σφίσι καὶ τἆλλα προσχωρῆσαι [thinking that, if they could win back Miletos, they would easily regain the others] (Thuc. 8.25.5).

The Athenian response brings up the question of what defenses the Milesians enjoyed in 412 B.C.E., for there is no physical sign that the Milesians refortified their city when they refounded it in the early fifth century. Considering the devastation that they had suffered then and the fact that the Persian problem was far from being solved, this absence must be considered odd. They were either too poor to rebuild their fortification or did not think there was any need to do so. Poverty is an unlikely answer: they could have stacked together a makeshift wall out of the debris of the Archaic city, just as the Athenians did after 480. The Milesians must have thought it unnecessary.

Thucydides says that Ionia was unwalled in 427 B.C.E. (ἀτειχίστου γὰρ οὔσης τῆς Ἰωνίας, 3.33.2). The explanation for this dearth in fortifications in general cannot be that they never existed or that they were all destroyed by the Persians in 494/3, although certainly this may have been true for some cities other than Miletos. Rather, the Ionian city walls must have been systematically dismantled as another part of the Athenian imperial policy, imposing sanctions on rebellious and potentially rebellious allies in Asia, as at Samos in 440.[53] Since the Milesian walls had already been demolished in 494, the policy would have had the effect of discouraging or even forbidding the construction of a new wall, until the situation had changed so that either the Athenians saw the wisdom of such a wall or the Milesians did not feel constrained by Athenian regulations. Only after the Milesians rebelled against the Athenians in 412,

---

53. Thuc. 1.117; Meiggs 1972, 149–50.

departing permanently from the Athenian Empire, were they able to construct some kind of fortification.

Thucydides' narrative of the Athenian attempt to retake the city (8.24–27) implies that there was some barrier behind which the Milesians could hide. After blockading the city with twenty ships, the Athenians and their allies, including a large continent of Argives, made a landing and attacked the Milesians with their new Peloponnesian allies. While the Milesians routed the Argives, the Athenians managed to push back both the Peloponnesians and the general mass of the army. When the Milesians saw that their side was defeated, they fell back into their city (ὑποχωρησάντων ἐς τὴν πόλιν, 8.25.4). The Athenians pursued them to the city itself, where they grounded their arms (πρὸς αὐτὴν τὴν πόλιν τῶν Μιλησίων κρατοῦντες ἤδη τὰ ὅπλα τίθενται, 8.25.4). The Athenians considered putting up a blockading wall (περιτειχισμός) but realized the futility of that exercise, because the Spartans were as eager to hold the city—especially because it was walled in (ἀποτειχισθεῖσαν, 8.26.3)—as the Athenians were to retake it. The Athenians decided that their position was untenable, so rather than risk a battle, καὶ οἱ μὲν Ἀθεναῖοι ἀφ᾽ ἑσπέρας εὐθὺς τούτῳ τῷ τρόπῳ ἀτελεῖ τῇ νίκῃ ἀπὸ τῆς Μιλήτου ἀνέστησαν [in this way, on that very evening, the Athenians went away from Miletos with their victory unaccomplished] (8.27.6). However, since the battle only lasted one day and the siege was given up literally before it was started, this engagement with the Athenians need not imply the existence of a full-scale, permanent wall. It is likely that the fence was only a stopgap measure, raised up hurriedly against the immediate danger.

For the rest of the Peloponnesian War, the Spartans used Miletos both as the chief naval base of their fleet in Ionia and as a meeting place between the Spartan leaders and the representatives of the Persian king (Thuc. 8.28–109 passim). The Milesians seemed happy with this arrangement at first (οἵ τε Μιλήσιοι προθύμως τὰ τοῦ πολέμου ἔφερον [And the Milesians supported the war eagerly] Thuc. 8.36.1). Although they were keen for war against Athens, they were troubled to see Sparta making an alliance with Persia, which was immediately followed by Persian encroachment near Miletos. The Milesians acted on their apprehension when, taking advantage of a crisis in Spartan leadership, they struck out against the Persians (Thuc. 8.84.4–5). They fell on the satrap in a fort he had made in Milesian territory and threw out the garrison that was in it. When a Spartan officer complained about this ill-treatment of Sparta's most important ally (and the source of Spartan funds), he attracted

Milesian anger as well, so that when he later died from disease, they refused to bury him there.

Obviously the Milesians thought that they were falling back into the clutches of the Persian Empire and in this estimation they were correct. In the third treaty between the Peloponnesians and the Persians from the year 412/1, the two parties agreed that χώραν τὴν βασιλέως, ὅση τῆς Ἀσίας ἐστί, βασιλέως εἶναι· καὶ περὶ τῆς χώρας τῆς ἑαυτοῦ βουλευέτω βασιλεὺς ὅπως βούλεται [the land of the king, as much as in Asia, shall be the king's, and concerning this land that is his own, the king may wish whatever he wishes] (Thuc. 8.58.2). Instead of guaranteeing their freedom, the Spartans betrayed the Greeks of Asia Minor to the Persian king as the price of his financial and naval aid in the Peloponnesian War. The Milesians were not happy about this turn of events, but ultimately they could do little about it.

Thucydides' account of the war breaks off in 411, but it is picked up at the same point by Xenophon, who devotes the first two books of his *Hellenika* to the concluding decade. In those years, the fighting moved away from Ionia, mostly to the area around the Hellespont and Black Sea, but Miletos continued to be the Spartan base of naval operations (Xen. *Hell.* 1.5.1, 1.6.2, 1.6.7). The Milesians also contributed infantry to the struggle in 409, marching out to relieve an Athenian attack on Pygela, a town lying just to the south of Ephesos. The effort was ill conceived, however, and the Milesians were nearly all killed by the Athenian peltasts and hoplites (Xen. *Hell.* 1.2.2–3).

Throughout the war, the Milesian hostility toward the Persians seems to have continued unabated. In 406, when Cyrus, the brother of the Persian king and commander over Asia Minor, procrastinated in making his payment to the Lakedaimonian troops at Miletos, the Spartan general Kallikratidas grew angry and ashamed that the Greeks were waiting at the doors of the Persian king for the sake of money, but he had to obey his orders and attack the Athenian forces. Worse yet, he had to convince the Milesians to attack alongside him, despite their lack of pay. To do this, he played off their hostile feelings toward the Persians, convincing them that they should show up the Persians by attacking the Athenians without their help and their money (Xen. *Hell.* 1.6.8, 11).

ἐμοὶ μέν, ὦ Μιλήσιοι, ἀνάγκη τοῖς οἴκοι ἄρχουσι πείθεσθαι· ὑμᾶς δὲ ἐγὼ ἀξιῶ προθυμοτάτους εἶναι εἰς τὸν πόλεμον διὰ τὸ οἰκοῦντας ἐν βαρβάροις πλεῖστα κακὰ ἤδη ὑπ᾽ αὐτῶν πεπονθέναι. . . .

ἀλλὰ σὺν τοῖς θεοῖς δείξωμεν τοῖς βαρβάροις ὅτι καὶ ἄνευ τοῦ ἐκείνους θαυμάζειν δυνάμεθα τοὺς ἐχθροὺς τιμωρεῖσθαι.

[O Milesians, I have to obey those who are in charge at home, and I think it only right that you be the most eager in this war, since, dwelling among the barbarians, you have already suffered most numerous evils at their hands. . . . But with the help of the gods, let us demonstrate to the barbarians that, even without looking on them with awe, we are able to take vengeance on our enemies.]

As a result, private citizens came to the aid of the army, funding Kallikratides' successful assault on Methymna.

We know of one last episode of the Peloponnesian War involving the Milesians, a brutal oligarchic coup at Miletos in 405 B.C.E. remembered by Diodoros (13.104.5–6):

[5] καθ᾿ ὃν δὴ χρόνον ἐν τῇ Μιλήτῳ τινὲς ὀλιγαρχίας ὀρεγόμενοι κατέλυσαν τὸν δῆμον, συμπραξάντων αὐτοῖς Λακεδαιμονίων. καὶ τὸ μὲν πρῶτον Διονυσίων ὄντων ἐν ταῖς οἰκίαις τοὺς μάλιστα ἀντιπράττοντας συνήρπασαν καὶ περὶ τεσσαράκοντα ὄντας ἀπέσφαξαν, μετὰ δέ, τῆς ἀγορᾶς πληθούσης, τριακοσίους ἐπιλέξαντες τοὺς εὐπορωτάτους ἀνεῖλον. [6] οἱ δὲ χαριέστατοι τῶν τὰ τοῦ δήμου φρονούντων, ὄντες οὐκ ἐλάττους χιλίων, φοβηθέντες τὴν περίστασιν ἔφυγον πρὸς Φαρνάβαζον τὸν σατράπην· οὗτος δὲ φιλοφρόνως αὐτοὺς δεξάμενος, καὶ στατῆρα χρυσοῦν ἑκάστῳ δωρησάμενος, κατῴκισεν εἰς Βλαῦδα, φρούριόν τι τῆς Λυδίας.

[[5] At the same time in Miletos, certain men who were yearning for an oligarchy dissolved the democracy with the aid of the Lakedaimonians. First of all, when the Dionysia was being celebrated, they snatched up about forty of the leaders of the opposition while they were in their own homes and cut their throats. Afterwards, when the *agora* was full, choosing out the three hundred wealthiest men, they killed them too. [6] Then the most accomplished men of those who favored the democracy, being not less than one thousand in number, fearing the current state of affairs, fled to the satrap Pharnabazos. And that man, receiving them courteously and, giving to each of them a gold stater, settled them at Blauda, a fortress of Lydia.]

Two other sources back this account (Plut. *Lys.* 8; Polyain. 1.45.1), but they both put the blame for the events squarely on the shoulders of the Spartan general, Lysander. At any rate, we hear nothing more about this coup, so it could not have lasted very long: there is no reflection of it in the inscriptional evidence from Miletos.

When the Peloponnesian War ended in 404 B.C.E., all of the worst fears of the Milesians came true. Sparta abandoned Ionia to the Persians, and after a hiatus of nearly a century, Miletos was forced to settle unwillingly back into the status of a Persian subject. When Cyrus decided to rebel against his brother, the king, in 401, Miletos alone of the Ionian Greeks did not go over to his side, only because Tissaphernes stepped in quickly and executed or banished anyone sympathetic to the rebel cause. Cyrus responded in turn by besieging the city by land and sea (Xen. *Anab.* 1.1.6). His attack, though short-lived, was almost certainly against a city with a full circuit wall. The archaeological remains of the Classical wall date to the end of the fifth century or beginning of the fourth. Perhaps it was constructed immediately after 412, when the Milesians were free from Athenian imperial restrictions and while the Peloponnesian War was still raging, so that this important naval headquarters for the joint Spartan-Persian fleet could be properly defended.[54] In any case, Cyrus soon gave up the siege and withdrew to Sardis to prepare for his famous march up-country (Xen. *Anab.* 1.2.2), and Miletos continued under the control of the legitimate Persian king.

Although its continued economic prosperity can still be seen today in the visible ruins of the city, most of which date to the Hellenistic and Roman centuries, Miletos, the "ornament of Ionia" (Hdt. 5.28), the city that had once been the intellectual and economic center of the Hellenic world, would never again be free.[55] Instead, the Milesians were treated as pawns in the larger political game going on around them. A contingent of Milesians was still attending the satrap, Tissaphernes, at the time of his death in 395 (Polyain. 8.16), and Persian control over Asia Minor was formally accepted by the Greeks in the Peace of Antalkidas, also called the King's Peace, in 386 B.C.E. (Xen. *Hell.* 5.1.31). Several Carian rulers made inroads against the city during the fourth century,[56] but with the

---

54. The finds are best summarized in Müller-Wiener 1986a and Cobet 1997.

55. Miletos after 400: Kleiner 1970; *PECS* 578–82; Foss 1977, 477–79; Dunham 1915, 118–20.

56. Polyain. 6.8; Dunham 1915, 118–20.

arrival of Alexander the Great in 334, Miletos was again guarded by a Persian garrison and was the first city to present Alexander resistance (Arr. *Anab.* 1.18ff.). The Milesians themselves offered Alexander possession of the city in common with the Persians, but he refused and began a vigorous siege that led quickly to the fall of the city.[57] For the time being, it was back in Greek hands, but Alexander's premature death left Miletos as a point of dispute between the families of the generals who succeeded him. In the Hellenistic era, the Seleukids and Attalids competed for control of the city, and they were responsible for the construction of many buildings at the site, including the Council House, a large gymnasium, and probably the stadium.

In 133, King Attalos of Pergamon died and left his entire kingdom— western Anatolia, including Ionia—to the people of Rome. It was set up as the province of Asia. In this new Roman era, Miletos was esteemed much less than in earlier years, in part because its usefulness was diminishing as its harbors were rapidly filling with silt from the Maiandros River, thus requiring frequent and costly dredging projects to keep them functioning. Nevertheless, Miletos experienced a building boom, especially under Trajan and his wife, Faustina, who completed an improvement project for the processional road to Didyma and constructed the Baths of Faustina and the Nymphaeum. Miletos was home to the largest agora known from the entire Greek World, the South Market (33,000 sq. m.) with its towering Market Gate that has been reerected in modern times in the Pergamon Museum in Berlin. In addition, the city boasted a large Roman theater, which was 140 m. across and seated some fifteen thousand spectators in three tiers of seats. In the seventh century, this theater was converted into a fortress by the Byzantine powers that succeeded Rome. By then the fortification wall surrounded an area only one-quarter the size of the ancient city. Both it and the fortress were destroyed in an earthquake in the tenth or eleventh century C.E. They were rebuilt, but subsequently most of the city fell into ruin, except the fortress, which was maintained for many centuries by the Ottoman Turks, and which gave the site its modern name, *Balat*.

---

57. Sometime in the fourth century, a wall was built across the plain, separating Kalabaktepe from the city proper. This would have been the wall Alexander assaulted. See *Milet* 1.6.83–84, 1.8.109–11, 2.3.120–24; Mellink 1984, 454.

Appendix: The Milesian Colonies

Section 1. West of the Propontis

Abydos, one of the earliest colonies in this vicinity, was situated on the best natural harbor in the Troad and at the narrowest part of the strait (6 km. north of modern Canakkale). The site has been located but not excavated. The city was home to a pre-Milesian settlement already mentioned in Homer's Catalogue of Ships (*Il.* 2.836). It may have been a Phoenician colony originally, since it housed a cult of Aphrodite Porne, the great Eastern fertility goddess (Ath. 13.572–73).[1] Strabo (13.1.22) says that Abydos was founded by the Milesians with the permission of Gyges, king of the Lydians. This statement implies, first, a literary foundation date concurrent with Gyges' reign (ca. 680–652); second, that the Lydians controlled the Troad in the first half of the seventh century; and, third, that the Milesians enjoyed some sort of special relationship with them. This association may explain the Milesian control of the south shore of the Propontis: while Lampsakos was founded at the northeast corner of the Hellespont by the Phokaians in 654, no other non-Milesian colonies were placed on the south coast until Athens settled Sigeion, ca. 600.[2]

Abydos occupied a prime location on the Hellespont. It exploited the nearby forests and gold mines for trade,[3] and it may also have found a profitable livelihood in controlling the sea traffic between the Aegean and

---

Much of the archaeological scholarship on the Milesian colonies is written in Russian, Turkish, Romanian, or another eastern European language. In most instances, I cite sources in a Western language that give much more complete bibliographical references in their notes.

1. Abydos: Thuc. 8.61; Str. 13.1.22, 14.1.6; Eust. *GGM* 2.315, para. 513; Ath. 12.524; Steph. Byz. s.v.; Polyb. 16.29; Ehrhardt 1983, 32; Röhlig 1933, 13; Leaf 1923, 116–19; Bilabel 1920, 51; Busolt 1893, 1.271 (Phoenician origin).
2. Ehrhardt 1983, 31–48; Graham 1982a, 121.
3. Röhlig 1933, 14–15.

the Propontis and demanding tariffs for the right of passage, although no direct evidence of this remains. It was also the ideal place for the channeling of land transportation across to the Lesbian cities Sestos and Madytos, located on the European side of the Hellespont: precisely here Xerxes constructed his famous pontoon bridge to transfer his army across into Europe for the invasion of Greece in 480 B.C.E. (Hdt. 7.34).

Kardia was a joint foundation by the Milesians and the Klazomenians dating to ca. 600 B.C.E. It was located on the Thracian Chersonese (modern Gallipoli), in the northern corner of the inner part of the Bay of Melas, facing west. In the mid–sixth century, the Athenians took over this city when the Elder Miltiades seized the area. The situation of this city and Limnai (following) on a mountainous peninsula meant that agricultural opportunities were limited, but their Thraceward exposure indicates that they may have been involved with commercial enterprises with the natives there.[4]

Limnai was also on the Thracian Chersonese, probably on the west coast but possibly near Sestos on the eastern side. It was founded by Milesians alone at an unknown date, and very little else is known about it.[5]

Arisbe, along with Skepsis (following), was located on the Troad and was among the Milesian colonies listed by Anaximenes of Lampsakos (Str. 14.1.6). We know little about the city, about a dozen kilometers northeast of Abydos, except that it was attributed to the Milesians and was later a member of the Delian League.[6]

Skepsis was on the Skamander River in the Troad, about 70 km. inland. It was traditionally a pre-Greek settlement led by some Trojan princes, who were later joined by Milesians (Str. 13.1.52). It was certainly Milesian at some time: the personal name *Milesios* occurs there. No date is given for its

---

4. Ps.-Skym. *GGM* 1.223, lines 698–99 (in connection with another city on the west coast); Str. 7.51 (joint foundation), 53; Ehrhardt 1983, 33; Bilabel 1920, 53.

5. Str. 14.1.6; Ps.-Skym. *GGM* 1.223, line 705; Steph. Byz. s.v. (near Sestos); *ATL* 1.468; Ehrhardt 1983, 33; Bilabel 1920, 53.

6. Ehrhardt 1983, 35; Leaf 1923, 108–11; Bilabel 1920, 51; *IG* i³ 269.ii.2 [443/2], 270.ii.24 [442/1] (Delian League). Stephanos Byzantios confuses this city with one by the same name on Lesbos and wrongly attributes it to the Mytilenaians. The tradition of Milesian domination of colonization in the northeast is demonstrated when Strabo (13.1.9) assumes that Lampsakos is Milesian; we know that it was Phokaian: see Charon *FHG* 1 F 6; Plut. *Mul. vir.* 18. Stephanos Byzantios gives both mother cities.

foundation, and estimates range from the seventh century to the fifth. Its location so far inland is very unusual for a Milesian settlement, but that location may be explained in part by its proximity to the forests of Mt. Ida.[7]

Section 2. The South Shore of the Propontis

Paisos and *Kolonai,* the first colonies along the south coast of the Propontis, were located at the inlet of the Hellespont. Strabo says (13.1.19) that both were Milesian, but there is some dispute about them, because he wrongly attributes Lampsakos to Miletos in the same section. Perhaps we should consider Lampsakos to be a joint colony of Miletos and Phokaia (as was Amisos a century later), or perhaps Strabo is confused. The matter may be settled when the cities are excavated, but until then we may accept these two cities provisionally as Milesian and leave Lampsakos Phokaian. Paisos was never of much significance, since it was severely curtailed by the size of the coastal plain on which it sat. The site of Kolonai is not known for certain.[8]

Parion (modern Kemer) poses another problem for scholars. Strabo calls the very early settlement, dated to 709 B.C.E. (Euseb. 91b Helm), a joint colonization effort of Erythrai, Paros, and Miletos (Str. 10.5.7, 13.1.14), but elsewhere it is attributed solely to Erythrai (Paus. 9.27). There is a strong argument for the Erythraian role based on the titles of the magistrates (the *exetasiai*) and perhaps from the evidence of some personal names, but the Parian role cannot be overlooked, because Paros must be the origin of the colony's name. Thus two of Strabo's three mother cities are confirmed. Why not accept the third as well? Some reject the Milesian role for lack of evidence, despite the fact that the city in question is not well excavated, or because of outside considerations having to do with the alliances of the Lelantine War. Neither of these causes is sufficient, and the early date might favor a joint foundation: it was a gamble sending out a colony to an area not yet thoroughly colonized, and success

---

7. Ehrhardt 1983, 29; Bilabel 1920, 51–53. Perkote, lying between Arisbe and Lampsakos, may have also been a Milesian foundation, but the question remains open until more evidence is obtained (Leaf 1923, 111–14). Zeleia is denied by both Bilabel (1920, 47–49) and Ehrhardt (1983, 38).

8. Graham 1982a, 161; Leaf 1923, 98–102; Bilabel 1920, 50–51. Ehrhardt (1983, 35–36) and Dunham (1915, 57) discount Kolonai, reasoning that its position off the immediate coastline makes it an unlikely candidate for a Milesian city.

would be more likely if three cities pooled their resources. Finally, in view of Parion's location in the midst of other Milesian colonies, the Milesian role in the foundation of Parion should be accepted.[9]

Kyzikos was the earliest and most important of the colonies of the southern Propontis. It was located on the narrow neck of a much bigger peninsula (now called Kapidagi) that was an island in very early antiquity: it had harbors on both east and west and a swamp to the south. Today the Archaic section is underwater. Although the city is not mentioned in the Epic Cycle, there is a tradition of pre-Greek settlement, for in the *Argonautika* of Apollonios of Rhodes (1.956–1153), Kyzikos was the name of the pre-Greek eponymous king who ruled over the Doliones. Later the Milesians came with their double settlement in 756 and 679 (Euseb. 88b, 93b Helm) and established one of their most prosperous colonies. The Kyzikians obtained grain, meat, wine, metals, and timber from the mainland and produced unguents and salt fish themselves. The Kyzikene electrum stater, featuring the tuna fish, was made from the sixth century onward; trade was so successful that the stater quickly became the standard for international exchange in Thrace, Ionia, the Black Sea, the Greek mainland, Magna Graecia, and Sicily.[10]

Artake, located on the southwest corner of the peninsula above Kyzikos, is mentioned as a Milesian colony in the list of Anaximenes of Lampsakos, but no trace of the ancient city remains.[11]

Prokonnesos was situated on the southwest side of the Island of Marmara (modern Marmara Adasi), northwest of Kyzikos. It produced good vineyards, but its real wealth came in the quarries of white marble for which it was famous for centuries: this stone was used in the construction of the city of Kyzikos, the palace of Mausolos in Halikarnassos, and the Hagia Sophia in Constantinople. Prokonnesos was absorbed by Kyzikos in 362 B.C.E.[12]

---

9. Bilabel (1920, 49) and Ehrhardt (1983, 36–37) both argue against accepting Parion. Leaf (1923, 80–86) makes no judgment.

10. Str. 14.1.6; Sch. Ap. Rhod. 1.1076; Vell. Pat. 2.7.7.; Pliny *NH* 5.142; Ehrhardt 1983, 40–42; Röhlig 1933, 13–14; Bilabel 1920, 46–47; Hasluck 1910; *PECS* 473–74.

11. Str. 14.1.6 (cf. Steph. Byz. s.v.); Hasluck 1910, 16–23.

12. Str. 13.1.12, 16 (marble); Vitr. 2.8 (marble); Sch. Ap. Rhod. 2.279; Paus. 8.46 (absorbed by Kyzikos); Ehrhardt 1983, 38–40; Leaf 1923, 89–91; Bilabel 1920, 47; Hasluck 1910, 30–35.

Priapos was on the mainland west of Kyzikos, near the modern Biga River. It occupied a sharp triangular promontory (modern Kale Burnu, or "Castle Cape"), which provided a good anchorage. Strabo groups Prokonnesos and Priapos with Abydos (13.1.12), implying that they were colonized at about the same time early in the seventh century; alternatively, Priapos may have been a secondary colony founded by Kyzikos.[13]

Miletopolis, sometimes called Miletoteichos ("Milesian Fort"), is judged a Milesian city from its name. The oldest mention of it occurs in the Athenian tribute list for 410 B.C.E., and although the ruins have been located about 30 km. inland, near where the Koca River empties into Lake Uluabat (at modern Melde), little else is known about it, including the date of its initial foundation.[14]

Apollonia on the Rhyndakos has very little known about it except that it was Milesian and located on the northeast corner of the same lake as Miletopolis. The best evidence is late, a second-century B.C.E. inscription from Miletos on the occasion of the resumption of relations between colony and mother city (*Milet* 1.3 #185). The settlement was probably founded much earlier, in the late seventh or early sixth century.[15]

Kios was founded in 622 B.C.E. and is firmly attributed to the Milesians, both in a decree from the mother city dated ca. 228 B.C.E. (*Milet* 1.3 #141) and by Aristotle (fr. 514 Rose = Sch. Ap. Rhod. 1.1177), who says that Kios was founded first by the Mysians from Chios, then by the Carians, and finally by the Milesians. The ruins have been located in a bay in the eastern Propontis (near modern Gemlik), and similarities in calendar, cults, state officials, and personal names make the connection with Miletos unmistakable.[16]

---

13. Str. 13.1.12; Ehrhardt 1983, 37–38; Leaf 1923, 73–76; Bilabel 1920, 49.

14. *ATL* 1.343; 2.81, 86. At *IG* 1³ 100.5, the name *Miletoteichos* is preferred by the editors. According to Ehrhardt (1983, 42–44), the earliest dated items in the excavation are coins from the fourth century, and although the city was Milesian, about 410 it received Athenian colonists as well. See also Bilabel 1920, 46; Hasluck 1910, 74–77.

15. Ehrhardt 1983, 44–47; Bilabel 1920, 45–46.

16. Pliny *NH* 5.144; Hier. (date); Ps.-Skyl. *GGM* 1.63, para. 93; Mela 1.100; Ehrhardt 1983, 47–48 (archaeology); Bilabel 1920, 43–45.

Section 3. The South Shore of the Pontos

Sinope was the first and most famous city in the lower Pontos, acting as an anchor for a number of neighboring, secondary colonies on the south littoral (Str. 12.3.11). It was located about halfway along the coast, on a small peninsula that formed natural harbors on either side of it (modern Sinop). It also benefited from its situation at the narrowest point of crossing between the south shore and the Tauric Chersonese (the Crimea), enabling the Sinopeans to trade with the cities of the north, exporting wine in particular. Besides drying fish, they traded with the people of the Anatolian interior for wood, the pigmentation miltos (known to the Greek world as Sinopean red ocher), and ample supplies of iron, all trade goods highly valued in the mother city.[17]

Milesian roots are amply evidenced in literature and inscriptional evidence of cults, personal names, and magistrates, as well as frequent mentions of the mother city. According to legend, Sinope was founded first before 756 by a Milesian named Habron or Habrondas and quickly sent out a daughter colony, Trapezous (modern Trabzon), founded in 756 (Euseb. 1.80e Schoene [Armen.]). But Sinope, and presumably Trapezous as well, only survived a brief time before being wiped out by the Kimmerians (Ps.-Skym. *GGM* 1.236, lines 948–49 = 993–94 Diller, quoted in chap. 2). Herodotos says, φαίνονται δὲ οἱ Κιμμέριοι φεύγοντες ἐς τὴν Ἀσίην τοὺς Σκύθας καὶ τὴν χερσόνησον κτίσαντες, ἐν τῇ νῦν Σινώπη πόλις Ἑλλὰς οἴκηται [The Kimmerians appeared in Asia fleeing from the Skythians and settled the peninsula on which now the Greek city Sinope stands] (4.12.2). While the Kimmerians destroyed Sinope in the eighth century, the Milesian exiles Kretines and Koes refounded the city after the Kimmerian threat was gone, in 631 B.C.E. (Ps.-Skym. *GGM* 1.236, lines 949–52 = 994–97 Diller). The earliest pottery sherds date to the late seventh century.[18]

Trapezous, Kerasos, Kotyora, Kytoros, Armene, and *Pterion* were probably all founded as secondary colonies from Kyzikos.[19]

---

17. Fish: Str. 3.11. Wood: Theoph. *Hist. Plant.* 4.5.5; Str. 12.3.12; Pliny *NH* 16.197. Miltos: Str. 12.2.10. Iron: Aesch. *Prom. Vinct.* 714; Xen. *Anab.* 5.5.1. See also Röhlig 1933, 15.

18. Ivantchik 1998; Graham 1994; Hind 1983/84, 95–96 (archaeology); Ehrhardt 1983, 57 (Milesian roots). Boardman (1980, 254–55) says that the earliest remains are Corinthian pottery from a little after 600.

19. Ehrhardt 1983, 55–58; Bilabel 1920, 30–40. Trapezous: Steph. Byz. s.v. Kytoros: Str. 12.3.10; Arr. *Peripl. Eux.* 23 = *GGM* 1.390–91, para. 23. Armene: Str. 12.3.10. Pterion: Steph. Byz. s.v. (site unknown).

Amisos (modern Samsun) was located on a headland between Sinope and its colonies and was founded fairly late, ca. 564. This city presents a number of problems because the literary references to it are confusing. Strabo (12.3.14) quotes Theopompos (*FGH* 115 F 389) as saying that it was a Milesian foundation, but Pseudo-Skymnos (*GGM* 1.235, lines 917–20 = 956–59 Diller) attributes it to Phokaia with some other city: there is a lacuna in the text. Perhaps the Milesians should be restored in the gap and this city was a joint foundation, although a number of arguments can be made for settlement by Miletos alone. The archaeological remains above the surface are clearly Ionian and date to at least the middle of the sixth century B.C.E., but no excavation has been conducted.[20]

Tieion (later called Tios) was founded farther to the west, about a third of the way along the southern shore of the Pontos (near modern Bartin), but little is known about it other than its Milesian ancestry.[21]

Section 4. The East Shore of the Pontos

Phasis was located on the east shore, but we know neither its date nor its precise location. The *oikist* was said to be named Themistagoras, who may possibly be identified with the *aisymnetes* of 536/5 (or 521/0), but as with the other settlements in this region, the circumstances of settlement are ill understood because, as one scholar says, ". . . the Greek cities have been virtually ignored, so far, by those engaged in archaeological research."[22] Very little is known and current conclusions are tentative.

The basis of the economy in this area, known in antiquity as Kolchis, was agriculture, but the colonies were located near metal mines, and the gold dust panned from the rivers spawned the story of the Golden Fleece (Str. 11.2.19). As far back as the end of the second millennium or

---

20. Graham 1987, 126; Ehrhardt 1983, 58–60; Bilabel 1920, 29; *PECS* 49. Among the arguments used by Ehrhardt for a Milesian solo foundation are the fact that Apollo was the chief god of the colony, an argument from coinage, and the contention that, if it was indeed Phokaian, when the Phokaians abandoned their own city in 544 as the Persians approached, why did they go west to Alalia on Corsica instead of coming to this colony? I think this last argument is probably not strong: the Persians would have controlled Amisos as well as Ionia, so flight to the colony would not have escaped the king.

21. Mela 1.104; Arr. *Peripl. Eux.* 19 = *GGM* 1.384–85, para. 19; Theoph. in Ath. 8.331c; Steph. Byz. s.v. Τίος; Ehrhardt 1983, 52; Bilabel 1920, 42.

22. Tsetskhladze 1994, 121; Mela 1.108 (Themistagoras); Steph. Byz. s.v.; Str. 11.11.17; Pliny *NH* 6.13; Lordkipanidze 1985; Ehrhardt 1983, 85–86; Bilabel 1920, 28.

the beginning of the first, the native peoples were producing bronze tools, weapons, jewelry, and statuettes; in later centuries, they included bronze-work, pottery, gold, and silver. In addition, as Strabo reports (11.2.17), the region was generally rich in other resources.

> ἀγαθὴ δ᾽ ἐστὶν ἡ χώρα καὶ καρποῖς πλὴν τοῦ μέλιτος (πικρίζει γὰρ τὸ πλέον) καὶ τοῖς πρὸς ναυπηγίαν πᾶσι· ὑπολλήν τε γὰρ ὕλην φύει καὶ ποταμοῖς κατακομίζει, λίνον τε ποιεῖ πολὺ καὶ κάνναβιν καὶ κηρὸν καὶ πίτταν. ἡ δὲ λινουργία καὶ τεθρύληται· καὶ γὰρ εἰς τοὺς ἔξω τόπους ἐπεκόμιζον, . . .

[The land [of Kolchis] is fortunate, especially in its produce, except for its honey (which is mostly bitter), and in all the materials needed to build ships. For it produces a great deal of lumber and carries it by river. Also, it makes a lot of linen, as well as hemp, wax, and pitch. The linen-work is particularly famous, for they used to export linen to the outside world, . . .]

Dioskourias, renamed Sebastopolis by the Romans, was also in Kolchis, north of the presumed location for Phasis. The Greek remains date to the mid–sixth century B.C.E.[23]

Gyenos should also be sought in this region (Ps.-Skyl. *GGM* 1.61–62, para. 81), but its precise location is not known. Other Hellenic settlements whose names and foundation dates are yet unknown have been discovered at Pichvnari and Tsikhisdziri.[24]

Section 5. The West Shore of the Pontos

Istros (Histria) was the earliest settlement in this region. It was founded in 657 B.C.E. (Eus. 95b Helm), at the time when the Kimmerians entered

---

23. Pliny *NH* 6.5; Ps.-Skyl. *GGM* 1.61–62, para. 81; Arr. *Peripl. Eux.* 14 = *GGM* 1.378, para. 14; Tsetskhladze 1994, 121–22; Hind 1992/93, 110; Lordkipanidze 1985; Bilabel 1920, 28; *PECS* 277.

24. Tsetskhladze 1994, 122; Kacharava 1983/84; Kacharava 1990/91. Kacharava's articles are frustrating because they fail to distinguish clearly between Hellenic and non-Hellenic settlements. Kacharava (1990/91, 79–80) thinks that Gyenos is to be found at modern Ochamchire, where Attic black-figure ware, Ionian banded ware, and Chian amphoras have been uncovered.

Asia.²⁵ This city features one of the most extensive excavation projects of
the Black Sea region: the foundations of a temple of Zeus Polieus and a
number of graves date from the sixth century, and there is Middle Wild
Goat pottery from ca. 630. Located south of the Danube River delta, near
the city of Constanta, Romania, Istros featured Milesian cults and tribal
organization.²⁶

Tomis was located just south of Istros. Pottery sherds have been found
from the early sixth century, but the excavation is extremely limited by
the modern city on the site.²⁷

Odessos (modern Varna, Bulgaria) was founded during the reign of
Astyages, king of Media (Ps.-Skym. *GGM* 1.226, lines 748–50), and is
dated to the first half of the sixth century, a conclusion confirmed by the
physical evidence.²⁸

Apollonia Pontika is in modern Bulgaria, across the bay from Burgas, at
modern Pojani. Various sources say that the Milesians founded it fifty
years before the time of Cyrus (d. 530) and that the founder was the
philosopher Anaximander, leading to the conclusion that it was founded
in the first half of the sixth century. However, pottery from the site dates
back even further, to the last half of the seventh century, indicating that
the literary tradition must be mistaken.²⁹

Anchiale was a daughter colony of Apollonia (Str. 7.6.1), sent out probably in the fifth or fourth century. It was the site of a later war between

25. Ps.-Skym. *GGM* 1.227, lines 767–72 = 766–70 Diller. Sherds discovered at the site
date as early as the mid–eighth century (Graham 1990, 53), but they may be explained by
hypothesizing contamination with sherds from Al Mina in the Museum of Classical Archaeology at Cambridge: see Boardman 1991, accepted by Graham 1994, 5.
26. Hdt. 2.33; Str. 7.6.1; Tsetskhladze 1994, 117; Hind 1983/84, 76–77; Ehrhardt
1983, 71; Bilabel 1920, 19; *PECS* 419.
27. Ps.-Skym. (*GGM* 1.227, lines 765–66 = 764–65 Diller) says it is Milesian and
founded fifty years before Cyrus; cf. Ovid *Trist.* 1.20.41, 3.9.3–4. Strabo (7.6.1) and Pliny
(*NH* 4.44) do not mention the mother city. See also Hind 1983/84, 75–76; Ehrhardt 1983,
67–70; Bilabel 1920, 19; *PECS* 928.
28. Hind 1983/84, 74; Ehrhardt 1983, 64; Bilabel 1920, 15–19.
29. Ps.-Skym. *GGM* 1.225, lines 730–33 (Cyrus); Ael. *VH* 3.17.23 (Anaximandros);
Pliny *NH* 4.45 (Antheia); Str. 7.6.1. (Apollo); Ehrhardt 1983, 61–64; Bilabel 1920, 13–15.
Stephanos of Byzantium (s.v. Ἀπολλώνια) adds that the Rhodians contributed to the colony
of Apollonia, but this is generally discounted.

Apollonia and Mesembria, indicating that it was located just north of Apollonia.[30]

Section 6. The North Shore of the Pontos

Berezan/Borysthenes and *Olbia* were located in the northwest corner where the rivers Dnestr, Bug, and Dnepr empty into the Black Sea (in Ukraine). Berezan was founded in 647 B.C.E. (Euseb. 95b). The Greek name for it is unknown, although it might have been called Borysthenes after the name of the river (modern Dnepr) near which it was located. Berezan was a small island or perhaps a peninsula, now 2 km. from the coast. It did not possess a large harbor, but it was easily defensible: in short, it was positioned very typically for the earliest Greek settlement in a new area. The excavation there has yielded the remains of Greek earth huts, graves, and a rich and diverse collection of pottery, beginning in the second half of the seventh century B.C.E. and growing rapidly both in quantity and quality after that time—ample indication that the city grew to a high level of prosperity in the sixth and fifth centuries.[31]

There is some confusion between Berezan and Olbia, situated on the mainland to the northwest, at the mouth of the Bug: Pseudo.-Skymnos (*GGM* 1.229, lines 804–9 = 809–14 Diller) says that they were only one city, and by the late Archaic period, inscriptional evidence suggests that Berezan belonged to Olbia.[32] Since the Greeks were likely to start their settlement on an island or peninsula and then move to an unwalled city on the mainland, it is a natural conclusion that the original colonists settled at Berezan and then established Olbia shortly afterward. However, the finds at both sites are of equal antiquity, although those from Olbia are far richer. While Berezan, Olbia, and other small locations in the vicinity may have been of separate foundation, it is also possible that they were actually all part of one single state called Olbia.[33]

---

30. Ehrhardt 1983, 62–64; Bilabel 1920, 15.

31. Vinogradov and Kryzickij 1995, 127; Hind 1997; Hind 1992/93, 92–94; Hind 1983/84, 78–82; *PECS* 150. A small Greek hydria from the site dates to ca. 800–760 B.C.E.: see Graham 1990, 53.

32. Ehrhardt 1983, 74. Cf. Solovev 1998.

33. Hdt. 4.18.1; Str. 7.3.17; Ps.-Skym. *GGM* 1.229, lines 804–12 = 809–16 Diller; Mela 2.1.6; Hdt. 4.78.3; Steph. Byz. s.v. Βορυσθένης; Hind 1997; Hind 1992/93, 92–96; Vinogradov 1997, 133–45; Jacobson 1995, 41–45; Tsetskhladze 1994, 117–19; Graham 1994, 6; Ehrhardt 1983, 74–79; Bilabel 1920, 23–26. Vinogradov and Kryzickij 1995 is a

This polity constitutes what is probably the best-excavated Greek city on the Pontos, and the remains demonstrate a strong Milesian character that confirms the literary accounts of a Milesian foundation. The city was very prosperous, thanks to the resources of the location, enumerated by Herodotos (4.53.1–3).

τέταρτος δὲ Βορυσθένης ποταμός ὅς ἐστι μέγιστός τε μετὰ
Ἴστρον τούτων καὶ πολυαρκέστατος κατὰ γνώμας τὰς ἡμετέρας
οὔτι μοῦνον τῶν Σκυθικῶν ποταμῶν ἀλλὰ καὶ τῶν ἄλλων
ἁπάντων, πλὴν Νείλου τοῦ Αἰγυπτίου· τούτῳ γὰρ οὐκ οἷά τέ
ἐστι συμβαλεῖν ἄλλον ποταμόν· [2] τῶν δὲ λοιπῶν Βορυσθένης
ἐστὶ πολυαρκέστατος, ὃς νομάς τε καλλίστας καὶ εὐκομιδε-
στάτας κτήνεσι παρέχεται ἰχθῦς τε ἀρίστους διακριδὸν καὶ
πλείστους, πίνεσθαί τε ἥδιστός ἐστι, ῥέει τε καθαρὸς παρὰ
θολεροῖσι, σπόρος τε παρ'αὐτὸν ἄριστος γίνεται, ποίη τε, τῇ οὐ
σπείρεται ἡ χώρη, βαθυτάτη. [3] ἅλες τε ἐπὶ τῷ στόματι αὐτοῦ
αὐτόματοι πήγνυνται ἄπλετοι. κήτεά τε μεγάλα ἀνάκανθα, τὰ
ἀντακαίους καλέουσι, παρέχεται ἐς ταρίχευσιν, ἄλλα τε πολλὰ
θωμάσαι ἄξια.

[The fourth river is the Borysthenes [Dnepr], which is the biggest after the Istros [Danube] and supplies the most resources in my judgment, not only of the rivers of Skythia, but also of all other rivers except the Nile in Egypt (for no other river can be compared to that one). [2] But of the others, the Borysthenes supplies the most resources, since it furnishes the most beautiful pastures and the most well-tended flocks and far and away the best and most abundant fish, and it has the sweetest drinking water and flows clear alongside muddy rivers. The crops from it are the best, and also, where the land is not sown, the grass is very thick. [3] A limitless supply of salt is formed of its own accord at the mouth of the river. And it produces great huge spineless fish for preserving, which are called *antakaioi,* and many other amazing things.]

good source, especially for economic matters (72–97). Hind (1992/93, 92–94) claims that Berezan is nearly completely excavated though not completely published.

Solovev (1998) argues that Olbia was a later, discrete settlement. Certainly, if they were not one before, by the third quarter of the sixth century B.C.E., Berezan and Olbia underwent a *synoikism,* installing one polity for the two cities. The problem with this theory is that it requires us to explain away as originating at Berezan the pottery from the last third of the seventh century that has been found at Olbia: see Tsetskhladze 1994, 119; Hind 1992/93, 95.

Agriculture was already well established in the sixth century, since the remains of farms demonstrate that the *chore* by then extended far along the shore on ground that favored grain production over viticulture. Pastures farther inland fed sheep and goats first of all but later cattle and oxen as well. In addition, the forest-steppe furnished deer, wild pigs, wild donkeys, antelope, bear, rabbits, fox, wolves, and wildcats for hunting, while the water was rich in catfish, carp, pike, perch, other fish, and, of course, salt.

While agriculture and hunting provided for the day-to-day existence of the colonists, trade was an economic mainstay from the start. The citizens of Olbia acted as intermediaries between the Skythians in the interior and the Greeks in Ionia and elsewhere. In the second half of the seventh century, the Skythians were importing Greek wine and pottery: the Skythians had a general shortage of clay, which made the containers important in their own right. It is also likely that the Skythians imported the wool and woodwork for which Miletos was famous. In exchange, the Skythians sent back through Olbia to Miletos grain and other agricultural goods, livestock and its by-products, fish, wood, furs, slaves, and perhaps metals. By the first half of the sixth century, trade was extended even further. Amphoras containing wine were imported not only from Miletos but from Samos, Chios, Lesbos, and other places, especially in Ionia but also Rhodes and Athens. Imports included decorated ivory from Africa, precious and nonprecious worked metal (weapons, household items, toiletries, mirrors, jewelry, etc.), and large pieces of statuary, such as marble kouroi. In addition, the local industries at Olbia and Berezan were producing glassware and metal goods—weapons and jewelry of bronze and iron—for sale to the Skythians. Thus, Olbia was a prosperous city throughout the Archaic and early Classical period.

Tyras is much less known. It was located at the mouth of the river whose name it bore (modern Dnestr), though both the city and river were once called Ophioussa. No literary foundation date is given, but the earliest archaeological remains are Ionian pottery sherds dating to the sixth century. It was doubtless settled to facilitate trade with the tribes inland up the Dnestr River, after Berezan and Olbia had proven the economic potential of the region.[34]

---

34. Hdt. 4.51; Pliny *NH* 4.82; Steph. Byz. s.v.; Ps.-Skyl. *GGM* 1.57–58, para. 68; Str. 7.3.16; Ps.-Skymn. *GGM* 1.229, lines 802–3 = 799–800 Diller; Ehrhardt 1983, 72;

Tanais and Pantikapaion (following) are called the two greatest *emporia* for barbarian goods (Str. 7.4.5). Tanais was situated not on the Chersonese proper but on the mainland, where the river Tanais (Don) empties into Lake Maiotis (the modern Sea of Azov). Its precise location has not been agreed on. It may be identified as the ruins found near modern Elizavetovsk, where the earliest Greek archaeological remains date to ca. 625–600, or it may have been located at modern Taganrog, just to the southwest of Elizavetovsk, at a site that is now underwater but where Greek pottery from the seabed and shore can be dated to the last third of the seventh century. In either case, the economy of Tanais was based in part on trade in fish (Pliny *NH* 32.146, 149) and hides (Str. 11.2.3), bartered from the native Skythians.[35]

Pantikapaion is indisputably of Milesian origin, settled by the late seventh or early sixth centuries. Remains include semipit shelters, coins, and the sixth-century Temple of Artemis, as well as inscriptional evidence from the fourth century and beyond that ties the city to Miletos.[36] The city was located on the mouth of Lake Maiotis, on a strait called the Kimmerian Bosporos, at the location of the modern Ukrainian city Kerch. The intersection of these waterways made an ideal location for an *emporion*. In addition, Pantikapaion was on the east end of a very fertile plain that stretched along to Theodosia, about 95 km. to the southwest. As noted by Strabo (7.4.6), except for the strip of mountains along 120 km. of the lower half of the southeast coast (west of Theodosia), the entire Chersonese is enormously fertile.

Bilabel 1920, 19–23. According to Graham (1982a, 162) the archaeological remains date to ca. 600–500, but Ehrhardt says that while the excavators claim to have artifacts from the seventh and sixth centuries, these remain unpublished; the earliest datable item is a coin from the fourth century. *PECS* (943) agrees with the sixth-century date.

35. Tsetskhladze 1997, 42; Tsetskhladze 1994, 119; Graham 1982a, 130. No literary evidence connects Tanais to Miletos, and neither Bilabel nor Ehrhardt mention it, but Graham (1982a, 162) says that it may be Milesian, and Danoff (1962, 1138) says that it is Milesian. Hind holds the view that Tanais was located at Taganrog as a secondary foundation from the fourth century, along with Gorgippia and Kimmeris (1994, 484), and that the earlier city at Elizavetovsk was Skythian, implying that the Greek goods came through trade (1992/93, 104). The city at Elizavetovsk was founded or refounded in the third century (Hind in *PECS* 877) by the Greeks who held the Kimmerian Bosporos (Str. 11.2.3). Further excavation may clear up this dispute.

36. Str. 7.4.4; Pliny *NH* 4.87; Ammian. 22.8.26; Steph. Byz. s.v.; Tsetskhladze 1997, 44–49; Tsetskhladze 1994, 119; Jacobson 1995, 45–48; Hind 1994, 484; Hind 1992/93, 102–3; Ehrhardt 1983, 80; Bilabel 1920, 26–27; *PECS* 672–73.

τῆς δὲ Χεϱϱονήσου, πλὴν τῆς ὀϱεινῆς τῆς ἐπὶ τῇ θαλάττῃ μέχϱι
Θεοδοσίας, ἥ γε ἄλλη πεδιὰς καὶ εὔγεώς ἐστι πᾶσα, σίτῳ δὲ καὶ
σφόδϱα εὐτυχὴς τϱιακοντάχουν γοῦν ἀποδίδωσι, διὰ τοῦ τυχόντος
ὀϱυκτοῦ σχιζομένη. . . . κἂν τοῖς πϱόσθεν χϱόνοις ἐντεῦθεν ἦν τὰ
σιτοπομπεῖα τοῖς Ἕλλησι, καθάπεϱ ἐκ τῆς λίμνης αἱ ταϱιχεῖαι.

[Of the Chersonese, except for the mountainous land along the sea
up to Theodosia, the land is entirely flat and fertile, and it is very
prosperous in grain especially, giving off at least thirtyfold increase if
it is plowed by a digging tool. . . . In still earlier times [before
Mithradates], the Greeks used to import their grain from here, just as
they imported their supply of salt fish from the lake [Lake Maiotis].]

Besides receiving trade goods from the interior and from the other
Greeks, Pantikapaion could produce for home consumption and for ex-
portation abroad grain in abundance, salt from the Sea of Azov, and
fish.[37] The proof of the success of this location can be found in the
number of Greek cities that soon covered both shores of the Kimmerian
Bosporos, some of which may have been founded by Pantikapaion, "the
capital city of the [Kimmerian] Bosporos" (Str. 7.4.4).

Theodosia (modern Feodosiya, Ukraine) was a Milesian colony whose
archaeological remains date from ca. 580–560 B.C.E. Strabo (7.6) says it
was a fishing city.[38]

Kepoi was definitely Milesian, dating from ca. 580–560 B.C.E. It was
situated on the Asian mainland.[39]

---

37. One grave found at Pantikapaion has been advanced in arguments about the presence of native peoples in Greek colonies. Tychon the Taurian is clearly identified by an
inscribed stele in a cemetery dating to the sixth and fifth centuries B.C.E., and thus, some
would argue, there must have been a non-Greek population living in the city (the idea that
he was a slave was correctly dismissed because a slave would not have been buried with
such honor). Graham postulates that he may have been a distinguished visitor to the city,
perhaps one who shared a guest-friendship with a Greek family (an interesting explanation
for his Greek name). For a summary of the arguments (published in Russian), see Graham
1994, 7–8.

38. Str. 7.4.4.; Ammian. 22.8.26; Arr. (*Peripl. Eux.* 30 = *GGM* 1. 394, para. 30); Dem.
Lept. 33; Tsetskhladze 1997, 50–51; Tsetskhladze 1994, 119; Hind 1992/93, 100; Graham
1987, 128; Ehrhardt 1983, 82; Bilabel 1920, 26–27.

39. Ps.-Skym. *GGM* 1.234, line 899 = 898 Diller; Pliny *NH* 6.18; Tsetskhladze 1997,
57; Tsetskhladze 1994, 120; Hind 1992/93, 106–7; Hind 1983/84, 89; Graham 1987, 128;
Ehrhardt 1983, 81–82; Bilabel 1920, 27–28.

Nymphaion, east of Theodosia, was probably Milesian and possibly a secondary colony founded by Pantikapaion. It was a city with a good harbor (Str. 7.4.4), and its earliest remains are Attic black-figure pottery from the middle or early sixth century.[40]

Tyritake and *Myrmekion* on the Chersonese and *Hermonassa* on the mainland to the east were all probably either Milesian colonies or secondary settlements out of Pantikapaion. They all have remains dating to the early or middle sixth century B.C.E. Tyritake has been located near modern Yakovenkovo, on the south end of the Kimmerian Bosporos. Myrmekion was just north of Pantikapaion. Hermonassa was south of Kepoi. A site near it, called the Tuzlian Cemetery, has also revealed Greek pottery from ca. 580–560. The cities of the Kimmerian Bosporos were so closely tied together that in 480 all of them joined together under one government, a polity called the Bosporos, whose capital was Pantikapaion.[41]

The Milesian Colonies

Date	Name	Location	Comments
Pre-756 (first)	Sinope	South Pontos	Double foundation
756	Trapezous	South Pontos	From Sinope
756 (first)	Kyzikos	South Propontis	Double foundation
709	Parion	South Propontis	With Erythrai and Paros
Ca. 690	Prokonnesos	South Propontis	
Ca. 690	Artake	South Propontis	No ruins
679 (second)	Kyzikos	South Propontis	Double foundation
Ca. 668–652	Abydos	Hellespont	
657	Istros	West Pontos	
647	Olbia/Berezan	North Pontos	
Ca. 633–600	Tanais	Northeast Pontos	Site uncertain
631 (second)	Sinope	South Pontos	Double foundation
627	Kios	South Propontis	

40. Tsetskhladze 1994, 119 (ca. 580–570); Hind 1992/93, 100 (mid–sixth century).

41. Nymphaion, Myrmekion, and Tyritake are all listed by Graham (1982a, 161–62) but are not mentioned by Bilabel (1920) or Ehrhardt (1983). Hermonassa is mentioned as a possible colony by both Graham and Ehrhardt (1983, 83), but not by Bilabel. See Hind 1994, 484 (Hermonassa, sympolity); Hind 1992/93, 100–103 (summary); Hind 1983/84, 89–90 (Hermonassa); Tsetskhladze 1997, 49–50 (Nymphaion), 55–57 (Hermonassa), 60–61 (Myrmekion and Tyritake as dependent cities); Tsetskhladze 1994, 119–20 (Tuzlian cemetery).

Date	Name	Location	Comments
Ca. 610	Apollonia Pontika	West Pontos	
Ca. 600	Pantikapaion	Tauric Chersonese	
Ca. 600	Kardia	Thracian Chersonese	With Klazomenai
Ca. 600	Apollonia Rhyndakos	South Propontis	
Ca. 600–575	Tomis	West Pontos	
Ca. 600–575	Odessos	West Pontos	
Ca. 600–575	Hermonessa	Northeast Pontos	From Pantikapaion?
Ca. 600–575	Myrmekion	Tauric Chersonese	From Pantikapaion?
Ca. 600–575	Tyritake	Tauric Chersonese	From Pantikapaion?
Ca. 600–550	Nymphaion	Tauric Chersonese	From Pantikapaion?
Ca. 600–500	Tyras	North Pontos	
Ca. 580–560	Theodosia	Tauric Chersonese	
Ca. 580–560	Kepoi	Northeast Pontos	
Ca. 564	Amisos	South Pontos	With Phokaia?
Ca. 550	Dioskurias	East Pontos	
Ca. 512	Myrkinos	Makedonia	
Ca. 500–400	Anchiale	East Pontos	From Apollonia Pontika
No date	Arisbe	Hellespont	
No date	Armene	South Pontos	From Sinope
No date	Gyenos	East Pontos	Site uncertain
No date	Kerasos	South Pontos	From Sinope
No date	Kolonai	South Propontis	Site uncertain
No date	Kotyora	South Pontos	From Sinope
No date	Kytoros	South Pontos	From Sinope
No date	Limnai	Thracian Chersonese	Site uncertain
No date	Miletopolis	South Propontis	
No date	Paisos	South Propontis	
No date	Phasis	East Pontos	Site uncertain
No date	Priapos	South Propontis	
No date	Pterion	South Pontos	From Sinope; site uncertain
No date	Skepsis	Troad	
No date	Tieion	South Pontos	

Bibliography

Adiego, Ignacio J. 1997. "Fragment d'une inscription lydienne." In Graeve 1997, 156–57.

Adriani, A., et al., eds. 1970 *Himera I: Campagne di Scavo 1963–1965*. Rome.

Aly, W. 1911. "Delphinios: Beiträge zur Stadtgeschichte von Milet und Athen." *Klio* 11:1–25.

Ambaglio, Delfino. 1975. "Il motivo della deportazione in Erodoto." *Storia Antico, Istituto Lombardo (Rend. Litt.)* 109:378–83.

Andrewes, A. 1956. *The Greek Tyrants*. London.

Armayor, O. K. 1978. "Herodotus' Catalogues of the Persian Empire in the Light of the Monuments and the Greek Literary Tradition." *TAPA* 108:1–9.

Asheri, David. 1975. "Osservazioni sulle origini dell'urbanistica ippodamea." *Rivista Storica Italiana* 87:5–16.

Aubonnet, Jean. 1960. *Aristote Politique*. Paris.

Austin, M. M. 1970. *Greece and Egypt in the Archaic Age*. Cambridge.

———. 1990. "Greek Tyrants and the Persians, 546–479 B.C." *CQ* 40:289–306.

Balcer, Jack M. 1978. *The Athenian Regulations for Chalkis: Studies in Athenian Imperial Law*. Wiesbaden.

———. 1984a. "Miletos (*IG* 1².22 [1³.21]) and the Structures of Alliances." In *Studien zum attischen Seebund*, ed. Jack M. Balcer, 11–30. Konstanz.

———. 1984b. *Sparda by the Bitter Sea: Imperial Interaction in Western Anatolia*. Chico, CA.

Ball, Rashid. 1979. "Generation Dating in Herodotos." *CQ* 29:276–81.

Barceló, Pedro. 1993. *Basileia, Monarchia, Tyrannis: Untersuchungen zu Entwicklung und Beurteilung von Alleinherrschaft im vorhellenistischen Griechenland*. Stuttgart.

Barnes, Jonathan. 1979. *The Presocratic Philosophers*. Vol. 1, *Thales to Zeno*. London.

Barron, J. P. 1962. "Milesian Politics and Athenian Propaganda, c. 460–440 B.C." *JHS* 82:1–6.

Bean, George E. 1966. *Aegean Turkey: An Archaeological Guide*. New York.

———. 1980. *Turkey beyond the Maeander*. 2d ed. London and New York.

Bean, George E., and J. M. Cook. 1957. "The Carian Coast III." *ABSA* 52:58–146.

Belvedere, Oscar. 1976. "Tipologia e sviluppo delle abitazioni." In *Himera II: Campagne di scavo 1966–1973*, ed. A. Allegro et al., 1:575–94. Rome.

Benson, J. L. 1963. *Ancient Leros*. Durham, NC.

Berve, Helmut. 1967. *Die Tyrannis bei den Griechen*. 2 vols. Munich.

Bielohlawek, K. 1927. "ΜΕΛΠΕΣΘΑΙ und ΜΟΛΠΗ: Studien zur Überlieferungsgeschichte der antiken Homerischen Bedeutungslehre." *Wiener Studien* 45:1–11.

Bilabel, Friedrich. 1920. *Die Ionische Kolonisation*. Philologus Suppl. 14, no. 1. Leipzig.

Bittel, Kurt. 1975. "Altkleinasiatische Pferdetreusen." *MDAI(I)* 25:301–11.

Blamire, A. 1959. "Herodotus and Histiaeus." *CQ* 9:142–54.

Boardman, John. 1957. "Early Euboean Pottery and History." *ABSA* 52:1–29.

———. 1980. *The Greeks Overseas*. 2d ed. New York.

———. 1991. "Early Greek Pottery on Black Sea Sites?" *OJA* 10:387–89.

Boehringer, Erich, ed. 1959. *Von antiken Architektur und Topographie: Gesammelte Aufsätze von Armin von Gerkan*. Stuttgart.

Boffo, Laura. 1983. *La conquista persiana della città greche d'Asia Minore*. Roma.

Bowden, Hugh. 1996. "The Greek Settlement and Sanctuaries at Naukratis: Herodotus and Archaeology." In *More Studies in the Ancient Greek Polis*, ed. Mogens Herman Hansen and Kurt Raaflaub, 17–37. Stuttgart.

Boyd, Thomas D., and Wolf W. Rudolph. 1978. "Excavations at Porto Cheli and Vicinity, Preliminary Report IV: The Lower Town of Halieis, 1970–1977." *Hesperia* 47:333–55.

Bradeen, Donald. 1947. "The Lelantine War and Pheidon of Argos." *TAPA* 78:223–41.

Bradeen, Donald W., and Malcoln F. McGregor. 1973. "Regulations for Miletos." Chap. 2 in *Studies in Fifth-Century Attic Epigraphy*, 24–70. Norman, OK.

Branigan, K. 1981. "Minoan Colonization." *ABSA* 76:23–33.

Braun, T.F.R.G. 1982a. "The Greeks in Egypt." *CAH* 3³.3 32–56.

———. 1982b. "The Greeks in the Near East." *CAH* 3³.3 1–31.

Bresson, Alain, and P. Rouillard, eds. 1993. *L'emporion*. Paris.

Brett, Agnes Baldwin. 1955. *Catalogue of Greek Coins, Museum of Fine Arts, Boston*. Boston.

Brinkmann, Vinzenz. 1990. "Der Westbau [des Kalabaktepe]." *MDAI(I)* 40:51–55.

Brückner, Helmut. 1998. "Coastal Research and Geoarchaeology in the Mediterranean Region." In *German Geographical Coastal Research: The Last Decade*, ed. Dieter H. Kelletat, 235–57. Tübingen.

Bryce, Trevor R. 1985. "A Reinterpretation of the Milawata Letter." *AS* 35:13–23.

———. 1989. "The Nature of Mycenaean Involvement in Western Anatolia." *Historia* 38:1–21.

———. 1998. *The Kingdom of the Hittites*. Oxford.

Buck, Carl Darling. 1955. *The Greek Dialects*. Rev. ed. Chicago and London.

Buck, Robert J. 1970. "The Athenian Domination of Boeotia." *CP* 65:217–27.

———. 1978. *A History of Boeotia*. Edmonton.

Bürchner, L. 1912. *RE* 7.1249, s.v. "Gergithes."

Burkert, Walter. 1975. "Apellai und Apollon." *RM* 118:1–21.

———. 1994. "Olbia and Apollo of Didyma: A New Oracle Text." In *Apollo: Origins and Influences*, ed. Jon Solomon, 49–90. Tucson and London.

Burn, A. R. 1929. "The So-Called 'Trade-Leagues' in Early Greek History and the Lelantine War." *JHS* 49:14–37.

———. 1985. "Persia and the Greeks." *CHI* 2:292–391.

Burns, Alfred. 1976. "Hippodamus and the Planned City." *Historia* 25:414–28.

Burstein, Stanley M. 1976. *Outpost of Hellenism: The Emergence of Heraclea on the Black Sea*. Berkeley.

Busolt, Georg. 1893. *Griechische Staatskunde*. Handbuch der Altertumswissenschaft sect. 4, part 1, vol. 1. 2d ed. 2 vols. Munich.

Busolt, Georg, and Heinrich Swoboda. 1920. *Griechische Staatskunde*. Handbuch der Altertumswissenschaft sect. 4, part 1, vol. 1. 3d ed. 2 vols. Munich.

Cahn, H. A. 1950. "Die Löwen des Apollon." *Mus. Helv.* 7:185–99.

Cameron, G. G. 1973. "The Persian Satrapies and Related Matters." *JNES* 32: 47–56.

Camp, John McK. 1979. "A Drought in the Late Eighth Century B.C." *Hesperia* 48:397–411.

Carlier, Pierre. 1984. *La royauté en Grèce avant Alexandre*. Strasbourg.

Carpenter, Rhys. 1948. "The Greek Penetration of the Black Sea." *AJA* 52:1–10.

Carradice, Ian, and Martin Price. 1988. *Coinage in the Greek World*. London.

Caspari, M. O. B. 1915. "The Ionian Confederacy." *JHS* 35:173–88.

Cassola, F. 1957. *La Ionia nel mondo miceneo*. Naples.

Castagnoli, Ferdinando. 1971. *Orthogonal Town Planning in Antiquity*. Trans. V. Caliandro. Cambridge, MA, and London.

Cataldi, S. 1981. "La Secession dei βέλτιστοι milesi e le Ξυγγραφαί ateniensi per Mileto." In *Studi sui rapporti interstatale nel mondo antico*, ed. S. Cataldi et al., 161–233. Pisa.

Cawkwell, George L. 1992. "Early Colonisation." *CQ* 42:289–303.

Chadwick, John. 1975. "The Prehistory of the Greek Language." *CAH* 2³.2 805–19.

Chantraine, P. 1968. *Dictionnaire étymologique de la langue grecque*. 4 vols. Paris.

Chapman, G. A. H. 1972. "Herodotus and Histiaeus' Role in the Ionian Revolt." *Historia* 21:546–68.

Cobet, Justus. 1997. "Milet 1994–1995: Die Mauern sind die Stadt. Zur Stadtbefestigung des antiken Milet." *AA* 112:249–84.

Collingwood, R. G. 1956. *The Idea of History*. Ed. T. M. Knox. 1946. Reprint, Oxford.

Connor, W. R. 1993. "The Ionian Era of Athenian Civic Identity." *PAPhS* 137: 194–206.

Cook, J. M. 1946. "Ionia and Greece in the Eighth and Seventh Centuries B.C." *JHS* 66:67–98.

———. 1958/59. "Old Smyrna, 1948–1951." *ABSA* 53–54:1–34.

———. 1961. "Some Sites of the Milesian Territory." *ABSA* 56:90–101.

———. 1962. *The Greeks in Ionia and the East*. New York and Washington.

————. 1967. Review of Kleiner 1966. *Gnomon* 39:212–14.

————. 1975. "Greek Settlement in the Eastern Aegean and Asia Minor." *CAH* 2³.2 773–804.

————. 1983. *The Persian Empire*. New York.

————. 1985. "The Rise of the Achaemenids and Establishment of Their Empire." *CHI²* 200–291.

Cook, J. M., and D. J. Blackman. 1964/65. "Greek Archaeology in Western Asia Minor." *AR* 11:32–62.

————. 1970/71. "Archaeology in Western Asia Minor, 1965–70." *AR* 17:33–62.

Corsaro, Mauro. 1985. "Tassazione regia e tassazione cittadina dagli Achemenidi ai re Ellenistici: Alcune osservazioni." *REA* 87:73–95.

Coulton, J. J. 1977. *Greek Architects at Work: Problems of Structure and Design*. London.

Danoff, C. M. 1962. *RE* Suppl. 9.865–1175, s.v. "Pontos Euxeinos."

Danov [Danoff], C. M. 1990. "Characteristics of Greek Colonization in Thrace." In Descoeudres 1990, 151–55.

Davies, Malcolm. 1989. *The Epic Cycle*. Bristol.

Demand, Nancy. 1990. *Urban Relocation in Archaic and Classical Greece*. Norman, OK.

de Sanctis, Gaetano. 1931. "Aristagora di Mileto." *RFIC* 59:48–72.

————. 1976. *La guerra sociale: Opera inedita*. Ed. Leandro Polverini. Florence.

Desborough, V. R. d'A. 1964. *The Last Mycenaeans and Their Successors*. Oxford.

————. 1972. *The Greek Dark Ages*. New York.

Descoeudres, Jean-Paul, ed. 1990. *Greek Colonists and Native Populations*. Canberra and Oxford.

Develin, Robert. 1989. *Athenian Officials, 684–321 BC*. Cambridge and New York.

Dickinson, Oliver T. P. K. 1994. *The Aegean Bronze Age*. Cambridge.

Dittenberger, W. 1960. *Sylloge Inscriptionum Graecarum*. 4th ed. 4 vols. Hildesheim.

Donlan, Walter. 1989. "The Pre-state Community in Greece." *SO* 64:5–29.

Drews, Robert. 1972. "The First Tyrants in Greece." *Historia* 21:129–44.

————. 1973. *The Greek Accounts of Eastern History*. Cambridge, MA.

————. 1976. "The Earliest Greek Settlement in the Black Sea." *JHS* 96:18–31.

————. 1983. *Basileus: The Evidence for Kingship in Geometric Greece*. New Haven and London.

Drijvers, Jan Wilhelm. 1999. "Strabo 17.1.18 (801C): Inaros, the Milesians and Naucratis." *Mnemosyne* 52:16–22.

Dubois, Laurent. 1996. *Inscriptiones grecques dialectales d'Olbia du Pont*. Geneva.

Dubuisson, Michel. 1977. "ΟΙ ΑΜΦΙ ΤΙΝΑ, ΟΙ ΠΕΡΙ ΤΙΝΑ." Ph.D. diss., Université de Liège.

Dunham, Adelaide. 1915. *A History of Miletus down to the Anabasis of Alexander*. London.

Dunst, G. 1961. "Zu den altmilesischen Phylen." *Forschungen und Fortschritte* 35:272–73.

Dupont, Pierre. 1986. "Naturwissenschaftliche Bestimmung der archaischen Keramik Milets." In Müller-Wiener 1986c, 57–71.

Earp, A. J. 1954. "Athens and Miletos *ca.* 450 B.C." *Phoenix* 8:142–47.

Ehrenberg, Victor. 1948. "The Foundation of Thurii." *AJP* 69:149–70.

Ehrhardt, Norbert. 1983. *Milet und seine Kolonien.* Frankfurt am Main and New York.

———. 1987. "Die politischen Beziehungen zwischen den griechischen Schwarzmeergründungen und ihren Mutterstädten: Ein Beitrag zur Bedeutung von Kolonialverhältnissen in Griechenland." *Acta Centri Historiae Terra Antiqua Balcanica* 2:78–117.

———. 1998. "Didyma und Milet in archaischer Zeit." *Chiron* 28:11–20.

Eickstedt, Klaus-Valtin von. 1991. *Beiträge zur Topographie des antiken Piräus.* Athens.

Emlyn-Jones, C. J. 1980. *The Ionians and Hellenism.* London.

Erdmann, M. 1884. "Hippodamos von Milet und die symmetrische Städtebaukunst der Griechen." *Philologus* 42:193–227.

Evans, J. A. S. 1963. "Histiaeus and Aristagoras: Notes on the Ionian Revolt." *AJP* 84:113–28.

Fabricius, E. 1913. *RE* 8.1731–34, s.v. "Hippodamos (3)."

Falciai, Patrizia Benvenuti. 1982. *Ippodamo di Mileto, architetto e filosofo: Una reconstruzione filologica della personalità.* Florence.

Faraguna, Michele. 1995. "Note di storia milesia arcaica: Ι ΓΕΡΓΙΘΕΣ e la ΣΤΑΣΙΣ di VI secolo." *SMEA* 36:37–89.

Farnell, Lewis R. 1921. *Greek Hero Cults and Ideas of Immortality.* Oxford.

Finley, Moses I. 1975. "Myth, Memory, and History." In *The Use and Abuse of History,* 11–33. London.

———. 1977. *The World of Odysseus.* Rev. ed. New York.

Fol, A. 1996. "Thracia Pontica—Twenty Years Later." In Tsetskhladze 1996, 1–12.

Fontenrose, Joseph. 1978. *The Delphic Oracle: Its Responses and Operations with a Catalogue of Responses.* Berkeley.

———. 1988. *Didyma: Apollo's Oracle, Cult, and Companions.* Berkeley and Los Angeles.

Forbeck, Elke, and Huberta Heres. 1997. *Die Löwengrab von Milet.* Berlin.

Fornara, Charles. 1971. "The Date of the 'Regulations for Miletus.'" *AJP* 92: 473–75.

———. 1983a. *The Nature of History in Ancient Greece and Rome.* Berkeley.

———, ed. and trans. 1983b. *Archaic Times to the End of the Peloponnesian War.* Vol. 1, *Translated Documents of Greece and Rome.* 2d ed. Cambridge.

Forrer, Emil. 1924a. "Die Griechen in den Boghazköi-Texten." *OLZ* 27:113–18.

———. 1924b. "Vorhomerische Griechen in den Keilschrifttexten von Boghazköi." *MDOG* 63:1–22.

Foss, Clive. 1977. "Archaeology and the 'Twenty Cities' of Byzantine Asia." *AJA* 81:469–86.

Foti, G. 1964. "La ricerca del sito di Sibari." *Atti e Mem. Soc. Magna Graecia,* n.s., 13–14: 9–15.

Foucault, J. A. de. 1967. "Histiée de Milet et l'esclave tatoué." *REG* 80:182–86.

French, Elizabeth. 1971. "The Development of Mycenaean Terracotta Figurines." *ABSA* 66:101–87.

Frisk, H. 1960. *Griechisches etymologisches Wörterbuch.* Vol. 1. Heidelberg.

Furumark, A. 1950. "The Settlement at Ialysos and Aegean History, c. 1550–1400 B.C." *Opuscula Archaeologica* 6:150–271.

Gans, Ulrich. 1991. "Die Grabung auf dem Zeytintepe." In Graeve 1991, 137–40.

Gardner, P. 1908. "The Gold Coinage of Asia before Alexander the Great." *ProcBrAcad* 3:107–38.

———. 1911. "The Coinage of the Ionian Revolt." *JHS* 31:151–60.

———. 1913. "Note on the Coinage of the Ionian Revolt." *JHS* 33:105.

———. 1918. *A History of Ancient Coinage, 700–300 B.C.* Oxford.

Garland, Robert. 1987. *The Piraeus from the Fifth to the First Century B.C.* Worcester.

Gehrke, Hans-Joachim. 1980. "Zur Geschichte Milets in der Mitte des 5. Jahrhunderts v. Chr." *Historia* 29:17–31.

Genière, Juliette de la. 1975. "Saggi sull'acropoli di Selinunte: Relazione preliminare." *Kokalos* 21:68–107.

Georges, Pericles B. 2000. "Persian Ionia under Darius: The Revolt Reconsidered." *Historia* 49:1–39.

Gerkan, Armin von. 1924a. *Griechische Städteanlagen.* Berlin and Leipzig.

———. 1924b. "Hippodamos." In *Allgemeines Lexikon der bildenden Künstler,* ed. Ulrich Thieme and Felix Becker 17:124–25. Leipzig. Reprinted in Boehringer 1959, 4–5.

———. 1940. "Zur Lage des archaischen Milet." In *Bericht über der VI. internationalen Kongress für Archäologie: Berlin 21.–26. August 1939,* 323–25. Berlin. Reprinted in Boehringer 1959, 286–88.

———. 1950. "Zum Heiligtum des Apollon Delphinios in Milet." *IstForsch* 17:35–37. Reprinted in Boehringer 1959, 288–90.

Geyer. 1924. *RE* 12.1890–93, s.v. "Leleger."

Gilbert, Otto. 1907. *Die meteorologischen Theorien des griechischen Altertums.* Leipzig. Reprint, 1967.

Gillis, D. 1979. *Collaboration with the Persians.* Wiesbaden.

Glotz, Gustave. 1928. *La cité grecque.* Paris.

Gomme, A. W. 1945. *A Historical Commentary on Thucydides.* Vol. 1. Oxford.

Gorman, Robert J., and Vanessa B. Gorman. 2000. " 'The Tyrants around Thoas and Damasenor' (Plut. *Q.G.* 32.298c–d)." *CQ* 50:526–30.

Gorman, Vanessa B. 1995. "Aristotle's Hippodamos (*Politics* 2.1267b22–30)." *Historia* 44:385–95.

Graeve, Volmar von. 1973/74. "Milet: Bericht über die Arbeiten im Südschnitt an der hellenistischen Stadtmauer 1963." *MDAI(I)* 23–24:63–115.

———. 1975a. "Eine Sitzfigur aus Milet." *MDAI(I)* 25:61–65.

———. 1975b. "Milet: Vorläufiger Bericht über die Grabung im Südschnitt an der hellenistischen Stadtmauer 1966." *MDAI(I)* 25:35–59.

————. 1986a. "4. Grabung auf dem Kalabaktepe." In Müller-Wiener 1986b, 37–51.

————. 1986b. "Über verschiedene Richtungen der milesischen Skulptur in archaischer Zeit." In Müller-Wiener 1986c, 81–94.

————. 1987. "1. Grabung auf dem Kalabaktepe." In Müller-Wiener 1987, 6–33.

————. 1989. "Eine spätarchaische Anthemienstele aus Milet." *MDAI(I)* 39: 143–51.

————. 1990. "Der Schnitt auf dem Gipfelplateau des Kalabaktepe 1988." With R. Biering and I. Blum. *MDAI(I)* 40:39–43.

————. 1991. "Milet 1990: Vorbericht über der Arbeiten des Jahres 1990." *MDAI(I)* 41:125–86.

————. 1992. "Milet 1991: Vorbericht über der Arbeiten des Jahres 1991." *MDAI(I)* 42:97–134.

————. 1995. "Milet 1992–1993: Vorbericht über die Grabungsarbeiten und Geländeerkundungen, die Denkmälerrestaurierung und die naturwissenschaftlichen Begleitprogramme der Miletgrabung in den Jahren 1992 und 1993." *AA* 110:195–333.

————. 1997. "Milet 1994–1995: Vorbericht über die Grabungsarbeiten und Geländeerkundungen, die Denkmälerrestaurierung und die naturwissenschaftlichen Begleitprogramme der Miletgrabung in den Jahren 1994 und 1995." *AA* 112:109–88.

Graeve, Volkmar von, and R. Senff. 1990. "Die Grabung am Südhang des Kalabaktepe." *MDAI(I)* 40:44–50.

————. 1991. "Die Grabung auf dem Kalabaktepe." In Graeve 1991, 127–33.

Graf, David F. 1985. "Greek Tyrants and Achaemenid Politics." In *The Craft of the Ancient Historian: Essays in Honor of Chester G. Starr,* ed. J. W. Eadie and J. Ober, 79–123. Lanham, MD.

Graf, Fritz. 1974. "Das Kollegium der Μολποί von Olbia." *Mus. Helv.* 31: 209–15.

————. 1979. "Apollon Delphinios." *Mus. Helv.* 36:2–22.

————. 1993. *Greek Mythology: An Introduction.* Trans. Thomas Marier. Baltimore.

Graham, A. J. 1958. "The Date of the Greek Penetration of the Black Sea." *BICS* 5:25–42.

————. 1971. "Patterns in Early Greek Colonisation." *JHS* 91:35–47.

————. 1978. "The Foundation Date of Thasos." *ABSA* 73:61–101.

————. 1980/81. "Religion, Women and Greek Colonization." *CeRDAC Atti* n.s., 1:293–314.

————. 1982a. "The Colonial Expansion of Greece." *CAH* 3^2.3 83–162.

————. 1982b. "The Western Greeks." *CAH* 3^2.3 163–95.

————. 1983. *Colony and Mother City in Ancient Greece.* 2d ed. Chicago.

————. 1987. Review of Ehrhardt 1983. *Gnomon* 59:124–29.

————. 1990. "Pre-colonial Contacts: Questions and Problems." In Descoeudres 1990, 45–60.

————. 1992. "Abdera and Teos." *JHS* 112:44–73.

————. 1994. "Greek and Roman Settlements on the Black Sea Coast: Historical

Background." In *Colloquenda Pontica,* ed. Gocha R. Tsetskhladze, 4–10. Bradford, England.

Grundy, G. B. 1901. *The Great Persian War and Its Preliminaries.* London. Reprint, New York, 1969.

Gschnitzer, F. 1973. *RE* Suppl. 13.730–816, s.v. *Prytanis.*

Günther, Wolfgang. 1971. *Das Orakel von Didyma in hellenistischer Zeit.* Tübingen.

Güterbock, Hans G. 1983. "The Hittites and the Aegean World: Part 1. The Ahhiyawa Problem Reconsidered." *AJA* 87:133–38.

———. 1984. "Hittites and Akhaeans: A New Look." *PAPS* 128:114–22.

———. 1986. "Troy in Hittite Texts? Wilusa, Ahhiyawa, and Hittite History." In *Troy and The Trojan War,* ed. Machteld J. Mellink, 33–44. Bryn Mawr.

Guthrie, W. K. C. 1962. *A History of Greek Philosophy.* Vol. 1, *The Earlier Presocratics and the Pythagoreans.* Cambridge.

Hadzisteliou-Price, Theodora. 1971. "Double and Multiple Representation in Greek Art and Religious Thought." *JHS* 91:48–69.

Hägg, Robin, and Nanno Marinatos, eds. 1984. *The Minoan Thalassocracy: Myth and Reality.* Stockholm.

Haider, Peter W. 1996. "Griechen im vorderen Orient und in Ägypten bis ca. 590 v. Chr." In *Wege zur Genese griechischer Identität,* ed. Christoph Ulf, 59–115. Berlin.

Hajnal, Ivo. 1995. "Das Vokalsystem des Karischen: Eine provisorische Bestand-aufnahme." *Die Sprache* 37:12–30.

Halliday, W. R., ed. and trans. 1928. *The Greek Questions of Plutarch.* Oxford.

Hammond, N. G. L. 1967. *A History of Greece to 322 B.C.* 2d ed. Oxford.

———. 1998. "The Branchidae at Didyma and in Sogdiana." *CQ* 48:339–44.

Hanell, Krister. 1946. *Das altrömische eponyme Amt.* Lund.

Hanfmann, George. 1953. "Ionia, Leader or Follower?" *HSCP* 61:1–37.

Hansen, Mogens Herman. 1986. "The Origin of the Term *Demokratia.*" *LCM* 11, no. 3:35–36.

———. 1997a. "*Emporion.* A Study of the Use and Meaning of the Term in the Archaic and Classical Periods." In Nielsen 1997, 83–105.

———. 1997b. "A Typology of Dependent *Poleis.*" In Nielsen 1997, 29–37.

Harris, George. 1971. "Ionia under Persia, 547–477 B.C.—A Political History." Ph.D. diss., Northwestern University.

Hasluck, F. W. 1910. *Cyzicus.* Cambridge.

Haussoullier, B. 1897. "Dèmes et tribus, patries et phratries de Milet." *Rev. Phil.,* n.s., 21:38–49.

———. 1902. "Les îles Milésiennes: Léros-Lepsia-Patmos-les Korsiae." *Rev. Phil.,* n.s., 26:125–43.

Haverfield, F. 1913. *Ancient Town-Planning.* Oxford.

Hedreen, Guy. 1991. "The Cult of Achilles in the Euxine." *Hesperia* 60:313–30.

Hegyi, Delores. 1965. "Notes on the Origin of Greek *Tyrannis.*" *AAntHung* 13:303–18.

———. 1966. "The Historical Background of the Ionian Revolt." *AAntHung* 14:285–302.

———. 1977. "Der Ursprung der Aisymneteia." *ACD* 13:7–10.

Heilmeyer, Wolf-Dieter. 1986. "Die Einordnung Milets in die Siedlungszonen die griechischen Frühzeit." In Müller-Wiener 1986c, 105–12.

Heinlein, S. 1909. "Histiaios von Milet." *Klio* 9:341–51.

Heinrich, Hayo, and Reinhard Senff. 1992. "Die Grabung am Kalabaktepe." In Graeve 1992, 100–104.

Heinsius, Daniel. 1621. *Aristotelis Politicorum Libri VIII*. Lugduni.

Heinz, Margarete, and Reinhard Senff. 1995. "Die Grabung auf dem Zeytintepe." In Graeve 1995, 220–24.

Hermann, Karl Friedrich. 1841. *Disputatio de Hippodamo Milesio ad Aristotelis Politicis II.5*. Marburg.

Herrmann, Peter. 1965. "Neue Urkunden zur Geschichte von Milet im 2. Jahrhundert v. Chr." *MDAI(I)* 15:71–117.

———. 1970. "Zu den Beziehungen zwischen Athen und Milet in 5. Jahrhundert." *Klio* 52:163–73.

———. 1995. "Inschriften." In Graeve 1995, 282–92.

Hiesel, G. 1990. *Späthelladische Hausarchitektur*. Mainz.

Hill, D. K. 1932. "Boundary Stones from the Piraeus." *AJA* 36:254–59.

Hiller von Gaertingen, F. 1932. *RE* 15.2.1586–1622, s.v. "Miletos *(Geschichte)*."

Hind, John G. F. 1983/84. "Greek and Barbarian Peoples on the Shores of the Black Sea." *AR* 30:71–97.

———. 1992/93. "Archaeology of the Greeks and Barbarian Peoples around the Black Sea." *AR* 39:82–112.

———. 1994. "The Bosporan Kingdom." *CAH* 6^2 476–511.

———. 1996. "Achilles and Helen on White Island in the Euxine Sea: Side B of the Portland Vase." In Tsetskhladze 1996, 59–62.

———. 1997. "Colonies and Ports-of-Trade on the Northern Shores of the Black Sea: Borysthenes, Kremnoi, and the 'Other Pontic *Emporia*.' " In Nielsen 1997, 107–16.

Hoepfner, W., and G.-H. Schwandner. 1994. *Haus und Stadt im klassischen Griechenland*. 2d ed. Munich.

Hölbl, G. 1999. "Funde aus Milet VIII: Die Aegyptiaca vom Aphroditetempel auf dem Zeytintepe." *AA* 114:345–71.

Hommel, Peter. 1959/60. "II. Der Abschnitt östlich des Athena-Tempels." In Weickert 1959/60a, 31–62.

———. 1967. "Archaischer Jünglingskopf aus Milet." *MDAI(I)* 17:115–27.

———. 1976. "Die Grabungs Kampagne in Milet im Herbst 1973." *TürkAD* 22, no. 1:37–40.

———. 1980. *Der Gott Achilleus*. Heidelberg.

How, W. W., and J. Wells. 1912. *A Commentary on Herodotus*. 2 vols. Oxford.

Hussey, E. 1995. "Ionian Inquiries: On Understanding the Presocratic Beginnings of Science." In *The Greek World*, ed. Anton Powell, 530–49. London.

Huxley, G. L. 1966. *The Early Ionians*. New York.

———. 1968. *Minoans in Greek Sources*. Belfast.

Ivantchik, A. I. 1993. *Les Cimmériens au Proche-Orient*. Göttingen.

———. 1998. "Die Gründungvon Sinope und die Probleme der Anfangsphase der griechischen Kolonisation des Schwarzmeergebietes." In Tsetskhladze 1998b, 297–330.

Jacobson, Esther. 1995. *The Art of the Scythians: The Interpenetration of Cultures at the Edge of the Hellenic World.* Handbuch der Orientalistik sect. 8, vol. 2. Leiden, New York, and Cologne.

Jacoby, F. 1912. *RE* 7.2667–2750, s.v. "Hekataios (3)."

Janssen, T. H. 1984. *Timotheus Persae: A Commentary.* Amsterdam.

Jeffery, L. H. 1976. *Archaic Greece: The City-States, c. 700–500 B.C.* New York.

———. 1990. *The Local Scripts of Archaic Greece.* Rev. ed. Oxford.

Jenkins, G. K. 1972. *Ancient Greek Coins.* New York.

Jones, Nicholas F. 1987. *Public Organization in Ancient Greece: A Documentary Study.* Philadelphia.

Jowett, Benjamin. 1905. *Aristotle's* Politics. Oxford.

Judeich, W. 1931. *Topographie von Athen.* 2d ed. Munich.

Kacharava, D. D. 1983/84. "Archaeological Investigations on the Eastern Black Sea Littoral, 1970–80." *AR* 30:98–101.

———. 1990/91. "Archaeology in Georgia, 1980–90." *AR* 37:79–86.

Kahn, Charles. 1960. *Anaximander and the Origins of Greek Cosmology.* New York.

Kerschner, Michael. 1995. "Die Ostterrasse des Kalabaktepe." In Graeve 1995, 214–20.

Kerschner, Michael, and Reinhard Senff. 1997. "Die Ostterrasse des Kalabaktepe." With Irene Blum. In Graeve 1997, 120–22.

Kilian, K. 1990. "Mycenaean Colonization: Norm and Variety." In Descoeudres 1990, 445–67.

Kirk, G. S., J. E. Raven, and M. Schofield. 1983. *The Presocratic Philosophers.* 2d ed. Cambridge.

Kleine, Jürgen. 1979. "Milet: Bericht über die Arbeiten im Südschnitt an der hellenistischen Stadtmauer 1968–1973." *MDAI(I)* 29:109–59.

Kleiner, Gerhard. 1960. "Die Grabung in Milet im Herbst 1959." *TürkAD* 10, no. 1:39–41.

———. 1961. "Bericht über die Grabung in Milet im Herbst 1961." *TürkAD* 11, no. 2:46–48.

———. 1966. *Alt-Milet.* SB Frankfurt 4.1. Wiesbaden.

———. 1968. *Die Ruinen von Milet.* Berlin.

———. 1969/70. "Stand der Erforschung von Alt-Milet." *MDAI(I)* 19–20: 113–23.

———. 1970. *Das Römische Milet, Bilder aus der griechischen Stadt in römischer Zeit.* Wiesbaden.

Kleiner, Gerhard, Peter Hommel, and Wolfgang Müller-Wiener. 1967. *Panionion und Melie.* Berlin.

Kleiner, Gerhard, and Wolfgang Müller-Wiener. 1972. "Die Grabung in Milet im Herbst 1959." *MDAI(I)* 22:45–92.

Kochavi, Moshe. 1992. "Some Connections between the Aegean and the Levant in the Second Millennium BC: A View from the East." In Kopcke and Tokumaru 1992, 7–15.

Koenigs, Wolf. 1980. "3. Bauglieder aus Milet II." In Müller-Wiener 1980a, 56–91.

———. 1986. "Reste archaischer Architektur in Milet." In Müller-Wiener 1986c, 113–19.

Kondis, J. D. 1958. "Zum antiken Stadbauplan von Rhodes." *MDAI(I)* 73: 146–58.

Konstantinopolis, G. 1970. "Τὸ ϱυμοτικὸν σύστημα τῆς ἀϱχαίας Ρόδου." *Archaiologika Analekta ex Athenon* 3:52–55.

———. 1989. Ἀϱχαία Ρόδος. Athens.

Kopcke, Günter, and Isabelle Tokumaru, eds. 1992. *Greece between East and West, 10th–8th Centuries BC.* Mainz.

Koshelenko, G. A., and V. D. Kuznetsov. 1998. "Greek Colonisation of the Bosporus." In Tsetskhladze 1998b, 249–63.

Kostof, Spiro. 1991. *The City Shaped: Urban Patterns and Meanings through History.* London.

Kraay, C. M. 1976. *Archaic and Classical Greek Coins.* Berkeley and Los Angeles.

Kraay, C. M., and M. Hirmer. 1966. *Greek Coins.* New York.

Kuhrt, Amélie. 1988. "Babylonia from Cyrus to Xerxes." *CAH* 4² 112–38.

Kurke, Leslie. 1999. *Coins, Bodies, Games, and Gold: The Politics of Meaning in Archaic Greece.* Princeton.

Labaree, Benjamin W. 1957. "How the Greeks Sailed into the Black Sea." *AJA* 61:29–33.

Lambrino, Scarlat. 1927–32. *Dacia III–IV.* Bucharest.

Lang, M. L. 1968. "Herodotus and the Ionian Revolt." *Historia* 17:24–36.

———. 1984. *Herodotean Narrative and Discourse.* Cambridge, MA, and London.

Larsen, J. A. O. 1932. "Sparta and the Ionian Revolt: A Study of Spartan Foreign Policy and the Genesis of the Peloponnesian League." *CP* 27:136–57.

———. 1933. "The Constitution of the Peloponnesian League." *CP* 28:257–76.

———. 1934. "The Constitution of the Peloponnesian League." *CP* 29:1–19.

Lateiner, Donald. 1982. "The Failure of the Ionian Revolt." *Historia* 31:129–60.

———. 1989. *The Historical Method of Herodotus.* Toronto.

Lattimore, Richmond. 1939. "The Wise Adviser in Herodotos." *CP* 34:24–35.

Lavedan, Pierre, and Jeanne Hugueney. 1966. *Histoire de l'urbanisme antiquité.* 2d ed. Vol. 2. Paris.

Lawton, Carol. 1992. "Sculptural and Epigraphical Restorations to Attic Documents." *Hesperia* 61:239–51.

———. 1995. *Attic Document Reliefs: Art and Politics in Ancient Athens.* Oxford.

Lazarov, M. 1998. "Notizien zur griechischen Kolonisation am westlichen Schwarzen Meer: Schriftquellen und archäologische Denkmäler." In Tsetskhladze 1998b, 85–95.

Leaf, Walter. 1923. *Strabo on the Troad, Book XIII, Cap. I.* Cambridge.

Lenschau, Thomas. 1944. "Die Gründung Ioniens und der Bund am Panionion." *Klio* 36:201–37.

Lewis, D. M. 1990. "Public Property in the City." In *The Greek City from Homer to Alexander*, ed. Oswyn Murray and Simon Price, 245–64. Oxford.

Libero, Loretana de. 1996. *Die archaische Tyrannis*. Stuttgart.

Lohmann, Hans. 1995. "Survey in der Chora von Milet: Vorbericht über die Kampagnen der Jahre 1990, 1992 und 1993." In Graeve 1995, 293–328.

Lordkipanidze, Otar. 1985. *Das alte Kolchis und seine Beziehungen zur griechischen Welt vom 6. zum 4. Jh. v. Chr.* Constance.

Luria, S. 1928. "Ein milesischer Männerbund im Lichte ethnologischer Parallelen." *Philologus* 83:113–36.

———. 1963. "Kureten, Molpen, Aisymneten." *Acta Antiqua Akademiae Scientiarum Hungaricae* 11:31–36.

Macan, R. W. 1895. *Herodotus: The Fourth, Fifth, and Sixth Books.* 2 vols. London. Reprint, New York, 1973.

Malkin, Irad. 1987. *Religion and Colonization in Ancient Greece.* Leiden.

———. 1994. *Myth and Territory in the Spartan Mediterranean.* Cambridge.

———. 1998. *The Returns of Odysseus: Colonization and Ethnicity.* Berkeley.

Mallwitz, Alfred. 1959/60a. "V. Eine Kultstätte im Athenaheiligtum." In Weickert 1959/60, 76–85.

———. 1959/60b. "Zur Mykenischen Befestigung von Milet." In Weickert 1959/60, 67–85.

———. 1968. "Der alte Athena-Tempel von Milet." *MDAI(I)* 18:89–160.

———. 1975. "Gestalt und Geschichte des jüngeren Athenatempels von Milet." *MDAI(I)* 25:67–90.

Manganaro, G. 1963/64. "Le inscrizioni delle Isole milesie." *ASAA* 41–42:293–349.

Manning, Sturt W. 1995. *The Absolute Chronology of the Aegean Early Bronze Age: Archaeology, Radiocarbon, and History.* Sheffield.

Manville, P. B. 1977. "Aristagoras and Histiaeus: The Leadership Struggle in the Ionian Revolt." *CQ* 27:80–91.

Martin, Roland. 1951. *Recherches sur l'agora grecque: Études d'histoire et d'architecture urbaines.* Paris.

———. 1972/73. "Problèmes d'urbanisme dans les cités grecques de Sicile." *Kokalos* 18–19:348–65.

———. 1974. *L'urbanisme dans le Grèce antique.* 2d ed. Paris.

———. 1975. "Rapport sur l'urbanisme de Sélinonte." *Kokalos* 21:54–67.

———. 1977. "Histoire de Sélinone d'après les fouilles récentes." *CRAI* 46–63.

———. 1978. "Thasos: Quelques problèmes de structure urbaine." *CRAI* 182–97.

Mattingly, H. B. 1961. "The Athenian Coinage Decree." *Historia* 10:148–88.

———. 1981. "The Athenian Decree for Miletos (*IG* I², 22+ = *ATL* II,D 11): A Postscript." *Historia* 30:113–17.

———. 1997. "The Date and Purpose of the Pseudo-Xenophon *Constitution of Aristotle*." *CQ* 47:352–56.

Mayer, M. 1932. *RE* 15.2.1622–49, s.v. "Miletos *(Topographie. Bauwerke)*."

Mazzarino, Santo. 1947. *Fra Oriente e Occidente: Ricerche di storia greca arcaica.* Florence.

McCredie, James R. 1971. "Hippodamos of Miletos." In *Studies Presented to George M. A. Hanfmann,* ed. D. G. Mitten, J. G. Pedley, and J. A. Scott, 95–100. Mainz.

McKeon, Richard, ed. 1941. *The Basic Works of Aristotle.* New York.

Mee, C. 1978. "Aegean Trade and Settlement in Anatolia in the Second Millenium B.C." *AS* 28:121–55.

Meiggs, Russell. 1943. "The Growth of Athenian Imperialism." *JHS* 63:21–34.

———. 1963. "The Crisis of Athenian Imperialism." *HSCP* 67:1–36.

———. 1966. "The Dating of Fifth-Century Attic Inscriptions." *JHS* 86:86–98.

———. 1972. *The Athenian Empire.* Oxford.

———. 1982. *Trees and Timber in the Ancient Mediterranean World.* Oxford.

Meiggs, Russell, and David Lewis, eds. 1988. *A Selection of Greek Historical Inscriptions to the End of the Fifth Century B.C.* Rev. ed. Oxford.

Melas, E. M. 1988. "The Dodecanese and W. Anatolia in Prehistory: Interrelationships, Ethnicity and Political Geography." *AS* 38:109–20.

Mellaart, J. 1966. *The Chalcolithic and Early Bronze Ages in the Near East and Anatolia.* Beirut.

Mellink, Machteld J. 1961. "Archaeology in Asia Minor." *AJA* 65:37–52.

———. 1962. "Archaeology in Asia Minor." *AJA* 66:173–90.

———. 1963. "Archaeology in Asia Minor." *AJA* 67:149–66.

———. 1972. "Archaeology in Asia Minor." *AJA* 76:149–66.

———. 1974. "Archaeology in Asia Minor." *AJA* 78:105–30.

———. 1975. "Archaeology in Asia Minor." *AJA* 79:201–22.

———. 1976. "Archaeology in Asia Minor." *AJA* 80:261–89.

———. 1980. "Archaeology in Asia Minor." *AJA* 84:501–18.

———. 1983. "The Hittites and the Aegean World Part 2. Archaeological Comments on Ahhiyawa-Achaians in Western Anatolia." *AJA* 87:138–41.

———. 1984. "Archaeology in Asia Minor." *AJA* 88:441–59.

———. 1987. "Archaeology in Anatolia." *AJA* 91:1–30.

———. 1989. "Archaeology in Anatolia." *AJA* 93:105–33.

———. 1991a. "Archaeology in Anatolia." *AJA* 95:123–53.

———. 1991b. "The Native Kingdoms of Anatolia." *CAH* 3^2.2 619–65.

Meritt, B. D. 1972. "The Tribute Quota List of 454/3 BC." *Hesperia* 41:403–17.

Meritt, B. D., and H. T. Wade-Gery. 1957. "Athenian Resources in 449 and 431 BC." *Hesperia* 26:163–97.

———. 1963. "The Dating of Documents to the Mid–Fifth Century—II." *JHS* 83:100–117.

Mihailov, G. 1991. "Thrace before the Persian Entry into Europe." *CAH* 3^2.2 591–618.

Miller, Stephen G. 1978. *The Prytaneion: Its Function and Architectural Form.* Berkeley and Los Angeles.

Millon, Charles, ed. 1803. *Politique d'Aristote.* 3 vols. Paris.

Mitchel, Fordyce. 1956. "Herodotos' Use of Genealogical Chronology." *Phoenix* 10:48–69.

Mitchell, S. 1984/85. "Archaeology in Asia Minor, 1979–84." *AR* 31:70–105.

———. 1989/90. "Archaeology in Asia Minor, 1985–1989." *AR* 36:83–131.

Mitchell, S., and A. W. McNicoll. 1978/79. "Archaeology in Western and Southern Asia Minor, 1971–78." *AR* 25:59–90.

Mitchell, T. C. 1991. "Judah until the Fall of Jerusalem (c. 700–586 B.C.)." *CAH* 3².2 371–409.

Moles, John. 1996. "Herodotus Warns the Athenians." *Papers of the Leeds International Latin Seminar* 9:259–84.

Möller, Astrid. 2000. *Naukratis: Trade in Archaic Greece.* Oxford.

Mordtmann, J. H. 1980. "Epigraphische Mitteilungen: II. Archaische Inschrift aus Kyzikos." *Hermes* 15:92–98.

Mørkholm, Otto. 1991. *Early Hellenistic Coinage from the Accession of Alexander to the Peace of Apamea (336–188 B.C.).* Ed. P. Grierson and U. Westermark. Cambridge.

Müller-Wiener, Wolfgang. 1967. "Das Theaterkastell von Milet." *MDAI(I)* 17: 279–90.

———. 1977. "Die Grabungskampagne in Milet im Herbst 1977." *TürkAD* 25, no. 2:135–40.

———. 1977/78a. "Milet 1973–1975." *MDAI(I)* 27–28:93–125.

———. 1977/78b. "1. Michaelskirche und Dionysos-Tempel—Baufunde und Phasengliederung." In Müller-Wiener 1977/78a, 94–103.

———. 1979. "Milet 1977." *MDAI(I)* 29:161–203.

———. 1980a. "Milet 1978–1979." *MDAI(I)* 30:23–98.

———. 1980b. "Untersuchungen auf dem Humeitepe." In Müller-Wiener 1980a, 30–38.

———. 1981a. "Milet 1980." *MDAI(I)* 31:95–147.

———. 1981b. "Untersuchungen auf dem Humeitepe." In Müller-Wiener 1981a, 99–105.

———. 1985. "Milet 1983–1984." *MDAI(I)* 35:13–138.

———. 1986a. "Bemerkungen zur Topographie des archaischen Milet." In Müller-Wiener 1986c, 95–104.

———. 1986b. "Milet 1985." *MDAI(I)* 36:5–57.

———. 1987. "Milet 1986." *MDAI(I)* 37:1–81.

———. 1988a. "Milet 1976–1986: Ergebnisse aus 10 Jahren Ausgrabungstätigkeit." *Antike Welt* 19:31–42.

———. 1988b. "Milet 1987." *MDAI(I)* 38:251–90.

———. 1988c. "Notgrabung in der archaischen Nekropole von Milet." In Müller-Wiener 1988b, 253–78.

———. 1988d. "2. Untersuchungen im Bischofspalast in Milet (1977–1979)." In Müller-Wiener 1988b, 279–90.

———, ed. 1986c. *Milet 1899–1980: Ergebnisse, Probleme und Perspektiven einer Ausgrabung.* Tübingen.

Müller-Wiener, Wolfgang, and Walter Voigtländer. 1980. "1. Arbeiten im Stadtgebiet." In Müller-Wiener 1980a, 24–47.

Müller-Wiener, Wolfgang, and B. F. Weber. 1985. "1. Arbeiten im Stadtgebiet." In Müller-Wiener 1985, 15–38.

Murray, Oswyn. 1980. *Early Greece.* Brighton, Sussex, and Atlantic Highlands, NJ.

———. 1988. "The Ionian Revolt." *CAH* 4² 461–90.

Naumann, Rudolf. 1971. *Architektur Kleinasiens von ihren Anfängen bis zum Ende der hethitischen Zeit*. 2d ed. Tübingen.

Naumann, Rudolf, and Klaus Tuchelt. 1963/64. "Die Ausgrabung imm Südwesten des Tempels von Didyma 1962." *MDAI(I)* 13–14:15–62.

Nenci, G. 1962. "La monetazione della rivolta ionica nei suoi aspetti economici e politici." In *Studi in onore di Amintore Fanfani*, 1:71–83. Milano.

Newman, W. L., ed. 1887. *The Politics of Aristotle*. 4 vols. Oxford.

Nielsen, Thomas Heine, ed. 1997. *Yet More Studies in the Ancient Greek Polis*. Stuttgart.

Niemeier, Barbara, and Wolf-Dietrich Niemeier. 1997. "Milet 1994–1995: Projekt 'Minoisch-mykenisches bis protogeometrisches Milet': Zielsetzung und Grabungen auf dem Stadionhügel und am Athenatempel." *AA* 112:189–248.

Niemeier, Wolf-Dietrich. 1998. "The Mykenaeans in Western Anatolia and the Problem of the Origins of the Sea Peoples." In *Mediterranean Peoples in Transition: Thirteenth to Early Tenth Centuries BCE*, ed. Seymour Gitin et al., 17–65. Jerusalem.

———. 1999. " 'Die Zierde Ioniens': Ein archaischer Brunnen, der jüngere Athenatempel und Milet vor der Perserzerstörung." With A. M. Graeves and W. Selesnow. *AA* 114:373–413.

Nissen, H. 1877. *Pompeianische Studien*. Leipzig.

Noonan, Thomas S. 1973. "The Grain Trade of the Northern Black Sea in Antiquity." *AJP* 94:231–42.

Nordin, Richard. 1905. "Aisymnetie und Tyrannis." *Klio* 5:392–409.

Oliver, James Henry. 1935. "The Athenian Decree concerning Miletus in 450/49 BC." *TAPA* 66:177–98.

Onyshkevych, Lada. 1998. *Archaic and Classical Cult-Related Graffiti from the Northern Black Sea Region*. Ph.D. diss., University of Pennsylvania.

Ormerod, Henry A. 1924. *Piracy in the Ancient World*. Liverpool and London.

Ostwald, Martin. 1969. *Nomos and the Beginnings of the Athenian Democracy*. Oxford.

———. 1986. *From Popular Sovereignty to the Sovereignty of Law: Law, Society, and Politics in Fifth-Century Athens*. Berkeley.

Owens, E. J. 1991. *The City in the Greek and Roman World*. London and New York.

Page, Denys L. 1959. *History and the Homeric Iliad*. Berkeley.

Papalas, Anthony J. 1992. *Ancient Icaria*. Wauconda, IL.

Parke, H.W. 1985a. "The Massacre of the Branchidai." *JHS* 105:59–68.

———. 1985b. *Oracles of Apollo in Asia Minor*. London.

———. 1992. *Sibyls and Sibylline Prophecy in Classical Antiquity*. Ed. B. C. McGing. London.

Parke, H. W., and D. E. W. Wormell. 1956. *The Delphic Oracle*. Vol. 2, *The Oracular Responses*. Oxford.

Parker, Victor. 1997. *Untersuchungen zum Lelantischen Krieg und verwandten Problemen der frühgriechischen Geschichte*. Stuttgart.

———. 1998. "Τύραννος: The Semantics of a Political Concept from Archilochos to Aristotle." *Hermes* 126:145–72.

Parzinger, Hermann. 1989. "Fur frühesten Besiedlung Milets." *MDAI(I)* 39: 415–31.

Pearson, Lionel. 1939. *Early Ionian Historians*. Oxford.

Petit, Thierry. 1985. "L'integration des cites ioniennes dans l'empire Achemenide (VIe siecle)." *REA* 87:43–52.

Petrakos, Basile Chr. 1963. "Dédidace des ΑΕΙΝΑΥΤΑΙ d'Érétrie." *BCH* 87: 545–47.

Pfrommer, Michael. 1985. "2. Studien zu einzelnen Fundgruppen." In Müller-Wiener 1985, 39–138.

———. 1986. "Ein Bronzebecher des 6. Jahrhunderts aus Milet." In Müller-Wiener 1986b, 34–36.

Piérart, M. 1969. "Les ΈΠΙΜΗΝΙΟΙ de Milet." *AntCl* 38:365–88.

———. 1974. "Milet dans la première liste de tributs." *ZPE* 15:163–67.

———. 1979. "La Constitution de Milet à la lumière des institutions de ses colonies." In *Acta de VIIᵉ congrès international d'épigraphie grecque et latine*, ed. D. M. Pippidi, 439–40. Paris.

———. 1983. "Athènes et Milet. I: Tribus et dèmes milésiens." *Mus. Helv.* 40:1–18.

———. 1985. "Athènes et Milet. II: L'Organisation du territorire." *Mus. Helv.* 42:276–99.

Poland, F. 1935. *RE* Suppl. 6.509–20, s.v. Μολποί.

Pounds, N. J. G. 1973. *An Historical Geography of Europe, 450 BC–AD 1330*. Cambridge.

Powell, Anton. 1988. *Athens and Sparta*. Portland, OR.

Powell, Barry. 1991. *Homer and the Origin of the Greek Alphabet*. Cambridge.

Quiller, Bjorn. 1981. "The Dynamics of the Homeric Society." *SO* 56:109–55.

Raaflaub, Kurt. 1987. "Herodotus, Political Thought, and the Meaning of History." *Arethusa* 20:221–48.

———. 1998a. "A Historian's Headache: How to Read 'Homeric Society'?" In *Archaic Greece: New Approaches and New Evidence*, ed. Nick Fisher and Hans van Wees, 169–93. London.

———. 1998b. "Homer, the Trojan War, and History." *CW* 91, no. 5:386–403.

Radt, Wolfgang. 1973/74. "Pidasa bei Milet." *MDAI(I)* 23–24:169–74.

Rainey, F. G. 1964. "The Location of Ancient Greek Sybaris." *AJA* 73:261–73.

Real, Willi. 1977/78. "2. Ausgewählte Funde aus dem Dionysos-Tempel." In Müller-Wiener 1977/78a, 105–16.

Rehm, A. 1958. *Didyma*. Vol. 2, *Die Inscriften*. Berlin.

Renfrew, Colin. 1982. "Polity and Power: Interaction, Intensification, and Exploitation." In *An Island Polity: The Archaeology of Exploitation in Melos*, ed. Colin Renfrew and Malcolm Wegstaff, 264–90. Cambridge.

Rhodes, P. J. 1972. *The Athenian Boule*. Oxford.

———. 1992. "The Delian League to 449 B.C." *CAH* 5² 34–61.

Robert, Louis. 1928. "Mémoires de l'Académie des Inscriptions." *BCH* 52: 158–78.

Robertson, Noel. 1987. "Government and Society at Miletos, 525–442 B.C." *Phoenix* 41:356–98.

Roebuck, Carl. 1955. "The Early Ionian League." *CP* 50:26–40.

———. 1959. *Ionian Trade and Colonization*. New York. Reprint, Chicago, 1984.

———. 1961. "Tribal Organization in Ionia." *TAPA* 92:495–507.

Röhlig, Johannes. 1933. *Der Handel von Milet*. Hamburg.

Roisman, J. 1988. "On Phyrnichos' *Sack of Miletos* and the *Phoinissai*." *Eranos* 86:15–23.

Röllig, Wolfgang. 1992. "Asia Minor as a Bridge between East and West: The Role of the Phoenicians and Aramaeans in the Transfer of Culture." In Kopcke and Tokumaru 1992, 93–102.

Romer, F. 1982. "The *Aisymnêteia*: A Problem in Aristotle's Historical Method." *AJP* 103:25–46.

Rosenbloom, David. 1993. "Shouting 'Fire' in a Crowded Theater: Phrynichos's *Capture of Miletos* and the Politics of Fear in Early Attic Tragedy." *Philologus* 137:159–96.

Roussel, D. 1976. *Tribu et cité*. Paris.

Rudolph, Wolf W. 1984. "Excavations at Porto Cheli and Vicinity, Preliminary Report VI: Halieis, the Stratigraphy of the Streets in the Northeast Quarter of the Lower Town." *Hesperia* 53:123–70.

Ruge, W. 1933. *RE* 16.1.995–96, s.v. "Mydones."

Rusjaeva, Anna S. 1979. *Zemledel'ceskie Kul'ty v Ol'vii Dogetskogo Vremeni*. Kiev.

Ruzé, Francoise. 1985. "Le style ionien dans la vie politique archaïque." *REA* 87:157–67.

Sakellariou, M. B. 1958. *La migration grecque en Ionie*. Athens.

Salviat, F. 1984. "Les Archontes de Thasos." In Πρακτικὰ τοῦ ἡ συνεδρίου ἑλληνικῆς καὶ λατινικῆς ἐπιγραφικῆς, 233–58. Athens.

Samuel, Alan E. 1972. *Greek and Roman Chronology: Calendars and Years in Classical Antiquity*. Handbuch der Altertumswissenschaft sect. 1, part 7. Munich.

Scherer, Anton. 1934. *Zur Laut- und Formenlehre der milesischen Inscriften*. Ph.D. diss., Universität München.

Schiering, Wolfgang. 1959/60. "I. Südabschnitt." In Weickert 1959/60a, 4–30.

———. 1968. "Der alte Athena-Tempel von Milet." *MDAI(I)* 18:144–60.

———. 1975. "Die monisch-mykenische Siedlung in Milet vor dem Bau der grossen Mauer." *MDAI(I)* 25:9–15.

———. 1979. "Milet: Eine Erweiterung der Grabung östlich des Athenatempels." *MDAI(I)* 29:77–108.

———. 1984. "The Connections between the Oldest Settlement at Miletus and Crete." In Hägg and Marinatos 1984, 187–89.

———. 1986. "Zu den Beziehungen zwischen der ältesten Siedlung von Milet und Kreta." In Müller-Wiener 1986b, 11–15.

Schneider, Carsten. 1997. "Grabung an der Stadmauer 1995." In Graeve 1997, 134–36.

Schneider, Peter. 1987. "Zur Topographie der Heiligen Strasse von Milet nach Didyma." *AA* 102:101–29.

Schofield, Elizabeth. 1984. "Coming to Terms with Minoan Colonists." In Hägg and Marinatos 1984, 45–48.

Schröder, Bernt, et al. 1995. "Geowissenschaftliche Umfelderkundung." In Graeve 1995, 238–44.

Schuller, Wolfgang. 1974. *Die Herrschaft der Athener im ersten Attischen Seebund.* Berlin and New York.

Schwarz, Christiane. 1989. "Drei dädalische Terrakotten aus Milet." *MDAI(I)* 39:507–16.

Seltman, C. 1933. *Greek Coins.* London.

Senff, Reinhard. 1995a. "Die Grabung am Kalabaktepe." In Graeve 1995, 208–13.

———. 1995b. "Sondierungen am Südhang des Mengerevtepe ('Assessos')." In Graeve 1995, 224–28.

———. 1997a. "Arbeiten am Zeytintepe im Jahre 1994." In Graeve 1997, 114–18.

———. 1997b. "Das Wohnviertel am Südhang des Kalabaktepe." In Graeve 1997, 118–20.

Senff, Reinhard, et al. 1992. "Die Grabung auf dem Zeytintepe." In Graeve 1992, 105–8.

———. 1997. "Die Grabung auf den Gipfelplateau des Kalabaktepe 1995." In Graeve 1997, 122–24.

Shipley, Graham. 1987. *A History of Samos, 800–188 B.C.* Oxford and New York.

Singer, I. 1983. "Western Anatolia in the 13th Century B.C. according to the Hittite Sources." *AS* 33:205–17.

Snodgrass, Anthony M. 1971. *The Dark Age of Greece: An Archaeological Survey of the Eleventh to the Eighth Centuries B.C.* Edinburgh.

Sokolowski, F. 1955. *Lois sacrées de l'Asie Mineure.* Paris.

Solovev, S. 1998. "Archaic Berezan: Historical-Archaeological Essay." In Tsetskhladze 1998b, 205–25.

Stahl, M. 1987. *Aristokraten und Tyrannen im archaischen Athen: Untersuchungen zur Überlieferung, zur Sozialstruktur und zur Entstehung des Staates.* Stuttgart.

Stahr, Adolphus. 1839. *Aristotelis Politicorum Libri Octo.* Lipsiae.

Starke, Frank. 1997. "Troia im Kontext des historisch-politischen und sprachlichen Umfeldes Kleinasiens im 2. Jahrtausend." *Studia Troica* 7:447–87.

Ste. Croix, G. E. M. de. 1972. *The Origins of the Peloponnesian War.* London.

Stein, Heinrich, ed. 1894. *Herodotus.* Vol. 3. Berlin. Reprint, 1963.

Stubbings, Frank H. 1975. "The Expansion of the Mycenaean Civilization." *CAH* 2³.2 165–87.

Stümpel, Harald, et al. 1997. "Stand der geophysikalischen Messungen im Umfeld von Milet." In Graeve 1997, 124–34.

Sulimirski, T., and T. Taylor. 1991. "The Scythians." *CAH* 3².2 547–90.

Szanto, Emil. 1894. *RE* 1.477–78, s.v. Ἀειναῦται.

———. 1909. *RE* 6.178–79, s.v. Ἐπιμήνιοι.

Szidat, Joachim. 1980. "Hippodamos von Milet: Seine Rolle in Theorie und Praxis der griechischen Stadtplanung." *BJ* 180:31–44.

Tausend, Klaus. 1987. "Die Lelantische Krieg—ein Mythos?" *Klio* 69:499–514.

———. 1992. *Amphiktyonie und Symmachie*. Stuttgart.

Taylour, Lord William. 1983. *The Mycenaeans*. Rev. ed. New York.

Theodorescu, Dinu. 1975. "Remarques préliminaires sur la topographie urbaine de Sélinonte." *Kokalos* 21:108–20.

Tod, Marcus N., ed. 1946. *Greek Historical Inscriptions: From the Sixth Century B.C. to the Death of Alexander the Great in 323 B.C.* 2d ed. 2 vols. Oxford: Reprint (2 vols. in 1), Chicago, 1985.

Tozer, H. F. 1971. *A History of Ancient Geography*. 2d ed. Ed. M. Cary. New York.

Tozzi, Pierluigi. 1977. "Erodoto e le responsabilità dell'inizio della rivolta ionica." *Athenaeum* 55:127–35.

———. 1978. *La rivolta ionica*. Pisa.

Triebel-Schubert, Charlotte, and Ulrike Muss. 1983/84. "Hippodamos von Milet: Staatstheoretiker oder Stadtplaner?" *Hephaistos* 5–6:37–59.

Tsetskhladze, Gocha R. 1994. "Greek Penetration of the Black Sea." In *The Archaeology of Greek Colonisation: Essays Dedicated to Sir John Boardman*, ed. Gocha R. Tsetskhladze and Franco de Angelis, 111–35. Oxford.

———. 1997. "A Survey of the Major Urban Settlements in the Kimmerian Bosporos (with a Discussion of their Status as *Poleis*)." In Nielsen 1997, 39–81.

———. 1998a. "Greek Colonisation of the Black Sea Area: Stages, Models, and Native Population." In Tsetskhladze 1998b, 9–68.

———, ed. 1996. *New Studies in the Black Sea Littoral*. Oxford.

———, ed. 1998b. *The Greek Colonisation of the Black Sea Area*. Stuttgart.

Tuchelt, Klaus. 1973. *Vorarbeiten zu einer Topographie von Didyma*. Tübingen.

———. 1988. "Die Perserzerstörung von Branchidai-Didyma und ihre Folgen— archäologisch betrachtet." *AA* 103:427–38.

———. 1989. "Didyma. Bericht über die Ausgrabungen 1985 und 1986 an der heiligen Strasse von Milet nach Didyma." *AA* 104:143–217.

———. 1991a. *Branchidai-Didyma: Geschichte, Ausgrabung und Wiederentdeckung eines antiken Heiligtums, 1765 bis 1990*. Mainz.

———. 1991b. "Drei Heiligtümer von Didyma und ihre Grundzüge." *Revue Archéologique* 85–98.

———. 1996. *Didyma*. Vol. 3, *Ergebnisse der Ausgrabungen und Untersuchungen seit dem Jahre 1962*. Part 1, *Ein Kultbezirk an der Heiligen Strasse von Milet nach Didyma*. Mainz.

Ure, P. N. 1922. *The Origin of Tyranny*. Cambridge.

Vallet, Georges. 1973. "Espace privé et espace public dans une cité coloniale d'Occident: Mégara Hyblaea." In *Problèmes de la terre en Grèce ancienne*, ed. M. I. Finley, 83–94. Paris.

Vallet, Georges, François Villard, and Paul Auberson. 1976. *Mégara Hyblaea*. Vol. 1, *Le Quartier de l'agora archaïque*. Rome.

————. 1983. *Mégara Hyblaea.* Vol. 3, *Guide des fouilles.* Rome.

van der Horst, P. W. 1978. *Admonationes: The Sentences of Ps.-Phocylides.* Leiden.

van Wees, Hans. 1992. *Status Warriors: War, Violence, and Society in Homer and History.* Amsterdam.

Vettori, Piero. 1576. *Comentarii in VIII. Libros Aristotelis de Optimo Statu Civitatis.* 2d ed. Florence.

Vinogradov, Jurij G. 1981. *Olbia: Geschichte einer altgriechischen Stadt am Schwarzen Meer.* Stuttgart.

————. 1997. *Pontische Studien: Kleine Schriften zur Geschichte und Epigraphik des Schwarzmeerraumes.* Mainz.

Vinogradov, Jurij G., and Sergej D. Kryzickij. 1995. *Olbia: Eine altgriechische Stadt im nordwestlichen Schwarzmeerraum.* Leiden.

Vlastos, Gregory. 1953. "Isonomia." *AJP* 74:337–66.

Voigtländer, Walter. 1975. "Die mykenische Stadtmauer in Milet und einzelne Wehranlagen der späten Bronzezeit." *MDAI(I)* 25:17–34.

————. 1981. "2. Grabung westlich des Buleuterion." In Müller-Wiener 1981a, 106–30.

————. 1982. "Funde aus der Insula westlich des Buleuterion in Milet." *MDAI(I)* 32:30–173.

————. 1983. "Frühe Funde vom Killiktepe bei Milet." *MDAI(I)* 33:5–39.

————. 1985. "Zur Topographie Milets: Ein neues Modell zur antiken Stadt." *AA* 100:77–91.

————. 1986a. *Antike aktuell: Didyma und Milet im Modell.* Frankfurt am Main.

————. 1986b. "Zur archaischen Keramik in Milet." In Müller-Wiener 1986c, 35–56.

von Fritz, Kurt. 1967. *Die griechische Geschichtsschreibung.* 2 vols. Berlin.

Wallace, Robert W. 1987. "The Origin of Electrum Coinage." *AJA* 91:385–97.

Wallinga, H. T. 1993. *Ships and Sea-Power before the Great Persian War.* Leiden.

Ward-Perkins, J. B. 1974. *Cities of Ancient Greece and Italy: Planning in Classical Antiquity.* London.

Warren, Peter. 1969. *Minoan Stone Vases.* Cambridge.

————. 1975. *The Aegean Civilizations.* Oxford.

Warren, Peter, and Vronwy Hankey. 1989. *Aegean Bronze Age Chronology.* Bristol.

Weber, Berthold F. 1995. "Ein spätarchaischer Tempel auf dem Mengerevtepe bei Milet." In Graeve 1995, 228–38.

————. 1999. "Die Bauteile des Athenatempels in Milet." *AA* 114:415–37.

Weickert, Carl. 1940. "Ausgrabungen in Milet 1938." In *Bericht über den VI. Internationalen Kongress für Archäologie, Berlin 21.–26. August 1939,* 325–32. Berlin.

————. 1958. "Bericht über die Ausgrabung in Milet Im Jahr 1957." *TürkAD* 8, no. 1:31–32.

————. 1959. "Neue Ausgrabungen in Milet." In *Neue deutsche Ausgrabungen im Mittelmeergebiet und im vorderen Orient,* ed. E. Boehringer, 181–96. Berlin.

———. 1959/60a. "Die Ausgrabung beim Athena-Tempel in Milet 1957." *MDAI(I)* 9–10:1–96.

———. 1959/60b. "III. Der Westabschnitt." In Weickert 1959/60a, 63–66.

Weickert, Carl, et al. 1957. "Die Ausgrabungen beim Athena-Tempel in Milet 1955." *MDAI(I)* 7:102–32.

Werner, R. 1955. "Die Dynastie der Spartokiden." *Historia* 4:412–44.

Wernicke, K. 1896. *RE* 2.1–111, s.v. "Apollon."

West, M. L. 1978a. "Phocylides." *JHS* 98:164–67.

———. 1978b. *Theognidis et Phocylidis Fragmenta et Adespota Quaedam Gnomica.* Berlin and New York.

West, Stephanie. 1991. "Herodotus' Portrait of Hecataeus." *JHS* 111:144–60.

Wiegand, Theodor. 1901. "Zweiter vorläufiger Bericht über die von den Königlichen Museen begonnenen Ausgrabungen in Milet." *SBBerlin* 903–13.

———. 1904. "Dritter vorläufiger Bericht über den Königlichen Museen begonnenen Ausgrabungen in Milet." *SBBerlin* 72–91.

———. 1911. *Siebenter vorläufiger Bericht über die von den Königlichen Museen in Milet und Didyma unternommenen Ausgrabungen.* Berlin.

Wiener, M. H. 1984. "The Tale of the Conical Cups." In Hägg and Marinatos 1984, 17–26.

Wiesehöfer, J. 1987. "Kyros und die unterworfenen Völker: Ein Beitrag zur Entstehung von Geschichtsbewusstsein." *Quaderni di Storia* 26:107–26.

Wilamowitz-Moellendorff, Ulrich von. 1903a. "Apollo." *Hermes* 13:575–86.

———. 1903b. *Timotheos, die Perser, aus einem Papyrus von Abusir im Auftrage der Deutschen Orientgesellschaft.* Leipzig.

———. 1904. "Satzungen einer milesischen Sängergilde." *SBBerlin* 619–40.

———. 1906a. "Panionion." *SBBerlin* 38–57. Reprinted in *Kleine Schriften,* ed. Paul Mass et al. Vol. 5, no. 1. (Berlin, 1937), 129–51.

———. 1906b. "Über die ionische Wanderung." *SBBerlin* 59–79. Reprinted in *Kleine Schriften,* ed. Paul Mass et al. Vol. 5, no. 1. (Berlin, 1937), 152–76.

———. 1914. Review of *Milet* 1.3, *Das Delphinion in Milet* by Georg Kawerau and Albert Rehm. In *GGA* 65–109. Reprinted in *Kleine Schriften,* ed. Paul Mass et al. Vol. 5, no. 1. (Berlin, 1937), 417–66.

Wiseman, D. J. 1991. "Babylonia, 605–539 B.C." *CAH* 3^2.2 229–51.

Woodard, Roger D. 1997. *Greek Writing from Knossos to Homer.* New York and Oxford.

Wycherley, R. E. 1964. "Hippodamus and Rhodes." *Historia* 13:135–39.

———. 1973. *How the Greeks Built Cities.* 2d ed. London.

Yaker, J. 1976. "Hittite Involvement in Western Anatolia." *AS* 26:117–28.

Young, T. Cutler, Jr. 1988. "The Consolidation of the Empire and Its Limits of Growth under Darius and Xerxes." *CAH* 4^2 53–111.

Zgusta, Ladislav. 1984. *Kleinasiatische Ortsnamen.* Heidelberg.

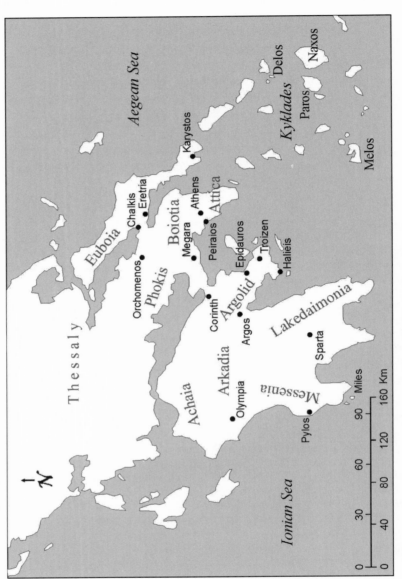

Map. 1. The Greek mainland

Map 2. Asia Minor

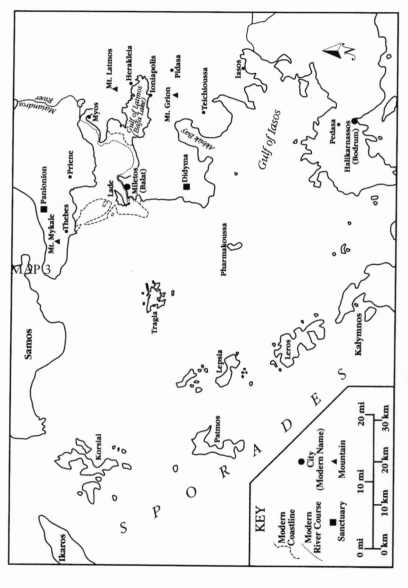

MAP 3

Samos

Matandros River

Mt. Mykale ▲
Panionion ■
Thebes ●
Priene ●

Myos ●
Lade
Miletos (Balat) ■

Mt. Latmos ▲
Herakleia ●
Ioniapolis ●
Pidasa ●
Gulf of Latmos
Bafa Lake)

Mt. Grion ▲
Teichioussa ●

Iasos ●

Didyma ■

Abbuk Bay

Gulf of Iasos

Pedasa ●
Halikarnassos (Bodrum) ●

Pharmakoussa

Tragia

Lepsia

Leros

Korsiai

Patmos

Kalymnos

Ikaros

S   P   O   R   A   D   E   S

KEY

⌇⌇ Modern Coastline
┈┈ Modern River Course
■ Sanctuary
● City (Modern Name)
▲ Mountain

0 mi   10 mi   20 mi
0 km   10 km   20 km   30 km

Map 3. The territory around Miletos

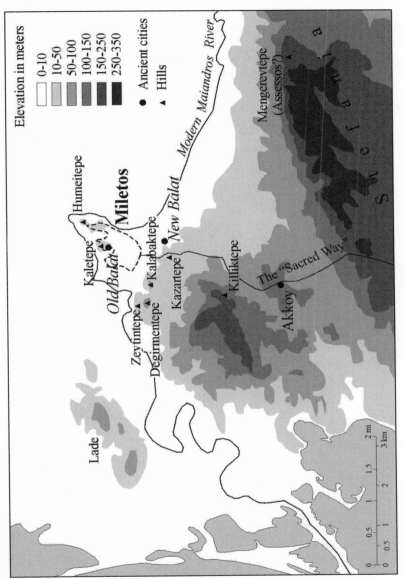

Map 4. The Milesian *chore*

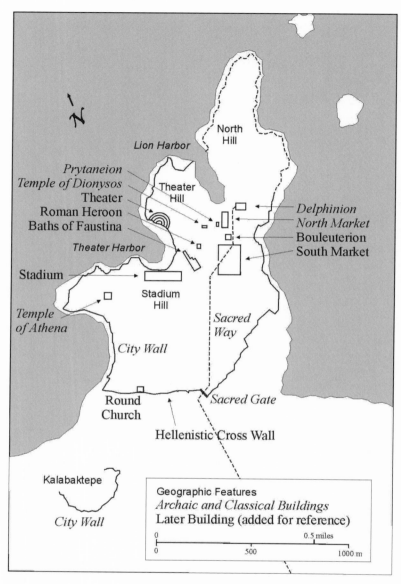

North
Hill

Lion Harbor

Prytaneion
Temple of Dionysos   Theater
Theater   Hill
Roman Heroon   Delphinion
Baths of Faustina   North Market
                                                    Bouleuterion
Theater Harbor   South Market

Stadium
                           Stadium
                           Hill
Temple
of Athena
                                        Sacred
                                        Way
            City Wall

                        Round
                        Church   Sacred Gate

                    Hellenistic Cross Wall

Kalabaktepe

            City Wall
                                Geographic Features
                                Archaic and Classical Buildings
                                Later Building (added for reference)
                                0   0.5 miles
                                0   500   1000 m

Map 5. The city of Miletos

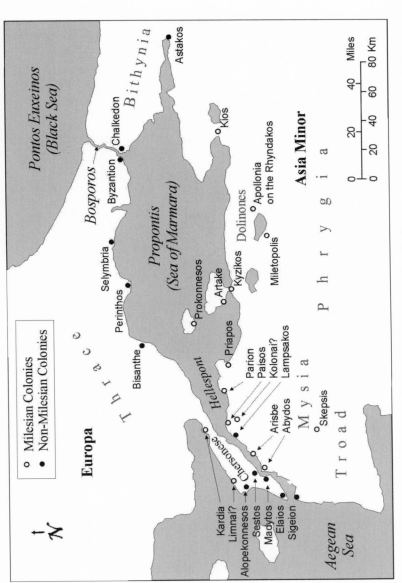

Map 6. The Propontic colonies

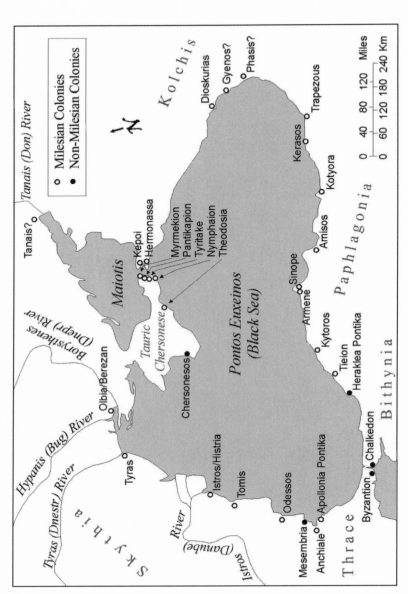

Map 7. The Pontic colonies

Index Locorum

Aelian, *Varia Historia*
  3.17.23: 251n. 29
  3.43: 106
  8.5: 17n. 8, 32, 34n, 41
Aeschylus
  Prometheus Vinctus 714: 60n. 32,
    248n. 17
Agathemeros, *GGM* 2.471, 1.1: 84
Ammianos, 22.8.26: 255n. 36, 256n.
  38
Anaximenes of Lampsakos, *FGH* 72 F
  26: 49
Andokides, *de Mysteriis* 45: 159n. 60
Anecdota Graeca 1.266.28 Bekker (s.v.
  Hippodameia agora), 159n. 60
Anonomous, *Periplus Euxini* 64 =
  GGM 1.419: 175n. 23
Anthologia Palatina 12.131 = Gow
  and Page 3082–85: 209n. 93
Apollodoros
  2.167–80: 9n
  3.1.2.1: 19
Apollonius of Rhodes, *Argonautika*
  1.956–1153: 246
  1.958–60: 193
Aristophanes
  Aves 995–1009: 163
  Equites 361: 48n. 3
  Plutus 1002: 2
  Ranae 543: 48n. 3
Archilochos, fr. 22 Diehl, 91
Aristides, *Orationes* 16.237 Jebb =
  1.383 Dindorf, 192–93
Aristokritos of Miletos *FGH* 493 F 3:
  19n. 12

Aristotle
  Athenaion Politeia 5: 34
  de Caelo
    2.294a28–31: 77n. 77
    2.294b1: 80n. 84
    2.295b10–296a3: 79
  fragments (Rose)
    98: 51n. 14
    514: 247
    524: 97
    557: 13
  Historia Animalium
    5.15.3: 48n. 3
    8.13.2: 60n. 32
  Metaphysica
    1.983b6–24: 76–77
    1.984a5–10: 80n. 84
  Meteorologica 2.365b6–20: 80n.
    84
  Poetica 9.1451a36–b11: 8
  Politica
    1.1259a9–18: 48n. 3, 76
    2.1260b30–37: 157–58
    2.1260b36–40: 157
    2.1261b38–40: 157
    2.1267b22–30: 158
    2.1267b37–1269a12: 158n. 57
    2.1268a16: 158
    3.1279a22–1280a6: 90n. 6
    3.1284a31–b4: 95
    3.1285a31–b4: 98
    3.1305a15–19: 101
    7.1330b21–31: 155, 162
Arrian
  Anabasis 1.18ff.: 242

General Index

Hyetis (riverlet), 209
Hyrtakina, 170

Iasos, 44, 46
Ikaros, 49–50
Indigenous people of Anatolia, 14–18,
    67–69
Intellectuals, 72–85
Ionia, 1, 47, 81, 124, 143, 167, 241,
    246
Ionian League. *See* Panionion
Ionian Migration, 31–42
Ionian Revolt, 34–37, 49, 102, 129–
    45, 219
Isonomia, 136
Isopoliteia, 147–51
Istrian Bridge, 130
Istros, 93, 209, 250–51

Jason, 61

Kadmos of Miletos, 82
Kalabaktepe, 4, 122, 146–47, 151,
    166, 203–6, 212; East Terrace,
    172, 203–5; sanctuary on, 205;
    Summit Terrace, 204, 206
Kalamaion, 38
Kaletepe. *See* Theater Hill
Kallikratides, 239–40
Kalymnos, 49–50
Kamarina, 150, 154
Kambyses, 127
Kanachos, 190
Kardia, 244
Kaunos, 16, 137
Kazartepe, 4, 206–7
Kekropis, 217
Kepoi, 209, 256
Keraiites, 179, 184–85
Kerasos, 248
Kimmerians, 65, 68, 122, 203, 248,
    250
King's Peace, 241
Kios, 93, 137, 150, 247
Klazomenai, 57, 125, 137, 237, 244
Knidos, 57

Knossos, 170
Kodros, 32
Koes, 132, 136, 248
Kolchis, 249–50
Kolonai, 245
Kolophon, 119, 122, 125, 228, 230
Koos, 65
Koroneia, Battle of, 221, 236
Korsiai, 49
Kotyora, 248
Kretines, 65, 248
Kroisos, 2, 68, 75, 119, 123–24, 188
Kroton/Krontoniates, 105–6
Kurotrophos, 172
Kyanepsion, 38
Kyklades, 126, 134
Kyme, 63, 97–98, 106, 137, 188
Kythera, 236
Kytoros, 248
Kyzikos, 39, 64–66, 68, 150, 192–93,
    246, 247

Lade, 15, 48, 50, 237; Battle of, 138–
    40, 144
Lakedaimonia/Lakedaimonians, 210–
    11, 222, 240
Lakonia, 210
Lampsakos, 137, 243, 245
Latmos, Gulf of, 3, 46
Lebedos, 100, 125
Lelantine War, 51–52, 137, 245
Leleges, 17
Lenaion, 38
Leodamas, 45, 90–91
Leontis, 218
Lepsia, 49–50
Leros, 49–50, 126, 140–42, 223–24,
    235
Lesbos, 70, 137–38, 237, 244, 254
Leto, 172, 175, 194
Leukos, 175
Leukos Promontory, 224
Levant, 52–54
Limnai, 244
Linear A, 22
Linear B, 25, 37